THE HIBBERT LECTURES,
1892.

THE HIBBERT LECTURES, 1892.

LECTURES

ON THE

ORIGIN AND GROWTH OF RELIGION

AS ILLUSTRATED BY THE RELIGION OF THE

ANCIENT HEBREWS.

BY

C. G. MONTEFIORE.

SECOND EDITION.

Wipf & Stock
PUBLISHERS
Eugene, Oregon

Wipf and Stock Publishers
199 West 8th Avenue, Suite 3
Eugene, Oregon 97401

Lectures on the Origin and Growth of Religion as illustrated by the Religion of the Ancient Hebrews
The Hibbert Lectures, 1892
By Montefiore, Claude C.J.
ISBN: 1-59244-480-6
Publication date 1/16/2004
Previously published by Williams & Norgate, 1893

T. G. M.

Born October 27, 1864. Died June 10, 1889.

To the Memory of Her,

BY WHOSE ADVICE AND ENCOURAGEMENT

THE OFFER TO PREPARE THESE LECTURES WAS ACCEPTED,

THEY ARE NOW

VERY HUMBLY AND REVERENTLY

DEDICATED.

Μὴ εἰκῆ περὶ τῶν μεγίστων συμβαλώμεθα.—HERACLITUS (*Rel.* xlviii., ed. Bywater).

And so in all religions: the consideration of their morality comes first, afterwards the truth of the documents in which they are recorded, or of the events natural or supernatural which are told of them. But in modern times, and in Protestant countries perhaps more than in Catholic, we have been too much inclined to identify the historical with the moral; and some have refused to believe in religion at all, unless a superhuman accuracy was discernible in every part of the record. The facts of an ancient or religious history are amongst the most important of all facts; but they are frequently uncertain, and we only learn the true lesson which is to be gathered from them when we place ourselves above them.—JOWETT's *Dialogues of Plato*, 3rd edition, Vol. III. p. xxxvii.

PREFACE.

My purpose in these Lectures is to give a short history, as clear as I can make it, of the Religion of the Old Testament. By this I mean that I have endeavoured to group the religious material contained in that book in chronological order, and to trace the historical development, which then becomes visible, from its beginning to its end. This beginning has been but lightly touched upon, partly because of its extreme obscurity and partly because of my own insufficient equipment to deal adequately with so complex a problem; but more space has thus been won for the delineation of that phase of the Jewish religion in which it stood at the close of the Old Testament period, and on the lines of which it was destined to develop for many subsequent centuries.

I have also found it necessary either entirely to omit or to dismiss with bare allusion many topics which, though connected with the main subject, were of subsidiary importance for my special purpose as here defined. Thus I have said nothing about Alexandrian or Hellenistic Judaism, because, while that phase of religion was of great interest in itself, and of great importance for the history of Christianity, it lay aloof from and outside the main course of religious development both in the Old Testament itself and in the Rabbinical literature.

The early or Biblical history of the Jewish religion, as of the Jewish people, is still in many important respects shrouded with obscurity. Some four years ago, in a review of Stade's "History of Israel," Prof. Kamphausen said that in the then existing condition of our knowledge he for one would not have ventured to undertake the task. That I should have dared to grapple with a subject from which such a scholar as Kamphausen shrinks, may indeed seem to indicate the rashness of ignorance or conceit. My partial excuse is that the subject was allotted to me and not chosen by myself. The rare liberality of the Hibbert Trustees led them to think that it might be interesting to have the story of the Old Testament religion put forward from a point of view little known to or hitherto considered by the general public. Hence it was that, at the close of 1888, I received the honourable, but very responsible, offer of which the present book is the result. Whether in accepting that offer I sufficiently weighed the difficulty of the work or my own incapacity, is, I admit, very doubtful. I am painfully conscious that lack of time and of preliminary knowledge has prevented me from giving to many a disputed question that "discipline of hard and minute investigation," without which, as Prof. Cheyne has recently said, a man's opinions on Biblical criticism, as on any other department of human science, are not worth having. How far the somewhat novel point of view, which, I hope, has yet always been compatible with impartiality, may have compensated for these various deficiencies, I must leave others to decide. But the dogmatic appearance of many of my statements is assuredly only due either to the exigencies of space or to a necessary avoidance of that constant iteration of qualification and uncertainty which tends to put too heavy a burden upon the patience of the reader. Following M. Renan in the Preface to his "Histoire d'Israel," I would say, Be pleased to think that a legion of "possibly's" and "probably's" is scattered over the pages of my book.

It is unnecessary to point out in detail what I owe to previous writers in the same field. But I cannot forbear to mention the names of some distinguished scholars, on the results of whose labours my own small work is chiefly based, and to whom I owe the most both for direct information and for suggestive stimulus. From Germany, then, I must single out Stade and Wellhausen; from Holland, Kuenen; and from England, Prof. Cheyne and Mr. Schechter. Of these five, Kuenen is no longer with us. May I add here that this great scholar, in my single interview with him at Leiden in 1889, showed the most kindly interest in my work, and afterwards more than once wrote me valuable (and touchingly modest) letters in answer to permitted inquiries on difficult points? It is a pleasure to be able to associate my book even in this small way with the man who was at his death the acknowledged chief and master of the subject with which it deals. To Mr. Schechter I owe more than I can adequately express here. My whole conception of the Law and of its place in Jewish religion and life is largely the fruit of his teaching and inspiration, while almost all the Rabbinic material upon which that conception rests was put before my notice and explained to me by him.

To several other friends I desire here to offer my grateful thanks: to Mr. Estlin Carpenter, Vice-Principal of Manchester New College, Oxford, who read through the Lectures in proof, and made many valuable suggestions and corrections; to Mr. Israel Abrahams, who performed the same tiresome office, and also helped me considerably at an earlier stage; and, above all, to my old teacher and friend, Mr. Arnold Page, Rector of Tendring, Essex, who read the Lectures in a type-written form and made innumerable verbal corrections. Any measure of clearness and simplicity which I may have reached is largely owing to him.

To Mr. Ashton, the Chairman, and to the Hibbert Trustees generally, I beg herewith to express my very grateful acknowledgments, not only for their great liberality in entrusting me with this task, but also for allowing me to extend the length of the course beyond what was originally intended, and for much sympathy and encouragement shown to me in the delivery of the Lectures.

That this book, in spite of all the help which I have received, will contain many errors, is certain. The last and not the least of the German commentators upon Isaiah ends his Preface with these memorable words: "If one might not believe that even errors, when they are the outcome of honest work, may have good results, no one would venture to write about religion or the Bible at all." To this I would fain add the hope that I have approached this solemn subject in the spirit of one to whom in matters of religion I owe more than to any other living man. Had not a higher and holier duty constrained, I should have asked his permission to dedicate my book to him; as it is, he has allowed me to use as a kind of motto a quotation from his printed words. They are simple words doubtless, and some may think their warning obvious; but how much would the world have gained if the investigation of religion and of the Bible had been always conducted from the point of view and in the spirit enjoined upon us by the Master of Balliol!

TABLE OF CONTENTS.

Lecture I.

ORIGIN AND FOUNDATION OF THE HEBREW RELIGION.

	PAGE
Subject of the Lectures	1
Point of view here adopted: criticism and tradition	2
Results of Old Testament criticism	4
Authorities: the Old Testament	5
No indisputably authentic and homogeneous writings older than the eighth century B.C.	6
Results of this limitation	7
The eighth-century prophets and their religion	8
Origin of their religion: origin of Hebrew "monolatry"	10
Three periods of Hebrew history up to eighth century	11
(a) The age of the patriarchs: a pre-historic period	12
(b) The Mosaic age: beginnings of history	14
(c) The pre-prophetic age: from Moses to the eighth century	15
Whether monolatry dates from the third period	16
Traditional view of this period and its origin	17
Monolatry known in the third period, but not its creation	19
Whether it was the custom of the pre-historic age: nature of Semitic religion generally	22
The nearest kinsmen of the Hebrews	27
Edom, Ammon and Moab, and their religions	28
Arguments to prove that origin of monolatry must be sought for in the creative doctrine of Moses	31

xiv   TABLE OF CONTENTS.

	PAGE
Character of Mosaic monolatry	32
To be partially inferred from character of pre-prophetic monolatry	34
Existence of other gods recognized in pre-prophetic period, but their worship in Israel forbidden	35
Yahveh's character: his connection with fire	37
Yahveh's wrath and its results	38
His nature	41
His worship under material forms	42
The bull images and the ephods	43
Yahveh the God of justice: the priestly Torah	44
Inference as to the Mosaic conception of Yahveh and his character	46
Origin of Mosaic monolatry: an obscure and perhaps insoluble question. Two main hypotheses	50
Historic period of Israel's religion still to be dated from Moses	54

Lecture II.

THE HISTORY OF THE HEBREW RELIGION BETWEEN THE MOSAIC AGE AND THE EIGHTH CENTURY B.C.

From Moses to Samuel	55
Unhistorical view of period by editor of Book of Judges	57
Canaanite religion: its chief divinities	59
Influence of Canaanite on Hebrew religion	62
Yahveh the God of Israel	64
The priesthood: its origin and functions	65
The sacred lot: the priest as teacher and judge	68
Hosea's view of the priestly office	70
The seers: Samuel	72
The prophets, their origin and early history: Gad and Nathan	76
The Nazirites	80
David and Solomon	81
Jeroboam's revolt and its results	84
The early kings of Judah and Israel	86
Ahab and the worship of the Tyrian Baal	90

	PAGE
Elijah, Elisha and Micaiah	91
Jehu and the suppression of Baal worship	95
Athaliah and Jehoiada	96
The Syrian wars and their effects	97
The religious progress of the ninth century	99
General character and estimate of pre-prophetic religion	100

LECTURE III.

THE PROPHETS OF THE EIGHTH CENTURY B.C.

	PAGE
The prophets of the eighth century	106
External history of Israel and Judah in the eighth century	107
The end of the northern monarchy	109
Deportations to Assyria and their result	110
Hezekiah and Sennacherib	111
Moral and religious condition of the two kingdoms in the eighth century	112
"Prophetic" narratives of the Pentateuch	113
Religious and moral decay	114
Coincident advance	116
The priests and their legislative codes	117
The four prophets of the eighth century: Amos, Hosea, Isaiah and Micah	119
Characteristics common to their prophecies	120
Their teaching: Yahveh's character and his relation to Israel	122
Israel's duty to Yahveh	125
Moral ideals of the prophets	126
The true worship of Yahveh	127
Hosea's polemic against images	128
The place of sacrifices: form *versus* substance	130
Assyria and its office	133
The prophetic advance towards monotheism	134
The gods of the nations	136
The conception of the judgment	137

	PAGE
Isaiah's predictions of punishment and retrieval	139
The Messianic age and the Messianic king	142
Judgment on Assyria	144
Origin and first stages of prophetic universalism	146
Disputed passages in Isaiah: the nineteenth chapter	147
General estimate of prophetic teaching	150
Political views of the prophets	151
Prophets as social reformers	152
Prophets as religious teachers	153
Wellhausen's conception of prophecy	154
The effect of the prophetic teaching	156
Difficulties produced by it	157
Its essential uniqueness and nobility	159

LECTURE IV.

THE SEVENTH CENTURY: DEUTERONOMY AND JEREMIAH (700—586 B.C.).

Judah after the retreat of Sennacherib	161
Hezekiah's reform	163
The growing importance of Jerusalem and its temple	165
The reign of Manasseh: religious reaction	167
Assyrian idolatries and the worship of Moloch	168
Active persecution of the prophetical party	170
Accession of Josiah	171
The invasion of the Scythians	172
Zephaniah and Jeremiah	173
The early prophecies of Jeremiah and their present form	174
Convergence of prophets and priests	175
Increasing prevalence of idolatry: the party of reform	176
The idea of a single sanctuary for all Judah	177
A new law-book and its origin	178
The Book of the Law brought to Josiah	179
Josiah's reform	180

	PAGE
The abolition of the "high places"	182
The Book of Deuteronomy and its general character	184
The attack on idolatry and its symbols	185
The single sanctuary	186
Prophetic and priestly elements in Deuteronomy	188
The introductory chapters	189
A new commandment: the love of God	190
Whether the authors of Deuteronomy were hopeful of success	192
The Deuteronomic school and its work	193
Condition of Judah after the proclamation of Deuteronomy, and Jeremiah's attitude towards it	194
Death of Josiah and its effects	196
Disappointment and reaction	197
The lower nationalism: "Yahveh will protect his own"	198
The advance of Babylon: the battle of Carchemish: Jehoiakim the vassal of Nebuchadrezzar	199
Jeremiah under Jehoiakim and his teaching	200
Jehoiakim's revolt: the first deportation (597)	201
Religious condition under Zedekiah	205
Habakkuk and Hananiah	206
Jeremiah and the exiles in Babylonia	207
The fall of Jerusalem and the second deportation (586)	208
Jeremiah in Egypt	209
Religious progress in the seventh century	210
The Book of Lamentations	211
Religious literature of the seventh century	213
Monotheistic advance: Jeremiah's conception of Yahveh	215
Growth of religious individualism	216
Jeremiah's view of the relation of the individual to God	218
The new covenant and its meaning	220

Lecture V.

THE BABYLONIAN EXILE: EZEKIEL AND THE SECOND ISAIAH.

	PAGE
The Jewish exiles in Babylonia	222
Religious ideas current among them	224
Effects of the fall of Jerusalem	225
The two main results of the exile	228
The Sabbath in the exile	229
The worship of Yahveh	230
Editing of the historical books: views of the editors	231
Codification of priestly laws	234
The law of holiness	236
Prophecy in the exile	237
Ezekiel: his general position	238
His early history and prophetic call	240
His visions	242
Character of his book and work	244
His conception of God	246
The glory of Yahveh	248
Yahveh's relation to Israel and its results	250
Ezekiel's individualism	251
The sins of Israel	254
Ceremonial and morality	255
Ezekiel's legalism	257
Cyrus and his victories	260
Their effect upon the Jewish exiles	261
The new prophecy	262
The second Isaiah	264
Character of his teaching	265
His absolute monotheism	268
Yahveh the Creator and only God	270
The polemic against idolatry	271
Cyrus and the nations	273
The mission of Israel and its purposes	274

TABLE OF CONTENTS.

	PAGE
The conception of the Servant	276
Universalism	277
The fifty-third chapter	279
The new Jerusalem	281
Cyrus in Babylon: the Jewish exiles permitted to return home	283

Lecture VI.

THE RESTORATION AND THE PRIESTLY LAW.

Priests and Levites	286
Sheshbazzar, Zerubbabel and Joshua	289
Attitude of returned exiles to descendants of old population and to their northern neighbours	291
Delay in rebuilding the temple and its causes	294
The interval between 536 and 520	295
Haggai and Zechariah: character of their teaching	297
Contents of their prophecies	299
The temple rebuilt and consecrated (516 B.C.)	301
From 516 to 458: a gloomy interval	302
Help from Babylon: Priests and Levites and their work	304
Ezra the priest and scribe: his mission to Jerusalem and its objects	306
Ezra at Jerusalem: the mixed marriages	309
Failure of Ezra's plans	310
Nehemiah and the rebuilding of the walls of Jerusalem	311
Introduction of a new Law-book	314
Origin and character of this book: the sections of the Pentateuch which belong to it	315
Its religious conceptions	318
Its fusion of priestly and prophetic ideas	320
The sanctuary God's dwelling-place	321
The conception of holiness	324
Sin and atonement	327
Sacrifices and sin-offerings	330

xx   TABLE OF CONTENTS.

	PAGE
The Day of Atonement	333
The Sabbath and its observance	338
The relation of Israel and Yahveh to the outer world	340
Criticisms on the priestly code and their accuracy	342
The reading of the Law and its immediate results	345
Departure of Nehemiah from Jerusalem: the Law neglected and disobeyed	349
Nehemiah's second visit to Jerusalem	350
The foundation of the Samaritan community and its results	352

LECTURE VII.

FROM NEHEMIAH TO THE MACCABEES: EXTERNAL
INFLUENCES AND INTERNAL ORGANIZATION.

No Old Testament history but much Old Testament literature after Nehemiah	355
Persian and Greek periods	356
Method and object of last three Lectures	357
Survey of Persian period	359
Artaxerxes III. Ochus and the Syrian revolt	360
Story of Bagoses	361
Alexander the Great and the Jews	362
Judæa from Alexander to Antiochus Epiphanes	363
Joseph the son of Tobias	366
Relation of the Jews to the outer world	367
Opposition to heathenism	368
Proselytizing tendencies	369
Ruth and Jonah	371
Universalist fragments in the Book of Isaiah	372
Influence of Persian rule upon Judaism	373
Influence of Hellenism	374
The Hellenistic party	375
The party of vigorous opposition	376
Moderate Hellenism	377

	PAGE
The Book of Ecclesiastes	379
The introductory chapters of Proverbs (i.—ix.)	380
Sirach or Ecclesiasticus	381
Effect of the persecutions of Antiochus Epiphanes	382
The Temple and its worship	383
The Book of Chronicles	384
The Temple and the Psalter	385
The Psalter and post-exilic piety	386
Religious effect of the Temple and its ceremonial	387
The Scriptures	389
The synagogue and its services	390
The priesthood and the Levites	392
The Scribes and their origin	394
Literary products of the early Scribes in the Old Testament: the Book of Proverbs	396
The conception of Wisdom	398
The Law and the teaching which it fostered	400
The final redaction of the Pentateuch	402
How far the editors are to blame	404
Redaction of the Prophets: additions and interpolations	405
Their general character and purpose	406
Jonah and Daniel	408
Religious activity and variety in the post-exilic period	409
Causes of this variety	410
Religious fervour of post-exilic period	413

LECTURE VIII.

FROM NEHEMIAH TO THE MACCABEES: GOD AND ISRAEL.

The post-exilic religion	415
Point of view from which it is here regarded	416
Classification of the material and its dangers	417
Undogmatic character of early Judaism	418

	PAGE
Religion the only spiritual interest	419
The three factors of religious life: God, Israel and the Law	420
Conception of Deity: Yahveh identical with God, but God still Yahveh	421
The divine transcendence	423
Its supposed evil effects	424
God of heaven	425
God's relation to Nature	426
His relation to the Israelite: God's "nearness" and how the sense of it was won	427
Angels and their function	429
The divine Spirit	431
God's relation to Israel and its effects	432
His presence in the temple	433
The object of God's special relation to Israel	434
The divine honour	436
The Messianic hope	437
Religious effects upon the individual of the belief in God's special love of Israel	439
Humility a Jewish virtue	440
The conception of the divine character	442
God's rule and its methods: theory of divine retribution	444
The past history of Israel: the Book of Chronicles	447
Doubts and theodicies	449
Explanations of suffering	450
Outward good and outward misfortune	452
Evil angels: Satan	453
Origin and growth of the belief in a future life	454
Influence of Zoroastrianism	456
Resurrection of the body	457
References to a future life in the Psalter	458
Religious effects of belief in future life	460
Justice and goodness of God: the Divine Fatherhood	462

TABLE OF CONTENTS. xxiii

LECTURE IX.

FROM NEHEMIAH TO THE MACCABEES: THE LAW AND ITS INFLUENCE.

	PAGE
The Torah: its meaning and place in post-exilic religion	465
Ethics and religion dominated by the law	468
The effects of religion as law, and of the Jewish law in particular	470
Main contents of the ceremonial law	472
Dietary laws	473
Agrarian laws, and laws of clean and unclean	474
The rigorists on "clean and unclean"	477
The effect of the law upon men's conception of goodness	479
Supposed evil results	480
Humility and confidence	481
The "heart" recognized as the source and seat of good and evil	483
General character of Jewish morality	484
Enemies of Israel and enemies of the individual Israelite	486
Enthusiasm of Rabbinic religion and morality	488
Modification of the penal law	489
Tendency towards monogamy: the praise of chastity	491
Evil influence of the ceremonial law	492
Supposed false "intellectualism" of a legal religion: how far a true indictment of post-exilic and Rabbinic religion	493
The 'Am ha-Arets: their origin and decline	497
Gradual penetration of the law through all layers of society; its fulfilment a religious satisfaction	502
The theory that the law was a burden entirely mistaken	503
The Sabbath and prayer: two crucial examples	504
Mr. Schechter on the "burden of the law"	506
Tendency towards diminution in evil results of ceremonial law when obeyed by all	508
The distinction between the ceremonial and the moral never forgotten; case of fasting as illustration	509
Effect of the law upon the conception of sin and sinfulness	512
National self-righteousness and individual humility	514

TABLE OF CONTENTS.

	PAGE
The sense of individual sinfulness sometimes obscured through the law	516
Human free-will and divine grace	518
Atonement and forgiveness: fusion of prophetic and priestly doctrine	521
Repentance the condition of forgiveness	523
Tendency towards doctrines of "good works" and "merit"	525
The potency of almsgiving	526
The motives of the observance of the law	529
Wrong emphasis usually given to utilitarian or mercenary motive	530
Prof. Schultz and Prof. Schürer	532
The mercenary or eudæmonistic motive strongest in Deuteronomy and weakest with the Rabbis	533
The law obeyed from purely religious motives: the love of the law	534
How a belief in reward and a disinterested love of the law and of its Giver are quite compatible with each other	536
How through the law the Jew felt himself to be God's child and God to be his Father	539
General estimate of post-exilic religion: Wellhausen and St. Paul	541
Undogmatic and unsystematized character of post-exilic religion, its causes and its effects	543
Legalism and its ethical and religious results	547
The future of Judaism	550

APPENDIX.

I. THE DATE OF THE DECALOGUE	553
II. LEGAL EVASIONS OF THE LAW	557
ADDITIONS AND CORRECTIONS	564

Lecture I.

ORIGIN AND FOUNDATION OF THE HEBREW RELIGION.

These Lectures have for their subject the Origin and Growth of the Religion of the Hebrews. Whatever view may be held as to the natural or supernatural derivation of that religion, its history has a higher and more immediate interest for us than the history of any other religion of antiquity. For, while it would be unjust exclusively to identify the history of the Hebrew religion with the history of Monotheism, inasmuch as the monotheistic conception was attained by chosen individuals of other races independently, that form of monotheism which Europe and its colonies have adopted is based upon, and is descended from, the ancient Hebrew faith. Thus our attitude towards the old Hebrew religion is different from our attitude towards other religions, such as those of Egypt or Assyria or Mexico, which have formed the subject of Hibbert Lectures in previous years. There are many million souls to whom the sacred books of the old Hebrews are sacred still; sacred, either because they are believed to be inspired in higher measure than the sacred literature of other races, or else because of that ethical sanctity which attaches to the written origins of the greatest spiritual possessions of civilized mankind.

Upon any one, therefore, who deals with Israel's religion, there rests a peculiar responsibility. No one can be more conscious of this than I am, or better aware of the difficulties of the task which has been entrusted to my care.

It is, perhaps, hardly necessary for a Hibbert Lecturer to say anything of the point of view from which he intends to treat his subject, even though that subject is the religion of Israel. He has only to take care that no personal opinions of his own shall obscure or prejudice the story he has to tell. That story must be told in the spirit and method of criticism as distinguished from the spirit and method of tradition. Tradition has been accustomed to regard the fundamental religious teaching of the entire Old Testament as one and the same throughout. Abraham and Moses and David and Isaiah and Ezra were assumed to have been, one and all of them, monotheists of the same pure type. Tradition has taken for granted the accuracy of the Biblical narratives, and, speaking very generally, has regarded each book of the Old Testament as a contemporary record of the age with which it dealt. In this view the chronological order of the different books is predetermined. The religious institutions of the Israelites and their system of sacred law become coincident in time with the beginnings of their national life. Criticism, on the other hand, makes the discovery that the Laws of the Pentateuch are not always consistent with one another: Deuteronomy contradicts Leviticus, and Exodus contradicts itself. The David of the Books of Samuel is very different from the supposed David of the Psalms, and both are different from the David of Chronicles. The religious institutions of the monarchy are often flagrantly opposed to Pentateuchal ordinances; and the older prophets, who, upon the traditional hypothesis, must have regarded the Mosaic writings as the basis of their religious ideas, maintain complete silence about them.

Criticism finds, in fact, that the Old Testament is neither homogeneous in doctrine nor consistent in standard of practice, and it attempts to establish some sort of relation between such divergences as these and differences of date: it seeks to arrange them in some order, and to show, if possible, their logical connection one with another, and the historical development of the later out of the earlier stage. We may ultimately find that an unbroken chronological development from the most immature doctrines and practices which are discoverable in the Biblical books to the noblest and most mature, is unhistorical. There may be a period of decline intervening between two periods of progress. The general tendency of Biblical criticism has been to emphasize the originality and importance of the Prophets, and to place the Law and the Poetical Books in a new relation to them in the chronological order. The dates assigned by tradition to Amos, Hosea and Isaiah, are not affected; but whereas, according to tradition, the Psalms and the Proverbs were earlier than these Prophets, according to criticism they are later; and the legal portion of the Pentateuch, all of which tradition would fain believe anterior to the Prophets, stands almost in its entirety after them.

As to the "growth" or "development" of the ancient

Hebraic religion, criticism has reached many results which may be regarded as well ascertained and sure, or which, at any rate, are winning their way more and more decisively to general acceptance, and changing from hypothesis into fact. Such conclusions we may gladly receive with that cautious readiness which should welcome the results of scientific investigation, and with the reverence which the subject to be illustrated demands. But as to the "origin" of this religion, criticism still speaks with no certain voice. In the main, its verdict is chiefly negative: it has shown the inadequacy of traditional views, but replaced them with no unquestionable construction of its own: it has revealed where legend was masquerading in the dress of history, but it has not yet been able to substitute for the unmasked legends a positive narrative of truth. The rule that all origins are obscure is nowhere more true than in the religious history of Israel. And yet the origin of Israel's religion must be the subject of this initial Lecture. It is thus inevitable—and this point needs emphatic insistance—that the results to be obtained are purely inferential and argumentative. Out of a variety of conflicting hypotheses, one will be adopted and defended as the most probable. Now the probability of any hypothesis upon the origin of the Hebrew religion is in proportion to the extent with which it squares with the facts of the subsequent historic period, and best explains how these facts may have come to be.

It is necessary to indicate the causes of this deep obscurity which rests over the beginnings of our subject. And here I may premise that a certain familiarity with the contents of the Old Testament, and with the course of the history which it embodies, will be throughout assumed.

The material from which an investigation into "the origin and development" of the Hebrew religion must be built up, is twofold in character. There is, in the first place, the evidence won from the religions of other kindred or neighbouring peoples—the evidence, in other words, of comparative religion, and more particularly of that portion of it which deals with the Semitic races. This evidence is obviously indirect: it may explain a fact or suggest an hypothesis; the facts themselves must come from another source. That source is the Old Testament itself. In the absence of religious inscriptions and works of art, we possess no other first-hand and immediate authority. What the Old Testament has to tell us of the origin and development of its religion may be illustrated, emended or rejected, both by the comparative evidence of other races and by historical criticism; there is no fresh and external material upon which to construct a new account independent of the old.

It is true that the religion of Israel is professedly an historical religion, and possesses documents which claim to give an historical account of its origin and fortunes. But the earliest portions of these documents, like the sacred traditions of other races, embody not history but legend, the unhistoric character of which, in the light of comparative religion, is pretty easily determined. Where legend passes into history, the difficulties are not overcome, for the history is narrated to us by writers who lived many centuries after the events which they describe, and who habitually allow the past to speak in the language of their own age.

We possess no unquestionably authentic and homogeneous contemporary writings older than the second half of the eighth century B.C. It is important to realize definitely the bearing of this statement. Let us assume that upon Israelite history, as distinct from Israelite legend, the curtain rises at the moment when the Hebrew clans, under the guidance of a common leader, are about to leave their settlements upon the borders of Egypt and to seek a new home in Canaan. The date of this movement was perhaps somewhere about 1250 B.C. The fortunes of the tribes from the exodus from Egypt till the age of Isaiah, in other words till the eighth century, are in their outline familiar to us all. These five hundred years include the settlement of the tribes in Canaan, the period of the Judges, the establishment of the monarchy under Saul and its transference to David, the disruption of the kingdom on the death of Solomon, and then a series of rulers in the two monarchies during the two hundred years that lie between Solomon and Jeroboam the Second. Many great names are familiar to us in the course of this period. First and foremost come Moses himself, his brother Aaron, and his successor Joshua; then, in the time of the Judges, Deborah and Barak, Gideon and Abimelech, Jephthah and Eli. We pass on to Samuel, whose figure is prominent in the history of the early monarchy; to Nathan and Gad, the seers who were bold enough to censure the wrong-doings of their master and king; to the prophet Ahijah, who foretold to Solomon the insurrection of Jeroboam; and, some hundred years later, to the majestic figures of Elijah and Elisha, who lived and taught about a century before Amos and Hosea.

And now let us recall to mind that from all these centuries, with their long roll of great events and great names, there remains not one homogeneous and complete literary work. Once more let us look at the same fact from another point of view. When we open an English Bible we find the writings of the Old Testament arranged upon a certain plan. First come historical books, then poetical books, then prophetical books. Now the poetical books are one and all, in the light of a criticism which I believe to be assured, later than the eighth century. Of the prophetical books, Hosea, Amos, and certain portions of Isaiah and Micah, are authentic documents of the eighth century; the rest are all later. There remain the historical books. Exclude Ruth, Chronicles, Ezra, Nehemiah, Esther, which are all subsequent to the eighth century, and we are left with the Pentateuch and the books of Joshua, Judges, Samuel and Kings. Now the word "book" is here misleading. We think of a book as written by a single person within a limited time; but not one of these books was written by a single person, or even within the limits of a single century. They contain isolated documents, such as the Song of Deborah and the Blessing of Jacob, which are comparatively ancient; but in their present form, and even in much of their matter, they are later than the eighth century. Their earlier portions may belong to the ninth, a very small element to the tenth century. They are derived from many sources, and these sources had themselves a history, during which they did not retain their original shape, but, in the process by which they were fused together to form each of these so-called books, underwent many modifications. We shall presently see the reason why the fact that these books have undergone repeated revisions, and that they incorporate increments from different centuries, compels us to use their evidence as to the origin and early growth of the religion of Israel with the utmost caution.

Be it granted, then, that the earliest authentic and homogeneous writings of the Old Testament belong to the eighth century B.C. They belong, therefore, to a period which had left the first formative stages of religion a long way behind. And secondly, they are the writings of men whose religious standpoint was an ethical monotheism, if not theoretically absolute, yet already practically master of the field. Thus here, where for the first time we reach an unyielding foothold, we find the religion whose growth and origin we investigate, in some of its main principles almost full-grown. The men whose writings I refer to are the four prophets of the eighth century—Amos, Hosea, Isaiah and Micah.

To their teaching I shall naturally have to direct your attention later on in some detail; but I wish here to summarize its heads, in order that we may see what the religion of our first authentic witnesses actually was. For it is from their words that, following the example of Prof. Kuenen, we must begin our investigation into the origin of the religion of Israel. From what is certain we must trace our steps back to the uncertain, and, starting from the known faith of Amos and Isaiah, attempt to determine its origin and development in doubtful and disputed sources.

The religious faith of these great teachers was on the border-land which separates monolatry from monotheism. For practical purposes it was, however, distinctly monotheistic, and as such it may be now regarded. Yet their monotheism strikes us at once as different from our own in one important point, which was, however, essentially connected both with its religious and with its popular character. Their Deity is the God of their race, and is addressed by a proper name. For us, the unity of God is as much a necessity of our thought as the unity of the world. A distinctive appellation for Deity is as absurd as a distinctive appellation for the universe: it is not necessary to distinguish them from other members of the same categories, for each is co-extensive with its class. God exhausts deity, and the universe exhausts the world. But for our eighth-century prophets monotheism meant something different: its meaning was, that one particular God, with one particular name, the God of their own particular nation, had driven all other gods out of the field. Yahveh—for that is his name—is still the God of the Israelites, though he be also the Creator of heaven and earth. Practically, indeed, he has become the only God, for his power and his interest are not limited to Israel; other divine agencies, even if they exist, are beside him of no account. But his personality is so marked that he is more familiar to the prophets under the name Yahveh than as simply God.

In spite of this limitation, as well as in spite of the

fact that to the prophets Yahveh is far more closely related to, and interested in, one particular race than we can conceive it possible for God to be, there are yet essential features of their doctrine in which, after seven- and-twenty centuries of progress, we are still largely at one with them. What Yahveh's exact nature is, they do not tell us, beyond implying that, like the angels whose Lord he is, it is spirit and not flesh.[1] But of his character they speak clearly. He is wise and just and good. The duties which he imposes upon his worshippers are civic righteousness, purity and compassion. For himself he claims only a rigid abstention from the worship or acknowledgment of "other gods." Ceremonial worship, in antiquity equivalent to sacrifice, is indifferent to Yahveh; but where united with injustice and unchastity, it becomes a moral abomination. Sacred images and material representations of the Godhead in any human or animal form are abhorrent to the prophets: their religion is almost wholly free from the superstitious elements which disfigured other religions of antiquity. Sorcery and witchcraft are hateful to their God. His will is made known by special revelations which he gave and gives to chosen individuals. The form and manner of these revelations are not clearly defined, but there is no adequate evidence to show that the prophets shared the belief of antiquity, and of their contemporaries, in the possibility of ascertaining the Divine will by the casting of a sacred lot.

The object, then, of the present Lecture is to find a

[1] Isaiah xxxi. 3.

working hypothesis as to the origin of this religion,— the historic origin, if that be still possible, of that phase of monotheism which the prophets of Israel and Judah taught publicly in the eighth century B.C. And as we can see that this monotheism is still young and immature, and must clearly have sprung from a monolatry out of which it has scarcely become emancipated, the problem may at once be pushed one stage farther back, and resolved into the question as to the origin of the monolatry which preceded the nascent monotheism of the prophets. Monolatry must be here understood to imply a faith, the primal law of which is, that only one particular god must be worshipped by its adherents, but which does not deny the existence of other gods beyond its own pale. Monolatry is the worship of one god; monotheism, of the one and only God.

Now the history of the Hebrew people and of its religion up to the era of the eighth-century prophets may be divided into three periods of very unequal length, to any one of which the origin of Hebrew monolatry may be, and has been, assigned. The first period is traditionally known as the age of the Patriarchs, and is supposed to stretch from Abraham to Joseph. It is described in the Book of Genesis, and comprises the history of four generations. But from the narratives in Genesis we can make no safe or cogent deductions as to the religious condition and opinions of the Hebrews in the pre-Mosaic era.

The Patriarchal age of the Hebrews corresponds with the heroic age in Greece. As they are presented to us in Genesis, Abraham, Isaac and Jacob, and Jacob's

12   I. ORIGIN AND FOUNDATION OF

twelve sons, are not historical personalities, but legendary heroes.[1] This is freely admitted even by so cautious a critic as Dillmann. He asserts: "At the present day it is self-evident that all the stories about the Patriarchs belong to the domain of legend, not to that of rigorous history. It must be unreservedly allowed that of no people on earth are its actual ancestors historically trace-

[1] It is impossible here to attempt any proof of this apparently startling statement. But before the "general reader" argues that it has been rashly made on inadequate evidence, let him first read the authorities referred to in this note. As Kuenen said in 1870, it is in the abstract possible that such persons as Abraham, Isaac and Jacob should have existed; but the question at issue is, "whether the progenitors of Israel and of the neighbouring nations who are represented in Genesis, are historical personages. It is this question which we answer in the negative." Since Kuenen wrote, the discovery of the two Palestinian localities, Yaqbal = Jacob-el, and Ishpal = Joseph-el, in the Karnak list of places conquered by Thothmes III. (16th century) of Egypt, shows that Jacob and Joseph were names of tribes, and then, perhaps, of the places where they dwelt, long before they became the names of individualized *heroes epongmi*. Cf. Meyer, *Z. A. W.*, 1886, pp. 1—16; 1888, pp. 42—46; Groff, *Revue égyptologique*, 1885, Vol. IV. pp. 95—101, 146—151; Renan, *Histoire du peuple d'Israel*, Vol. I. pp. 107, 112; *Records of the Past*, N.S., Vol. V. pp. 48, 51. It is another question whether Abraham, Sarah, &c., were originally divinities. Nöldeke still maintains this view; cf. his article on the Hebrew Patriarchs in *Im neuen Reich*, 1871, pp. 497—511, and *Z.D.M.G.*, 1888, p. 484; and generally for the legendary or mythical character of the Patriarchs, Kuenen, *Religion of Israel*, Vol. I. pp. 108—115; *De stamvaders van het Israelitische volk: Theol. Tijdschrift*, 1871, p. 255, &c.; Review of Popper's *Ursprung des Monotheismus*, ditto, 1880, p. 461, &c.; Matthes' Review of Goldziher, *Der Mythus bei den Hebräern*, ditto, 1877, p. 188, &c., p. 241, &c.; Stade, *Geschichte des Volks Israel*, Vol. I. pp. 126—129; *Z. A. W.*, 1881, pp. 112—116, pp. 347—350; Renan, *Revue des études juives*, 1882, p. 162; Wellhausen, *History of Israel*, p. 318, &c.; Piepenring, *La livre de la Genèse: Revue de l'histoire des religions*, 1890, pp. 1—62.

able. For a nation is not formed like a family, but grows together out of a variety of heterogeneous materials. The Biblical representation of all the Hebrew tribes as descended from twelve sons of one father does not imply the historic result of an actual blood relationship or of natural consanguinity: it was rather the product of artifice and purpose, and depended on geographical, political, and even religious considerations. The personifications of nations, tribes, territories and periods, universally acknowledged for the stories contained in the first eleven chapters of Genesis, do not suddenly cease with chapter twelve. They still recur, and not only in the mere genealogies of nations. And now that we have a wide knowledge of the legendary poetry of the most various peoples, it is no longer necessary to prove that the life-like individuality of the Genesis stories is in itself no evidence of their historic truth, but, on the contrary, is a characteristic peculiarity of legend."[1] For the earliest history of the Hebrew religion, the only positive conclusion to be drawn from the stories of the Patriarchs is purely inferential. Our estimate of the Mosaic period may induce us to believe that even before Moses, and partially explaining both his teaching and its success, there existed among the Hebrew clans an inner circle of purer religious faith, which, as Dillmann plaintively pleads, if it was in any sense a reality, must almost necessarily have been realized and carried forward by certain special, or even exceptional, individuals. But this is no more than shadowy hypothesis, and our first period therefore remains a pre-historic age, in which, so far as direct evidence

[1] Dillmann, *Die Genesis*, 5th ed., 1886, p. 215.

goes, the outward events and the inward spiritual development are alike unknown.

Between the first and second period—between Genesis and Exodus—the family of Abraham has become the people of Israel. The second period is the age of Moses and Joshua, of the exodus from Egypt, and of the settlement in Canaan. It is described by the sacred history of the Pentateuch as the age in which the true national life was begun, and the national religion established, by special and novel revelations of the national God to Moses, his servant. Moses is the traditional founder of the national religion, and with this estimate of tradition the prophets of the eighth century substantially agree. Criticism regards this period as a mixture of legend and of fact, in which legend predominates. Yet the departure of the Hebrew clans from Egypt marks the moment in which the semi-historical, as contrasted with the purely legendary, epoch of both the political and religious life of Israel may be considered to begin, and criticism has accepted, and still accepts, the exodus itself and the personality of Moses as assured historical realities.

But why, it will be asked, does criticism regard Moses so differently from the Patriarchs? Why are Abraham, Isaac and Jacob, legendary heroes, but Moses, on the contrary, a figure of history? Must he not also be assigned a place among that dim band of sacred founders and legislators whose personality has faded away under the fierce light of an inexorable science? Is not his history one uninterrupted sequence of miracles and impossibilities? The answers to these questions are manifold. The historic reality of Moses is mainly a matter of inference. Yet any one can see that there is a real difference between the narratives of Genesis, and those of the remaining books of the Pentateuch. In the former we deal with individuals; in the latter, with a people and its leaders. The strong and uniform tradition that Israel's religious and national life began with the deliverance from Egypt and the entry into Canaan, accepted and emphasized by the eighth-century prophets as well as by the authors of the Pentateuch, is not to be lightly set aside. It would, indeed, have to be rejected if the course of the subsequent history appeared resolutely to contradict it. But this is not so. As we shall see, the course of religious development and its explanation support tradition to this extent, that they posit and demand a higher and purer religious belief for the Hebrews than for the Canaanites. And if this be so, there is nothing in the way of accepting tradition in the further step of connecting the origin and inculcation of this higher religious faith with the person and the work of Moses.

The third period extends from the end of the Mosaic age to the eighth-century prophets—an interval of some five hundred years. In one of the earliest stories related to us from this third period—though two centuries may perhaps have already elapsed since the first settlements in Canaan—we pass out of the legendary epoch, and are presented with a piece of contemporary evidence—the Song of Deborah, the oldest fragment, in all probability, preserved to us in the Hebrew Scriptures. And, from Deborah onwards, allowing for certain gaps, the story of Israel can be recounted in a continuous and historic narrative.¹ There are still occasional legends, and the documents from which such a narrative is drawn are of composite material and in their preponderating bulk of later date than the events which they describe, but the course of the *outward* history, at least, can be sufficiently ascertained.

In which, then, of these three periods did the law and practice of monolatry take their rise? Was monolatry the gradual acquisition of the third or historic period; was it the novel teaching of Moses; or, lastly, is its origin to be relegated, as an immemorial custom rather than a conscious enactment, to the earliest and pre-historic age?

If the first appearance of monolatry, either as custom or law, be denied not only to the pre-historic but also to the Mosaic age, such a decision runs counter to the narratives of the Pentateuch, to the editors of the historical books, and, above all, to the prophets of the eighth century. For, while the prophets are wholly ignorant of any comprehensive Mosaic Law, regulating alike the social life of the people and the ceremonial worship of Yahveh, so that the Pentateuch, as we now possess it, was indisputably unknown to them, they allude to Moses as a prophet, though not as a lawgiver. While they are in marked and strenuous opposition to the popular religion of their day, they throughout represent themselves as restorers rather than as innovators. Theirs is the legitimate religion of Israel; and more than once the exodus from Egypt is referred to as the epoch which witnessed

¹ Deborah's date may perhaps be assigned to the eleventh century B.C.

THE HEBREW RELIGION. 17

the establishment of that true national faith which is also their own.[1]

The editors of the historical books—Judges, Samuel and Kings—who arranged, manipulated and annotated material of very various dates, put forward a view of Israel's religious history between the age of Moses and that of the prophets which has become traditional, and with which we are all familiar. They agree with the prophets in their estimate of the Mosaic age, but they represent the history of Israel from the first settlement in Canaan as a long record of perpetually recurrent apostasy. Monolatry was, indeed, the law, but it was broken again and again.

Thus they tell us that "the people of Israel served Yahveh all the days of Joshua and all the days of the elders that outlived Joshua, who had seen all the great works of Yahveh which he did for Israel," but that after their deaths "the children of Israel did evil in the sight of Yahveh and served the Baals and Ashtoreths."[2] This idolatrous impulse was never suppressed till the Israelites were driven from their land into exile; its action was, however, interrupted by spasmodic intervals of repentance and reform, during which the false gods were abandoned, and Yahveh was served alone.

Criticism is unable to accept this interpretation of the religious history of Israel in the period between Joshua and the eighth-century prophets. But while scholars are agreed in its rejection, there are opposing theories

[1] Amos ii. 10, iii. 1, v. 25, ix. 7; Hosea xi. 1, xii. 13, xiii. 4; cf. also Micah vi. 4 (? 7th century); Jer. vii. 22, xv. 1, ii. 2.

[2] Judges ii. 7, 13.

which they would substitute in its place. According to the one theory, the *law* of monolatry would be ascribed to, and have originated in, our third or post-Mosaic period; according to the other, to which I myself adhere, it would be relegated to one of the two periods preceding. In the short presentment and discussion of these theories, it will be necessary to allude to some matters which will have to be treated of again in their proper place when we have reached a probable, if only hypothetical, starting-point for our narrative, and can deal with the religious history of Israel progressively in chronological sequence. That starting-point of our whole subject is the quest of the present Lecture: we shall find it—let me add by anticipation—in the teaching of Moses.

The question in dispute is really twofold, being concerned with a fact and with the fact's interpretation. The fact to discover is, whether between Joshua and the eighth century there was in truth so much actual idolatry as the editors of the histories aver; the interpretation to be formed is, whether, if such idolatry existed, it was natural and innocent, or a conscious infraction of a known monolatrous law. How far was the commandment, "Thou shalt have no other gods but Yahveh," observed by the men of the post-Mosaic period; and if it was broken, was it, at any rate, known? The material with which to ascertain the fact is contained in the documents which form the substratum of the histories, and are easily to be detached from the editorial nexus.

The first theory accepts the view of the editors that there was much idolatry between Joshua and Amos, and holds that there is in the earlier documents sufficient proof and basis for that opinion. Yahveh was the chief divinity; but the law claiming for him an exclusive worship was a very gradual growth, which did not ripen fully till the age of Ahab and Elijah. A modification of this theory was put forward some twenty years ago by Prof. Kuenen in his famous book, "The Religion of Israel." While it was there admitted that Moses had proclaimed the law, "No God but Yahveh," it was argued that this principle of monolatry was neither accepted nor understood by the great majority of his contemporaries. After his death it was lost sight of altogether, partly through the seductive influence of Canaanite polytheism, partly by the recrudescence of primitive Hebrew paganism. The mistake of the historical editors consists in regarding the idolatry of that time as a conscious abandonment of Yahveh, or as a wilful breach of his law. For the worship of other local (i.e. Canaanite) or neighbouring divinities was not supposed to be inconsistent with the pious service of Yahveh as the chief or tutelary God.

The second and opposing theory, of which Prof. Stade is one of the ablest exponents, denies, not only the editorial interpretation, but also, to a considerable extent, the existence of the supposed facts upon which the interpretation is imposed.

According to this theory, which, so far as I can see, is nearer to the facts, there is no such amount of idolatry recorded in the period between Joshua and Amos, which is not consistent with an acknowledged law of monolatry, put forward, let us provisionally assume, by Moses, and never forgotten or wholly ignored since the founder's death. It is true that when the Israelites entered Canaan, lived among, and largely assimilated to themselves, the native population, and gradually exchanged a pastoral for an agricultural life, their religious practices and views underwent considerable modification. It is generally believed that their subsequent forms of worship—their feasts and sacrificial rites, their altars upon high places and under green trees—were borrowed from the Canaanites. Many may also have borrowed the deities to whom the rites were originally devoted. "The apostasy to Baal," the chief deity of the Canaanites, says Professor Wellhausen, " upon the part of the first generation which had quitted the wilderness and adopted a settled agricultural life, is attested alike by historical and prophetical tradition."[1] By degrees, however, Baal came to be identified, rather than merely co-ordinated, with Yahveh, whose worship, and, in the minds of some, whose character, approximated more and more closely to the worship and character of his rival.

But as a set-off to this partial infiltration of Canaanite belief, there is very much to be said upon the other side. Our oldest prophetic sources, imbedded in the historical books, say and imply nothing of general and constant fluctuations from idolatry to monolatry, and from monolatry to idolatry. The eighth-century prophets, whose evidence is unimpeachable, though they do accuse the people of idolatrous practices, show so marked a tendency to identify a corrupt and material worship of Yahveh with the service of other gods, that it becomes a grave question whether the idolatry with which they charge their con-

[1] *Abriss der Geschichte Israels und Judas*, in *Erstes Heft der Skizzen und Vorarbeiten*, 1884, p. 18.

temporaries ought not usually to be interpreted as equivalent to the irregular and unauthorized service, after heathen fashion, of the same God whom accusers and accused alike acknowledged. The national leaders, both martial and spiritual, from Deborah to David, were all worshippers of Yahveh. It stands out as a prominent and incontrovertible fact, that down to the reign of Ahab, by whom there is a distinct attempt to introduce the worship of a foreign god, no prominent man in Israel, with the doubtful exception of Solomon, known by name and held up for condemnation, worshipped any other god but Yahveh. In every national and tribal crisis, in all times of danger and of war, it is Yahveh, and Yahveh alone, who is invoked to give victory and deliverance.

Hence, since that which the Canaanites gave to the Israelites was idolatrous in texture, and certainly not the monolatrous worship of Yahveh, we may infer that monolatry was the recognized rule, the concurrent worship of other gods the irregular exception, in the post-Mosaic and pre-prophetic Israel. In other words, the origin of the Hebrew monolatry of which we are in search, must fall behind the limits of our third period, and be due either to the second or the first.[1]

[1] It should in fairness be stated that one objection, though not to my mind a convincing one, against this line of argument is, that whereas proper names compounded of Yahveh or Yah are frequent after Saul, they are rare in the earlier periods. Thus Nöldeke uses this fact to the following effect. The names of which Yahveh or Yah forms part, " entscheiden schon fast allein dafür dass mindestens seit der Theilung des Reichs Jahve allgemein als Hauptgott, wenn nicht als einziger Gott des Volkes angesehen ward. In älterer Zeit treten dagegen solche Namen höchstens vereinzelt auf. Von den Namen der Stämme und Geschlechter, die doch zum grossen Theil wohl erst nach

I. ORIGIN AND FOUNDATION OF

Does it, then, belong to the first period—the pre-historic age? If so, monolatry would have begun as a custom centuries before it was transmitted into a law. But is this not within the limits of probability? Have we not been told by a distinguished scholar of a Semitic instinct towards monotheism; and may not, therefore, monolatry, at any rate, have been the wonted practice of at least some Semitic tribes, of whom the Israelites were one?

It thus becomes necessary to glance at some illustrative features of Semitic religion in general, and at the place of the Israelites in the aggregate of the Semitic races.

A full discussion into the origin and development of Israelite monotheism should, indeed, include an adequate estimate of Semitic religion, and also, if this were possible, of the religions of that section of the Semitic family to which the Hebrews more immediately belonged. Yet such an estimate, it need scarcely be said, is beyond the limits of a course of Lectures such as these, as it is also wholly beyond the powers of the lecturer.

The problem most germane to our own inquiry would be the question already alluded to, whether there existed

der Ansiedlung in Kanaan enstanden sind, enthält keiner יהו. Die Mutter Mose's יוכבד mag für historisch halten, wer will. Der Heros der Ephraimiten der die Eroberung leitet, heisst zwar gewöhnlich יהושע, aber eigentlich הושע, Num. xiii. 16. Gideon's Vater יואש und sein Sohn יורם können nach יהוה genannt sein, aber diese Namen lassen auch andre Ableitungen zu. Erst mit der Gründung des Königthums werden solche Namen häufig. Das deutet darauf, dass dieser Gottesname verhältnissmässig neu ist, und sich erst allmählich verbreitet hat, und was vom Namen gilt, wird doch auch einigermassen von dem dadurch ausgedrückten Begriff gelten."—*Z. D. M. G.*, 1888, p. 477.

THE HEBREW RELIGION. 23

among the Semitic races generally anything approaching to a tendency or instinct for monotheism. It is well known how frequently this question has been debated hither and thither in recent years. To the course of its history since M. Renan started his famous theory of the monotheistic instinct of the Semitic races, it is unnecessary to allude. Although in the form proposed by him nearly forty years ago, and still maintained in his "History of Israel," it has not won general approbation, because it is unsupported by facts, modifications of it are still occasionally put forward and defended by eminent scholars. Where the Semitic races have been least subject to external influence, and have apparently preserved their individuality most strongly, certain general religious characteristics are observable which can be interpreted in a monotheistic direction. An exuberant mythology is markedly wanting in the religion of such purely Semitic races. Many names of Semitic deities are merely titular or descriptive. "Baal" or Master, "Moloch" or King, "Adonis" or Lord, would seem to be divinities of races who not only distinguished God from nature, but had not even created him out of it. Then, again, several Semitic races possessed one chief or tribal god, to whom worship was, if not exclusively, at all events mainly, paid; and with others there seems some evidence that a plurality of gods had resulted from the amalgamation of independent clans into a single nation.[1]

---

[1] Assyrian religion had better be put on one side, because of the adoption by the Semitic invaders of the older Accadian divinities. On the religion of other Semitic races, cf. Tiele, *Histoire comparée des anciennes religions de l'Égypte et des peuples Sémitiques*, 1882; Baeth-

A partially monotheistic view of the oldest Semitic religion has lately been again put forward by Professor Baethgen. He believes that the Semites started, not indeed with monotheism, but with what he calls "monism;" they worshipped El or God, and the word indicated, not the totality of the separate gods, but the undivided and impersonal divine essence. There are, however, many objections to such hypotheses, if they imply that the earlier or pre-historic faith of the Semites was higher and purer than the faiths which succeeded it. No single theory has yet been able to explain all the phenomena of Semitic religions. Besides the Semitic deities whose names indicate dominion or power, there are others which are clearly nature-gods whose names explain their origin.[1] A nature-myth peeps out at least of one story in the Old Testament, the appearance of which cannot with any certainty be ascribed to a non-Semitic influence.[2] Just as the origin of all religion is

gen, *Beiträge zur semitischen Religionsgeschichte*, 1888; Wellhausen, *Reste arabischen Heidentumes*, 1887; Pietschmann, *Geschichte der Phönizier*, 1889, pp. 152—237; Nöldeke, *Z. D. M. G.*, 1887 and 1888, in reviews of Baethgen and Wellhausen; Meyer, *Geschichte des Alterthums*, 1884, Vol. I. pp. 210—212; Chantepie de la Saussaye, *Lehrbuch der Religionsgeschichte*, 1887, Vol. I. pp. 214—223 : *Die semitische Familie* (many other references are there given); Robertson Smith, *Religion of Semites*, 1889, especially pp. 66—69, 92—94.

[1] Der Satz, dass die Semiten im Gegensatz zu den Indereuropäern keine eigentliche Naturvergötterung gekannt hätten, ist wenigstens in der Schroffheit ganz unrichtig. Wo Sonne Mond und Venusstern verehrt werden, da ist es spitzfindig den einfachen Naturdienst zu leugnen. Nöldeke, *Z. D. M. G.*, 1888, p. 485.

[2] The story of Samson : but Prof. Wilken has lately thrown doubt upon this. See his interesting essay, *De Simsonsage* in the *Gids* of March, 1888.

due to more than one source, ancestor-worship, spirit-worship, and nature-worship, all contributing to its production and development, so in the formation of Semitic religions must there have been more than one operating cause. Analogy does not lead us to believe that if we were to go further and further back into pre-historic times we should find a higher or purer religion, but rather one vaguer, meaner and more trivial. It may be true we should reach a stage in which the divine powers would have received no name and no marked personality; but this would not be because they were higher or more universal, but because they were incoherent, characterless and chaotic. Nameless divine powers may have composed the contents of the earliest chapters of Semitic religion, rather than one nameless but single Being of unlimited might and range. Or if we assume that the tendency of the earliest Semitic clans was to worship one divinity only as the protector of their flocks and herds, this deity was in no sense conceived as a supreme God, but only as the tribal or tutelary spirit. If there was any original monolatry, it did not rise above the level of spirit-worship, for nameless deities are not gods in the personalized sense of the word at all, but merely energies with power to harm or help, and without character or individuality. When the spirits pass into gods and receive names, a more polytheistic tendency begins, for then sexual differentiation steps in, and to the patron god there is often added a goddess of similar nature, but separate personality. Then, too, the other sources of religion create other deities, so that, as the historic period opens, we have no certain evidence of any Semitic tribe worshipping only a single god. On the other hand, the worship of a chief divinity is undoubtedly a characteristic feature of Semitic religion. Pietschmann, the latest historian of Phœnicia, thinks there must have been a time when the common ancestors of the Canaanites and Phœnicians worshipped, each in their own small clan, one single deity only.[1] Here, perhaps, will lie the crucial point. If they ever did so, that single clan deity must have been one of very small capacity, and rather, as I have ventured to maintain, of the nature of a spirit than of a god. If the appellatives, Ruler, Lord, and King, were the titles of the clan deities from the beginning, this only shows how vague in outline and indefinite in character these local and tribal gods must necessarily have been. The personal God of the Hebrews had a name, the meaning of which must have been already lost in very early times. Yahveh could even be addressed as Baal without relinquishing his own proper and peculiar name. But the many Baals of the different Canaanite localities in all probability never received any more definite nomenclature.

There is no complete evidence or adequate proof that within the historical period any Semitic tribe worshipped one deity only with a peculiar proper name of his own. It is, however, necessary to look for a few moments more narrowly at the particular group of tribes of which the Israelites were one.

It would seem that the Israelite people was formed by

[1] *Geschichte der Phönizier*, 1889, p. 170.

the gradual closer cohesion of various clans belonging to the family of the "Hebrews."[1] From Mesopotamia to the north-east of Palestine, nomad Semitic tribes had journeyed west and south, and this, the first wave of migration, crossed the Jordan and established an agricultural and city life. Thus were constituted the "Canaanites," a people closely allied to Israel both in blood and speech. Another wave moved in a more southerly direction, and formed the conglomerate of tribes which we now know as the Arabians. Between these waves there was a third, consisting of tribes which in their aggregate included Israel and its nearest kinsfolk, Edom, Moab and Ammon. The Israelite clans appear to have lived a wandering nomad life on the eastern shores of Jordan. Then, from whatever causes, they proceeded southwards, and, settling upon portions of Egyptian territory, became subject to and oppressed by their Egyptian overlords. When, with Moses for their leader, they escaped from servitude, and journeyed once more towards Palestine, they subsequently not only acquired settlements on the east of the Jordan, but gradually made themselves masters of much of the land upon the west which lies between Carmel northwards and the steppes of Judæa towards the south. Their relations to and dealings with the Canaanites will come before us hereafter. Yet it may here be noted that in the long period which elapsed

[1] "Hebrews" means "the men of the other side," i.e. beyond Jordan. They were so called by the inhabitants of Canaan before their own occupation of the land. That the word "Hebrews" had ever a wider connotation than the Israelites, which is implied, chiefly on Stade and Wellhausen's authority, in the above sentence, is denied by Meyer, Z.A. W., 1886, p. 11.

before the various loosely connected tribes had become one people—a period of some three hundred years, reaching from Moses to David—many clans of alien, though Semitic, blood were absorbed into fellowship with them, and adopted their religion. With the Kenites there existed even into historical times a close and peculiar relationship, so that it has been suggested that the distinctive religion of Moses was of Kenite and not of Israelite origin. Kenites and Midianites belonged to the Arab nomads of the south; though akin, they were not so near in blood to the Israelites as were the men of Edom, Moab and Ammon. Of the subsidiary evidence to be drawn from comparative religion to illustrate or explain the religion of the Israelites, the most important chapter would unquestionably deal with the religions of these three kindred and neighbouring tribes. For if their religions were monolatrous, the argument from analogy would lead us to surmise that Israelite monolatry, like the monolatry of its neighbours, must be referred to the pre-historic age. We should need no Moses to account for its appearance, and our task would rather be to seek out and find, if that were feasible, the causes and circumstances which changed the monolatry of immemorial custom into the monolatry of conscious principle and national law.

Unfortunately, we know very little about the religions of Edom, Ammon and Moab. As regards the first, Baethgen has shown that, fragmentary as our knowledge is, it goes to establish the polytheistic character of the Edomite religion, rather than the contrary. It is not absolutely certain that the Edomites had even reached the stage of a chief divinity for all their clans. The case, however, is markedly different with Ammon and Moab. In the Book of Kings, reference is made in two or three places to Milcom, the god of the Ammonites; and Baethgen is compelled to acknowledge that, beside Milcom, there is no certain record of the worship of any other god. While he considers that this absence of evidence is solely due to the scantiness of our sources, it is open to scholars who start from different premises, and are not, like Baethgen, intent upon defending a particular hypothesis—the uniqueness of Hebrew monotheism, and its origin in revelation—to draw a different, and not merely negative, inference even from such fragmentary notices as we possess.[1] As regards Moab, we are fortunate enough to possess in the Moabite stone a first-hand authority. The chief god of the Moabites was Chemosh, and he undoubtedly stood to Moab in a relation very similar to that in which Yahveh stood to Israel. This fact we can even deduce from the Old Testament, in which Moab is called the people of Chemosh. On the Moabite stone, king Mesa speaks of Chemosh much as an early Israelite king would speak of Yahveh. At the bidding of Chemosh, the king fights against Israel, and by his help he wins the victory. But this very stone of Mesa seems to show that Chemosh was not the only deity acknowledged in Moab. The king speaks of having devoted the town of Nebo to Ashtor-Chemosh, a compound deity clearly distinct from the simple god. Here, then, we have evidence of a (probably female) deity who was worshipped alongside of Chemosh, and so

[1] Cf. Kuenen, *Theol. Tijd.*, 1888, pp. 570—588.

closely connected with him that the two in their union were regarded as a new and single divinity. Chemosh is, therefore, no exclusive god like Yahveh; he admits a female associate, and from their alliance a third divinity is compounded. Whether the Baal or Lord of Peor is identical with Chemosh, or, as is more probable, a distinct and separate deity, may be left undecided.[1] The Moabite stone is sufficient to show that in historical times the principle of monolatry was unacknowledged in Moab. Thus two out of the three nations nearest akin to Israel were certainly not monolatrous in the same sense as Israel. While the character of their neighbours' religions would lead us to expect among the Hebrews the worship of a chief divinity, it is not sufficient to make us prepared for *a law* of monolatry, or to explain to us its origin upon the simple method of analogy.

If the three nearest kinsmen are thus unable to establish the existence of a Semitic monolatry beyond the pale of Israel, it may be safely asserted that no other Semitic tribe less closely related to Israel—and certainly not any tribe or city of the Canaanites—can be shown to have practised monolatry, whether as custom or as law. Now the light thrown by the Old Testament itself upon the pre-historic age—our first period—is conflicting, but it cannot with any propriety be used to substantiate the hypothesis of a pre-Mosaic and customary monolatry. We are, therefore, pushed forward to our second period; and we must now ask whether there is not good reason to follow the Pentateuchal narratives and the eighth-cen-

[1] Numbers xxv. 3. Cf. Stade, *Geschichte Israels*, Vol. I. p. 114, 2nd ed.

tury prophets to the extent of connecting the foundation of the national faith, the origin of its monolatry, with the person and teaching of Moses.

Let me here sum up the evidence in favour of thus assigning the origin of monolatry to the creative doctrine of Moses. The post-Mosaic ages were substantially monolatrous, but their monolatry was neither their own discovery nor a new inspiration. It reaches back beyond the opening, with Deborah, of the third period. Secondly, there is no likelihood that monolatry preceded Moses: the Old Testament, critically examined, is itself scarcely favourable to such a supposition, and the analogy of other races contradicts it. With the combined force of these two arguments, we have, thirdly, no sufficient justification to reject the allusions of the prophets and the statements of the Pentateuchal narratives so utterly as not to ascribe a commanding religious position to the person of Moses. And, lastly, we have the great implication involved in the conquest of Canaan. When the Israelite tribes made their gradual entry into Canaan, they must have been at a low level of material civilization. The indigenous population was admittedly their superior in general culture. The Canaanites were tillers of the soil and dwellers in cities; the new-comers were shepherds and nomads. And yet how strange was the result of the intermixture of the two races! So far from the Canaanites absorbing the Israelites, it was the Israelites who began to absorb the Canaanites, the few who overcame the many. And as in the historical age Hebrew patriotism centres in religion, as the Israelite *esprit de corps* is bound up and identified with the name and cause of Yahveh, we are entitled to infer that the victory of semi-barbarous Israel over the arts and culture of Canaan could only have been due to the religion of Yahveh. And if the religion of Yahveh triumphed over Baal and Astarte and the whole Canaanite pantheon, this was just because, while they were many, Yahveh was one, who demanded as an acknowledged right the undivided allegiance of his worshippers. Monolatry as law, not as custom, will alone explain the supremacy of Yahveh's religion in the midst of Canaanite environment. Monolatry, it is true, implies more than the abstract assertion of the worship of a single God. Nor is it in ignorance of this wider implication that we are now led to infer that in the principle of monolatry lay the essential feature and excellence of the Mosaic faith. "Thou shalt have no other god besides me:" if any Pentateuchal law, in substance though not in words, represent the Mosaic religion at all, it must be the opening injunction of the Decalogue.[1]

With this conclusion, significant as it is, we can, nevertheless, in no wise remain content. Two questions immediately present themselves. The first is, What was the character of the Mosaic monolatry? the second, How was it obtained, and what kind of religion preceded it?

A religious law of monolatry, imposed by one man upon a people who had not known it hitherto, implies definite and peculiar characteristics in the Founder's conception of the Deity, whose single worship he has induced his nation to accept. If it was borne in upon Moses that Yahveh demanded an undivided worship, so novel a con-

[1] Cf. the analogous arguments of Stade, *Geschichte*, Vol. I. pp. 439 and 516.

ception could only have arisen in his mind because Yahveh seemed to him different in quality from all the other gods, who had never yet required so exclusive an allegiance. This difference in quality could be of two kinds. A law of monolatry might have been conceived by Moses either because his god was regarded as jealous to an extreme degree of any attention paid to another deity but himself, and both able and likely to punish such parallel worship with extremest violence; or, again, it might have been conceived by him as the necessary and consistent consequence of the ethical superiority of the one chosen and accepted deity over all his rivals.

How are we to discover which of these two possibilities conditioned the monolatry of Moses, since we cannot with confidence assume that any single portion of the Pentateuch reflects back to us the true character of the Mosaic religion?

Recurring once more to the sure foothold and starting ground of our eighth-century prophets, it will be remembered that their monotheism or monolatry was distinctly ethical. To them the single worship of Yahveh is inseparable from his unique character. Can we trace this character of Yahveh back from them to the mind of Moses? Or is there a distinct cleavage and wide difference between their opinions and those of former generations? The literary material from which any answer to these questions must be attempted is primarily contained in the oldest sections of the Pentateuch and of the historical books. There is also the evidence of the prophets themselves, who often contrast, directly or indirectly, their own religious conceptions with those of their contemporaries.

Thus the next stage in our inquiry would seem to be an estimate of the pre-prophetic monolatry. Important peculiarities appear to distinguish it from the monolatry of the prophets. Several and even crucial passages, however, on which many historians and theologians rely to prove the contrast between the Yahveh of the prophets and the Yahveh of the pre-prophetic age, are themselves as late as the prophetic period; and it has been strongly urged that such passages cannot fitly be used to show that higher conceptions of the Godhead were not the possession of a Mosaic minority throughout the pre-prophetic era.[1] The supposed contrast or difference may be, not between period and period, but between popular superstition and Mosaic doctrine. But this objection will, I think, only hold if there were clear and positive evidence of specifically prophetic conceptions having been held by such a Mosaic minority before the eighth century and upwards. And this we shall not find to be the case. If the prophetic teaching was in many respects novel or progressive, it is clear that it could not have been immediately apprehended and adopted to the full by every writer or historian. There must have been a considerable period of overlapping, in which old and new ideas would co-exist in the same mind, and both be expressed in words. It is therefore, I think, legitimate to use even those passages which are subsequent to Amos and Isaiah as evidence of lower and more restricted views about God in the pre-prophetic period, unless there be special reason to suppose that they represent either primitive

---

[1] Davidson, "The Prophet Deborah:" *Expositor*, 3rd Series, Vol. V. p. 49, n. 1. Robertson, *Early Religion of Israel*, 1892, p. 303, and *passim*.

survivals, or a graft of foreign superstition upon the genuine line of religious development. A deterioration of the Founder's teaching through Canaanite influence, imperfect apprehension or a recrudescence of pre-Mosaic idolatry, must not indeed by any means be overlooked; but if we would not place Moses in too violent a contrast, not only to his contemporaries, but also to his successors, such arguments must not be pushed too far.

In the first place, then, the prophets of the eighth century seem to have made a distinct advance in the direction of monotheism. Before their time, men appear to have more fully recognized the existence of other independent divinities outside and beyond Israel. The very fact that Israel's God was addressed by a proper name shows that he was thereby contra-distinguished from the gods of other peoples and lands. It is not said in the Decalogue, There is no God but Yahveh, but, Beside Yahveh there shall be for the Israelite no other God. As Israel is the people of Yahveh, so is Moab the people of Chemosh,[1] and this parallelism must have at least arisen and been established while some considerable measure of reality was ascribed to the Moabite god. A corrupt passage in the Second Book of Kings would appear to imply that the power of Chemosh in his own land was the cause of a signal Israelite defeat.[2] Palestine is frequently called the "inheritance of Yahveh;" and in two famous passages, which are repeatedly quoted and emphasized in this connection, it would seem as if the habitual rule and interest of Yahveh were conceived as coterminous with his own land. Both of them, how-

[1] Numbers xxi. 29.
[2] 2 Kings iii. 27; cf. Stade, *Geschichte*, Vol. I. p. 431.

over, are probably as late as the eighth, and one may even belong to the seventh century. The first is where David curses those "who have driven him out from abiding in the inheritance of Yahveh, saying, Go, serve other gods." The second is a sentence in Jephthah's message to the king of Ammon, reproaching him for his attack upon Israel. "Is it not thus? That which Chemosh thy god gives thee, thou takest in possession; and whatsoever Yahveh our God has dispossessed before us, that take we in possession."[1] If we are justified in making any use of this comparatively late passage for our estimate of the pre-prophetic religion, it would certainly seem as if the older conception of Yahveh had not advanced very far beyond monolatry to monotheism.

But if in the pre-prophetic period Israelites believed frankly in the existence and power of other gods besides their own, the supremacy of Yahveh was as unquestioned by them as the supremacy of Chemosh was doubtless unquestioned by the Moabites. Nor was a belief in the mere existence of other gods, and of their power in their own lands, at all incompatible with the full acknowledgment that Yahveh was the one and only object of worship to be tolerated in Israel.

[1] 1 Sam. xxvi. 19; Judges xi. 24 (Variorum Reference Bible). For the date of the former passage, cf. Kittel, *Geschichte der Hebräer*, Vol. II. p. 38; Kuenen, *Onderzoek*, 2nd ed., Vol. I. p. 385: for that of the latter, Kittel, Vol. II. p. 80; Kuenen, Vol. I. p. 349; Wellhausen, *Composition*, p. 228 (Bleek's *Einleitung*, p. 195). Both Wellhausen and Stade use the passages as illustrations of pre-prophetic thought. For the same purpose, 2 Kings v. 17 is often made use of, which seems to contrast oddly with verse 15, and 2 Kings i. 6, which however, is again not pre-prophetic in date. Cf. Kittel, Vol. II. p. 184.

The next point of difference is more important. It relates to the inferior character of the pre-prophetic deity, and to the imperfect nature of his worship.

If we compare Yahveh as represented in the oldest sections of the historical books with what we know of other Semitic deities, we are struck by certain likenesses as well as by certain differences. Though he is a person, there is no mythology connected with him; he has no relative—above all, no goddess—either beneath him or beside him.[1] Sexual licentiousness was never connected, so far as we know, with his native and uncorrupted worship. If he be allied to any of the Semitic gods, it is rather to those severer deities whose natural affinities are with the lightning and the storm.

Thus it is that fire and thunder are the concurrent signs of a theophany. Within the burning bush lurks Yahveh himself. Fire is the symbol of his presence, and the instrument of his wrath.[2] It consumes the murmurers in Israel who have aroused his anger. In a pillar of fire and cloud he leads his people through the wilderness. It is only gradually that an effort is made to distinguish these natural phenomena from the divine nature, and to picture Yahveh as present rather in the still, small voice than in the earthquake and the fire.[3]

---

[1] Our existing Hebrew vocabulary possesses no separate word for goddess.

[2] Exod. iii. 4; 2 Kings i. 10; Judges xiii. 20; Gen. xix. 24, &c.

[3] 1 Kings xix. 11, 12. In one of his somewhat mocking moods, Wellhausen (Bleek's *Einleitung*, 4th ed. p. 246, n. 1) has warned us against the *sentimentale Ausdeutung* of this sequence of storm, earthquake, fire, and still, small voice. But cf. also Kuenen, *Nieuw en Oud,*

With the eighth-century prophets the wrath of Yahveh is a moral wrath, though even in their writings it is represented as manifesting itself upon a scale and with an intensity which are hardly consonant with our notions of divine justice and self-containment. But in the pre-prophetic period it appears occasionally as disconnected with moral motives, resembling rather the insensate violence of angered nature, than the reasonable indignation of a moralized personality. Yahveh—to borrow Wellhausen's phrase—had unaccountable moods. The holiness of Yahveh meant nothing more than an awful inviolability; he shared that common quality of the gods which makes it dangerous for man to approach them too closely, or to meddle with what belongs to them. He was not always invisible to mortal eye, but the sight of him was fraught with peril.[1] Any infringement of his rights, any trespass upon ground which was hallowed by his localized presence, was visited with extreme punishment. Thus, when the sons of Jechoniah among the men of Beth-Shemesh gaze too curiously upon the Ark of Yahveh, he kills seventy of them for their presumption.[2] When Uzzah ventures to support the Ark upon the cart, he too is killed, although his motive is good.[3] At Mount Sinai, God bids Moses caution the people against drawing too near to the mountain, lest God should break forth upon them to their destruction.[4] The priests must sanc-

1864, p. 141 (*De Profeet Elia*), reprinted now in the collected edition of the *Schetsen uit de geschiedenis van Israel*.

[1] Cf., e.g., Judges xiii. 22, &c.
[2] 1 Sam. vi. 19. For the text, see Driver's *Samuel, ad. loc.*
[3] 2 Sam. vi. 6—8.   [4] Exod. xix. 21—24.

tify themselves, otherwise, when they come near, the same fate will befal them. The wrath that follows upon sacrilege seems to be regarded by Yahveh himself as almost a mechanical reaction. Again, while the early Israelite was accustomed to attribute any strange or untoward event to the direct agency of Yahveh, he did not always regard calamity as retribution for sin. This is another indication that Yahveh's character was as yet imperfectly moralized. A frequently quoted instance of this defect is the suggestion of David that Saul's undeserved enmity may be owing either to the accusation of man or to the motiveless incitement of God.[1] In another instance, the anger of Yahveh is said to have been kindled against Israel, like the anger of Chemosh against Moab in the stone of Mesa, without any cause for indignation which the historian can discern; for, seemingly, it is mere wantonness which prompts Yahveh to move David to take the census, in order that he may punish the people thereafter for the sin which he himself had instigated.[2]

In harmony with these wrathful and fiery elements in Yahveh's character is his proclivity for battle and war. "Yahveh is a man of war, Yahveh is his name"—such is the triumphant outburst of an old song of victory.[3] "The Wars of Yahveh" was the title of a lost book in which the battles of Israel were described.[4] The spirit of Yahveh in the oldest sections of the Book of Judges

[1] 1 Sam. xxvi. 19.
[2] 2 Sam. xxiv. 1; cf. 1 Chron. xxi. 1.
[3] Exodus xv. 3. Date of song is uncertain, but it is clearly post-Mosaic (ver. 13).
[4] Numbers xxi. 14.

drives on the leaders of the people to martial exploits.[1] Enemies of Yahveh can expect no mercy from him; utter destruction is their lot. When a city was devoted to him, every living thing within it was given to the sword. The ban properly included the cattle and even the inanimate spoil, though these were sometimes specially exempted from the general destruction. Its victims were sacrosanct, and the withdrawal of any of them from their prescribed doom was an unpardonable offence. The stories of Achan and Agag are instances in point. It does not surprise us that a deity to whom the votive offering of an entire community could be agreeable, should be propitiated in exceptional circumstances with human sacrifices. Unsuccessful efforts have been made to explain away the few instances of these sacrifices in the historical books. The most obvious is that of Jephthah's daughter; but there are others which, if not sacrifices in the technical sense, are yet, as the offering of human lives to appease the wrath of God, of practically equivalent nature. Such is the hanging up of Saul's seven sons before Yahveh in Gibeon, or, again, the execution of the leaders of the people in Shittim, who are "hung up unto Yahveh against the sun that his fierce wrath might be turned away from Israel."[2]

The actual nature of the Godhead was conceived, as

[1] E.g. Judges xiv. 19.

[2] Numbers xxv. 4. Whether the sacrifice of first-born sons was an ancient custom in the religion of Yahveh, revived in the eighth and seventh centuries, is a disputed point. That it was so has been lately re-argued with much ability in a dissertation by B. D. Eerdman *Melekdienst en vereering van hemellichamen in Israel's Assyrische periode*, 1891.

we should expect, upon lines parallel to the general estimate of his character. While the prophets were beginning to spiritualize the nature of Yahveh, so that their anthropomorphic phrases and elaborate theophanies are probably little more than poetic symbolism or metaphor, by the people generally Yahveh was conceived as existing under conditions of space like ourselves; he resided in a definite locality, and moved, if necessity required, from place to place. In the oldest period his dwelling appears to have been Mount Sinai;[1] but when the Israelites settled in Canaan, it was identified with their own. Originally, men probably believed that God's shape was the same as man's. When Moses, Aaron, Nadab, Abihu and the seventy elders, go up "unto Yahveh," they apparently see, not merely a manifestation of God, but Yahveh himself visibly present.[2] This story represents an earlier phase of thought than the verse in a subsequent chapter, "There can no man see me and live," although, in that story too, it is assumed that God really possesses hand, face and back parts; it was, therefore, easy for a popular imagination to picture God as walking in a garden, or appearing to Abraham as a guest in human form. Such stories are the links between the manifestation of Yahveh himself and the manifestation of his angel, who is closely connected and even frequently identified with Yahveh, but whose appearance in one place would not, I imagine, have precluded in the popular idea his appearance at the same time in another place. For, although Yahveh is present in his angel, the very

[1] Cf. Exod. xix. 4 (iii. 1—5); Judges v. 5.
[2] Exod. xxiv. 10.

fact that it *is* the angel, and not the unmediated God, shows that the whole Yahveh is not exhausted in a single manifestation. As the dwelling-place of Yahveh was shifted afterwards from earth and mountain-tops to the sky above, this change had an influence upon men's conceptions of his bodily form. Yahveh can march above the mulberry-trees, or travel in a moving pillar of cloud and fire.[1] That the human form could not have been habitually regarded as his permanent shape, is also apparent from his mysterious relation to the Ark. It is not certain whether this sacred palladium was empty, or contained certain sacred stones in which an earlier age had believed a spirit to reside. The story of the Ark's construction to receive the tablets of the Decalogue is late and unhistorical. But the close connection of the Ark with Yahveh we have already witnessed in those appalling punishments which were supposed to have visited its unauthorized handling or inspection. In some places in the narrative of Samuel, the Ark is almost identified with Yahveh.[2]

Where such conceptions of God are still prevalent, it is not surprising that little reluctance is shown to worship the Deity under material forms. The most prevalent symbol, borrowed from the Canaanites, was that of the bull. In the historical books of the Old Testament, such a representation of Yahveh is always described by the later editors as gross idolatry. It is, however, clear that in early times it was not regarded as open to objection even by fervent worshippers of Yahveh. Jeroboam's

[1] 2 Sam. v. 24; Exod. xiii. 21.
[2] 1 Sam. iv. 7, 8, vi. 9.

famous bulls were not an unheard-of innovation, but the outcome of a calculated, conservative movement. Even prophets like Elijah and Elisha, and practical reformers like Jehu, raise no objection to the bull-worship at Bethel and at Dan. In the southern kingdom this idolatrous symbolizing of God does not appear to have taken such firm root. In the central temple at Jerusalem, at any rate, we never hear of any certain image of Yahveh. It has been conjectured that the Ark, the possession of which was a kind of fetish even in Jeremiah's age, supplied the place of any material image.[1] It is also possible that the purest Mosaic tradition was hostile to image-worship, and that this tradition was handed down by the priests, first at Shiloh, and then at Jerusalem. Image-worship, however, existed in many other places besides Dan, Bethel and Samaria. There was an image, the form of which is still unascertained, called an Ephod. The verb from which the noun is derived means to cover, or overlay; and we can thus infer that the Ephod image was overlaid with a coating of some precious metal. We hear of these Ephods several times. Gideon sets one up out of the spoils of his victory in the sanctuary at Ophrah. Micah, the Ephraimite, possesses one in his own private chapel. There is another Ephod in the sanctuary of Nob, which Abiathar takes with him in his flight as a valuable piece of priestly property.[2] From the use subsequently made by David of this Ephod, we learn that the image was used in throwing the sacred lot. There must also have been many other images of Yahveh in existence

---

[1] Stade, *Geschichte*, Vol. I. p. 465.
[2] Judges viii. 27, xvii. 5; 1 Sam. xxi. 10, xxiii. 6, 9.

during the eighth century, some in local sanctuaries and some in the possession of private individuals. The Teraphim, which were of human form, were not symbols of Yahveh; their meaning as well as their connection with the Ephod and the lot are obscure; but it has been conjectured that they were images of household divinities, antagonistic to the exclusive religion of Yahveh, but yet admitted even by such a man as David into his own house. In addition to them, the prophets allude to other images which most probably were symbols of Yahveh himself; thus we find Isaiah complaining that "Judah has become full of idols, so that men do homage to the work of their hands." In the good time coming, "they will defile the covering of their silver graven images, and overlaying of their golden molten images, and scatter them as loathsomeness."[1] Some of these idols may have been images of other and foreign divinities, but the majority were probably images of the national God.

From the foregoing summary of some elements in the character and worship of the pre-prophetic Yahveh, it would appear as if the motive of the Mosaic monolatry could only be sought in the first of the two suggested causes—in the power, jealousy and vindictive wrath of the Deity whom the founder chose for his own and for his people's God. But there is something to be said upon the other side, which, although incapable of much illustration and instance, is yet highly significant and suggestive.

Yahveh was the God of justice. His severity did not merely vindicate his own outraged honour; it was also

[1] Isaiah ii. 8, 20, xxx. 22.

the guardian of morality. It is true that the clear distinction between ritual and religion inculcated by the eighth-century prophets is unparalleled in any earlier narrative of the histories or of the Pentateuch. Yet the belief in Yahveh's retributive action, and in his consistent refusal to allow breaches of the people's moral customs to remain ignored or unavenged, was vividly present to the national consciousness.[1] Most signal and characteristic was the moral influence of Yahveh in the domain of law. Yahveh, to the Israelite, was emphatically the God of Right. This conception, though here indicated so briefly—in the next Lecture it will again come before us—was of enormous importance.

From the earliest times onward, Yahveh's sanctuary was the depository of law, and the priest was his spokesman. / The oracle of Yahveh, of which the priests were the interpreters, decided suits and quarrels, and probably gave guidance and advice in questions of social difficulty. The *Torah*—or teaching—of the priests, half-judicial, half-pedagogic, was a deep moral influence; and there was no element in the religion which was at once more genuinely Hebrew and more closely identified with the national God. There is good reason to suppose that this priestly *Torah* is the one religious institution which can be correctly attributed to Moses. If that be so, then not only did the pre-prophetic religion itself include an important ethical element, but this very element was part and parcel of the original Mosaic teaching, so that

[1] E.g. Judges ix. 56, 57; cf. Wellhausen, *History of Israel*, E. T. p. 393.

a spiritual feature becomes a constituent portion of the Mosaic monolatry.

So far the result of our inquiry has been to prove that there was a fusion of good and evil elements in the character and worship of the pre-prophetic God. Both, in all probability, reach back to the Mosaic age. Violent severity and easily-excited wrath seem no less native to the original conception of him than a guardianship of social morality and a zealousness for right. It is something more, however, than the leaven of early affections which leads me to suggest that the motive for the Mosaic monolatry, though not without its modicum of the lower cause, was yet mainly stimulated by the higher—the ethical superiority of his chosen God.

For that successful resistance to Canaanite polytheism on which we laid so much stress when ascribing the origin of monolatry to the Mosaic age, would surely not have been possible unless the Yahveh whom Moses taught differed from the Canaanite deities, not only in his numerical uniqueness, but in his higher and more consistent ethical character. The violent elements in Yahveh's character he shared with Moloch and Baal, and many another divinity of the neighbouring Semitic tribes; but in no single case did this corresponding violence produce a corresponding monolatry. We are therefore entitled to doubt whether the exclusive worship of the national God would ever have been ordained, had there not lain in the original conception of Yahveh the "promise and potency" of the monotheism of Amos and Isaiah. To quote the earlier words of Professor Kuenen, "the great merit of Moses lies in the fact of his connection of the religious idea with the moral life."[1] The exclusive worship of Yahveh on the one hand, God's moral character and the moral duty of man upon the other hand, must have acted reciprocally in the production of the Mosaic teaching as a whole. The first element, to which Stade would confine the creative originality of the Founder, would hardly have arisen without the second, and could scarcely have produced those historic results of which we seek the cause. One of the most sober and trustworthy of Old Testament critics, Professor Kamphausen, maintains the same argument. "I recognize," he says, "in the fact that the small number of the Israelites was not absorbed by the Canaanites, who were by far their superiors in all matters of external culture, a convincing proof of the ethical power of the Yahvistic religion. But this superiority consisted in the nature of that Yahveh whom Moses proclaimed, not in a dogmatic assertion of Semitic exclusiveness."[2]

Yet it is not necessary, whatever views we may hold as to the natural or supernatural origin of the Founder's religion, to place the religious teaching of Moses upon a level with that of Amos or Isaiah. We must endeavour to assess it neither too low nor too high. If too low, it becomes well nigh impossible to account for the continued existence of Yahveh-worship, for the comparatively successful absorption of the Canaanites, and for the share of the national faith in the establishment of the monarchy, two hundred years after the death of Moses. If, on the

[1] *Religion of Israel*, Vol. I. p. 282 (1870).
[2] *Theologische Studien und Kritiken*, 1890, p. 201, n. 1.

contrary, we assess it too high, it is hard to understand how so many superstitions could have crept in, or rather how almost the whole outward embodiment of the religion was modelled upon Canaanite lines. We could not explain how eager Yahveh-worshippers, such as David, could countenance practices and make use of expressions little removed from the level of heathenism. While the great merit of Moses lies in the fact that he connected the religious idea with the moral life, it does not necessarily follow that he possessed a refined or matured conception of either religion or morality. His Yahveh had many features which we should regard as incompatible with a moralized notion of deity. A belief in the fierceness of Yahveh's wrath, and the violence of the punishment he inflicts upon those who have incurred it, might easily co-exist in the soul of Moses with the conviction that Yahveh was a just God who required the establishment and maintenance of justice among his people. One must not forget the number of inconsistent and incongruous ideas which can all find storage in the recesses of the same human mind. Directly the contrariety is perceived, the old combination seems impossible.

Summing up, then, all that we may legitimately infer of the Mosaic religion, it cannot with any measure of certainty be said to have included more than that Yahveh was a God of justice, as well as a God of power; that no God but Yahveh was to be worshipped in all the tribes of Israel; and that he would not only lead the hosts of Israel to victory, but, through his ministers and interpreters, become Israel's lawgiver and judge. At the sanctuary of Yahveh, where the God was invisibly present among his people, were the fountain of justice and the judgment-seat. The priests, whose judicial and didactic functions were in early days the most important part of their office, traced, as we have already learnt, their origin to Moses, who, in Yahveh's name, was not only his people's leader, but their supreme judge. ' "If Moses did anything at all," says Wellhausen, "he certainly founded the Sanctuary of Kadesh, and the Torah there, which the priests of the Ark carried on after him."[1] We may, then, reasonably infer that Moses taught his contemporaries, not theoretically but practically, as occasion demanded, and as part and parcel of Yahveh's religion, the fundamental elements of social morality. He taught them that Yahveh, if a stern and often a wrathful Deity, was also a God of justice and purity. Linking the moral life to the religious idea, he may have taught them, too, that murder and theft, adultery and false witness, were abhorred and forbidden by their God.[2]

There is, however, no sufficient evidence to exclude the Decalogue from the general verdict that the laws of the Pentateuch in their written form are one and all subsequent to the Founder.[3] We can abandon the Mosaic authorship of the Ten Words with less reluctance, if we are justified in the conclusion that the morality which

[1] *History of Israel*, E. T. p. 397, n. 1; cf. p. 438.

[2] I have only recently read the analogous arguments of Piepenring on Moses and his religion in his essay, "Moses et le Jahvisme:" *Revue de l'histoire des religions*, Vol. XIX. 1889, pp. 312—332.

[3] See *Recent Criticism on Moses and the Date of the Decalogue: Jewish Quarterly Review*, January, 1891, and Appendix I.

they teach not unfairly represents the character of the Mosaic faith.

Having thus arrived at certain definite, if necessarily hypothetical, conclusions as to the quality of the Mosaic monolatry, the second question—far harder, far less soluble—still remains: Whence was this monolatry obtained, and what kind of religion preceded its adoption? As this question is wrapped in darkest obscurity—for of the pre-Mosaic religion we know practically nothing—and as all the hypothetical answers are compatible with our estimate of the Mosaic monolatry itself, it will be needless to do more than indicate in barest outline the nature of the solutions which have hitherto been proposed.

There are two main hypotheses. The first is that the name and worship of Yahveh were utterly unknown to the Israelites before their introduction by Moses. In that case, as it is unlikely that Moses invented the name himself, we must suppose that he borrowed it from an outside source. Yahveh would be the God of some alien nation. That the name is Egyptian is a theory now almost universally abandoned.[1] But two great scholars, Profs. Tiele and Stade, have sought Yahveh's original home, not in Egypt, but in Midian.[2] Upon the basis of various superstitious observances, still prevalent in Israel even in historic times, Stade essays to prove the existence

[1] Not, however, by Nöldeke, Z. D. M. G., 1888, p. 483.

[2] Tiele, *Histoire comparée des anciennes religions*, 1882, p. 350; Stade, *Geschichte*, pp. 131, 132, and divers passages in his seventh book, pp. 358—518.

THE HEBREW RELIGION. 51

of a very low religious level in the pre-Mosaic age, and more particularly of a system of ancestor and spirit-worship, which, in other nations usually preceding polytheism, in Israel preceded monolatry.[1] The Old Testament itself alludes in a few passages to a pre-Mosaic period of idolatry.[2] Now tradition ascribes to Moses before his assumption of leadership a prolonged residence in the wilderness of Sinai; he married there a daughter of Jethro, a priest of Midian. In an old chapter of the Book of Judges, the relatives and descendants of Moses' father-in-law are called, not Midianites, but Kenites, and are in close alliance with Judah.[3] In the rebellion of Jehu, the usurper receives assistance from Jonadab the son of Rechab, who shows himself an active adherent of Yahveh. We learn from Jeremiah that the Rechabites were a family who had preserved the simple customs of nomads as a kind of family tradition, and from the Book of Chronicles we gather that the Rechabites were originally Kenites.[4] It has, therefore, been conjectured that Yahveh was originally a God of the Kenites, and borrowed by Moses from his Kenite (or Midianite) hosts. It by no means follows that the Mosaic conception of

[1] My space being limited, I have purposely omitted any description of these various superstitions, as also of the evidence of early stone and tree worship, both in the pre-Mosaic and post-Mosaic periods. Besides Stade, *loc. cit.*, cf. for convenient summary, Piepenring, *La Religion primitive des Hebreux: Revue de l'histoire des religions*, Vol. XIX. 1889, p. 179, &c.

[2] Josh. xxiv. 2—14 (Gen. xxxi. 19, xxxv. 4); Ezek. xxiii. 3, xx. 7.

[3] Judges i. 16; cf. iv. 11; Numbers x. 29—32 (see Dillmann); 1 Sam. xv. 6, xxvii. 10, xxx. 29.

[4] 2 Kings x. 15; Jer. xxxv. 2—11; 1 Chron. ii. 55.

E 2

Yahveh was not different from and higher than the conception of him among the Kenites; still less that the Kenites knew and worshipped no other God than Yahveh. The Old Testament gives this further support to the hypothesis that one of the two earlier Pentateuchal narratives denies that the name of Yahveh was known before Moses, and ascribes its origin to a special revelation vouchsafed to the Founder by the God of the patriarchs, who had hitherto refrained from communicating to man his special and peculiar name. But as the date of this narrative is probably not earlier than the eighth century, its evidence is counterbalanced by the other, probably older, chronicle which relegates the first employment of the name to the period before the Flood. Nor have philologians yet been able to discover with certainty the precise signification of the word. The etymology put forward in the famous story in Exodus, whereby it is connected with the verb "to be," is by no means above suspicion.

The second hypothesis assumes that Yahveh was already known to the Israelites as one God out of many, or even as the chief and common Deity of all their clans. To this hypothesis, in its turn, the Old Testament gives the support that Moses is represented as charged by Yahveh to accredit himself to the children of Israel as the emissary of their fathers' God. There is also this further argument, that it is difficult to imagine the Israelites rallying round the leadership of one who spoke to them in the name, and urged them to adopt the worship, of a foreign and hitherto unknown divinity.[1] More-

[1] Kittel, *Geschichte der Hebräer*, Vol. I. p. 157 (1888).

over, as Dillmann urges, the higher religion of Moses must surely have had its points of connection with preexisting beliefs within his people or tribe. This argument gives to a form of the second hypothesis, once briefly indicated by Wellhausen, a certain degree of superior probability. Yahveh, according to that great scholar, "is to be regarded as having originally been a family or tribal God, either of the family to which Moses belonged or of the tribe of Joseph, in the possession of which we find the Ark of Yahveh, and within which occurs the earliest certain instance of a composite proper name with the word Yahveh for one of its elements (Jeho-shua, Joshua)."[1] But why, it may be asked, upon this assumption is Yahveh's earliest residence upon the mountain of Sinai? Does not this fact, if it be such, go rather to substantiate the hypothesis of Stade, which would place in the Sinaitic peninsula, and not in Palestine or Canaan, the home and origin of Yahveh? On Wellhausen's theory, we must then apparently make the additional hypothesis that the Israelites had heard of this mountain God in their wanderings before the settlement in Goshen, that he had been included in their pantheon, and in the family of Moses or in the tribe of Joseph had obtained the place of honour. By the force of the Mosaic teaching, and by the great event which proved the power and favour of Yahveh, the combined Israelite tribes accepted the God of Moses as their own. Religion welded them together. In the name of Yahveh they achieved their earliest victories, and their common patriotism became identified with their common religion.

[1] Wellhausen, *History of Israel*, p. 433, n. 1.

Beyond suggestions such as these, criticism will probably never be competent to advance. Why the pre-Mosaic religion and the origin of Yahveh must continue in the main unknown, we have already learnt. For behind Moses there stretches back the dark and limitless pre-historic age. But with Moses the historic period begins. Of the history of Israel's religion he constitutes the first chapter.

Through the thick veil which hangs over its former phases we cannot hope to penetrate. Let us be satisfied if we may still believe that at the fountain-head of Israel's religion there stood a man of high inspiration or exalted genius, whose new and spiritual teaching, accepted, though ill-understood, by his people in the flush of a new-born enthusiasm, was destined to break forth, after a long period of danger and decay, into wider and more glorious developments.

Lecture II.

THE HISTORY OF THE HEBREW RELIGION BETWEEN THE MOSAIC AGE AND THE EIGHTH CENTURY B.C.

OUR task in this Lecture is to trace the course of religious history in Israel from the death of Moses in the thirteenth, to the teaching of Amos in the eighth century before Christ, a period of some five hundred years.

In the last Lecture we arrived at the conclusion that the evidence to. be derived from the prophets and the general history of the Israelites is most judiciously explained upon the supposition that the traditions and legends of the Mosaic age contain a certain residuum of historical fact, and that the story of Israel's religion opens with the work of a great personality, who taught his people to worship one God only, a severe but just deity, demanding from the tribes which acknowledged his dominion the practice of the simplest rules of civic morality. We must not be surprised if the ideas of Moses were ill-understood by his contemporaries and successors. He did not leave behind him elaborate institutions capable of preserving and developing his fundamental conceptions; he did not compose, as tradition represents, a code of written laws both moral and ceremonial. The Hebrew festivals are all later than the Mosaic age, for they imply a settled agricultural life; originally borrowed from the Canaanites, they were only afterwards connected with incidents in the national history. The Sabbath, even if Moses enjoined its observance, was of no considerable religious importance till a far later period. The one means by which the higher teaching of Moses could be maintained and handed down was the agency of the priests.

To gain an accurate conception of the early priesthood, one must put entirely aside the picture of an organized hierarchy which the latest elements of the Pentateuch attribute to the Founder; for, in the period between Moses and Samuel, there was no operative inter-tribal organization either in the political or in the religious sphere.

The tribes only gradually became masters of the land beyond Jordan. In their struggles with the Canaanites they fought in comparative isolation, each for its own hand. The Canaanites were not extirpated, but either lived on in cities of which the Israelites were unable to dispossess them, or were gradually absorbed by, and assimilated to, the new-comers who spoke a kindred language and belonged to the same race. Yet resistance upon a more extensive scale was sufficient to draw the tribes together for a common end, and the recognition of a common God was the rallying-point of national feeling. Yahveh, as the God of all the Israelite tribes, was chiefly realized in war, for the battles of Israel were the battles of their God. The Song of Deborah mentions all the tribes with the exception of Levi and Simeon, who apparently had disappeared before her time, and of

Judah, whose clans, largely mixed with alien blood, were for a long time only loosely connected with the main Israelite community. The picture of the course of history from the death of Joshua to the establishment of the monarchy, drawn by the latest editor of the Book of Judges, is unhistorical. He imagines a kind of irregular kingship appearing at intervals between Joshua and Samuel. This idea is part of his equally unhistorical conception of the religious history. According to him, the Israelites fall away, again and again, from the pure worship of Yahveh, who suffers them, by way of punishment, to be defeated and oppressed by their enemies. Then follow repentance and prayers for rescue. A deliverer intervenes, who, after freeing the people from their foes, "judges" them until his death, when the same round of apostasy, punishment, contrition and deliverance, re-commences anew. As a matter of fact, this wholesale apostasy and repentance are alike imaginary. Equally imaginary is the idea of a judge with a jurisdiction over all Israel. The supposed "judges" were mere tribal captains, exercising, after the successful repulse of hostile invasions, a purely local authority, which, except in one instance, they were unable to hand down to their sons. Gideon was, indeed, succeeded by his son Abimelech; but his dominion, which came to an untimely end, was nearly limited to Manasseh. Samuel was not a political ruler at all.

Between Joshua and Samuel there lies an interval of some two to three hundred years. It was an epoch of high importance in the history of the Israelite religion, although we can but dimly guess at the religious forces which then acted and re-acted upon each other. While we abandon the unfavourable view which the editor of the Book of Judges has made familiar to posterity, it is also clear that this period was by no means one of unchequered advance. The larger patriotism born at the exodus from Egypt, and raised to a high pitch of ardour by the genius or inspiration of the great leader, sank down again after his death to a lower level. But, at the same time, the knowledge that they were all branches of one tree must have gradually, though quietly, spread among the tribes; for a monarchy such as that of Saul, still more such as that of David, would scarcely have been possible under Barak and Gideon, even although the Philistine oppression had been anticipated by a hundred years. The same partial decay and partial advance must also be postulated in the sphere of religion. There, too, the enthusiasm which Moses had inspired for a time, and among some sections of the people, grew cold and feeble; but there, too, the religion of the highest spirits at the close of this period and the opening of the next shows that, in spite of partial corruption, there must also have existed a coincident advance.

As the Canaanites were by no means annihilated, but either lived on side by side with, or were assimilated by, the Israelites, it was only natural that they should have exercised a considerable influence upon the uncultivated though martial Hebrews, whose religion was far too unstable and immature to be unaffected by the long established religion of the older population. It becomes, therefore, of importance to obtain some faint idea of what that Canaanite religion actually was.[1] Out of the small material from which an estimate of them can be deduced, we gather that the chief deities of Canaan were personifications of natural forces, and more especially of the sun. Very early in their history the Canaanites seem to have perceived in the divine powers a twofold aspect, the one beneficent, the other destructive; and, like the Hebrews, they generally ascribed both qualities to one and the same deity. As the essence of divine beneficence, or at all events its most mysterious feature, seems to lie in generation and reproduction, this idea, with other and lower causes, may have contributed to the frequent co-ordination of goddess with god in Canaanite religion. Seeing that the sexual and religious instincts are so strangely connected, it is not surprising that sensuality should have become a leading feature of Canaanite worship. It would appear as if, at the period when the Israelites were settling down in their new homes, the native gods and goddesses had received no more than the vaguest and most inadequate moralization. When we speak of God's goodness, we mean by it the essential quality of his uniform and permanent character. The goodness of Baal meant something very different: it merely expressed in a pictorial and personal form the fact that the sun produces the harvest, that the rain causes fertility, that long life, numerous flocks and a large family, are incidents that

[1] Cf., for the succeeding few paragraphs, Baudissin's articles upon Canaanite deities, in Herzog Plitt's *Encyklopädie*, 2nd ed.; Baethgen's *Beitraege;* Pietschmann's *History of Phœnicia*, &c.

befall the more fortunate children of humanity. The principles of Phœnician and Canaanite worship seem to oscillate between the idea that the prosperities and joys of life are almost automatic functions of particular deities, and the idea that they are only to be wrung from the gods by servility, bribery, or craft.

It was thus an undeveloped polytheism with which the Israelites were brought into close and daily contact. Not only were the local Baals, though varieties of the same god, regarded as separate and distinct divinities, but, whatever may have been their primordial faith, the Canaanites during the period of the Judges worshipped many gods and goddesses with a goodly variety of names.

The three Canaanite divinities most frequently mentioned in the Old Testament are Baal, Astarte and Moloch. The word Baal means "lord" or "owner;" and the god Baal, like Adonis, Moloch, and others, belongs to a class of deities whose appellations denote power and mastery, whether over nature or over man. Baal is the supreme Phœnician and Canaanite god, so that the Greeks identified him with Zeus. A variety of evidence points to his solar origin; his sacred pillars are called *Chammanim*, and *Chamma* in the Old Testament is a poetical synonym for the sun. But Baal never became a regular proper name, like Zeus among the Greeks, or like Yahveh among the Hebrews. Each separate community could, and often did, possess its own Baal or chief divinity; hence we get the plural Baalim, so frequent in the Old Testament, primarily indicating, not images of Baal, but the many local varieties of the god, which, as I have already said, were regarded as separate personalities. Melkart, the chief god of Tyre, is also called its Baal. Baal was also distinguished from the sun, and worshipped as the Lord of Heaven. In accordance with the general principles of Canaanite religion, his character was conceived as both beneficent and hurtful, as the sun is the cause both of fertility and of drought. To the Baal of Carthage human sacrifices were offered, and it is supposed that when Grecian authors speak of children being sacrificed among the Phœnicians to Cronos, this Hellenic deity must be identified with Baal. Astarte, the Babylonian Ishtar, is the female revelation or complement of Baal. In one inscription she is called the name of Baal, as the goddess Taanith is called his face: she is the moon-goddess, and it is to her probably, under the title of Queen of Heaven, that the Israelite women burnt their incense and baked their cakes in the days of Jeremiah. Like Baal, she had a dual character, both amiable and fierce; it is with her worship that the sensual and licentious elements in the Canaanite religion were mainly connected. The sacrifice most consonant with her nature was the sacrifice of her votaries' chastity.

Moloch, more properly Melech or Milk, was not only the chief god of the Ammonites, but also a divinity of Canaan. He is merely the same sun-god under a different name. As the god of Tyre, he was known by the special name of Melkart, king of the city. Though the darker features of the Canaanite gods and of their worship seem to have clustered around Moloch, he is not, according to Baudissin, to be regarded as a purely malignant deity, just as Baal is not purely beneficent.

The sacrifice of children formed an element of his worship at Tyre; and the adoption of this horrible rite at a later age by Ahaz, king of Judah, marks the beginning of a period of gross idolatry in the history of the southern monarchy.

Canaanite worship was mainly carried on, as in all the ancient world, by sacrifices and offerings. We can infer with tolerable certainty that the Israelites borrowed from the Canaanites their habit of building altars upon the tops of hills and under the shade of trees. To the Canaanites was also familiar the practice of erecting sacred pillars at consecrated spots, as well as of placing wooden poles with a sensual connotation near the altars of the gods. Their festivals were mainly agricultural, connected, like those of the Israelites, with the first-fruits, the harvests, the wool-shearing and the vintage. Licentious usages were part and parcel of their worship. Sacred prostitution of both sexes was one of the ways by which the sensual elements in their faith found its most corrupt and terrible expression. Human sacrifices, culminating, as we have seen, in the offerings of first-born children, cannot have been uncommon.

That diverse elements of this religion should have been adopted by the new-comers was not unnatural. In entering Canaan, the Hebrews did not conceive themselves as entering a country which was destitute of divine protectors. For the monolatry of Moses was itself very different from monotheism, while the monolatry of his people was less advanced than his own. Even if they had accepted the principle, "No God but Yahveh," while the Founder was among them, and while the memories of the great deliverance were fresh in their minds, it was not probable that they would all maintain monolatry in Canaan, where the deities of the land and their attractive worship were constant and impressive realities. But the open and concurrent service of Baal and Astarte was less widely spread, as well as less lasting, than the influence of these deities upon the worship of Yahveh. For in Wellhausen's words, "It was not to be expected that the divinity of the land should permanently be different from the God of the dominant people. In proportion as Israel identified itself with the conquered territory, the divinities also were identified. Hence arose a certain syncretism between Baal and Yahveh which had not been got over even in the time of the prophet Hosea."[1]

The nature of the Canaanite influence upon the religion of Moses must mainly be sought in matters of sacred worship and external form. But the partial co-ordination of Baal with the Israelite God, and the subsequent syncretism to which Wellhausen has alluded, could not but leave their mark upon the conception of Yahveh. This is illustrated by the fact that no objection was felt to the use of Baal as an appellation of the national God. It must have tended to dilute the moral elements in Yahveh's character, and to make his connection with his people more mechanical, or even physical, than it had appeared to Moses. The idea of a covenant between God and Israel lay beyond the Mosaic horizon; but yet for Moses, novel as his teaching was, there must have been something of free choice on the part of Yahveh towards Israel, and of response from Israel to Yahveh. To the Israelite of the

[1] *Abriss*, pp. 18, 19.

pre-prophetic period, Yahveh was as naturally the God of Israel, and Israel as naturally his people, as a cloud drops rain or as the sun gives light. This dual relationship, like that which existed between the Canaanites and their gods, was neither begun by mutual treaty, nor was it the effect of divine grace; it was part of the scheme of things, accepted without question as an inevitable and indissoluble bond.

It is, however, a signal evidence of the grip which the Mosaic religion had won upon the national consciousness that the apostasy to Baal and Astarte was not far more overwhelming. It shows also, as we were led to infer in the previous Lecture, the comparative purity of the conception of Yahveh's character formed by the higher minds among the people, as well as his ethical superiority to Baal even in that early and pre-prophetic age. Yahveh never gave place to any other deity in his power over the popular patriotism. Baal may have been worshipped in times of peace in isolated localities; it was Yahveh, and Yahveh alone, in whose name the battles of Israel were fought, and by whose help the victories were won. In peace it was the sanctuary of Yahveh which was connected with the giving of judicial decisions, the utterance of oracles, the ascertainment of the divine will by oral teaching or the lot's decree. This side of Yahveh's religion brings us back again to the priesthood.

Though Moses was not the author of the written law, he was unquestionably the founder of that oral teaching, or *Torah*, which preceded, and became the basis of, the codes of the Pentateuch. Thus the false and late tradition which ascribes the whole Pentateuchal legislation to

THE MOSAIC AGE AND EIGHTH CENTURY B.C. 65

Moses is not entirely wanting in a small substratum of truth. His Torah was a direct consequence of his connection of religion with morality. The sanctuary of Yahveh was more than the place at which sacrifices were offered and vows discharged. To the tent of meeting, which was the Mosaic sanctuary, whether originally associated with the Ark or not, tradition asserts that every one who sought Yahveh made his way. It was before the tent of meeting that Moses is probably conceived as sitting to judge the people when they came to him to inquire of God.[1] Thus justice and the equitable settlement of disputes between man and man became associated with religion. The influence of the sanctuary had, however, a still wider range. Moses and his successors would give advice and help to those who sought their counsel in matters of difficulty or importance. By means of the sacred lot the future was inquired into, and predictions were uttered.[2] In all religious problems the priests of the local sanctuaries were the expounders of Yahveh's will.

To understand the position of the priests in old Israelite society, it has to be remembered that the performance of sacrificial rites was neither their most important nor their most characteristic function. The power to sacrifice was not limited to a priest: kings like Saul and David, prophets like Elijah, private persons like Gideon and Manoah, freely sacrificed with their own hands.[3] Nor

[1] Exod. xxxii. 7, 8, xviii. 15.
[2] 1 Sam. xxiii. 9, xxx. 7, &c.
[3] E.g. 1 Sam. xiv. 34, 35; 2 Sam. vi. 17, 18; 1 Kings xviii.; Judges vi. 24—26, xiii. 19.

F

was the priesthood in the earlier pre-prophetic period exclusively recruited from a single tribe. In the eighth and seventh centuries, Levite and Priest are synonymous terms; but this had not always been the case, and the story of the coalescence is one of the most obscure and disputed chapters in Israelite religion—too obscure and disputed to be touched upon here.[1]

We may, however, surmise that Moses, himself a Levite, entrusted the guardianship of Yahveh's sanctuary and the casting of the sacred lot, with the pronouncement of legal decisions and divine oracles, to the members of his own clan. Though we hear of no priest of note between the Founder's age and that of Samuel, the importance of the priesthood during this long period must not be underestimated. After the settlement in Canaan, a number of local sanctuaries sprang naturally into existence; but the best Mosaic tradition would centre round the Ark of Yahveh, and it would be at the sanctuary in which this Ark was placed that the spirit of the Mosaic teaching would be maintained most purely. That wandering priest from Bethlehem in the strange story of Micah the Ephraimite, in the 17th and 18th chapters of Judges, would represent a lower level of the order. But upon the whole the work of the priesthood cannot have been of insignificant worth, although it was silently carried on and has left no record. It must, indeed, be assumed, to account for subsequent developments.

The first priest of note mentioned by name in the

---

[1] See Baudissin, *Geschichte des alttestamentlichen Priesterthums*, 1889; art. "Levi," by Kautzsch, in *Ersch und Gruber's Encyklopädie*, 1889, and the references there given.

post-Mosaic era is Eli. He is the head functionary of the central sanctuary at Shiloh, where the Ark had been placed after the settlement in Canaan. When the story of Samuel opens, Eli is already an old man, and his two sons, priests like their father, officiate at Yahveh's altar. Their greed in these sacred ministrations is a matter of common notoriety and a grief to Eli.[1] In the reigns of Saul and David we hear a good deal of the priests in their capacity of soothsayers. At Nob, a town not far from Jerusalem, there was a sanctuary at which Achimelech, the grandson of Eli, was the chief priest. Together with him, there were eighty-five other priests belonging to the same sanctuary. That this large number was unusual is clearly shown by Nob being called specifically the City of the Priests.[2] Abiathar, who escapes when the city is destroyed by Saul, takes with him the Ephod, and by means of it serves David with divine oracles. He and Zadok become the king's chief priests, and their position gives them political as well as liturgical importance; they are high officers of state.[3]

From the meagre evidence which we possess, and by the analogy of kindred phenomena in other religions, it would therefore seem that in the manipulation of the sacred lot lay the most potent function of the earlier priest. Whether as teacher, soothsayer or judge, he was in each case the interpreter of Yahveh's will, the human

---

[1] 1 Sam. ii. 12—25. [2] 1 Sam. xxi. xxii.
[3] 1 Sam. xxiii. 6—12, xxx. 7; 2 Sam. viii. 17. It should also be noted that David seems to have appointed some of his sons to the priestly office: 2 Sam. viii. 18.

mouthpiece of a supernatural revelation.[1] But the man who could peer into futurity and ascertain the divine counsel or monition by magical processes, in the truth of which he himself believed, would acquire concurrently a moral influence over his contemporaries. He would be consulted upon matters which did not directly require the casting of the lot, and quietly and gradually his functions as teacher and judge would become emancipated from magical adjuncts. Stade has pointed out that the exponents of Yahveh's oracle enjoyed a moral authority to which all society in old Israel bowed down.[2] It is true that it was only the chief priest at the various sanctuaries who manipulated the lot, but every priest was at least capable of doing so, and the whole body was thus invested with a similar authority, and regarded with equal awe.

In his capacity of judge the priest maintained the Mosaic connection of morality with religion. Tradition speaks of a Well of Judgment at Kadesh, where the Mosaic sanctuary was perhaps first established.[3] At Marah, "Moses made for the people law and judgment, and there he proved them;" in other words, he judicially settled their disputes.[4] In the oldest Penta-

---

[1] I cannot enter here into the question as to the etymology of the word "Torah." See König, *Offenbarungsbegriff des alten Testamentes*, 1882, Vol. II. p. 343, with his references; Wellhausen, *History of Israel*, p. 394, and *Reste arabischen Heidenthums*, 1887, p. 167; and Stade and Siegfried's *New Hebrew Dictionary*, s. v. יָרָה.

[2] *Geschichte*, Vol. I. p. 474.

[3] Genesis xiv. 7; cf. Wellhausen, *History of Israel*, p. 343.

[4] Exod. xv. 25.

teuchal legislation the sanctuary is the scene of all legal operations.[1]

Questions of ceremonial and of purity fell naturally within the priests' province, and their answers were regarded as the judgment of God. But in all these departments of their activity there is no proof that they judged or taught upon the basis of a written law. Their Torah was purely oral, even where it was not given through the lot. It was, however, natural that, at the main sanctuaries in both Israel and Judæa, there should grow up a kind of consuetudinary law in matters which were of continual recurrence. The priests who regarded themselves as successors of Moses attributed their Torah to him as its founder; but there is no sufficient evidence that attempts were made to codify and write down these laws before the middle of the ninth century B.C.

Between the period of the Judges and that of the first canonical prophets, the priesthood must gradually have risen in moral dignity and spiritual power. Of the Ephod and the manipulation of the lot we hear no more after the reign of David. This was, doubtless, partly due to the rise of the prophets, and to their being consulted upon important occasions instead of the priests; but it was also due to the religion gradually freeing itself from its heathen associations. The essential ideas of the Mosaic religion were incompatible with superstitious practices, and as these ideas became more recognized and developed, the superstitions fell naturally into the background, the Torah becoming less oracular and more ethical. The Blessing of Moses reflects the highest

[1] Exod. xxii. 8, &c.

point in religious development which Israel had reached before the eighth-century prophets. Though its author alludes to the *Urim* and *Thummim* as belonging by right of inheritance to the Levites, he assigns to the priests a larger duty than the casting of the lot.[1] "They shall teach Jacob thy judgments and Israel thy instruction"— here the juridic and teaching office ascribed to them is surely independent of, or at least supplementary to, the lot.

The older prophets, and more especially Hosea, regard the priest's office as a very high one. They attack the priests for being false to their charge, and for having forgotten the Torah of their God. Hosea complains in God's name: "My people are destroyed for lack of knowledge. Because thou, the priest, hast rejected knowledge, I will also reject thee, so that thou shalt be my priest no longer. As thou hast forgotten the Torah of thy God, I will also forget thy children. The more they increased, the more they sinned against me; they exchanged their Glory for dishonour."[2] The Torah of the priests is here clearly conceived as a moral agency, which depends for its proper ministration upon the knowledge of God. Professor Stade, while emphasizing, as it appears to me, too one-sidedly the connection of the priesthood with casting the lot, yet clearly recognizes its importance for religion and morality. In a passage that merits quotation as summing-up the priestly influence with power and precision, he says: "No one in old Israel was more capable of

[1] Deut. xxxiii. 10.

[2] Hosea iv. 6, 7. For the slight correction of the text, see Cheyne's *Hosea, ad loc.*

protecting the unfortunate from oppression, of punishing the injustice of the mighty, and thus of strengthening the moral conscience, softening public manners, and educating society, than the priests. As in ancient Greece, they are the spiritual leaders of the clans and localities in which their sphere of office lies, the true representatives of the religious and national idea. Their importance for the development of religion, justice and public morality, cannot be too highly estimated. No other institution makes an impression of being so purely Israelite as the priesthood and its Torah. It is with good reason that they are referred back to Moses as their founder."[1]

Throughout the period of the "Judges," the priests remained the only official exponents of Yahveh's will and the teachers of his religion. The last deliverer mentioned in Judges, though himself a legendary or even mythical character, connects that book in one important respect with the Books of Samuel. For Samson fights against the Philistines, and when the Book of Samuel opens, this struggle is still being carried on. Its result is given in the very ancient story of the battle of Eben-ha-Ezer, in which Israel succumbs to the Philistines, and the Ark of Yahveh is captured.[2] The Philistines appear to have followed up their victory by the destruction of the sanctuary at Shiloh and the gradual establishment of their supremacy over all Israel. To put an end to Philistine subjection was the true occasion and object of the Israelite monarchy. As in other crises of Israelite history, the establishment of the monarchy was accompanied and partly brought about by a new religious development.

[1] *Geschichte*, Vol. I. p. 474.   [2] 1 Sam. iv.

It is now that prophecy makes its first appearance. The age of Samuel and David seems one of transition from old to new, and important religious personalities of every class come upon the stage. In Samuel we have the seer, who is perhaps also a Nazirite; in Eli, Abiathar and Zadok, priests of the first rank; in Gad and Nathan, representatives of the new order of prophets.

Unfortunately, our records do not speak with the clearness we could desire as to the exact mutual relations of these different religious orders. The Book of Samuel contains, as is well known, two diametrically opposed accounts of the origin of the monarchy. In the older version, Samuel is called a seer; in a later narrative, a prophet.[1] A note of an early editor explains this variety of usage in the following way: "Beforetime in Israel, when a man went to inquire of God, he spoke thus: 'Come and let us go to the Seer,' for he that is now called a Prophet was beforetime called a Seer."[2] According to this note, the seer and the prophet are identical persons; the difference is one of nomenclature only—as one might say that he that is now called a Conservative was beforetime called a Tory. The accuracy of this explanation is doubtful. Originally, seer and prophet appear to have been distinct, though cognate, personalities, and in the history of the Hebrew religion the former precedes the latter. The seer, as his name implies, is one who possesses an insight into the unknown, and reveals it to ordinary men. His name did not originally refer to the faculty of seeing visions, though it afterwards acquired a connotation of this kind. Primarily the seer is a soothsayer.

[1] 1 Sam. ix., iii. 20.   [2] 1 Sam. ix. 9.

As to the method of the seer's divination, we know nothing. The priests, as we have seen, made use of a sacred lot in pronouncing their oracles. It would rather seem as if the seer employed no implements of this kind, but spoke in virtue of his own direct inspiration.[1] His utterances were delivered in the name of Yahveh, and it was from Yahveh that he believed his supernatural knowledge to be derived. Soothsaying by the invocation of spirits was hostile to the principle of the Mosaic command, "Thou shalt have no other god beside me;" and it is consistent with the religious revival of the time of Samuel that Saul, not perhaps without Samuel's instigation, should have "put away those that had familiar spirits and the wizards out of the land."[2] We may therefore conclude that the seers spoke exclusively in Yahveh's name, and were free from heathen accessories of sorcery or witchcraft.

As Samuel is the first seer whose name is recorded, the inference seems to be that the earlier seers did not play any leading part in the religious history of Israel.[3] They were probably consulted by private individuals on private concerns, and seldom came forward as commissioned messengers of Yahveh on public or national affairs. The way in which Samuel is introduced to us in the oldest narrative is very significant. Saul's servant repre-

[1] Cf. Tiele, *Vergelijkende geschiedenis van de Egyptische en Mesopotamische Godsdiensten*, 1872, p. 603; *Histoire comparée*, p. 378.

[2] 1 Sam. xxviii. 3.

[3] But Deborah would form an exception. She is called a prophetess (= seer) in Judges iv. 4. This chapter is later than the song of chapter v. Stade, *Geschichte*, 2nd ed., Vol. I. pp. 178, 179.

sents to his master that there is in the city of the land of Zuph a man of God of great repute: all that he says comes surely to pass. Saul determines to consult this seer about some strayed asses, whither he should direct his way to find them. Other points in the story are also worthy of notice. It is assumed to be necessary that the seer should receive payment for his services, and the servant lends Saul the fourth part of a shekel of silver to give to the man of God. In those days, therefore, it was no disgrace for the seers to divine for money. We can also observe the close relation in which Samuel the seer stood to the priesthood: yet he is not described as a regular priest, and it does not follow that that version of Samuel's history whereby he was dedicated from his birth to the priesthood, and brought up as an acolyte in the temple of Shiloh, was known to, or adopted by, this older narrator.[1] But though not identified with the priesthood, Samuel fulfils priestly functions. Saul happens to approach the city just while a solemn sacrifice is being offered upon the "high place." "Lo, he is before you," say the young maidens who answer Saul's inquiry as to the whereabouts of Samuel; "for at this very time he is now come to the city, for there is a sacrifice of the people to-day in the high place." Saul meets Samuel just as he is returning to the city from the high place to eat, "for the people will not eat until he come, because he blesses the sacrifice."[2] Apparently, therefore, a seer of

[1] For the critical analysis of the Books of Samuel, cf. Cheyne's *Aids to the Devout Study of Criticism* (1892), chapter i., with the references given on p. 15.

[2] 1 Sam. ix. 6—14.

great repute like Samuel was wont to go about from place to place within a certain circumscribed locality, and lend to the city festivities a special solemnity and grace. He is not necessarily to be regarded as a priest because he takes a chief part in the sacrifice, and a complete identification of seers with priests is very precarious and doubtful. Connected they undoubtedly were, and many a seer may have been originally a priest; but even in the oldest period there is no reason to assume that it was not possible to be a seer without being a priest at the same time.

Samuel himself, though ready to be consulted by individuals, like others of his order, was yet intent upon higher things. His power of insight into the unknown was directed to the good of his nation, and his patriotism heightened the religious value of his office. If Deborah was a seer, that would be another indication how the patriotic feeling tended to elevate religion; for in a time of danger and distress she inspired Barak with confidence, and revived the drooping faith of the tribes in the power of their God. Religion and patriotism in old Israel re-act upon and stimulate each other. There must clearly have been some basis for the part which Samuel is made to play in the establishment of the monarchy, though in the oldest narratives it is not quite certain what that part actually was. The campaign against the Ammonites is not ascribed to Samuel, but to Saul's own ardour and enthusiasm; and it was his victory on that occasion which secured for him the kingdom. Yet it is quite possible that Samuel may have marked him out as the one man capable of saving the people from subjection to the Philistines, and urged him in Yahveh's name to attempt the task. And his overthrow of the Ammonites was but the prelude to the attack upon the Philistines.

The same narrative which gives us our main information respecting Samuel the seer, also introduces us to the prophets. Samuel foretells to Saul certain things which will befall him upon his journey homewards, as a sign of the truth of his prediction respecting the kingdom. The third of these events is to be that, when Saul reaches Gibeah where the Philistine garrison or viceroy resides, he will meet "a company of prophets coming down from the high place with a psaltery, and a tabret, and a pipe, and a harp, and they will be prophesying; and the spirit of Yahveh will come upon him, and he will prophesy with them and be turned into another man." The prediction is fulfilled. Saul meets the prophets, and prophesies among them, to the astonishment of his acquaintances at Gibeah. They say one to another, "What is this that has come unto the son of Kish; is Saul also among the prophets?"[1] In this narrative it is clear that Samuel the seer is not himself regarded as one of the prophets. His calm sobriety contrasts with their excited emotionalism. It is, moreover, difficult to conceive what the narrator would have us understand by the "prophesying" of these enthusiasts. It was probably neither rebuke nor prediction, but more likely some form of sacred song, improvised under the impulse of the moment.

How are we to account for the rise of this new order? The most probable theory is that prophecy is of Canaanite origin, and was borrowed or imitated from the Canaanites

[1] 1 Sam. x. 5—11.

THE MOSAIC AGE AND EIGHTH CENTURY B.C. 77

by the Hebrews.[1] This would account for its comparatively late appearance in the history of Israel, and for its earliest characteristics. The writer of the note which I have already quoted, that "those who are now called prophets were beforetime called seers," is aware that the word seer is older than the word prophet, although he wrongly imagines that the two names stand for identical personalities. We have, on the contrary, observed that, though Samuel may have had certain relations with the prophets, he was not himself one of their number; there is nothing excited or dervish-like about his action and speech. Nor, as far as we know, could Deborah have resembled the prophets in her ministrations or manners. Seeing that the company of singing and playing enthusiasts who met Saul upon the road to Gibeah is scarcely in keeping with what we conceive to be the purest and most characteristic elements in the old religion of Yahveh, the presumption increases that the word and the thing were alike borrowed from the Canaanites. When we recollect that Baal, too, had his prophets, and call to mind their strange behaviour in the contest with Elijah upon the slopes of Carmel, the presumption is changed into probability.

We thus surmise that Hebrew prophecy had a twofold origin in the old Hebrew "seers" and in the Canaanite "prophets." The two orders, the one native, the other foreign, coalesced with results unique in character and importance. But the stages of the coalescence are hard to trace. What we should like to know is, how far the grafting of Canaanite prophecy upon the old stock of Hebrew seers may have helped to produce the typical

[1] See Kuenen, *Onderzoek*, Vol. II., 2nd ed., p. 6, and n. 19.

prophets of the eighth century. Its influence one may imagine to have been in the direction of making the seers less concerned with individuals and more concerned with the nation at large. The prophetical movement imitated from the Canaanites received its first impulse from the Philistine supremacy. The prophets were stimulated by political as well as by religious enthusiasm, and the two motives were so closely connected as to be indistinguishable in their own minds. They began to give up their lives to the work of prophesying. While that work was by no means of an elevated order, it yet presented the spectacle of bodies of men living together for religious purposes. Higher minds, to whom the merely physical aspects of the earlier prophesying were by no means so repugnant or unnatural as they are to ourselves, were not unlikely to be influenced by, or attracted to, such associations, seeing that their object was the glorification and service of the national God. Samuel the seer may have countenanced and supported them; other seers may have regularly joined their ranks. They would not spend their whole time in ecstatic excitement, but would occupy part of it in the study and recital of the national songs and traditions, all of which would tend to that religious and national revival upon which the prophets were bent.

In some such manner we may conjecture that the coalescence of prophet and seer was gradually brought about. With the troops of prophets the isolated seers became incorporated, receiving back from the prophets something of their national enthusiasm and their detachment from narrower interests; and, on the other hand, providing the prophets in many cases with calmer and more intelligent leaders, who might teach them to modify or to avoid the wilder excesses of a purely physical exaltation. From the historical books of the Old Testament we can, unfortunately, gather but very little in support of this conjecture. The bands of prophets mentioned for the first time in the two narratives about Saul and Samuel are heard of no more till the period of Elijah, an interval of a hundred and fifty years.

On Samuel there follow quickly the two prophets, Nathan and Gad. What connection these two men bore to the prophetical associations we cannot discover. The stories told about them have clearly been adapted by writers of a later age, who were probably familiar with the more developed prophecy of the eighth century. If, however, these stories contain a considerable basis of historical truth, Gad and Nathan aptly represent a transitional period in the prophetical history. They are closely connected with the court. David appears to have made it part of his policy to conciliate and win over to his own side the distinguished religious personalities of his day. Saul's ill-timed vengeance upon the priests of Nob secured for him the hostility of the priesthood. Zadok and Abiathar are the devoted servants of David. With the quick intuition of a born leader of men, he probably recognized the growing importance of the prophetical order, and attached two of its most prominent members to his own person. Gad is called David's seer, and Nathan takes an active part with Bathsheba in the court intrigue against Adonijah.[1] But, on the other hand, both Nathan

[1] 2 Sam. xxiv. 11; 1 Kings i.

and Gad, upon two critical occasions, reprove their king in Yahveh's name and in no measured strain. Samuel, according to a story the date of which seems later than that of his first meeting with Saul, but which in its main outlines is probably authentic, had already paved the way.[1]

Moreover, one of these occasions displays the prophet in a novel character of supreme significance, as a preacher of social morality. Though limited to a single individual and to a particular incident and time, Nathan's condemnation of David in the matter of Uriah and Bathsheba seems to mark the true beginning of that great movement which was to culminate in Amos and Hosea.

Besides the prophet and the priest, there existed in the early monarchy a third class of holy men, whose exact measure of influence it is difficult to estimate with accuracy. These were the Nazirites. Unlike the Nazirites of the Pentateuch, the older Nazirites appear to have observed their rules of abstinence for life. The two main features of Nazirite asceticism were abstention from wine and from cutting the hair. Of any important Nazirites we know nothing; for the figure of Samson is too legendary to enable us to assign him a place in the history of Israel, and Samuel, in the oldest accounts we have of him, is not clearly represented as a Nazirite. It has been suggested that the class of Nazirites represented a protest against the luxury and sensuality of Canaanite life, a practical demonstration in favour of the old purity and stern simplicity of the most ancient Yahvistic religion. The Rechabites, who com-

[1] 2 Sam. xii. (Bathsheba), xxiv. (the Census); 1 Sam. xv. (Agag).

bined abstinence from wine with an aversion to agricultural life, must have been closely allied to the Nazirites, and have owed their origin to a similar cause.

Priest, Seer, Prophet and Nazirite: these, then, are the four classes of holy men who furthered the progress of Israel's religion from Samuel to Elijah. But the political influences themselves were also of the greatest importance, and even in a sketch of the religious history they cannot be passed over in complete silence.

David (1010—978 B.C.) for a short time made the kingdom of Israel a first-rate power. It was natural that the dignity of his own position should be reflected back upon the national God. Nor is Abigail merely using the language of politeness, when she prophesies that Yahveh will make David a sure house because he fights the battles of Yahveh.[1] It was not only that the glory of Israel was equivalent to the glory of Israel's God, but that David, as we have already seen, made it part of his policy to identify his cause with the cause of religion, and to secure its leading representatives upon his own side. David may well have been ardently and sincerely attached to the national faith; with all the intensity of his impulsive nature he may have fully believed that his own advancement was synonymous with the glory of his God. In a sense other than he knew, this was the fact. The prophets of the eighth century could not have attained to the height of their argument, unless Israel had been lifted out of the petty political condition in which it had remained during the period of the Judges.

[1] 1 Sam. xxv. 28.

With David, too, the centre of gravity shifted southwards to Judæa and Jerusalem. By his removal of the Ark to his newly-captured capital, he laid the foundation of that fresh development in the external organization of the religion which was to culminate some four hundred years later in the law of the single sanctuary and the Book of Deuteronomy.[1] Solomon so far followed up his father's policy as to build a royal temple in Jerusalem, which, by the splendour of its services, its close connection with the court and its possession of the Ark of Yahveh, soon became the chief house of God in the entire realm. But all the other "high places" or local sanctuaries retained their recognized position, and there was no idea that the temple of Jerusalem would or should dispossess them of their functions and legality. Yet it was only natural that the chief and royal sanctuary within the capital should attract to its services the most cultivated and enlightened ministers, and, as the Ark of Yahveh never appears to have been associated with material images, the worship at the temple of Jerusalem was comparatively the purest in all the land.

The important political movements in the reigns of David and Solomon, though affecting religious worship and ceremonial, do not seem to have been accompanied by an immediate elevation of religious doctrine. Of Solomon's faith we know even less than of David's; yet in one important respect he seems to have differed

[1] "Little could David have guessed the issues which hung on this important step, but it is to him that the world is historically indebted for the streams of spiritual life which have proceeded from Jerusalem." Cheyne, *Aids*, &c., p. 56.

from his father. David was an enthusiastic, если not an elevated, worshipper of Yahveh; of Solomon we are told that on the hill that is east of Jerusalem he built "a high place for Chemosh, the abomination of Moab, and for Molech, the abomination of the children of Ammon. And likewise did he for all his strange wives, who burnt incense and sacrificed unto their gods."[1] These altars for foreign divinities seem to have been suggested originally by motives of policy, but they remained untouched until the reign of Josiah, and familiarizing the men of Judah with idolatrous rites, tempted them to participate in the forbidden worship of other gods. But the very fact that they continued undestroyed till the great reformation of the seventh century, shows that they may well have been erected, not in ignorance, but in despite, of the Mosaic command, "Thou shalt have no other gods but Yahveh." Though the rigorists may have disapproved of their existence, they were powerless to suppress them, for political advantages would outweigh all other considerations. But, with this exception, there is no reason to suppose that much idolatry was prevalent in the days of David and Solomon. Yahveh had shown his might and grace too significantly to make men inclined to traverse his command, and to seek for favour from other divinities more distant and less powerful.

While the death of Solomon was once more the beginning of a new epoch, Jeroboam's revolt can no longer be estimated as in the pre-critical age. The men of Israel did not regard their kingdom as apostate, or believe

[1] 1 Kings xi. 7, 8.

that its rulers lacked divine sanction and approval. So religious a writer as the author of the "Blessing of Moses" can yet utter the prayer, "Hear, Yahveh, the voice of Judah, and bring him back unto his people."[1] If Jeroboam was instigated to revolt by a northern prophet, Ahijah the Shilonite, it is far from probable that Ahijah viewed the formation of the new monarchy merely in the light of a divine punishment upon the errors of Solomon. Ahijah, like many another patriot, may well have sympathized with the discontent of the northern tribes at the oppressive government of Solomon, and yearned to free his people from the harsh Judæan yoke. It is just possible that the Israelite prophets were unfavourable to Solomon's attempt to make the new temple at Jerusalem overshadow the other and older sanctuaries of the realm, and that the revolt partook, therefore, to some extent, of a religious character. If there was any such element in the movement, it sprang from religious conservatism. The measures taken by Jeroboam to increase the attractiveness of the northern temples would appear to substantiate such an hypothesis. These measures constitute the sin of Jeroboam in the eyes of the Deuteronomistic redactor of the Books of Kings. In no other point does that writer more thoroughly misinterpret the spirit of the older age. The sin of Jeroboam is to him the central motive and cause of the entire tragedy which ended in the ruin of Israel. But in the eyes of Jeroboam and his contemporaries there was no sin and no idolatry. The bare facts of the case are, that Jeroboam made two new golden bulls, of which one was set up in

[1] Deut. xxxiii. 7.

Bethel and the other in Dan; these bulls, images of Yahveh,[1] were certainly no innovation, for such images were customary, and Jeroboam would clearly have been more inclined to appeal to the old conservative instincts of his subjects than to create a religious novelty just after the establishment of his rule. If he won his throne by the help of the prophets, it is unlikely that his bulls can have met with the hot opposition of men whose favour he had every reason to court.

Jeroboam's bulls were a kind of counterblast to Solomon's temple. But whereas the absence of image worship from the Judæan sanctuary enabled it to retain the affection of the more advanced prophets, and its priests to participate in a religious reform, the royal bulls, erected by the ruler's own orders, permanently fixed the worship of the northern kingdom at the same low level, and stamped it with the sanction and authority of the king. The higher prophetical movement of the eighth century could acquiesce in the temple of Jerusalem; it was brought into open and violent hostility with the sanctuaries of Israel. But for some considerable period these more indirect effects of Jeroboam's action did not declare themselves. To suppose that the northern kingdom was for the most part hopelessly given up to idolatry, and that the pure religion of Yahveh was almost exclusively maintained in the kingdom of Judah, rests upon misunderstanding and a too ready acceptance of the bias of later historians and editors against Israel and its kings. At first the religious condition of the two kingdoms was closely similar. It even happened, as

[1] 1 Kings xii. 26—33.

we shall see, that a forward movement in the history of prophecy began, not in Judah, but in Israel. But the instability of the throne in Israel, the number of revolutions and the frequent external wars hindered the gradual growth of a slow but thorough religious advance. By exaggerated opposition to the old tradition, some historians of the critical school are now inclined to forget the effect of these political troubles upon the religious condition of Israel.[1] Still the essential superiority of Judah must be abandoned, and if the Assyrian empire at the close of the eighth century had overthrown, not merely Israel, but also Judah, it is probable that the southern as well as the northern Hebrews would have lost their religious identity. More than three hundred years were still needed before the religion of Yahveh could become even temporarily independent of its temple and its land.

Jeroboam left the kingdom of Israel to his son Nadab, but he was soon slain by Baasha, "who reigned in his stead." Baasha's son Elah, after a year's rule, was murdered by Zimri, "his servant," who, after a short seven days' experience of regal power, was succeeded by Omri in the year 890.[2] Thus, omitting Zimri, we have three dynasties in less than fifty years. Omri was a powerful monarch, as we learn, not from the Book of Kings, but from the stone of Mesa and the Assyrian inscriptions. For it was he who once more brought Moab under the government of Israel, and his land became known in

[1] E.g. Stade in his *Geschichte*. He heads his account of Jeroboam's revolt thus : "Der Abfall *Judas* vom Reiche."

[2] 1 Kings xv. 25—xvi. 28.

Assyria as the "kingdom of Omri." The redactor of Kings tells us that in his twelve years' reign he wrought evil in Yahveh's eyes, and did worse than all who were before him; but he does not inform us wherein this special wickedness consisted, and it is possibly an invention of the historian to blacken the memory of Ahab's father and predecessor. The accession of Ahab took place about 878, sixty years after the death of Solomon.

The kingdom of Judah during this period was possessed by three monarchs only, Rehoboam, Abijam and Asa. Of its religious condition during these sixty years we know very little. Rehoboam and Abijam incur the historian's reprobation. In the days of the former, " Judah did evil in the sight of Yahveh, and they provoked him to jealousy with the sins which they committed above all that their fathers had done. For they also built them high places and pillars and Asherahs on every high hill and under every green tree. And there were also sodomites in the land, and they did according to all the abominations of the nations which Yahveh had cast out before the children of Israel."[1] These charges, it will be noticed, refer exclusively to matters of cultus, and do not deal directly with the worship of other gods. As to the high places and the pillars, no one before the seventh century and the reform of Deuteronomy imagined that they were displeasing to Yahveh; and of the Asherahs, the sacred poles of Canaanite origin, the same may probably be said. Prostitution as a form of divine service, which is the meaning of the second count in the historian's indictment, was a vice

[1] 1 Kings xiv. 22—24.

clearly borrowed from the Canaanites, in whose religion it held an acknowledged and honourable place. This horrible custom must have been widely imitated by the Israelites, for in the story of Judah and Tamar the words "harlot" and "Kedesha" are used as synonymous terms; but there is no evidence that it was at any period accepted by the better minds, in either the northern or the southern kingdom, as an integral part of their religion.[1]

The third king of Judah, Abijam's son Asa (917—877), is characterized very differently by the historian from either his father or his grandfather. He and his son Jehoshaphat, Ahab's contemporary and ally, did that which was right in the eyes of Yahveh, as did David, their ancestor. The measures by which Asa won this golden opinion are said to have been that he took away the sodomites out of the land, and removed the idols of his father; moreover, that he destroyed the "horrible thing" which his mother had made for Asherah and burnt it in the brook Kidron.[2] This statement about Asa is of extreme interest and importance: its authenticity is unquestionable; for the historian had no interest or motive to exempt Asa and Jehoshaphat from a general censure, unless their conduct had really differed from that of their immediate predecessors. We thus have to deal with a religious reform at the end of the tenth century. Saul's persecution of the witches and sorcerers we have already ascribed to the influence of Samuel. May not Renan be right in ascribing the reform of Asa to the growing influence of the prophets?[3] Its details, however, are not entirely

---

[1] Genesis xxxviii. 21 (R.V.).   [2] 1 Kings xv. 12, 13.
[3] *Histoire*, Vol. II. pp. 240—249.

clear. Whereas the offences ascribed to his predecessors were Canaanite accretions upon the worship of Yahveh, Asa seems to have destroyed the symbols of absolute idolatry. For the idols which he removed can scarcely have been images of Yahveh, unless we assume that in Judah, owing to the imageless worship in the temple, the prophets forbade the material representation of Yahveh earlier than in the northern kingdom. At any rate, the "horrible thing" which the queen-mother had erected for Asherah was probably a sacred pole set up in honour of Astarte, the two words being here, as in several other places, confused by the historian. He ought to have said that Maachah made an Asherah for Astarte; in which case the objection would not have been to the Asherah as such, but to the fact that it was an Asherah raised to the honour, not of Yahveh, but of Astarte. If this interpretation be correct, the inference follows that the Mosaic command of monolatry was thoroughly recognized by Asa, who sought to give effect to it by active measures of liturgical reform.

The reigns of Asa and Jehoshaphat extend over a period of sixty-five years (917—852). Under these powerful monarchs the dignity of the royal temple and of its worship gradually increased. Prophets and priests may have formed the beginnings of that alliance, the outcome of which can be traced in Isaiah and Deuteronomy. The seeds of much which we find in fresh growth or ripe maturity in the ninth and eighth centuries must have been sown in this tenth century, of which we would gladly know so much, of which we do know so little. Higher and lower elements of religion were gradually being parted off and differentiated from each other. Corresponding representatives of either element in the two orders of priesthood and prophecy embodied the growing contrast. But no great teacher, so far as we know, arose to carry forward the Founder's work. In the last portion of the century and in the first quarter of the next there was a religious calm. In the north, things were not very different under Omri from what they had been under Jeroboam and Solomon. In the south, while the reforms of Asa had been an augury of future developments, they can scarcely have been widely felt, or, perhaps, even widely known beyond the capital. But if calm there was, it was the calm before the storm. When a sufficient impetus from without gave signal and opportunity, the silent religious advance, implying also the growing religious conflict and contrast, was to declare itself openly upon the historic stage. The great men, never wanting in noble races at supreme moments of spiritual or national crisis, were also to be at hand.

Ahab, king of Israel, succeeded to the throne about the year 878 B.C. To secure himself the better against the enmity of the Syrians, or Aramæans, as they should properly be called, he appears to have entered into an alliance with Ethbaal, the king of Sidon, whose daughter Jezebel he took to wife. In his willingness to secure for his consort the full exercise of her religion, he went further than Solomon. He built a temple for Baal in his capital, and upon its altar he himself, together with his wife, paid worship to the Sidonian god.[1] The example of the king found many imitators; but

[1] 1 Kings xvi. 31.

whether other altars than that in Samaria were erected to Baal, and how far the Baal cultus spread through Israel generally, it is impossible to say. In any case, Ahab and his followers did enough to rouse the growing prophetical power to vigorous resistance. The soul of the Yahvistic opposition was Elijah the Tishbite. Of this great prophet we have, unfortunately, but little information which is free from legendary exaggeration and misstatement. With his usual concise eloquence, Wellhausen, in his inimitable sketch, characterizes the position of Elijah in Israel's religious history. "In solitary grandeur did this prophet tower over his time. Legend, and not history, could alone preserve the memory of his figure. One has rather the vague impression that with him one enters upon a new stage in the history of religion, than any precise data by which it can be ascertained wherein lay the contrast between the old and the new."[1] The main stories respecting him seem borrowed from a separate work dealing with his life and doings. Though it must have been drawn up within about half-a-century after the prophet's death, it is, nevertheless, legendary in character, and decidedly misinterprets or exaggerates the historical situations, to magnify the importance and lonely uniqueness of its hero. It is clear that both of Elijah, as well as of his disciple and follower Elisha, there must have been a large number of popular tales in circulation, only a few of which have been incorporated into the Books of Kings. Those which we possess are not by any means always consistent with each other, and

[1] *Abriss*, p. 33.

the same miracles are freely reported both of Elijah and Elisha.[1]

In the story of the famous challenge which Elijah threw down to Ahab and the prophets of Baal upon Mount Carmel, the author alludes to a systematic persecution of the more rigid adherents of Yahveh by Jezebel and the followers of Baal among the party of the court. Yahveh's altars are thrown down, and of all his prophets Elijah only is left. The inroads of Baal-worship have gone so far that there are only seven thousand in Israel who have not bowed the knee to Baal or kissed his image with their mouths. But these statements are exaggerated. Not only do Ahab's children bear names of which that of the national God forms part, but Jehu, even if we accept the stories of his violent reform as literally accurate, is able to exterminate all the worshippers of Baal by a single stratagem. Independently, moreover, of the Elijah stories, we possess a most valuable record of another great prophet of Yahveh, who carried the torch of religion forward in the reign of Ahab. This was Micaiah, the son of Imlah.[2] The long feud between Israel and Judah was brought to a close by Ahab and Jehoshaphat. The two monarchs formed an alliance, cemented by the marriage of Ahab's daughter, Athaliah, to Jehoshaphat's son, and they arranged a joint expedition against the Syrians to recover Rama in Gilead for

---

[1] The last German bit of work on Elijah is, I believe, an essay by Rösch, in *Theol. Studien und Kritiken*, 1892, pp. 551—572. It is very negative in its results.

[2] 1 Kings xxii.

the realm of Israel. Before leaving Samaria, Jehoshaphat desired to consult Yahveh as to the prospects of the undertaking. Ahab accordingly collected the prophets of Yahveh together to the number of about four hundred men. This story runs directly counter to the Elijah episode, in which all the prophets have been persecuted and murdered by Ahab. Here, on the contrary, they come forward in willing obedience to the royal will. They prophesy success: "Yahveh will deliver Rama into the hands of the king." But Jehoshaphat is not satisfied. He suspects that this unhesitating unanimity can scarcely be genuine, and he therefore asks whether there is not yet another prophet of Yahveh, that they may inquire of him. Ahab answers, that "there is yet one man, Micaiah, the son of Imlah, by whom we may inquire of Yahveh; but I hate him, for he does not prophesy good concerning me, but evil." Jehoshaphat urges that Micaiah should nevertheless be summoned. Ahab consents, and Micaiah is sent for. After obviously mimicking the four hundred prophets in their predictions of success, he is urged by Ahab himself to speak the truth only in the name of Yahveh. Micaiah then utters a short oracle of menace and foreboding, and proceeds to explain how it is that the true prophets of Yahveh predicted the success of the expedition. Their prophetic gift was perverted by the will of Yahveh himself, who by their means was luring Ahab on to his inevitable doom.

In this story we have the first indication of a wide ethical and religious cleavage in the ranks of the Yahveh prophets themselves, and the fact is sufficiently novel to call forth a special and supernatural explanation. The very type or model of the canonical prophets is already revealed in Micaiah. As Jeremiah stands alone in predicting ruin, while Hananiah and his followers foretell smooth and pleasant things—unable, perchance, to realize how Yahveh can show himself most supreme amid the disasters and downfall of his people—so, two centuries and a half earlier, did Micaiah withstand Zedekiah and the compliant four hundred before the gates of Samaria. One of the stories about Elijah is another harbinger of coming events. After Ahab's judicial murder of Naboth the Jezreelite, Elijah confronts Ahab, as Nathan had confronted David for the murder of Uriah. No mention is made of the apostasy to Baal; the punishment is to fall upon Ahab and his house because of the moral wrong which had been wrought in Jezreel. For the rest, the whole bulk of the narratives respecting the prophets of this period presents a fusion between old and new. The Yahveh of Elijah and Elisha was little softened from the Yahveh of Samuel.[1] In Yahveh's name Elijah slaughters the prophets of Baal at the brook of Kidron, and an unnamed prophet sternly reproves Ahab for sparing his enemy Ben-Hadad, who had fallen under the ban of Yahveh. Elisha curses the little children who laugh at his strange appearance, and two bears, the instruments of Yahveh's wrath, destroy forty-two of them. On the other hand, Elisha forbids the king of Israel to slay the Syrians who, smitten with sudden blindness, had followed him into Samaria. There are contrasts, too, in the manner

[1] 1 Kings xix. 12 must not be pressed too far, when one remembers that it is followed by verse 17.

of prophecy. Elisha, on one occasion, needs the impulse of music before he can reveal the oracle of Yahveh; and the four hundred prophets, who prophesy by Ahab and Jehoshaphat's request at the gates of Samaria, must clearly be conceived as in a condition of unnatural excitement and exaltation. Yet Elijah and Micaiah (and Elisha, too, upon other occasions) speak, like Isaiah and Jeremiah, from the pressure of momentary inspiration and without artificial stimulus.

The attempted addition of the Sidonian Baal as partner, if not as rival to Yahveh, ended in disastrous failure and bloody revolt. Elisha instigated Jehu to rebel against Jehoram, Ahab's son and younger brother of Ahaziah, his immediate predecessor. The rebellion took place in 843, thirty-five years after Ahab's accession to the throne. But the Baal movement was already slackening. Jehoram, according to the historian's own verdict, "wrought evil in the sight of Yahveh, but not like his father and like his mother, for he put away the pillar of Baal which his father had made."[1] Jehu, however, in exterminating the race of Omri, posed as an instrument of divine vengeance, and apparently slew, besides the royal family, many of the worshippers of Baal. In this bloody purgation, and in the destruction of Baal's images and temple, he was assisted by Jehonadab the Rechabite, who, himself of Kenite origin, had preserved the purest and simplest traditions of the oldest forms of Yahvistic faith. How far Jehu's violent zeal and bloodshed won him the approval of Elisha we do not know; a century later the prophet Hosea foretold the destruction

[1] 2 Kings iii. 1.

of the northern kingdom because of the bloodshed at Jezreel.

The experiment of introducing Baal-worship and the failure of the attempt were both repeated upon a smaller scale in the kingdom of Judah. Keen follower of Yahveh as Jehoshaphat was, he did not scruple to enter into close alliance with Ahab, and his son Jehoram was married to Athaliah, a daughter of Ahab, and probably, therefore, a daughter of Jezebel as well. Both Jehoram and his son Ahaziah (who had reigned only one year before he fell a victim to Jehu at Jezreel) are reported to have "walked in the way of the house of Ahab." A temple of Baal, with images and altars, was erected at Jerusalem. Priests were consecrated to his service. Athaliah, after her murder of the seed-royal, upon the news of Ahaziah's death reaching Jerusalem, followed naturally, so far as the worship of Baal was concerned, in the footsteps of her father. Nor do we hear of any opposition from the prophets; and when, after a lapse of six years (857), the idolatrous queen Athaliah is dethroned and slain, and Joash, Ahaziah's son (who had been saved by his aunt from his grandmother's clutches), is proclaimed king, it is Jehoiada, the chief priest of the temple, who is the ringleader of the revolt, and the destroyer of the worship of Baal.[1] Why the prophets take no part in the struggle is very obscure. Were the seers of Judah at that time more compliant and more courtly than those of Israel? Or is the omission of their co-operation with Jehoiada a mere accident? The argument from silence is proverbially dangerous.

[1] 2 Kings xi.

Between the accession of Ahab and the revolt of Jehu there is an interval of thirty-six years. These years were signalized, not only by the conflict between Baal and Yahveh, but also by the beginning of the Syrian wars. In Jehu's reign the Syrian king Hazael ravaged Israel with fire and sword. The victories of Ahab were not repeated by the destroyer of Ahab's house. Under Jehoahaz (814—796) things went from bad to worse, and it was not till the reign of his son Joash, and his grandson Jeroboam the Second, that the Syrian foe was finally vanquished, and Israel's power for one last brief period restored. The introduction and collapse of the worship of Baal, the prophetic opposition and its success, and the subsequent calamities at the hands of the national foe, cannot but have had a considerable effect upon religious development. It was not out of harmony with the religious ideas of those days that the punishment of the guilt incurred by the apostasy to Baal should appear to be visited upon subsequent generations. Nor was Judah exempt from trouble. A predicted invasion of Hazael was bought off at great expense by Jehoash; but Amaziah, his son, though he did that which was right in the eyes of Yahveh, was compelled to witness Joash of Israel break down the wall of Jerusalem, and enter into the capital with all the insolence of a foreign conqueror.[1] It is, therefore, not improbable, as Kuenen has suggested, that these external calamities, following closely upon the internal religious dissensions, suggested to the faithful that there was a causal connection between the two orders of events.[2] Nor was it possible for Elijah to resist the

[1] 2 Kings xiv. 13.   [2] *Religion of Israel*, Vol. I. p. 367.

Baal-worship of Ahab, without his conception of Yahveh being raised by the very process and strength of his opposition. In proportion as Yahveh's cause was held high by Elijah's party—fought for, perhaps even died for, through Jezebel's hostility—the contrast between Yahveh and Baal would grow larger and more distinct. As the one became holier, purer, greater, the other became viler, more impotent and less real. Professor Schultz has asserted that this supposed result of the events under the reign of Ahab and his immediate successors has no foundation in fact. "Kuenen's opinion that the persecution of the worship of Yahveh under Ahab gave occasion to a higher and more monotheistic conception of God, is nowhere supported by the original authorities."[1] But the opinion of Kuenen is an interpretation of the facts, not another fact beyond them. We know that the measures of Ahab awoke men like Elijah and Micaiah to active resistance, and that in the course of that resistance they displayed a moral power and reached a religious height above the previous level of the prophetic body. Now for the sixty years which lie between Elisha and Amos, we have no record of the religious condition of either Israel or Judah. In the latter kingdom Jehoash's two successors, Amaziah and Azariah, are both described as sincere followers of Yahveh. In Israel, Joash and Jeroboam II. continue the policy of Jehu; no change, in other words, is made in the customary worship, and the golden calves are still revered as the symbols of Yahveh. Then suddenly, amid the comparative prosperity of Jeroboam's reign, there sounds the

[1] *Alttestamentliche Theologie*, 4th ed., 1889, p. 144.

warning voice of Amos, the shepherd-prophet. He stands as high above Elijah, as Elijah, in all probability, stood above Samuel. The hypothesis of Kuenen is meant to account for the possibility of his advent and of his teaching. The religion of Yahveh was stirred to its depths by the policy of Ahab: the reaction which ensued, if it showed itself in acts of violence and ferocious vengeance, showed itself also in the noble figures of Elijah, Elisha, and Micaiah, and, after an interval of national calamity, which may have also helped to purify the religious conceptions of the higher minds, in the more developed teaching of the canonical prophets.

But the religious progress of the ninth century is only to be understood as a development; in no wise as a creation *ex nihilo*. The exclusive worship of Yahveh and the moral elements of his character were, as we have seen in the last Lecture, co-ordinated and causally connected from the very first. It is not without significance that the same Elijah who withstands Ahab as the introducer of a foreign cult, withstands him also as the murderer of Naboth. Had not Baal and Yahveh been alien deities from the first, there could have been no Elijah to fight till death for the worship of Yahveh. The religion of Moses only very gradually unfolded the promise which it contained, and it even seems to have occasionally sunk down close to the level of its Canaanite surroundings. But if external circumstances helped its ethical development, they would have been powerless to do so unless there had been *ab initio* something ethical to develop.

Nor does an impartial estimate of the pre-prophetic religion as a whole point in a contrary direction. Standing as we do now on the confines of old and new, it is well to collect together some general characteristics of the religion at the average level it had reached before the prophetic advance.

The nature of the pre-prophetic religion was determined by the character of its God. As Yahveh was conceived, so, in a great measure, was the religion of his worshippers. Let us, then, briefly recall to mind some central features of Yahveh's character. Yahveh is a person like ourselves, only wiser and more powerful. Even in the pre-prophetic stage, he is well marked off from the forces of nature which he controls, and thus ready to receive a uniform and self-consistent character. He already possesses many ethical attributes, and their possession points the way to the future development of an harmonious union of these qualities in a complete ethical ideal. But though Yahveh is a person, his life and doings are withdrawn from mortal ken, except in his relations to humanity. The taint of mythology is wanting. Yahveh has no associate or relative. Then, secondly, the religious custom, or, for the higher or more thoughtful minds, the religious law, of Israel was monolatry. Yahveh was a jealous God who did not tolerate the worship of other gods in his own land. The consequence was that the whole accumulation of supernatural agencies and effects was centred upon Yahveh; and as the conception of his character advanced in moral firmness and consistency, it became easier to arrange all religious phenomena upon a moral basis and to regard them from a moral point of view. As all fortunes of the national life, its calamities no less than its successes, were the ordered effects of one God's rule, every incident could only be explained in consonance with the character of that single divinity. It was not a malignant deity who had sent a famine, a beneficent deity who had brought the rain; it was one and the same Yahveh who had done all these things. As Yahveh's actions were more and more regarded, not as the inexplicable expressions of wayward and inconstant moods, but as the reasoned and justifiable display of a settled and unique character, the way was paved for the prophetic conception that national adversity could only betoken national sin, and finally that the ruin of the people might be compatible with the triumph of their God.

It is true that the moralization of Yahveh's character was by no means completed at the close of the pre-prophetic period. There was much left for the prophets to do. He still retained many aspects of the nature-gods out of whom he was derived, some of which still clung to him in the Mosaic teaching, while others may have been adopted from qualities of the Canaanite divinities. These lower aspects, however, mainly resolve themselves into one, Yahveh's wrath. That he should show no mercy to Israel's foes, who are identical with his own, is no more than natural, and but slightly affects the conception of him for an ordinary citizen in times of peace. But his wrath is not limited to the enemies of his people. We have seen that it bursts forth with equal vehemence against his own nation, where any violation, however unintentional, of his honour and sanctity may be involved. And this wrath, as it often arose from unethical causes, must be appeased by savage and unethical means. On the other side there is the fact that Yahveh's religion, ever since the Mosaic period, had linked religion and morality together both theoretically and practically. Every Israelite knew that injustice and adultery and violence were hateful to his God, and in every-day life the disputes of man with man were settled by the arbitrament of Yahveh. The priesthood judged and taught as Yahveh's interpreters, and in ordinary times the Israelites would be more frequently reminded of Yahveh's maintenance of, and desire for, social morality than of his jealousy and wrath.

With these considerations the evidence coheres which points to the religion of Israel being, on the whole, a source of happiness and satisfaction. The Israelites could exult in their God, who usually directed his divine capacities to the advancement and well-being of his people. But both the blessings and the difficulties of religion were very different to the old Israelites from what they became, let us say, to the authors of the Psalter. In many respects their religious views were closely similar to those of other nations of antiquity. So far as we can gather from our scanty records, the blessings of religion were conceived as material—a numerous progeny, fruitful harvest and long life. It was only on earth that one could hope to taste of Yahveh's bounties; after death there was one cheerless lot alike for all, whether rich or poor, evil or good. The Biblical *Sheol*, the home of the Shades, is the counterpart of the Homeric Hades, and the famous expostulation of Achilles would have found an echo in every Hebrew heart. At the close of the Old Testament period, doctrines of immortality gradually became the means of reconciling the just rule of God with the painful problems of human life; but to the old Israelites these problems had scarcely begun to appear above the furthest horizon of their thought. They did not perceive in the misfortunes of individuals anything inconsistent with the providence of Yahveh, for their God was mainly concerned with Israel as a whole, and not with the individual Israelite. It needed, therefore, we may imagine, some special calamity to awaken religious alarm, and then the explanation would be probably found in the idea of an unknown offence by which the wrath of Yahveh had unwittingly been aroused. For unintentional error would be as liable to incur divine punishment as the most voluntary crime, if it infringed the tolerably wide province in which the right or sanctity of Yahveh was involved. Personality was not sharply conceived in ancient society. The Israelites, therefore, saw no injustice in a deliberate chastisement of unintentional offences, in the sins of fathers being visited upon their children, or in the merited calamity of one bringing with it the undeserved ruin of many. Their religion was far more often a source of genial satisfaction than of painful perplexities. There was much in the ordinary rural life of those days to remind the people of their religion and their God. Enough indications remain to show that an altar of Yahveh was a necessary and usual feature in every larger village, and that here, on every sabbath and new moon, sacrifices and prayers were offered up to the national God. Besides the three great annual festivals of Passover, First-fruits and Ingathering, when everybody was expected to provide for and take part in the general rejoicing; the different families and clans had also their own yearly sacrifices,[1] and individuals upon special occasions could come before Yahveh and seek his favour with votive offering or free-will gift. Round the larger and more famous of these local sanctuaries, legendary stories grew up of their supposed foundation by the patriarchs before the departure of the people's progenitors to the land of Goshen. Some of these stories we can still read in the two oldest pre-prophetic sources of the Pentateuch, which must have been compiled at least as early as the beginning of the eighth century. The local sanctuaries were in so far a danger to the progress of spiritual religion as they helped to maintain the view that "to the ordinary man it was not moral but liturgical acts which seemed to be truly religious,"[2] and they were that part of Yahveh's faith which was most susceptible to, and received most of, Canaanite corruption.

Yet the religion of old Israel was simple, and comparatively free from degrading superstition. And though the view was widely prevalent that sacrifice could appease God's wrath or win his favour, it was not thought that Yahveh was compelled to change his mood, or hear his suppliant's prayer, by any human means. The religion of Yahveh was not tainted by sorcery. Moreover, the Yahveh of the priest was also the Yahveh of the layman. There is no trace of any esoteric priestly doctrine kept back from society at large. The business of Israel's teachers is to communicate their knowledge of Yahveh to his people: neither they nor the prophets are familiar with the idea that the highest conceptions of

[1] 1 Sam. xx. 29.   [2] Wellhausen, *History of Israel*, p. 468.

Yahveh and his religion need be limited to the possession of a few. Perhaps that is also the reason why, in all the various phases of Old Testament religion, we find no vestige of Pantheism.

The Israelite was proud of his religion and of his God. How enthusiastic are the words of the author of the "Blessing of Moses," presumably written shortly before the opening of the newer prophetical movement in the eighth century! "There is none like unto the God of Jeshurun, who rideth upon the heaven for thy help, and in his glory on the sky. Happy art thou, O Israel! who is like unto thee, O people saved by Yahveh, the shield of thy help, the sword of thy glory!" But proud as he is of Yahveh's help, and of the unique power of his God, the old Israelite has no knowledge of his nation's peculiar position or destiny. The idea of a theocracy is wanting. Israel is not marked off from other nations as the possessor of the one and only true religion. Israel hates its enemies as the other nations of antiquity hate theirs; but there is a world-wide difference between this natural hostility and that peculiar religious hatred of the heathen which was produced by far later developments. There is no thought of the religion of Yahveh being extended beyond the borders of Israel, or of supernatural vengeance being inflicted upon a heathen world for its opposition to the chosen people of the Supreme God. The light and shade of the prophetic religion are, in these respects, wholly wanting. Monolatry had not yet begun to pass into monotheism. The course of that transition, which corresponds with the teaching of the prophets, will come before us in the next Lecture.

Lecture III.

THE PROPHETS OF THE EIGHTH CENTURY B.C.

We have now reached a turning-point in our history. For the prophets of the eighth century are our subject, the men whose teaching, upon the basis of the founder's work, sufficed to make their people's religion unique among the religions of the world, just as their writings constitute a unique chapter in the annals of universal literature. We have already traced the origin and early development of the prophetical movement; we now approach the stage of its maturity, in which unrecorded speech was supplemented, or even replaced, by written words, and the value of the message was confirmed by the greater permanency of its form.[1]

Four prophets of the eighth century are known to us by their writings; already we have more than once had occasion to use these writings as indirect evidence in dealing with the earlier religious history of Israel; we

[1] Written prophecy corresponds with a change in prophecy's purport. The message of the eighth-century prophets was no longer directed to momentary needs or particular individuals, but dealt with the people as a whole and with subjects of lasting significance. It was therefore possible to teach by writing as well as by speaking, just as it was advisable to record the teaching as a witness of the present and a lesson for the future.

III. PROPHETS OF THE EIGHTH CENTURY B.C. 107

have now to study them for their own sakes, and obtain, if we can, a clear picture of their character and teaching. For this purpose it will be necessary to take a glance at the external history of Israel and of Judah in the last sixty years of the eighth century.[1] Jeroboam II. (781—741), the most powerful monarch of the house of Jehu, was reigning in Israel at the beginning of this period; Uzziah or Azariah (777—736), in Judah. The twofold fact that the Assyrian monarchy, having first greatly weakened the kingdom of Damascus, was itself about this time in partial and temporary eclipse, enabled Joash and Jeroboam to wage successful war against the Syrians, and to restore, unchecked by the greater power, the ancient borders of Israel towards the east and north.[2] But the recovered dignity of Israel was not long maintained. Within twenty years of the death of Jeroboam it was again lost. These two decades were crowded with trouble and horror for the inhabitants of the northern kingdom. Zechariah, the son of Jeroboam, was dethroned and killed after a six-months' reign, and with him ended the royal house of Jehu. Zechariah's murderer, Shallum, reigned for a month only, falling in his turn a victim to Menahem, "who slew him and reigned in his stead."[3] Meanwhile, an abler warrior had ascended the throne of Assyria, Pul or Tiglath-pilesar II. (745—728).[4] In a great battle at Arpad

---

[1] The dates in Lectures II.—IV. are taken from Kamphausen's *Die Chronologie der hebräischen Könige*, 1883.

[2] Tiele, *Babylonisch-assyrische Geschichte*, pp. 206—209; 2 Kings xiii. 25, xiv. 25—28.

[3] 2 Kings xv. 14.   [4] 2 Kings xv. 19.

(743) he destroyed the armies of northern Syria. Subsequent revolts were easily quelled, and by 738 all resistance was at an end. In that same year Menahem paid tribute to Tiglath-pilesar, and was confirmed, as Assyrian vassal, in the kingdom of Samaria. After a brief reign, Menahem was succeeded by his son Pekahiah, who, two years later, was slain by Pekah, his shield-bearer, who usurped the throne. Thus, since Jeroboam's death, four kings had rapidly come and gone, of whom three had died by the hands of their successors.

Pekahiah's death and Pekah's accession bring us to the year 736. In Judah, the reigns of Uzziah and Jotham (777—735) had, upon the whole, been fortunate and peaceful. Both monarchs are commended by the redactor of the Books of the Kings, and credited with doing "that which was right in the sight of Yahveh."[1] It is otherwise with Jotham's son Ahaz, under whom the history of Judah becomes again connected with the history of Israel. For in the last year of Jotham's reign, and the first year of Ahaz', a war broke out between Judah and the confederated forces of Pekah, king of Israel, and Rezin, the king of Damascus. Ahaz, fearful for his capital, sent a present of silver and gold, taken from his own and the temple treasures, to Tiglath-pilesar, thus formally becoming the vassal of the Assyrian monarch, and besought his aid against the kings of Israel and Damascus. Tiglath-pilesar thereupon entered Syria, and shut up Rezin in his capital. The Assyrian invasion appears to have occasioned another conspiracy in Israel, as a result of which "Hoshea, the son of Elah, smote and

[1] 2 Kings xv. 3, 34.

slew Pekah, the son of Remaliah, and reigned in his stead."[1] Hoshea became the creature of Assyria; but Tiglath-pilesar punished the independence of Pekah and his war against the newly accepted Assyrian vassal, by incorporating the Israelite territories east of Jordan and north of Mount Ephraim in his own empire, and transporting a portion of their inhabitants into Assyria. This was the beginning of the end. Tiglath-pilesar's death in 727, and the accession of a new monarch (Shalmanesar IV., 727—723), appear to have been the occasion for Hoshea (and for Elulaios, king of Tyre) to revolt. A fresh Assyrian invasion brought Hoshea to speedy submission. But soon afterwards he formed an alliance with Shabako, king of Egypt, and once more refused to pay tribute to his Assyrian lord.[2] Shalmanesar penetrated into Israel and took Hoshea captive, whether after a pitched battle or by voluntary submission is uncertain. But Samaria, the capital, refused to surrender, and offered a desperate resistance. For three years the city held out, till famine probably compelled capitulation. The date of its fall is 722, about 215 years after the death of Solomon and the foundation of the northern kingdom by Jeroboam the First. Shalmanesar died in the same year, and was succeeded by Sargon II. (722—705).

The capture of Samaria was followed by the customary deportations. Sargon speaks of having carried away 27,280 inhabitants into Assyria. This was sufficient to arrest and stifle the entire national life. The most educated and cultivated sections of the people were exiled from their land, and new colonists were gradually intro-

[1] 2 Kings xv. 30.   [2] Tiele, *Geschichte*, p. 223.

duced from other quarters of the Assyrian empire. A passing revolt of Samaria in 720, as well as more important movements in Hamath and Damascus, was easily put down, and the combined armies of Egypt and Gaza, on whose assistance the rebels had relied, suffered a crushing defeat at Raphia. The kingdom of Israel became a province of Assyria, and with the extinction of its national independence, its religious development ceased. For although the majority of its inhabitants remained in their old homes, even after the further deportations which may have followed the revolt of 720, the religion of Yahveh had not attained sufficient purity and vigour to survive the loss of political freedom. The higher prophecy had not had time to attract a large circle of disciples. Hosea, as a witness of the troubles which succeeded the reign of Zechariah, speaks in despairing tones of the religious corruption around him. Moreover, the introduction of foreign colonists and the deportation of the flower of the native population, including, as it would seem, the entire priesthood,[1] exposed the national religion, corrupt as it was, to manifold dangers. The new-comers, though they brought their idols with them, adopted also the God of the land. A process of fusion set in. Yahveh may have remained the chief, and afterwards have again become the only, God of the old Israelite provinces, so that upon the return of the Jewish exiles from Babylon, the descendants of the "ten tribes" claimed religious partnership with Jerusalem; but henceforward northern Israel contributed nothing to religious development, and the interest of the story wholly centres in Judah. From

[1] 2 Kings xviii. 27.

the strange incident recorded in the Book of Kings concerning the lions which were sent by Yahveh, and slew some of the new colonists because they knew not the religion of the God of the land, we learn something of the superstitious elements which formed part of the popular faith at the close of the eighth century.[1] From a mixed population, out of which the more educated members had been removed to make room for heathen settlers, a religious advance was not to be expected. But even the 27,000 exiles from Samaria were unable to maintain their religion apart from their nation and their land. After their deportation to Assyria we hear of them no more.

Would not a similar religious collapse have befallen the southern kingdom, had it also been incorporated into the Assyrian empire? Most probably. The different religious issue of the Babylonian captivity was doubtless due to the maintenance of the State, and, with the State, to the continuance of prophetical teaching for another hundred years. Meanwhile, during the troubles which culminated in the fall of Samaria, Ahaz remained faithful to his Assyrian lord, and even paid homage to Tiglath-pilesar at Damascus after its capture in 732. Hezekiah, Ahaz' son, probably succeeded him about the year 714. The first ten years of his reign were undisturbed by rebellion or war. Sargon had died in 705; his successor was Sennacherib. But about the year 703 a coalition was formed against Assyria, led by Egypt, and comprising the states of Tyre, Ashkelon, Ekron and Judah. With Sennacherib's invasion of Judah, and the remarkable preservation of Jerusalem from capture and spoliation,

[1] 2 Kings xviii. 25—41.

several of Isaiah's prophecies are closely concerned. The details of the campaign remain obscure, in spite of the Assyrian inscriptions; the upshot, however, was that though Hezekiah, after Sennacherib's hasty retreat from Palestine, remained the vassal of Assyria, his position was improved both in material power and comparative independence, and Jerusalem's escape from the fate of Samaria, which at one time seemed impossible, took shape in the mind of Isaiah, and indeed of all Judah, as a special divine deliverance. Hezekiah's reign was subsequently undisturbed. He died in 686.[1]

To complete the picture of the circumstances amid which the prophets spoke and wrote, it would be necessary to supplement our skeleton outline of the external history with a description of the internal moral and religious condition of the two kingdoms during the same period. But for an adequate description there is insufficient material, seeing that we are mainly confined to the prophetical writings themselves, and to such portions of the earlier Pentateuchal strata as we may be able, with any measure of certainty, to assign to the eighth century. If we could use it with greater confidence, the second of these two sources might enable us to correct, or counterbalance to the right degree, the sombre sketch which, like *censores morum* in all ages, the prophets have drawn for us of the society in which they lived.

The strata of the Pentateuch referred to are the two

[1] For Sennacherib's campaign in Judah (2 Kings xviii. 13—xix. 37) see Tiele, *Geschichte*, pp. 291—295, 315—318; Stade, *Z. A. W.*, 1886, pp. 172—183; Kuenen, *Onderzoek*, 2nd ed., Vol. I. pp. 414—417; Cheyne's *Isaiah*, Historical Introduction to xxxvi.—xxxix., &c.

so-called "prophetical" narratives, with the short legislative pieces connected with or contained in them. Unfortunately, scholars are still in some disagreement as to the date of these narratives, which, moreover—a feature seriously adding to the complexity of the problem—show many traces of revision and amplification. Though now so closely woven together that in our present Pentateuch we are often unable to disentangle the two threads, they were originally of independent origin. One of the narratives was compiled in northern Israel, the other in Judah. They contain an account, drawn partly from oral tradition and partly from earlier documents now lost, of the origin and early history of Israel, reaching back, in one of them, to the creation of the world by Yahveh, and brought down by both to the death of Joshua and the conquest of Canaan. It is also very possible that the earlier historical books are partly composed of materials that once formed the unbroken continuation of these same two narratives.[1] This question is, however, not yet fully decided.

The hypothesis as to their date, to which I would myself incline, essays to prove that at least the larger portion of both narratives, as well as of the legislation which belongs to them, was already in existence before Amos. Without expressing any opinion upon their relative ages, we may follow the hypothesis which assigns their compilation to the close of the ninth or the beginning of the eighth century. The religious material to be elicited from them is of a conflicting nature, representing partly the dual character of the pre-prophetic

[1] Budde, *Die Bücher Richter und Samuel*, 1890.

religion in general, and partly the special period of transition in which they were composed. But in view of the uncertainty still prevailing as to their date, and of the extent to which a plurality of recensions may have caused the existing differences in tone and teaching, we must use them but sparingly in our estimate of the moral and religious condition of the prophetic age, and, while remembering its obvious one-sidedness, rely in the main upon the evidence of the prophets themselves.[1]

Both decline and progress would seem to have been characteristics of the age which preceded, and of the age which witnessed, the coming of the prophets. Society in the Assyrian period was passing through an epoch of corruption and decay. Public morality was at a low ebb. The prophets bring the gravest charges against the officials and aristocracy of either kingdom. We hear much of the violation of justice, the venality of priests and judges, the land-hunger of the large proprietors, the oppressive cruelty of the rich and the monstrous luxury of their wives. Old social bonds were being broken up, and the process was accompanied, especially in the north, by rapine and even bloodshed.[2]

The moral iniquity of the ruling classes was sometimes associated with a religious scepticism, which, in times of danger and distress, was converted into hopeless despair or grovelling superstition.[3] Forbidden practices, hostile

[1] Kuenen's *Hexateuch* gives the references to the literature on this subject up to 1885. See also Kittel, *Geschichte der Hebräer*, Vol. I. 1888, &c.

[2] E.g. Amos ii. 7, iii. 10, vii. 12, viii. 4—6; Hosea iv. 2, 8, v. 2, vi. 9; Isaiah iii. 16—23, v. 8—22, x. 1—3; Micah ii. 2, iii. 1—3, 11.

[3] Isaiah v. 18—21, xxii. 12, xxxi. 1.

to the religion of Yahveh, such as the consultation of spirits, and various forms of sorcery and witchcraft, were also prevalent.[1] While the worship of Yahveh in material forms was not, as we already know, an erring innovation of the eighth century, it would yet seem as if the outward popular religion underwent debasement in the prophetic age. More than ever the attempt was made to purchase God's favour and appease his wrath by costly and varied sacrifices; while in the northern kingdom, at any rate, the worship of Yahveh was too frequently associated with a gross licentiousness, imitated from the rites of Astarte. Direct idolatry—the worship of other gods— was a not unknown offence in either kingdom.[2]

Exponents of religion suffered in the general decline. The "prophets of the school" sank lower and lower. Prophecy became more and more a convenient trade, securing a certain amount of popular admiration, and an easily acquired, if not luxurious, competency. Many members of the priesthood must have deserved the castigation which our four prophets often mete out to them.[3]

But while so much must justly be said upon the side of corruption and decay, there is also another side to the picture which cannot be neglected. For parallel with decline there must have been a coincident spiritual advance.

In the two oldest Pentateuchal narratives we find a

---

[1] Hosea iv. 12; Isaiah ii. 6, 8, viii. 19.

[2] Amos ii. 7, 8; Hosea iii. 1, iv. 13, 14; Isaiah i. 29, xvii. 10, xxx. 33; Micah i. 7, 13.

[3] Amos vii. 14; Hosea iv. 5, 6, vi. 9; Isaiah iii. 2, xxviii. 7; Micah ii. 11, iii. 5, 7.

fairly developed religious and ethical ideal. Though both show sincere attachment to the local sanctuaries, the syncretistic worship at which excited the indignation of our four prophets, neither alludes to a customary and approved worship of Yahveh under material forms.[1] Antagonism to this aberration may possibly have begun to show itself between Elijah and Amos. Again, this intervening period, while it witnessed a partial degeneracy in the dual orders of prophecy and priesthood, must also have produced a corresponding elevation. Here and there, whether within the prophetic guilds or outside them, were prophets in whom the fire of Elijah was not quenched, and who formed the necessary connection between the prophet of Gilead and Amos of Tekoa. Our primary eighth-century authorities allude to good prophets as well as to bad.[2] In at least one instance, Isaiah incorporates a passage from an earlier prophet into his own writings,[3] and he, as well as Amos and Hosea, bears witness to an upward development in prophecy beyond and above Elijah. For the seers, who according to Isaiah were bidden by his people, "Prophesy not unto us right things, but speak unto us smooth things, prophesy deceits," were clearly men of his own stamp, preachers of social rectitude as well as of religious purity.

Nor can the priesthood have been wholly corrupt. We may well remember the delineation of the priestly character and duties in the "Blessing of Moses," which was

[1] The date of Genesis xxxv. 2 (E) is uncertain.
[2] Amos ii. 11, iii. 7; Hosea xii. 11, 14, vi. 5; Isaiah xxx. 10, 20; Micah ii. 6.
[3] Isaiah xv. xvi. 1—12: ii. 1—4, is a possibly post-exilic insertion.

EIGHTH CENTURY B.C. 117

probably written shortly before Amos. The removal of Baal-worship in Judah during the rule of Athaliah was the work of the priest Jehoiada, and it is noteworthy that Jehoash (836—797) is recorded to have done "that which was right in the sight of Yahveh, according as Jehoiada the priest had instructed him."[1] Among the chosen friends of Isaiah, whom he is bidden to take as witnesses to his "large tablet," is Uriah the priest.[2] In Judah, at any rate, there had been one effort at religious reform even before Jehoash, and the contrast which Isaiah draws between the days of Ahaz and those earlier times when Jerusalem was still called the faithful city, is not without its significance, though it may easily be pressed too far.[3]

To priests who lived before Amos may also be assigned the compilation of those legislative chapters of the Pentateuch which are now embodied in the two so-called prophetical narratives, but have all of them probably an independent origin. These chapters include the "Book of the Covenant" or "First Legislation" of Exodus xxi.—xxiii., and the Decalogue of Exodus xx. in its shorter and more original form. It is true that many of the "judgments" in the former seem to us harsh and immature; but considered in the light of age and place, apparent cruelty frequently assumes the aspect of religious progress and enlightenment. Nor must we forget that the Book of the Covenant contains laws which breathe a pure spirit of rectitude and humanity. "Thou shalt not raise a false report; thou shalt not countenance

[1] 2 Kings xii. 2.   [2] Isaiah viii. 2.
[3] 1 Kings xv. 12, 13; Isaiah i. 26, with Dillmann's notes.

a rich man or a poor man in his cause; thou shalt take no gift; thou shalt not oppress a stranger;" these and other enactments of similar strain help to show us that the religion of Israel in the beginning of the eighth century, if characterized by much corruption and immorality, also contained elements which paved the way for, and even pointed forward to, the teaching of the prophets.[1] How far these codes were known beyond the limits of the sanctuary, where we may presumably place their compilation, is very uncertain. Yet Hosea appears to imply that, even in his age, there was a "law" recognized as God's and wrongly neglected by the people. "Though I write for him the words of my law, they are accounted a strange thing."[2] In other references of the eighth-century prophets to Yahveh's law (Torah) and to his ordinances, it is, more probably, the oral instruction of priests and prophets to which allusion is made. For in their teaching the eighth-century prophets do not appeal to any acknowledged standard of religion embodied in a legal code—the Law of Moses is a factor unknown to them—but to the general religious and moral consciousness of the people of Yahveh. To that teaching we can now advert. But, by way of final introduction, a few words must yet be said as to the life, personality and method of the four teachers.

[1] Cf. Kuenen, *Hexateuch*, p. 245, § 13, n. 23; and also Baentsch, *Das Bundesbuch*, 1892, who is inclined to think that the finest passages in the code are the latest, and due to prophetic influence and teaching.

[2] Hosea viii. 12. The emendation on which the translation is based was suggested by Graetz, *Geschichte der Juden*, Vol. II. i. p. 469. Cf. Kuenen, *Hexateuch*, § 10, n. 4, p. 178.

Amos is the oldest. He prophesied towards the end of the reign of Jeroboam II. (781—741). Hosea comes next; for while the earliest of his prophecies were written in the lifetime of that monarch, most of them were composed in the short and troubled reigns of his four immediate successors (741—736). Isaiah's prophetic career extended over some forty years, including the entire reign of Ahaz and more than half Hezekiah's (736—700 ?). Micah, a contemporary of Isaiah, though probably younger in years, only prophesied, so far as we know, in the reign of Hezekiah.

Of these four prophets, three were natives of Judah, only one, Hosea, belonging to the north. But Amos, though resident in Judah, received the divine call to prophesy against Israel, and travelled northwards from the pastures of Tekoa to deliver his message of denunciation and woe at Bethel, the sanctuary of the king.[1] It is not likely that any one of them belonged to the prophetic order. They were men of various social conditions and circumstances. Amos was a herdman, and began to prophesy in virtue of an inward call. "The lion roars, who will not fear? the Lord Yahveh speaks, who can but prophesy?" When Amaziah, the priest of Bethel, protested against his minatory predictions, and bade him "flee away into the land of Judah and there eat bread and prophesy there," he urged that he was no prophet and no prophet's son, but a herdman and a

[1] Some scholars maintain that Amos was himself an Israelite, not a Judæan. On this question, see Kuenen, *Onderzoek*, Vol. II. pp. 355, 356, with the further reference in the added page of "Verbeteringen en toevoegsels;" and, lastly, Oort in *Theol. Tijd.*, 1891, pp. 121—124.

dresser of fig-trees. "And Yahveh took me as I followed the flock, and Yahveh said unto me, Go, prophesy unto my people Israel." This appeal is significant. The "true" prophets, those who realized Yahveh's character and will most truly, and whose lives answered to their teaching, arose more and more rarely in the prophetic guilds.

Of Hosea, beyond that he was a native of the north, we know nothing. He was possibly a priest, and probably, unlike Amos, belonged to the higher rather than to the lower sections of Israelite society.

Such a contrast in social rank is pretty certain as regards the two Judæan prophets, Isaiah and Micah. Micah was "a native of Moresheth, a small town in the maritime plain near Gath," and probably belonged to the class of the peasantry.[1] Isaiah, though we know nothing positive as to his family or connections, was unquestionably a native of the capital and familiar with its leading citizens. Though a great prophet was no longer, as in the days of David, the seer of the court, Isaiah was ready to advise, as well as to denounce, the kings of Judah, and occupied an acknowledged position of authority in the state.

Thus the higher prophetic movement of the eighth century extended to both kingdoms, and found its spokesmen in all classes of society. But in the method of their teaching and in the manner of their speech, all our four prophets show common characteristics. Their combined usage both of the spoken and of the written word distinguishes them from the earlier prophets on the one hand, and from the later, more apocalyptic, prophets upon

[1] Cheyne, *Micah*, p. 9.

the other. Again, while the older type was marked by an access of physical exaltation (a lower concomitant of prophecy which was not, indeed, unknown throughout the pre-exilic period), our four canonical prophets appear never to have delivered even their spoken message in a state of ecstasy or excitement. The literary form of their prophecies, which is often artistically elaborate, could only have been the product of a perfectly calm mind, reflecting upon the spoken word, and emending it to suit the requirements of written discourse. Similarly, in the writings of all four prophets, visions occupy a very secondary place, or even become mere artifices of expression. Thus the visions of Amos are figurative and allegorical; Hosea and Micah are without them; while Isaiah only records one, and that in a highly developed literary form, written down long after the occasion of the original vision, which had seemed to accompany his inward call to the prophetic office. So, too, the strange symbolic actions of either older or less ethical prophets are almost wholly wanting. In Amos and Micah they are altogether absent; in Hosea, a lamentable incident in his past life is described *post eventum* as a divine command. The one symbolic action mentioned in Isaiah, which it is difficult to regard as a mere figure of rhetoric, forms an isolated exception.[1] Upon the whole, then, we have to deal with the teaching of men who, while firmly convinced of their divine mission, and assured that the word they spoke or wrote was the expression of Yahveh's will, were yet sober, as they were accurate, observers of the events and conditions of their time.

[1] Isaiah xx. 2.

The conception of Yahveh's character and of his relation to Israel is the first point in their teaching to which our attention must be directed. For all others are essentially dependent upon this.

The moral element in the divine nature which, as I have endeavoured to show, was the novel but specific feature in the Mosaic teaching, was all-pervading in the prophets of the eighth century. To them, Yahveh's moral attributes were co-extensive with his nature, so that there remained behind no non-ethical residuum. He was the God of Righteousness, not merely of justice in a purely juridic sense, but of Righteousness in the more extended connotation of ordinary modern usage. Righteousness is the fundamental virtue of the prophetic Yahveh. Not only can his dealings with man, and more especially with Israel, never be inconsistent with this sovereign quality, they must always be its direct outcome and issue. The consequence is, that he cannot leave the sins of Israel unrequited and unpunished. Ephraim and Judah are both sinful—sinful civilly, publicly, politically; therefore the punishment that must befall them is also outward and general. The main business of the prophets is to denounce iniquity, and foretell the judgment. They call to repentance, but without belief in the efficacy of their warning; the judgment of God must cause amendment; therefore they are prophets of trouble—"of war and of evil and of pestilence."[1] On the other hand, while these sins of Israel must inevitably call forth Israel's punishment, so that the triumph of the national foe is nothing more

[1] Jeremiah xxviii. 8.

than the fulfilment of divine purpose, Yahveh's anger is now no longer a merely fitful outburst, unrelated to Israel's own wrong-doing. It is an essential element of his righteousness, and, however seemingly passionate, it is always ethically pure.

But Yahveh's righteousness, which, to the prophets, was in the main necessarily manifested in retribution—for Israel was sinful—was tempered by other and gentler qualities, depending not upon the partiality of favouritism, but upon fidelity to a covenant promise and to persistency in a chosen purpose. Both sides of the divine character are expressed in the terms of the second betrothal, which, according to Hosea, Yahveh will contract with Israel after the purification of the judgment: "I will betroth thee unto me in righteousness and in justice, and in loving-kindness and in mercy."[1] God was not yet conceived as a "lover of souls" generally; his loving-kindness was not yet "philanthropy;"[2] but it was his love for Israel which ultimately generated his love for man.

We remember the popular view of Yahveh's relation to Israel. He was still in many respects the patron Deity. To the prophets, Yahveh is as much as he ever was the God of Israel; but his love for Israel is a thousand times deeper, as it is a thousand times purer, than the partiality of the popular God. Just because he stands in a nearer or closer relation to one people than to any other, the fulness of his being, the totality of his qualities and powers is brought to bear upon Israel. And as the essence of the divine character is its righteousness, the

[1] Hosea ii. 21. [2] Wisdom of Solomon xi. 26; Titus iii. 4.

punishment of Israel, to be executed by Assyria, is the direct consequence of Israel's relationship to its God. This thought is most sharply expressed by Amos: "You only have I known of all the families of the earth; therefore will I visit you for all your iniquities."[1] This terrible "therefore" must have been as a bolt from the blue to the popular religious consciousness in the days of king Jeroboam.

Israel is Yahveh's people; but it had not achieved this position through its own merit. Its relation to its God is the result of Yahveh's unfettered choice, a free exercise of his sovereign will. Yahveh's election of Israel is most clearly brought out by Amos and Hosea. The beginning of the relationship is assigned to the exodus from Egypt: "When Israel was a child, then I loved him, and called my son out of Egypt." "I am Yahveh thy God from the land of Egypt." So writes Hosea.[2] Amos alludes to the exodus in a similar strain, but he is at pains to add that the mere fact that Yahveh brought up the Israelites from Egypt was no unexampled manifestation of his interference in, or management of, the affairs of men. He is not bound to them because of the deliverance from Egypt by any tie beyond his own free will. If he brought up the Israelites from Egypt, he equally "brought up" the Philistines from Caphtor and the Syrians from Kir.[3] Yahveh as the moral God, and Yahveh as the ruler of the world (an aspect in which we have yet to regard him), can only have become connected with Israel upon the basis of an agreement, entered into by God for a purpose of his own. The idea of a covenant between Israel and

[1] Amos iii. 2. [2] Hosea xi. 1, xiii. 4. [3] Amos ii. 10, ix. 7.

Yahveh was more fully developed by the writers of the seventh century. But the germs of it are already traceable in Hosea, just as a contract between God and Israel in the Mosaic age upon the tenure of a fixed code had been described even before Hosea in the two earlier narratives of the Pentateuch.

Yet as to the nature of the purpose for which Israel was chosen, the prophets imply more than they say. Abstract theological meditation was alien to their nature, and inconsistent with the practical character of their work. They seem, however, already to have roughly conceived the idea, subsequently to be elaborated, that Yahveh was training up out of Israel a holy nation, who, by undivided allegiance to their God, and by the practice of social morality, should sanctify his name. The goal will not be reached, according to Isaiah, until "through the judgment blast every one that is left in Zion shall be called holy."[1] From this object of Israel's election, an object primarily confined to Israel's own spiritual glory and God's sanctification through Israel's means, there grew the fuller and larger conception of a conversion of the heathen nations to the true religion.

But Israel's election, while it conferred a privilege, imposed a duty. That duty we already know to have consisted in moral goodness and in the pure worship of Yahveh. Israel must seek Yahveh, and to seek Yahveh is equivalent to seeking goodness.[2] Israel is Yahveh's vineyard, and the fruits which it should have borne to its husbandman were justice and righteousness.[3] But very different fruits were yielded. "God hoped for

[1] Isaiah iv. 3.   [2] Amos v. 6, 14.   [3] Isaiah v. 1—7.

justice, but behold bloodshed; for righteousness, but behold a cry." Thus the purpose of Israel's calling was defeated by its own sinfulness, and a judgment had become necessary in order that Israel might fulfil in good earnest its divinely appointed mission. The judgment process would combine punishment of the wicked with purification for the good: it would put an end to existing iniquity and oppression, in order to substitute for them a perfect state of civic righteousness and of inward and outward well-being.

The moral ideals of the prophets corresponded to the sins which they denounced. "As to the contents of their conception of righteousness," says Wellhausen, with his wonted conciseness and power, "it was not righteousness in the sense of the gospel. They do not so much demand a pure heart as just institutions: they think less of the individual than of the state and society, showing the while a remarkable sympathy with the lower classes, which even exercised a permanent effect upon the religious terminology."[1] We are reminded of the prophetical manner by the sermons of Savanarola, and, to a certain degree, by the denunciations of Carlyle. As public men, they dealt with public affairs. They were preachers to a whole nation, inveighing against national sins. It was the nation of Israel which was chosen by Yahveh, and it was the nation which had transgressed against him, and which would meet with punishment. To the Hebrew prophets, as to the Greek philosophers, the state possessed a moral unity of its own. God's instrument of wrath, the power of Assyria, was a scourge of

[1] Wellhausen, *Abriss*, p. 52.

nations, not of individuals. The writing of God must first be traced writ large in the fortunes of kingdoms, before it can also be discerned upon the tablets of every human heart.

To the mind of the prophets, Israel had neglected the second portion of its duty as wofully as it had neglected the first. It was as deficient in the pure worship of Yahveh as in the practice of morality. In their eyes, the people's religious and moral delinquencies were intimately connected, for either element of Israel's duty towards its God was complementary to the other. In Hosea's writings, denunciation of moral iniquity occupies a less primary place than a constant lament over the false worship of Yahveh, of which moral wrong-doing is the natural and necessary result.

What would have been the character of that pure worship of Yahveh desiderated by the prophets? We are able to tell what it would not have been, rather than what it would. For on this subject we find much polemic against what was, but little explanation as to that which ought to be. Why this is so will shortly be apparent. Negatively, the worship of Yahveh must possess two chief characteristics, both of which were violated, the one occasionally, the other habitually, in the Israel of the eighth century. It must be rendered to Yahveh alone, and it must be performed without the help of material representations of deity. More briefly, it must be monolatrous and imageless.

The first requirement was no novelty. It was an obvious and necessary demand from the successors of Moses and Elijah. How far the worship of other gods was practised in the latter half of the eighth century is not wholly easy to ascertain. There is, however, a significant allusion in Amos to a form of Assyrian star-worship, which was being introduced into Palestine in the eighth century and became prevalent in the seventh. Hosea seems to imply that the Canaanite god Baal received separate adoration, and Isaiah, in two or three passages, refers with his peculiar irony to the service of foreign gods in Judah and Jerusalem.[1] As the prophets so habitually regard a material worship of Yahveh as equivalent to a breach of the law of monolatry, it often becomes difficult to determine to which kind of idolatry they are alluding.

As regards the second requirement, it was previously noticed that an imageless cultus of Yahveh is apparently presupposed in the two earlier Pentateuchal narratives, and the conjecture was hazarded that a silent antagonism to material representations of the national God may have begun in certain select circles between Elijah and Amos. But in the literature of the Old Testament a direct polemic against idols starts from the prophets of the eighth century, and more especially from Hosea In Amos there is only one sarcastic allusion to the bulls of Samaria.[2] But Hosea is never weary of denouncing the bull-images of Yahveh, and herein lies the most important, as it is undoubtedly the central, element of his teaching. Iden-

[1] Amos v. 26; Hosea ix. 10, xi. 2; Isaiah i. 29, ii. 18, 20(?), xvii. 10, xxx. 33.

[2] Amos viii. 14. This seems more probable than the view advocated by Robertson Smith, *Prophets of Israel*, p. 140. See Gunning, *Godspraken van Amos*, p. 179 (1885).

tifying this degraded worship of Yahveh with the Canaanite worship of Baal, he does not hesitate to call the idols of the national god Baalim, and the service thus rendered to Yahveh, Baal service.[1] This identification was the more intelligible because of the still prevalent usage of addressing Yahveh as Baal. If, in some passages, Hosea charges his contemporaries with the direct worship of other gods, including the actual Canaanite Baal, it is still significant that, whether he is referring to the debased service of Yahveh or to the worship of alien divinities, it is in either case the image-worship as such against which his chief indignation is directed.

It is useful to mark the stage of development at which Hosea has arrived in the purification of religious thought in this important matter. He plainly recognizes that an image is a mere combination of wood and gold, and therefore lifeless and undivine; but he does not definitely say either that the idol was an image of Yahveh, or that it is impious and idle to represent or symbolize Yahveh in material forms. Hence we may infer that, although it was originally Yahveh who was worshipped by the populace under the guise of a bull, the idol was widely confused or even identified with the God which it was fashioned to represent. Thus the true Yahveh was lost in the symbol: the bull became the god.[2] The prophet is consequently rather concerned to rebuke the worship of the idol as such, than to censure the prin-

[1] See, e.g., Cheyne on Hosea ii. 13 (E.V.).

[2] Cf. Exodus xxxii. 4, 8, in the story of the golden calf: "This is thy god, O Israel, which has brought thee up out of the land of Egypt."

ciple which led to the representation of a God like Yahveh in so coarse and puerile a form.

In reviewing the condition, and censuring the sins, of Judah, Isaiah does not make its idolatry, in either sense of the word, a principal count of his indictment. When he alludes to images, he does so sarcastically, and without that embittered wrath in which he censures the oppression of the poor. He couples the idols with divination and sorcery, and with the luxury which, in the early period of his ministry, after the prosperous reign of Uzziah, had become prevalent in Judah. "The land," he says, "has become full of idols; to the work of their hands men do homage, to that which their fingers have made."[1] The word he uses for "idols"—in most places, images of Yahveh are probably intended—is novel, and has a theological significance. It is a term apparently coined by himself; its meaning is literally "things of naught" or "nonentities." Its employment in one place to designate the deities of Egypt is clearly charged with a special intention.[2]

Upon the positive side, the prophets' conception of a pure worship of Yahveh was never elaborately defined. Such details lay outside their charge. It was their business to attack that mistaken and immoral importance assigned by their contemporaries to outward religion, and to demonstrate its worthlessness as a substitute for that moral service of God which is manifested in civic

---

[1] ii. 6—8.

[2] xix. 1. But in Siegfried and Stade's new dictionary, this etymology is rejected, and the word is derived from El (God), and not connected with 'Elil' (nothingness, Hosea xiii. 4; Zech. xi. 17).

rectitude and social well-doing. It must not be supposed that, in their polemic against sacrifices, the prophets start from the modern point of view that the slaughter of animals is an absurd and superstitious method of propitiating deity. To them, sacrifices were as much the ordinary expression of worship as church-going is with us. Nor did their hostility to sacrifices proceed from any objection to the high places or local sanctuaries, as contrasted with, or opposed to, the temple at Jerusalem. The law which made every sanctuary outside Jerusalem schismatic, was neither known nor written till the seventh century. It was the false importance assigned to sacrifices, and the false estimate attributed to their effect, which provoked the prophetic indignation. In this respect all the prophets are at one. Sacrifices, according to them, were never specifically enjoined by Yahveh as a portion of Israel's duty to its God. They were no equivalent for righteousness, just as no number of burnt-offerings could turn Yahveh from his purpose or atone for sin.

Never has the eternal antagonism of spirit to letter, substance to shadow, been more magnificently declared. Amos, the first of our four, is not the least emphatic. "I hate, I despise your feast-days, and I will smell no savour in your solemn assemblies. Though ye offer me burnt-offerings and meat-offerings, I will not accept them; neither will I regard the peace-offerings of your fat beasts. But let judgment run down like water, and righteousness as an ever-flowing stream. Did ye offer unto me sacrifices and offerings in the wilderness forty years, O house of Israel?"[1]

[1] Amos v. 21—25.

In Hosea we find the famous verse: "I delight in loving-kindness and not in sacrifice; and in the knowledge of God more than in burnt-offerings."[1]

More majestic still are the stately phrases of Isaiah: "Of what use is the multitude of your sacrifices to me? saith Yahveh; I am satiated with the burnt-offerings of rams, and the fat of fed beasts, and in the blood of bullocks and lambs and he-goats I have no pleasure. When ye come to see my face, who has required this at your hands—to trample my courts? Bring no more false offerings: a sweet smoke is an abomination to me; the new moon and the sabbath, the calling of a convocation . . . . I cannot bear wickedness together with a solemn assembly."[2]

Prayer itself is hateful from the lips of sinners: "Even if you make many prayers, I will not hear: your hands are full of blood. Wash you, make you clean, take away the evil of your works from before mine eyes; cease to do evil, learn to do well, seek out justice, righten the violent man, do justice to the orphan, plead for the widow."[3]

In the northern kingdom, at any rate, there was another reason of grave ethical import which compelled the prophets to take up an attitude of uncompromising hostility to the popular worship at the local sanctuaries.

---

[1] Hosea vi. 6.

[2] Prof. Cheyne's translation. I have borrowed from his translation in most of my quotations from Isaiah.

[3] Isaiah i. 11—17. "Righten the violent man" is doubtful. For an ingenious emendation, cf. Hoffmann, *Ueber einige phoenikische Inschriften*, p. 26, n. 2.

They were too frequently the scenes of debauchery and licentiousness; and among the rites there practised was often included the vile custom of sacred prostitution, borrowed from the worship of Astarte.

Upon some fundamental questions of religion and morality the teaching of the prophets was thus partly attained through a keen opposition to the actual moral and religious condition of the society around them. But the particular form in which their prophecies were generally cast—a prediction of the judgment and its results—was suggested to them by the outward history of the time, or, more accurately, by the conquests of Assyria. A corrupt society within, and the scourge of nations without, stimulated their utterance and determined its manner.

For that mighty Assyrian power, which in its career of victory was drawing nearer and nearer to Israel, shaped itself in the prophets' thought as Yahveh's chosen instrument wherewith to punish the sins of their own people and of the neighbouring political communities. It was a strange and novel explanation. For Assyria's triumphs, when they received a religious interpretation from the inhabitants of the conquered kingdoms, were commonly thought to imply either the anger of the gods of the vanquished states, or their inferiority to the gods of the Assyrians.

But Yahveh, from the days of Moses onwards, had been different from the gods of other lands, and the prophets, with their heightened ethical conception of deity and their intense belief in the moral future of Israel, interpreted the victorious advance of Assyria in a manner peculiar to themselves. Yahveh was just, Israel was sinful; but Yahveh's relationship to Israel was everlasting, and his object—the creation of a holy people to sanctify his name—unchanging and irresistible. But, as without the purifying fires of calamity a sin-polluted people could not become holy, the punishment of Israel assumed the form of a logical and ethical necessity, while the instrument of Yahveh's righteous wrath could be no other than the armies of Assyria. The temporary triumph of Assyria was the vindication of God's justice, the evidence of his will.

Postponing for the moment a closer examination into the prophetic conception of the judgment and its results upon Israel and the outer world, it is advisable to here consider what influence the ethical conception of Yahveh, and the inclusion of Assyria in the range of Yahveh's activity and control, exercised upon the monolatrous idea, which the prophets had received as an heritage of the past, and from which their own religious advance began. How far did the prophets of the eighth century transform monolatry into monotheism?

It may appear strange that my estimate of the entire prophetic teaching did not begin with this subject, instead of its being introduced, as it were, incidentally or by a side wind. But the truth is, that the prophetic advance beyond the monolatry of a previous age was only a silent consequence of fundamental axioms already arrived at. It was not from the side of Yahveh's power that the development began. When the national God of Israel, already numerically single, came to be regarded as equally unique in character and will, then his perfect justice and his indestructible purpose in regard to his chosen people, associated as they were with an admitted ascendancy over nature and over man, issued in the deduction, implied rather than stated, that Yahveh was the only true and living God in heaven and upon earth. In the eloquent words of Professor Kuenen, which I cannot forbear to quote, so admirably do they sum up the exact history of the Israelite monotheism, "When in the consciousness of the prophets, the central place was taken, not by the might, but by the holiness of Yahveh, the conception of God was carried up into another and a higher sphere. From that moment it ceased to be a question of 'more' or 'less' between Yahveh and the other gods, for he stood not only above them, but in very distinct opposition to them. If Yahveh, the Holy One, was God, if he was God *as* the Holy One, *then the others were not.* In a word, the belief that Yahveh was the only God sprang out of the ethical conception of his being. *Monotheism* was the gradual, not the sudden, result of this conception."[1]

Prof. Kuenen proceeds to state that monotheism in explicit terms was not taught till the last quarter of the seventh century in Deuteronomy and Jeremiah, but that implicitly it is to be found with unmistakable distinctness in the writings of our eighth-century prophets. This statement is quite borne out by the facts. The monotheism of our prophets shows itself in two directions, but in either rather by implication than by pronounced assertion. Direct references to other gods in Amos, Hosea, Isaiah and Micah, are exceedingly scanty. Count Baudissin has been able to collect very few of them in his exhaustive essay on the Old Testament views

[1] Kuenen, *Hibbert Lectures*, p. 119.

respecting the gods of paganism. The number is still further reduced if it be the case that several passages which he supposes to refer to foreign gods really refer to images of Yahveh. Only once, in the 19th chapter of Isaiah, is there a distinct allusion to foreign gods in their relation to their own lands, and not as imported objects of idol-worship in Israel. It is significant that Isaiah uses for the gods or idols of Egypt the same word which he had coined for the images of Yahveh that defiled the kingdom of Judah. In highly pictorial language he represents Yahveh as riding upon a swift cloud to Egypt, causing the not-gods of Egypt to shake before him, and the heart of the land to tremble. It is with no result that the people in their fear resort to the not-gods and to the sorcerers and the wizards.[1] Nothing is definitely said as to the unreality of the Egyptian gods, yet their association with the wizards and sorcerers in utter powerlessness to prevent the coming doom, seems sufficient evidence of the prophet's meaning. So, too, the uniqueness of Yahveh is strongly emphasized by sarcastic implication in the argument put into the Assyrian king's mouth to prove the ease with which he will add Judah to the number of his other conquests. "Is not Calno as Carchemish? or is not Hamath as Arpad? or is not Samaria as Damascus? As my hand has reached to these kingdoms, and their images exceeded those of Jerusalem — can I not as I have done to Samaria and her idols so do to Jerusalem and her images?"[2] The point

---

[1] xix. 1—3.

[2] Isaiah x. 9—11. For the slight emendation, cf. Giesebrecht, *Beiträge zur Jesaiakritik*, 1890, p. 72, n. 1.

of this sarcasm is clearly monotheistic. It is, however, noticeable that in his prophecies against Assyria, there is no allusion made to the Assyrian gods. They are simply ignored. Moreover, to Isaiah as well as to Hosea, the image and the god appear identified. As, then, the image was clearly considered lifeless, so we may presume were the deities they represented, or whose names they bore, considered lifeless too.

Another way by which the prophets were carried forward towards monotheism was the conception of the judgment. Both in its incidence and its results it became extended beyond Israel, and it gradually took the form of a universal transformation-scene. Of this enlargement the eighth-century prophets show only earlier phases, and their universalism is still occasional and tentative. For the inclusion of the nations in Yahveh's providence is only partly for their own benefit: it is mainly for Israel's advancement and for the divine glory. Yet in either case Yahveh assumes the solitary grandeur of universal rule.

We are thus by another route brought back again to the judgment, and may now briefly consider the manner of its onset, and the tenour of its effects upon Israel and the world.

For Israel (as I have already indicated) the judgment is partly punitive and partly educational. Yahveh punishes his people with an object beyond the direct satisfaction of outraged morality: he punishes to amend, he destroys to create anew. Thus it is that in the prophetical teaching there is always a combination, often very close, of two elements—the one denunciation, the other promise.[1]

[1] But cf. Giesebrecht, *Beiträge*, pp. 187—220.

Our four prophets do not precisely agree as to the details of the judgment process, or in their representation of its results. Nor are they always clear in their own language, or wholly consistent with themselves.

To Amos the judgment upon Israel involves exile in a foreign land: before or during this exile all the sinners of the people shall die by the sword. Whether captivity is to be the lot of Judah as well as of Israel, Amos does not say. It is clear that he contemplates the return of Israel from the captivity, though his attitude towards the separate northern kingdom is scarcely to be stated with any degree of certainty. In the renewed kingdom, or kingdoms, the old frontiers of David's monarchy will be restored. The Israelites will possess the remnant of Edom, and of all the nations which at any previous time had been conquered or controlled by Yahveh's people. There is no mention of any specially endowed or favoured king, and no hint of the knowledge of Yahveh extending beyond the borders of Israel's empire. The tokens of Yahveh's favour are the increased fertility of the land and the happy security of its inhabitants. How soon the renovated Israel shall return to its own land, and begin an uninterrupted era of outward and inward prosperity, is not stated or implied. But the judgment itself —nor was he mistaken—Amos evidently expects in the near future.[1]

Hosea, while also ignoring any claim of the heathen

---

[1] This paragraph assumes the authenticity of Amos ix. 11—15. But it must not be denied that weighty arguments can be brought to prove that they, or, at any rate, 11, 12, 13, are a later interpolation. Cf. Schwall, *Das Buch Ssefanjâ*, Z.A.W., 1890, p. 226.

world to the glories of the "Messianic" age, is a little more distinct and explicit upon the method of the judgment than his predecessor. An Ephraimite himself, he yet seems to regard the separate northern kingdom as apostate. As the cause of that apostasy was Yahveh's wrath, so destruction will be its sequel. The men of Israel will go into exile, but in exile they will turn to Yahveh, and Yahveh will gather them from the land of their captivity. Restored to their own homes, they will be united with the men of Judah—whose punishment, according to the prophet, is apparently not to extend to exile—under a common Davidic king.[1] The ideal monarchy of the future is painted in more peaceful and tender colours in Hosea than in Amos. What the interval will be between judgment and repentance, and between repentance and restoration, Hosea does not declare.

Isaiah's references to the judgment process and its effects are numerous and complicated. In considering them, one has to remember that his prophecies extended both to Israel and to Judah, and that in the middle of his ministry occurred the fall of Samaria and the exile of Israel's foremost citizens. Isaiah's earliest discourses are prior to the war of Pekah against Ahaz, and therefore before the vassalage of Judah to Assyria. Between this early period and the revolt of Hezekiah against Sennacherib, Isaiah frequently predicted the infliction of severe chastisement upon both Israel and Judah. Of the former state he speaks, as is natural, less frequently and more

[1] This view still seems to me to be the more probable, in spite of Oort's arguments in his essay on Hosea in *Theol. Tijd.*, 1890.

incidentally than of the latter; but it seems strange that in his prophecies after 722 he did not make more repeated use of, and allusion to, the fall of Samaria. The order and the date of Isaiah's prophecies are to a large extent still in dispute, and the subject has recently become more delicate and complicated because it has been shown, with tolerable certainty, that Isaiah must have been in the habit either of revising his utterances before they appeared in writing—and in this revision taking advantage of any intervening change of circumstance—or of re-issuing the written prophecies in a form accommodated to new events.[1] We know from one celebrated instance in the life of Jeremiah that the prophets, if occasion arose for re-publishing, or, as in Jeremiah's case, for rewriting their prophecies, saw no objection to modifying the pronouncements they had previously made.[2] Neither they nor their contemporaries appear to have thought that the guarantee of their inspiration consisted in an exact fulfilment of such of their statements as touched upon the issues of the future.

In his earlier period, Isaiah did not predict a sharper and more irrevocable catastrophe for Israel than for Judah. He did not contemplate the deportation of either kingdom from Canaan, or identify the chastened and purified remnant, in which he so ardently believed, with a band of exiles brought back from captivity. Assyria was to bring wide-spread desolation and ruin: in some

---

[1] See especially Giesebrecht, *Beiträge*, &c.; Cheyne, "Critical Analysis of the first Part of Isaiah," *Jewish Quarterly Review*, Vol. IV. p. 562, seq.

[2] Jer. xxxvi. 32.

of his prophecies before the invasion of Sennacherib, Isaiah apparently imagines an almost utter destruction of the kingdom; but the purified remainder, the tenth of the tenth, the new shoot from the stock of the felled tree, is always conceived as nearly, if not immediately, consequent upon the judgment process, the remnant left in the land after the withdrawal of the foe.[1] When the Assyrian invasion had actually begun, the emphasis of Isaiah's utterance was laid upon the coming deliverance. The nearer the judgment drew, the less was he inclined to insist upon its terrors. He was anxious to encourage as many as would to turn to Yahveh and be saved.[2] He predicted that the capital, Yahveh's dwelling-place, would be miraculously preserved, and the event justified his confidence.[3]

Amos had already spoken of Yahveh as roaring from Zion and uttering his voice from Jerusalem. Isaiah, himself a citizen of the capital, shared the growing pride of its inhabitants in their metropolis, the dwelling-place of Yahveh. For Yahveh's earthly seat, which had been formerly diffused over Palestine and manifested at every local sanctuary, was now confined to Jerusalem. In some respects this was, as we shall subsequently see, a perilous change, for it interfered with the wider conception of Yahveh as God of heaven and earth, and, still more, as God unlimited in space. Yahveh's residence

[1] Isaiah vi. 11—13, vii. 21, iv. 4.
[2] Cf. the more hopeful tone in xxix. xxx. xxxi.
[3] It is pleasant that Kuenen, as against Stade, has energetically maintained the authenticity of Isaiah xxxvii. 22—32. *Onderzoek*, 2nd ed., Vol. I. p. 417.

at Jerusalem, contrasted with his omnipresence in the world, typifies the painful dilemma in which post-exilic Judaism was involved between Yahveh as the God of the Jews, and Yahveh as the One and Only God of all races and lands. But in Isaiah's age these difficulties were still distant, and for the immediate present the exceptional importance assigned to Jerusalem was beneficial, conducing as it did to the great religious reform of the succeeding century.

Meanwhile, from the Jerusalem thus divinely delivered from imminent desolation, the new salvation of Judah was to proceed. Sinners, indeed, would be destroyed: but the negligent and indifferent would return to their God, while the poor and needy would rejoice in Yahveh, their saviour alike from native oppressor and foreign foe.[1]

In a few of his prophecies, Isaiah associated the good time of prosperity and righteousness, which was in store for Judah after its purgation by Assyria, with a scion of the Davidic house, who should inaugurate a new and golden era.[2] The eleventh chapter of the present book, of which the date is still disputed, and the authenticity not above suspicion, contains the fullest picture of this ideal king. It is, however, clear that Isaiah can have attached no such importance to this conception as it subsequently acquired in both Jewish and Christian theology; for he not infrequently depicts the happy future after deliverance from Assyria without any allusion to the ideal king. Some scholars hold that the two or three passages in which he predicts the individual

---

[1] Isaiah xxviii. 19—24.
[2] vii. 14(?), ix. 6, 7, xi. 1.

Messiah, all belong to the early period before the accession of Hezekiah.

The Messiah's relation to the reigning house is not exactly defined. His birth is announced in the ninth chapter—" For a child is born to us, a son is given unto us, and the government resteth upon his back, and his name is called, Wondrous Counsellor, Divine Hero, Everlasting Father, Prince of Peace." It is not certain when Isaiah anticipated that this child would be born, but an identification with Hezekiah is decidedly erroneous. The prophet probably imagined that his advent would not be long delayed; he may even have supposed that he was already living at the time when the prophecy was uttered. However this may be, he did not regard him as the deliverer from the Assyrian foe, but rather as the ideal monarch in whom the subsequent glories of the new era should culminate and centre. Yet the "Messiah," as such, adds scarcely anything to the prophetic ideal of the regenerate Israel. It makes little difference whether there is to be one kingly judge who "with righteousness shall judge the helpless and arbitrate with equity for the humble in the land," or whether, as in other places, the faithful counsellors and rulers are spoken of in the plural number. The essence of the ideal—an earthly polity based upon justice and loving-kindness, humility, righteousness and peace—remains in either case the same.[1]

Neither in its operation nor in its issue was the judgment, as we have already learnt, to be limited to Israel. For to the minds of the prophets, Yahveh, without

[1] Cf. Cheyne, *Origin of the Psalter*, p. 340.

renouncing or forfeiting his peculiar position as God of Israel, exercised control over other nations, and shaped their destinies according to his will. Not only were the heathen gods becoming lifeless and unreal, but all necessity for them was fast disappearing. Yahveh had usurped their province; he had driven them out of the field.

That Assyria was conceived as a tool in Yahveh's hand necessarily implied that the range of Yahveh's influence was not limited to Israel. In Amos and Isaiah, this implication assumes a more general aspect. Amos connects the coming judgment upon Israel with a contemporaneous judgment upon six neighbouring nations. Of these six, five are to be punished for wrongs done to Israel, but one, the kingdom of Moab, because of a cruel indignity inflicted upon the dead body of the ruler of Edom.[1]

Isaiah also addressed prophecies against neighbouring nations and predicted their castigation by Assyria. But though Assyria is the instrument, the moving power is Yahveh. "Who hath devised this against Tyre, the giver of crowns, whose merchants were princes?" And the answer is: "Yahveh of Hosts hath devised it."[2] Elsewhere Isaiah denounces Assyria for not recognizing its function as the instrument of Yahveh's wrath, and for seeking to overstep, in the insolence of success, the limits which had been assigned to its chastisements. "Woe to Asshur, the rod of mine anger, in whose hand as a staff is mine indignation."[3] Not, as he thinks, through the strength of his hand and by his own wisdom have his triumphs been achieved, but through the pur-

[1] Amos i. 3—ii. 3.   [2] xxiii. 8, 9.   [3] x. 5—15.

pose of Yahveh. And therefore when the work of Assyria is concluded, and judgment upon Zion and Judah meted out, Yahveh will hold visitation on the arrogance of his tool. "No longer shall the axe vaunt itself against him who heweth with it, or the saw bray against him who moveth it to and fro."

The judgment of the nations is thus only partially brought about by their own wrong-doing, and even when that is the cause, the people which is to suffer is not necessarily conscious of its supposed sin. Assyria is to be punished because it was blind to its position as the rod of Yahveh's anger, and had exceeded the limits of its commission. But Assyria was clearly innocent of any knowledge whether of its office or its delinquency. Moreover, the national basis of the prophetic teaching constantly makes itself felt. However disguised or explained, Yahveh's partiality towards Israel is still perceptible. In other words, the prophets cannot wholly overcome the so-called "particularism" inherent in the popular faith, which was the starting-point of their own. Five of the six nations whom Amos threatens with divine punishment had incurred Yahveh's wrath for the sake of Israel, while Isaiah's denunciations of Assyria are mainly due to the cruel injuries which it had inflicted upon Yahveh's people.[1]

In the main, then, the universalist effect of the nascent monotheism of our four prophets showed itself

[1] Possibly there must be included as a subsidiary cause the common prophetic conception of Yahveh's antagonism to everything proud and haughty in humanity—a conception which may be compared with the Greek ideas of the Godhead's envy.

by an extension of the area of the judgment beyond the limits of Israel. But at least one of them seems to have advanced a further stage in universalism, and allowed to the two typical and leading nations of his time a full share in the blessings of the golden age.

It is true that here also we tread upon debated ground. But thus much seems clear: in the eighth century Yahveh, to a few chosen minds, without losing his specific personality and his peculiar name as God of Israel, begins not only, for his own glory, to assert his sovereignty over other nations, but to take a qualified interest in them for their own sakes. Amos ascribes the migrations of other peoples besides Israel to the world-wide rule of Yahveh, and protesting against Israel's reliance upon the favouritism of its God, he even asks, though we must not press his words too far, "Are ye not as the children of the Ethiopians unto me, O children of Israel?" But it is only in Isaiah and Micah that we can find a few passages which allude to the religion of Yahveh, with its attendant blessings, as spreading, or to be spread, beyond the pale of Israel, and the authenticity of these passages is unfortunately by no means above suspicion.

The growth of the universalist conception is a puzzling problem and difficult to trace. The initial step would seem to have been a desire that other nations should recognize the power and divinity of Yahveh, and the unreality of their own gods. At first this recognition is conceived merely as an outward fact, and not as an inward blessing; its aim is the increase of Yahveh's reputation and Israel's, not yet the diffusion of truth or the spiritual welfare of humanity. An example of the idea in this stage of its development is Isaiah's prophecy concerning the Ethiopians. After the judgment upon Assyria has been accomplished, they are to "bring a present to Yahveh of Hosts to the place of his name, even unto Zion."[1] It is also noteworthy that this tribute to Yahveh's sovereignty, though scarcely equivalent to a religious conversion, is not wrung from the Ethiopians by calamity: it is, on the contrary, a willing gift of gratitude for deliverance from Assyria.

Complete universalism is only then attained when the nations are conceived as converted to Israel's God for their own benefit and edification. The interval from the former stages to this further and fuller conception seems also, at least once, to have been traversed by Isaiah. At the close of his long ministry he appears to have framed the idea of a true knowledge of Yahveh and his religion diffused permanently among Israel's two great enemies of the near and of the distant past, Assyria and Egypt. I do not venture to adduce here the celebrated fragment, found both in Isaiah and Micah, of the nations journeying to Jerusalem, to learn Yahveh's ways and to walk in his paths.[2] Its pre-exilic origin is, perhaps, not sufficiently assured. But we are still entitled to assign the noble end of the nineteenth chapter to Isaiah himself; and if the two greatest nations within his geographical horizon are there pictured as glad converts to Yahveh, it would surely seem as if the idea of an ultimate abolition of all idolatry, and of the establishment of the world-wide empire of Yahveh, had shed at least a passing glory upon his visions of the coming age. If this be so,

[1] xviii. 7.   [2] Isaiah ii. 2—4; Micah iv. 1—4.

it is very striking that even after the deliverance from Assyria, when the Messianic age still delayed to dawn upon an unrepentant and unbelieving world, Isaiah did not lose his hope in a great spiritual future, and that he took leave of the world in a splendid prophecy of universalism, in which the two typical enemies of Israel are to be united with him in common service of a common God, and recognized by that God as his worshippers and children.

"In that day there shall be an altar to Yahveh in the midst of the land of Egypt, and a pillar by its border to Yahveh, and it shall be for a sign and a witness to Yahveh of Hosts in the land of Egypt: when they shall cry unto Yahveh because of oppressors, he shall send them a deliverer and an advocate, and shall rescue them. And Yahveh shall make himself known to Egypt, and the Egyptians shall know Yahveh in that day, and shall serve with sacrifice and offering, and shall vow a vow unto Yahveh, and shall perform it. And Yahveh shall smite Egypt, smiting and healing; and when they return unto Yahveh, he shall receive their supplications, and shall heal them. In that day there shall be a highway from Egypt to Assyria; Assyria shall come into Egypt, and Egypt into Assyria, and the Egyptians shall serve with the Assyrians. In that day shall Israel be a third to Egypt and to Assyria, even a blessing within the earth, for as much as Yahveh of Hosts hath blessed him, saying, Blessed is my people Egypt, and the work of my hands Assyria, and mine inheritance Israel."[1]

If this passage be really authentic, as there still seems

[1] xix. 19—25. Prof. Cheyne's translation.

good reason to believe, it represents the high-water mark of eighth-century prophecy.¹ What a contrast to the thought that expulsion from Palestine involved the enforced worship of other gods, or that Israel and Ammon should each be content with the territories which their respective deities had given them! Truly the Bible is a strange book, with strange diversity of voices, and it is stranger still that for so many ages this diversity was neglected or unfelt.

Such are the main teachings of the four great prophets of the eighth century, teachings which, in the main, were common to them all, and which were possibly set forth also by other prophets now unknown. Indeed, the Old Testament itself probably contains citations from one or more of them. Isaiah certainly quotes an earlier prophet's utterance against Moab; and many authorities, including Kuenen, think that both he and Micah were indebted to a great contemporary or predecessor for that magnificent portraiture of the Messianic age and of the conversion of the nations which is now incorporated in their own prophecies. It is even by no means impossible that a part of Zechariah ix.—xii. is also the work of a prophet of the eighth century. But, for our present purpose, it is unnecessary to enter into this debated question. For our picture of the prophetic teaching would scarcely gain through its inclusion a single additional trait.

¹ Kuenen and Stade both accept it as Isaiah's. Kuenen also maintains the pre-exilic origin of Isaiah ii. 2—4, assigning it to an older contemporary of Isaiah. Cheyne, however, denies the authenticity of xix. 18—25 (*Origin and Religious Contents of the Psalter*, p. 170), and refers it to the time of Ptolemy Lagi. Cf. also *Expositor*, March. 1892, p. 212.

Let us now try to estimate more generally the place of the prophets in the history of Israel and in the development of its religion. So unique a phenomenon as Israelite prophecy has not unnaturally been interpreted and illustrated in many different ways. We have advanced beyond the antiquated view which, neglecting the human elements in prophecy almost entirely, regarded the prophets as mere foretellers of the future, entrusted with a fixed, precise and pre-arranged message from God, and repeating without change or flaw a lesson which had been verbally dictated to them by an automatic inspiration. But even though this view has been abandoned, yet, when the stress is laid upon any one particular side of the prophetical work, different interpretations of it as a whole are the result.

The prophets, for example, have sometimes been described as practical statesmen. But, in truth, their work as politicians was only an incident in their religious teaching. Of the four prophets with whom we are still immediately concerned, only Isaiah was consulted by the king and took a prominent part in affairs of state. And, though the genius of the prophets enabled them to cast a piercing glance into political affairs, and to show greater perspicacity than the mass of their contemporaries in interpreting the movements of Assyria and in recognizing the weakness of the neighbouring states, the political advice which they gave was suggested and controlled by their fundamental religious convictions. Professor Robertson Smith has clearly pointed out a marked difference between the older prophecy in which Elisha, during the period of the Syrian wars, " was the very soul of the struggle for independence," and the doctrine of Amos and Hosea, who "broke through the ancient faith in the unity of Jehovah's will with the immediate political interests of the nation," and taught that, "as the God of righteousness, Jehovah had nothing but chastisement to offer to an unrighteous nation." But when Isaiah bids Ahaz show no fear at the invasion of Resin of Damascus and Pekah of Israel, and make no alliance with Assyria, Prof. R. Smith regards "the delivery of this divine message" as an epoch in the work of Isaiah and in the history of Old Testament prophecy, because in it Isaiah, "no longer speaking of sin, judgment and deliverance in broad, general terms," appears "as a practical statesman, approaching the rulers of the state with a precise direction as to the course they should hold in a particular political juncture."[1] Yet when we reflect upon the character of this direction, and how entirely, although justified by the event, it corresponded with the general prophetical point of view in matters political, it would appear as if the term "practical statesman" were an appellation to which even Isaiah himself, the most political of the prophets, could lay no claim.

While Ephraim and Judah were yet free from entanglement in the meshes of the Assyrian net, the burden of the prophetical teaching in the domain of statescraft was, "Trust in Yahveh only; enter into no alliance with foreign powers." Israel, to the prophets, should be "the people which dwells alone, and is not reckoned among the nations."[2] Thus Isaiah was against any Assyrian, as he was against any Egyptian, alliance. When,

[1] *Prophets of Israel*, p. 254. [2] Numbers xxiii. 9.

however, the false step had once been taken, and Judah had become the vassal of Assyria, Isaiah, who recognized in Assyria the rod of Yahveh's wrath, acquiesced in the *fait accompli*, and protested against the hopelessness of rebellion. Lastly, when the revolt had been effected without his cognizance, Isaiah could but menace the infatuated rulers with divine punishment; but clinging, as he did, to the belief that when the night is darkest the dawn is nearest, he counselled resistance at the point when submission was apparently to signify the ruin of the national life. Again he was justified by the event, but the justification must be regarded either as purely accidental or as divinely controlled; it was certainly not an example of political prescience, for the chance that Judah would escape the forces of Sennacherib was infinitesimally small.[1]

By others, again, the prophets have sometimes been classified among social reformers. Their intense sympathy with the wrongs of the poorer classes has suggested the appellation "tribunes of the people," or "publicistes radicaux et journalistes intransigeants," as M. Renan calls them.[2] But it is scarcely advisable to apply such epithets to the prophets of the eighth or seventh century, even though the application be guarded by careful contrast between the prophetical oratory and that of the popular demagogue. For the prophets were in no sense popular leaders. In their frequent opposition to the patriotism of the day and to the favourite cult, they

---

[1] Cf. Driver's *Isaiah*, 1888, chapters vi. and vii., for the prophet's attitude during the rebellion and the invasion of Sennacherib.

[2] Renan, *Histoire du peuple d'Israel*, Vol. II. p. 425, and elsewhere.

provoked rather anger than sympathy. Their religious eagerness for social morality led them to denounce the oppression of the poor, because it was the most flagrant public iniquity of the age. Their invectives against luxury and debauchery were due to the fact that these were often co-ordinated with cruelty and vice, or seemed the consequence of that cold indifference to spiritual and divine agencies, or of that reckless and material temperament, which to Isaiah, and the prophets generally, was the completest type of enmity to Yahveh and his religion. It is for this reason that the judgment must fall with especial vehemence upon the class of rich oppressors and boastful scoffers, so that the day might dawn, "when the humble shall obtain fresh joy in Yahveh, and the poor among men shall exult in the Holy One of Israel."[1]

We are thus driven back, more and more exclusively, upon a purely religious interpretation of the prophetical work. We must regard the prophets as they regarded themselves—as religious teachers, as messengers of Yahveh, commissioned to explain to their people the immediate purposes and mandates of their God. In the discharge of this, their embassy, they now warned, now threatened, and now comforted. They read the gradual fulfilment of Yahveh's will in the events of their age, set forth the history and interpreted the lesson. But the less they were prophets by habit and by profession, the more were their utterances stimulated by special crises. They prophesied because, and when, they had a definite message to deliver. Yet it may well be surmised that

[1] Isaiah xxix. 19; cf. Robertson Smith, *Old Testament in the Jewish Church*, 2nd ed., 1892, p. 348.

in the intervals between these higher moments, their lives were devoted as religious teachers, in a modern sense of the word, to the more constant and normal duty of a gradual religious enlightenment. Isaiah gathered round him disciples,[1] and the very fact that the prophets of the eighth century began to publish and circulate their utterances, shows that they no longer confined themselves to the exigencies of the moment, but attempted a more continuous method of teaching, and a steadier and less fitful influence. Prof. Wellhausen, indeed, has taken a more restricted view of the prophetical office, and his words, short and incisive as usual, are capable, as they are deserving, of literal citation. "The newer prophets," he says, of whom Amos was the first, "resemble the former ones, not merely in the general form of their appearance and in the style of their speech, but also in that, like their predecessors, they are not preachers, but seers. It is not the sins of their people which cause them to speak, but the circumstance that Yahveh is about to do something, that great events are imminent. In quiet times, be they never so sinful, the prophets are silent— as, for example, in the long reign of king Manasseh—but immediately raise their voices when a fresh movement begins. They appear as storm messengers when an historic tempest is at hand; they are called watchers, because from their high roof they look forth and tell when anything suspicious shows itself upon the horizon."[2] Much of truth as this estimate by the great historian and critic contains, it is scarcely the whole truth nor is it devoid of exaggeration. Wellhausen himself ascribes

[1] viii. 16.   [2] *Abriss*, p. 50.

the last two chapters of Micah (with the exception of
the exilic verses at the close) to a writer of Manasseh's
age. Restraint and persecution may have forced the
prophets of that time into comparative silence. But
though their public work may have been interrupted, their
more private work in the construction of a *corps d'élite*,
a chosen few from out of the corrupt many, by means of
patient and continuous teaching, must have been carried
on notwithstanding. A considerable measure of activity
must be assumed in order to account at once for Manasseh's persecution and for Josiah's reform. The definition
of the prophets as religious teachers, whose highest and
most impressive work was reserved for special needs and
particular occasions, remains unaffected.

Though the previous history of Israel had prepared
the way, the appearance of the prophets is none the less
a striking and mysterious phenomenon. Its suddenness
is so extraordinary. Amos, the first example of the new
order in prophecy, was, in many respects, as Wellhausen
has observed, its purest exponent. Within thirty years
he was followed by Hosea, Isaiah and Micah, whose
united contributions to the store of prophetic teaching
left in some fundamental points little for the next century to supplement or improve. We are reminded of
the sudden rise of tragedy in Athens. Æschylus had his
predecessors, but they were of a totally different stamp,
and Sophocles, his younger contemporary, was the greatest
of the tragedians. In loftiness of style and perhaps in
fulness of inspiration, Jeremiah already represents a
prophetic decline, and in this respect, as in others, there
is a parallel between him, as compared with Isaiah, and

Euripides, the human, as compared with the author of the Œdipus.

It was the prophets, men few in number, but great in power, who gave to the religion of Israel its specific character and direction. The seed was sown by Moses, the Founder; the ground was watered by Samuel, by Nathan and Gad, by Elijah and Micaiah; but the harvest was gathered, or rather it was ripened, by the prophets of the eighth century. It was they who definitely connected the worship of Yahveh with the practice of morality, and conceived the idea of a holy nation, divinely chosen and divinely trained. They were the first to show how the triumph of a nation's God—his veritable "day" of glory—might be signalized by his people's punishment and defeat. It was the prophets who purified the conception of Yahveh as a God of righteousness and naught besides, and who began the transformation of the only God of a single nation into the only God of the entire world. And, lastly, it was the prophets of the eighth century who began to teach the doctrine—so strange to antiquity—that a single God of one people might become the One God of all. Thus the prophets point forward on the one hand to the Law, which sought by definite enactment and discipline to help on the schooling of the holy nation, living apart and consecrate to God, and on the other hand to the Apostle of Tarsus, who carried the universalist idea so nearly to its final and practical conclusion.

It was inevitable that the prophets should leave some room for future development. Their teaching contained the seeds of many subsequent antinomies. Their attitude towards the outward embodiment of religion was left vague and undefined. They had attacked the cultus, but they had suggested nothing in its place; they had inveighed against forms, but they had not given the people any vehicle of ceremonial expression for religious life: they had only said, "Seek God, seek goodness," counsels too elevated or too abstract for their generation to apply. Moreover, in spite of their denunciation of present abuses, they had been all too optimistic as to the not distant future. They had threatened a sinful society with summary punishment; but anticipating a speedy recovery from disaster, they had predicted a renovated community, chastened by suffering and purged of guilt. They contracted the progressive drama of history into a single scene.

All kinds of puzzling problems arose out of their teaching. The punishment and the deliverance came, but the Messianic age did not follow. Was sin still uneradicated, or were the children suffering for the iniquities of their fathers? Again, the prophetical unit was the nation and not the individual, and national wellbeing was characterized in outward and material terms. Sin brought adversity, but reform and penitence would bring welfare and content. Prosperity was the test of goodness and its reward. Even for nations this doctrine has its dangers; apply it, as later teachers did, to the individual, and you find yourself hopelessly at variance with fact. And lastly, although the prophets began to emancipate the religion of Israel from its tribalism—to turn Yahveh into God—they helped at the same time to produce a particularism narrower and more fatal than that which they had destroyed. For Yahveh, though the Only God, remained the God of Israel, and the nations were not solely regarded as independent creations of the One Creator—ends in themselves, as we should now say—but also, and sometimes mainly, as instruments to promote God's purposes in the training of his chosen people. For, as Wellhausen has finely said, " the present which was passing before the prophets became to them, as it were, the plot of a divine drama which they watched with an intelligence that anticipated the *dénouement*. Everywhere the same goal of the development, everywhere the same laws. The nations are the *dramatis personæ*, Israel the hero, Yahveh the author of the tragedy."[1] But in this tragedy, of which Israel is the hero, the nations only too readily assumed the villain's part. The eighth-century prophets did not yet so characterize the players, and the universalism of Isaiah enabled him to change Assyria, the rod of Yahveh's anger, into Assyria, the work of Yahveh's hands. But already in Ezekiel the nations are naturally and essentially the wicked enemies of Israel and of God, and the same identification was repeated again and again, though not without excuse, by subsequent writers after the captivity in Babylon. This, as we shall see, was the problem which the Judaism of Ezra and his successors, in spite of a never-forgotten and never-renounced idea of universalism, failed to solve. Only modern Judaism, upon the moral side at least, has effected a solution.

But these blemishes and imperfections of their teaching were as nothing to the greatness of the work which was

[1] *Abriss*, p. 49.

accomplished by the prophets for their own age and for posterity. Parallels to many of their noblest sayings can pretty easily be collected from other religious literatures both of the East and of the West. Deeper appreciation and fuller discussion of the dark problems of human destiny are to be found among the thinkers of India, and, here and there, among the thinkers of Greece. Ignorant as the prophets were of any bodily resurrection upon earth, still more of any spiritual life beyond the grave, a whole province of religious aspiration was cut off from them; and with that loss, the light which such beliefs alone can shed upon many important questions, such as sin and retribution, the transfiguration which they alone can effect upon the conception of earthly joys and earthly sorrows, could not be seen or anticipated. The very manner and occasion of their utterance are partly cause and partly result of the complete lack in all the prophetic writings of that mystic element in religion which hovers between the highest truth and the wildest vagary.

But no other teaching of the ancient world can show a similar grasp upon the essentials of true religion, with a like absence of refuse and of dross. Doubtless, this peculiar excellence was partly due to the comparatively severe and simple monolatry upon which the prophetic religion was based. While the God of the prophets possessed adequate personality, so as to enable their teaching to be generally understood, he was not disfigured by mythological taint. Separate and distinguished from the forces of nature, Yahveh, by the word of his chosen messengers, could denounce any intrusion of sexual impurity or symbolism into religious ceremonial. Chastity was no less specific a mark of the prophetic religion than its direct and close alliance with social morality.

To free the conception of God from the errors which still clung to the popular idea of him, it was not necessary to abandon Yahveh, but only to purify his attributes and to moralize his relation to Israel. Monolatry could be changed into monotheism; there was no need of the smallest pantheistic admixture. The prophetic teaching could thus maintain a close connection with its popular basis; it could become the religion of the many, and not a theology for the few. And here we can readily perceive one of its most characteristic and important features. There was nothing esoteric about it, no inner mystery which only the initiated might learn. If the doctrine, "Seek Yahveh, seek goodness," is elevated, it is also direct: it may be general, but all can understand it. Hence it is to the religion of these men, free at once from superstition on the one hand, and from mystery on the other, that the monotheism of the modern world owes its origin and its form. It is on this ground that the prophets can justly be regarded as the true founders of that phase of Theism which teaches a God who, while infinite, is yet self-conscious, who is both the Ruler of humanity and the Object of its prayer. Their business, as we have learnt, was with the nation and not with the individual. But it was their doctrine which supplied the indispensable basis of that Theism which discerns the purest efflorescence of religion in the relation and communion of the individual soul with the divine "Lover of souls," the Father who is in heaven.

LECTURE IV.

THE SEVENTH CENTURY: DEUTERONOMY AND JEREMIAH (700—586 B.C.)

In the present Lecture we have to deal with the history and development of the religion of Israel from the close of the eighth century to the fall of Jerusalem. Between the retreat of Sennacherib's army and the capture of the capital by Nebuchadrezzar there was an interval of little more than a century, yet meanwhile, upon the basis of the prophetical teaching, the foundations of Judaism were laid. Inveighing against the sins of the people and predicting their punishment, the prophets had elevated the conception of Yahveh, and changed monolatry into monotheism. While they bewailed the national deflection from an acknowledged standard of righteousness, they were half-unconsciously creating a new ideal of their people's function and destiny among the other peoples of the world. But in attempting to interpret the concrete incidents of their age by the light of abstract theories, they laid themselves open to discredit if their anticipations of the future were not fulfilled. One and all, as we have seen, foretold a judgment, and one and all believed that the effects of that judgment would be adequate and lasting. The Assyrian wars, or the captivity consequent upon them, would be the sure forerunners of the "Messianic" age. The crisis of their own country was conceived to be the crisis of the world, and the broad expanse of human history contracted into the narrow span of a few generations.

Amos and Hosea, who were mainly concerned with the kingdom of Samaria, had foretold Israel's exile as the condition precedent of future glory. Although they assigned no definite limit to the period of exile, their language indicates no clear anticipation that it would be more than sufficient for the extirpation of hardened sinners and for the growth of a real repentance. But the prophets of the north were unable to arrest the corruption of Samarian and Israelite society; and the hopes which they held out of pardon and return did not prevent the absorption of the exiles among the native population of Assyria, or effect any immediate religious improvement among those who were suffered to remain upon ancestral soil. In the south, Isaiah with emphasis and precision had proclaimed the inviolability of Jerusalem, and connected the advent of an ideal age with the end of the judgment process and with deliverance from the Assyrian foe.

The first part of Isaiah's prediction was literally fulfilled. Judah was delivered from the Assyrian army: the dawn of the ideal age was presumably at hand. Yet the actual result was only the first of a long series of experiences in which prophetical expectations were falsified by events.

The new era was to have included political independence as well as moral regeneration. But though Sennacherib had retreated from Palestine, Judah still remained the vassal of Assyria. The empire of Assyria was scarcely affected by the event which was to change the face of the world, and for more than half-a-century its power was undiminished and supreme. Yet, as regards the internal condition of Judah, the great deliverance was the occasion of a reform which at first may well have made Isaiah's heart beat high. It is clear that the prophet did not suppose that religious and moral regeneration would be brought about by purely supernatural means. By his own continuous teaching he had himself attempted to transform society, and we may also surmise that he gathered round him an inner circle of special and devoted disciples, who might be expected to become a leaven of purity, and to disseminate that teaching throughout the land.[1] Influential as he was at the court and with the king, and with reputation enormously enhanced by the fulfilment of his promise of deliverance, he probably urged and prompted Hezekiah to the execution of a religious reform.

The meagre verse in the Book of Kings which describes this reform is both inaccurate and misplaced.[2] There is no hint in the authentic writings of Isaiah or Micah that any religious innovations had been attempted before the Assyrian war.[3] It was the startling issue of Sennacherib's invasion which afforded the opportunity and suggested the idea. Moreover, wider changes are attributed to

[1] This is inferred from Isaiah viii. 16.

[2] 2 Kings xviii. 4; see Stade, *Geschichte*, Vol. I. p. 607 ff; *Z. A. W.*, 1886, pp. 172—182.

[3] Isaiah xxxvi. 7 (2 Kings xviii. 22) is not by Isaiah; cf. Kuenen, *Onderzoek*, 2nd ed., Vol. I. p. 414, seq.; Cornill, *Einleitung*, p. 145.

Hezekiah than he can actually have effected. He is reported to have "removed the high places and broken the pillars, and cut down the Asherah (or sacred pole), and broken in pieces the brazen serpent which Moses had made, and to which the people still burnt incense, calling it Nehushtan." There is, however, no clear indication that Hezekiah's reform corresponded so closely with the subsequent reform of Josiah; Isaiah and Micah do not appear to have impugned the sacred poles and pillars, or the legality of the high places; they confined themselves to an attack upon the worship of other gods, and more especially to a polemic against images. But so sweeping a reform can hardly be credited upon such slender authority, unless it were the natural result of prophetic teaching. Thus the residuum of fact contained in the 18th chapter of the Second Book of Kings must be probably limited to the destruction of the Nehushtan, or brazen serpent, that mysterious image in which the contemporaries of Hezekiah, whatever may have been its original signification, doubtless recognized a symbol of Yahveh. Yet indirect evidence would incline us to believe that Hezekiah's reform involved more than the annihilation of a single idol; it is more probably to be regarded as an attempt at a general abolition of images, as well as a suppression of the new Assyrian star-worship and of the "Moloch" sacrifices which had been introduced into Judah in the reign of Ahaz.

Whether this material iconoclasm betokened or generated any wide moral reformation is more than doubtful. It is unfortunate that we possess no certainly authentic prophecies of Isaiah bearing upon the condition of Judah after the year of deliverance. Some scholars, indeed, hold that the 22nd chapter was written after the retreat of Sennacherib.[1] In that case, the effect of Hezekiah's reforms must have disappointed Isaiah as cruelly as the effect of Josiah's disappointed Jeremiah. The date and meaning of this chapter are, however, not sufficiently clear to enable us to make with confidence so important a deduction. Yet if the 19th chapter be all Isaiah's, it must have been written down at a considerable interval after Sennacherib's departure from Palestine, and in it we see that Isaiah's expectations of an ultimate ideal future were not less sanguine than in the old days of the struggle with Assyria, while they were also wider in their scope.

But the prophecies of Isaiah had further influences, different from anything he could have foreseen or even desired. His predictions impressed the popular mind, and paved the way for serious issues. The reign of Manasseh, Hezekiah's son and successor, will show us some of these results; the reign of Josiah will show us others. Under particular circumstances and for a particular purpose, Isaiah had laid stress upon the indestructibility of Jerusalem, the mother-city of Judah, the dwelling-place of Yahveh.[2] This special prediction relating to a special occasion was much to the popular mind, and when the prediction had been fulfilled, was soon magnified into a permanent religious dogma. In natural consequence, the temple of Jerusalem grew

[1] So Kuenen, *Onderzoek*, 2nd ed., Vol. II. p. 63. But see Dillmann for objections to this view.

[2] Isaiah xxxvii. 22—32, xxx. 19, xxxi. 4—9.

rapidly in dignity and importance. Again, Isaiah had regarded the Assyrian invasion as the divine judgment which was to herald the Messianic age, and a certain measure of reform had followed hard upon deliverance. What more likely than that many honest, if narrow-minded, worshippers of Yahveh, who confounded external reform with spiritual regeneration, should be bitterly disappointed when the promised independence and glory were indefinitely postponed ? If they still believed in Yahveh's omnipotence and fidelity, they would suppose that the predicted golden age was only delayed for a time, not that any fresh judgment was necessary over and above the trial which they had only recently passed through; if, on the contrary, they were inclined to ascribe the non-fulfilment of Isaiah's prophecy to the insufficiency of Yahveh's power, they would be tempted to have recourse once more to Assyrian idolatries, seeing that the Assyrian gods were still supreme throughout the western Asiatic world. Or, perhaps, still believing in Yahveh's ability to exalt Israel above Assyria, some may have imagined that the sins of the past were not yet wholly atoned; grievously misunderstanding the teaching of the prophets, they may have thought that larger, more potent sacrifices were required before the wrath of God could be finally appeased.

Hezekiah's reign extended for about fourteen years after the deliverance of Jerusalem in 701. To the early part of this, its second division, the religious reformation must be assigned. A successful campaign against the Philistines, alluded to in the Book of Kings, probably fell within the same period. Beyond this, we know nothing, though we would gladly know much, of these fourteen concluding years of an eventful reign. In 686 Hezekiah died, and was succeeded by his son Manasseh, who occupied the throne for forty-five years (686—641).[1] The Book of Kings does not record a single external incident throughout his long reign. It must have been a time of profound peace and of comparative prosperity. Manasseh remained the vassal of Assyria, and the Assyrian inscriptions speak of him as paying tribute to the two kings, Esarhaddon (681— 669), Sennacherib's successor, and Asurbanipal (669— 626), till whose death the supremacy of Assyria in Palestine was wholly undisputed. Uneventful as Manasseh's reign was in foreign politics, it was all the more important in its internal and religious history. In it, and in the short reign of Amon, who maintained the policy of his father, there set in a period of strong religious reaction, extending over nearly half-a-century (686—638). Manasseh is singled out by the historian for special and repeated reprobation. In the eyes of the exilic redactor, his iniquities were the immediate cause of the destruction of the national life. Not even Josiah's reformation could turn Yahveh "from the fierceness of his great wrath, wherewith his anger was kindled against Judah, because of all the provocations that Manasseh had provoked him withal."[2] Jeremiah had said the same. Exile and dispersion are to come "because of Manasseh, the son of Hezekiah, king of Judah, for that which he did in Jerusalem."[3] It is not

[1] 2 Kings xxi. 1—18.   [2] 2 Kings xxiii. 26.
[3] Jeremiah xv. 4.

open to doubt but that the character of the Book of Deuteronomy, the product of Josiah's reign and the occasion of his reform, was coloured, in its fundamental attitude of uncompromising hostility to idolatry, by that which occurred under Manasseh. And the later editors of the Books of Kings, seeing in the state of religion and religious observances during that reign the crown and pinnacle of national iniquity, were thereby often induced to set the earlier history of Israel in a false light, and to identify vice with idolatry far more closely than the prophets of the eighth century.

What were the sins of Manasseh?

It has already been indicated that the Assyrians made their influence felt, not only in politics, but also in religion. It was the old Babylonian worship of the luminaries of heaven which was introduced into Judah in the eighth century, and which, after receiving a short check during the reign of Hezekiah, became very widely prevalent under his son. Altars were erected "and incense was burnt to the sun, and to the moon, and to all the host of heaven."[1] Manasseh, like a devoted vassal of Assyria, even polluted the temple of Yahveh with the worship of these foreign divinities; for we are told that "he built altars for all the host of heaven in the two courts of the house of Yahveh."[2] It appears that this form of idolatry rapidly acquired a great popularity, especially with women.[3] But together with this novel star-worship, there was also a recrudescence both of Canaanite idolatry and of old Israelite superstitions.

[1] 2 Kings xxiii. 5.   [2] 2 Kings xxi. 5.
[3] Jeremiah vii. 18, xliv. 15.

As regards the latter, we are told of Manasseh, that "he used soothsayings and divinations, and appointed workers with familiar spirits and wizards."[1] The special instance of the former was the adoption, or, as some would say, the revival, of the appalling rite of sacrificing children, especially the first-born son. Why this odious form of worship began to be practised in Judah in the eighth and seventh centuries is not wholly clear. Ahaz is the first king to whom it is attributed.[2] That it was still exceptional in the eighth century, we may infer from the silence of the prophets. Once only in a single passage in Isaiah is there any allusion to this worship; yet there, however, the language used seems to imply that it had already received a recognized locality for its performance in the neighbourhood of Jerusalem.[3] While both the authors of the Book of Kings and the prophets regard the barbarous offering as rendered to the Canaanite god Melech, or "the king," the actual sacrificers probably fused the two deities together, and devoted their children to Yahveh under the name of Melech. For the appellation "king" could be applied to Yahveh as it was to divers other neighbouring or kindred divinities. In addition to this syncretistic usage, there might also be co-ordinated a definite worship and acknowledgment of Melech or Moloch himself; such idolatry would be the more natural, inasmuch as Solomon's altar to Milcom, the Ammonite deity, who was only another form of the Canaanite "Moloch," was still in existence. Manasseh, like Ahaz, sacrificed his son, and many another during

[1] 2 Kings xxi. 6.   [2] 2 Kings xvi. 3.
[3] Isaiah xxx. 33.

his reign must have followed the example of the court.[1]

There are many tokens in the literature of the seventh century that the idolatrous reaction of Manasseh penetrated deep, making many converts. But the prophetic teaching of the preceding century had not fallen upon wholly barren soil, and the tendencies of Manasseh served to accentuate the distinction between the two sections of idolaters and monolatrists. For the very opposition which they encountered enabled Isaiah's doctrines, though not always in a shape which entirely conformed with the spirit of their author, to take firm root among those who were hostile to the religious innovations of the age. Manasseh would apparently brook no opposition to the idolatrous proclivities of his court; he met the indignation of Isaiah's disciples and of the prophetical party by open and relentless persecution.[2] Very probably the priests of the temple, or at any rate an important section of them, actively resented its pollution. The older historian of the Book of Kings speaks of "Manasseh shedding innocent blood very much, till he had filled Jerusalem from one end to another." This innocent blood must have mainly flowed from those who opposed his idolatrous tendencies. Jeremiah appears to allude to this persecution when he tells the men of Judah that their own

---

[1] The relation of Milcom, the Ammonite god, to the supposed Milk or Moloch of the Canaanites is, however, disputed. See Eerdman's *Melekdienst*, p. 112; and, on the wider question of the existence of a separate god whose *proper* name was Melech, Cheyne, *Jeremiah*, p. 45; n. 1 and 2, with the authorities there quoted, and Baethgen, pp. 37—40. &c.

[2] 2 Kings xxi. 16, xxiv. 4.

DEUTERONOMY AND JEREMIAH. 171

sword had devoured their prophets like a destroying lion. If some great critics are right in assigning the sixth and opening verses of the seventh chapters of Micah to a nameless prophet under Manasseh, they give us a vivid and painful picture of the moral corruption of the age.[1] And they show us also that Yahveh's favour was still solicited by sacrifices of immense size and cost, and that the crying abomination of "Moloch" worship had been successfully grafted upon the worship of the national God. But they also prove that the prophetical teaching of the eighth-century prophets was being continued in spite of opposition and enmity in the seventh, and not only continued, but advanced. One of the best examples of prophetical religion has been preserved to us out of the violence and injustice of the age: "Will Yahveh be pleased with thousands of rams, or with ten thousands of rivers of oil? Shall I give my first-born for my transgression, the fruit of my body for the sin of my soul? He has showed thee, O man, what is good; and what doth Yahveh require of thee, but to do justly, and to love kindness, and to walk humbly with thy God."[2]

From the accession of Manasseh to the death of Amon (686—638), a period of forty-eight years, this internal conflict continued; and in it, as always, the blood of martyrs was the seed of the Church. In 638, Amon was succeeded by his son Josiah, then only eight years old. It is possible that his accession brought about some amelioration in the condition of the prophetical party,

[1] So, e.g., Cheyne, Kuenen and Wellhausen, for vi. and vii. 1—7.

[2] Micah vi. 6—8; cf. Isaiah lvii. 5; Ezekiel xvi. 20, 21, xxiii. 37, xx. 25—31, &c.; Jer. xix. &c.

and that active persecution ceased. But the syncretistic and idolatrous worship was still maintained for another eighteen years, though those years are passed over without any notice in the Book of Kings. They were, however, years of great importance in the history of Asia, for they witnessed the break-up of the Assyrian empire, and the inroads of the Scythians. The collapse of Assyria followed hard upon the death of Asurbanipal in 626: Babylon revolted, the northern and north-western provinces of the empire fell into the hands of the Medes, and the authority of Assyria over the vassal kingdoms of the west was gradually weakened. We shall soon find Josiah venturing upon an independent expedition of his own into northern Israel, an integral portion at that time of the Assyrian empire. The Scythians are stated by Herodotus to have been rulers of "Asia" for twenty-eight years, but it is probable that he has over-estimated the period during which the Asiatic peoples were subject to this awful scourge. But what chiefly interests us to know is that the Scythians, penetrating into Palestine, pursued their march of rapine and desolation along the coast as far as the Egyptian border. Here, according to Herodotus, they were met by Psammetichus, king of Egypt, who, "by gifts and entreaties," prevailed upon them to return.[1] They seem, then, to have left Palestine by the same route by which they entered it, and neither in coming nor in going to have set foot in the kingdom of Judah. These events may be roughly assigned to the years 626—623. But though the Scythian invasion is unrecorded in the Book of Kings,

[1] Herod. i. 105.

and though Judah was unaffected by it directly, it left its mark upon Hebrew prophecy, and probably gave the impetus for plans of reformation which were matured and ready for execution not more than two years after the enemy's departure from Palestine.

Two prophets began their career at this period, and in striking accordance with Wellhausen's theory mentioned at the close of the last Lecture, it would seem as if for both of them it was the prospect of Scythian devastation which made them conscious of the divine call. The two prophets are Zephaniah, and his far more famous and important contemporary, Jeremiah. In the opening chapter of his book, Jeremiah tells us that "the word of Yahveh first came to him while still young, in the thirteenth year of king Josiah's reign." This would be about 626. The prophecies which were spoken by Jeremiah during the five earliest years of his ministry— that is, between his call in 626 and the reformation of 621—are professedly collected in the first six chapters of his book; but as, in their present form, they were written down far later, it is more than probable that they underwent considerable modification. Both Jeremiah and Zephaniah draw a very black picture of Judah's moral and religious condition in the days of Josiah; even if the king himself, according to Prof. Cheyne's opinion,[1] must be assumed to have come already for many years before the reformation under the influence of such men as Hilkiah the priest, there was as yet no general desistence either from idolatry or from those moral iniquities against which the older prophets had been wont to pro-

[1] Cheyne, *Jeremiah: his Life and Times*, pp. 16—20.

test so loudly. Both prophets saw in the approaching Scythians the instruments of God's righteous anger, and called upon the better-disposed to seek Yahveh in humility and justice, so that they might perchance be hid in the day of Yahveh's vengeance.

There are some faint indications that, while the danger was imminent, the national consciousness was stirred to fear, if not to repentance, by the invectives and menaces of Jeremiah, but that when it had passed away and the prophetic threats of judgment remained unfulfilled, idolatrous tendencies asserted themselves again with the augmented strength of a natural reaction. But the prophetic party was still undaunted by the recent failure. They did not believe the less in Yahveh because, in Prof. Cheyne's phrase, "God's dealings with his people were gentler than his threatenings."[1] Something must be done to check the downward progress of the nation into idolatry and corruption. What should that something be?

In the present form of Jeremiah's early prophecies, he speaks as if the true prophetic spirit was scarcely represented by any one but himself.[2] He attacks priests and prophets no less than rulers and judges. But this is the language of exaggeration, and reflects a later and more unanimous opposition in succeeding reigns. At this period, there must have been many priests who were not only opposed to the worship of foreign gods, but also keenly desirous for a purification of native ritual, so that the ceremonial religion of Yahveh might correspond the better with the spiritual teaching of the prophets. There was not necessarily any wide divergence in religious

[1] *Jeremiah*, p. 33.   [2] Jer. v. 1.

belief between prophet and priest, although naturally the latter would not take the same depreciatory view of all external observances which was customary with the former. Uriah, the chief priest of the Jerusalem temple under Hezekiah, had been Isaiah's chosen friend, and several of the prophet's disciples may have been drawn from the priesthood. Jeremiah himself belonged to a priestly family. Prophets and priests were now drawn into a closer alliance by a common danger. In Hezekiah's days, Yahveh himself, by the "judgment" of the Assyrians, had occasioned a partial reform: under Josiah the expected scourge had been withdrawn, and the people could afford to laugh at the prophets' miscalculation, and to neglect their teaching with a light heart. Even some, whom the retreat of the Scythians did not confirm in their idolatries, were tempted to become indifferent to the cause of religion. They would join the ranks of those who were "settled on their lees," and whose belief was limited to the atheistic doctrine: "Yahveh will not do good, neither will he do evil."[1] A reformation must now be attempted by human means, while the incitement to it must be effected by human effort, and be independent of external hazard.

More and more distinctly in the eyes of both prophet and priest did the evil condition of society appear to proceed from the corrupt worship of Yahveh and the idolatrous worship of other gods. The prophecies of Jeremiah show a marked contrast with those of Isaiah in this respect. They approach far more closely to the model of Hosea. Isaiah, as we saw, is mainly concerned with the moral

[1] Zephaniah i. 12.

offences of his contemporaries. To actual idolatry (the worship of other gods) he scarcely alludes at all; to the material representation of Yahveh, only occasionally in sarcastic contempt. But the incursion of new, and the recrudescence of old idolatries during the reign of Manasseh seemed a renewal of the Baal-worship of Ahab and Athaliah. Jeremiah accordingly places the apostasy from Yahveh in the head and front of Judah's offending.

How was this increasing prevalence of idolatry to be overcome? Isaiah, and Hosea before him, had protested against image-worship; but to the would-be reformers under Josiah it appeared that the attack must include more than the images, and that the work of destruction should take a wider sweep. It seemed to them necessary that the worship of Yahveh should be divested of all such material appurtenances as were common to it and to the worship of other gods. Free hitherto from prophetic censure, the sacred pillars and poles were in their eyes no longer innocuous. This ascription of illegitimacy to symbols, hitherto alike familiar and allowed, was, however, only a detail, and it was thrown into the shade by a gigantic innovation which was now apparently for the first time contemplated, and, as we shall soon see, was speedily carried into full effect. This innovation was nothing less than the abolition of all sanctuaries of Yahveh throughout the length and breadth of Judah, except the single temple at Jerusalem.

There were several reasons for an attempt of this kind. The difference between the country sanctuaries and the central sanctuary of the capital had gradually become marked and significant. Whereas originally, and for many generations after its foundation, Solomon's temple, in spite of its possession of Yahveh's Ark, was only first among its peers, it had now, partly through Isaiah's teaching and partly through the issue of the Assyrian wars, become identified with Yahveh's habitual dwelling-place. Here, and not elsewhere, was his nearer presence to be found, and hence it was (so many among the reformers would imagine) that Jerusalem had escaped destruction at the invasion of Sennacherib. Moreover, although the idolatrous reaction under Manasseh had penetrated within the temple precincts, so that the emblems of the host of heaven had been set up in close proximity to Yahveh's altar, yet upon the whole the temple ceremonial was purer than that of the country sanctuaries, and was administered by a more educated priesthood. If a successful reform movement were to throw the direction of public worship into the hands of its promoters, and if all worship of Yahveh were strictly prohibited except at a single sanctuary controlled by themselves, it would be far less difficult to prevent any revival of idolatry.

If these were the ideas which were ripening in the reformers' minds during the opening years of Josiah's reign, and more especially after the retreat of the Scythians from Palestine, the further question would arise, how they were to be translated into action, and how the king could be won over to accept and enforce them.

The reformers, or, as perhaps it would be more accurate to say, a small section of them, hit upon a method, which has been variously estimated by different historians. They determined to draw up a book of exhortation and law, suitable to the needs of the time, but set in a framework of fictitious antiquity. It was to be a book which the Founder himself might well have published, and would certainly have sanctioned, had he witnessed the condition of state and society under Josiah. It should begin with, and be based upon, the Decalogue, then regarded by one and all as of Mosaic origin, and it should include (with the modifications and improvements which changed circumstances and advanced religious ideas had rendered necessary) the substance of those older collections of laws (such as the Book of the Covenant) which perhaps had also acquired the stamp of Mosaic authenticity. The whole book, therefore, should be in thorough accordance with the spirit of the Mosaic religion; for we must remember that the purest conceptions of the seventh century would not have appeared to the reformers as new creations of their own or the preceding age, but as true expressions of the Founder's faith. In their eyes there would be no immoral deceit in placing the new code-book as a whole in the mouth of Moses.

One more step was wanting, even after the book itself had been completed. It was needful to have it publicly acknowledged by king and people as the law of the land. The older collections had never been widely known; in Prof. Cheyne's words, "There is no proof that they enjoyed any public, that is, national recognition, and their circulation was probably limited to the priests (if the collection was a ritualistic one), and to the few educated people among the laity (if the collection related to social duties)."[1] But now a bold effort was to be made to

[1] *Jeremiah: his Life and Times*, p. 61.

sweep the idolatries and immoralities of the age entirely away: hence the laws compiled to effect this great end must be publicly accepted and recognized throughout the kingdom as the binding Book of the Covenant ordained of God by the hands of Moses.

In some such manner as this we may imaginatively re-construct the course of events which preceded the scenes recorded in the Book of Kings for the eighteenth year of Josiah's reign. Among the prophets and priests responsible for the production of the new Book of the Covenant, if not among its actual writers, was Hilkiah, the chief priest of the Jerusalem temple, and to him was entrusted the duty of devising a favourable opportunity for submitting it to the notice of the youthful king. Hilkiah seems to have thought well to give the appearance of accident to a long preconcerted design. Josiah had sent Shaphan, his scribe or chancellor, to Hilkiah, with certain instructions relative to some repairs in the temple which were then being carried on. After Shaphan has delivered his message, Hilkiah informs him that he has found "the Book of the Law"—more accurately, "the Book of Teaching"—in the house of Yahveh. Shaphan, who, presumably, though known to be inclined to the reformers' views, was not himself a party to their scheme, reads the book, and returns with it to the king. After disposing of the business for which he has been sent to the temple, Shaphan adds: "Hilkiah the priest has given me a book." It is obvious that Shaphan must have informed Josiah what this book contained and from whom it was supposed to proceed. We are, however, merely told by the historian that "Shaphan read it before the king, and that when the king had heard the words of the book of the law, he rent his clothes."[1] Josiah (unlike Jehoiakim) was clearly susceptible to prophetic influences, and already inclined to follow, could he but see his way, in the footsteps of his grandfather.

Our general survey does not permit us to trace in detail from this point the stages of the reformation. It suffices to say that, confirmed by prophetic advice, the king summoned a national assembly, and in the court of the temple read before all the contents of the new code. Josiah was evidently convinced that the book was of genuine antiquity, and could thus affirm without difficulty that its provisions had been wilfully neglected by all previous generations. The men of Judah and Jerusalem, and all the elders, priests and prophets, who had not been previously admitted to the secret of its composition, would be under the same illusion. It is not, therefore, surprising that a considerable impression was produced. But the effect of its public recitation is only fully understood when we call to mind that, with the omission of certain chapters at the beginning and at the end, the new code was no other than our present Book of Deuteronomy. No wonder that the promises and threats of that remarkable book should have deeply moved the strange assembly collected together in the temple court. The immediate result is set forth in a single verse of the 23rd chapter of the Book of Kings: "And the king stood on the platform, and he made the covenant before Yahveh, to walk after Yahveh, and to keep his commandments and his testimonies and his

[1] 2 Kings xxii. 11.

DEUTERONOMY AND JEREMIAH. 181

statutes, with all his heart and all his soul, to perform the words of this covenant that are written in this book. And all the people entered into the covenant."[1]

After Deuteronomy had thus, in a moment of exaltation and excitement, been accepted by the people as the law of the land, Josiah proceeded to give practical effect to that acceptance by a series of active and sometimes violent reforms throughout the length and breadth of his kingdom. He began with the temple. In accordance with the provisions of the code, it was thoroughly purged of all idolatrous accretions, whether associated with the worship of other gods or with the worship of Yahveh. The sacred pole or Asherah was removed and burnt. The king "broke down" the houses in which, by the assimilation of Yahveh's worship to the most loathsome form of Canaanite idolatry, a kind of sacred prostitution was carried on within the very precincts of the temple. All the emblems of Assyrian star-worship, and all the instruments or vessels used in connection with it, were destroyed. Then the range of reform was advanced beyond the temple limits. The Topheth in which children were offered up to Moloch, or to Yahveh under the appellation of Moloch, was defiled, and the same fate befel those high places which Solomon had erected to the deities of Tyre, Moab and Ammon.

But the most trenchant and difficult reform was still to come. To obey the new Code, it was necessary to eradicate every sanctuary of Yahveh beside the one and

---

[1] Cf. the important remarks of Cheyne on the date of Deuteronomy, and the manner of its composition and introduction to Josiah, in the *Expositor*, 1892, February, pp. 94—104.

single temple of Jerusalem. It mattered not whether these sanctuaries were dear and holy to the inhabitants of the towns and villages which possessed them, whether they were hallowed by pious memories or local traditions, or whether, having escaped the general idolatrous tendencies of the age, they were consecrate to Yahveh and to him alone: all were swept away.

We are not told, but we can well imagine, that the execution of this provision of the new code caused poignant distress and met with bitter opposition. Its results could not have been realized in the assembly at Jerusalem, which would, moreover, be mainly confined to the inhabitants of the capital. The Levitical priests of the local sanctuaries were mostly removed to Jerusalem, where they were suffered to occupy an inferior position as servitors and assistants to the official priesthood of the temple.[1] The authors of Deuteronomy had not been unmindful of the cruel effect which the destruction of the sanctuaries would have upon their ministering priests, and they had generously intended that such priests should be admitted to equal rights with the priesthood of the central temple.[2] But as the temple of Jerusalem was already in all probability supplied with a full complement of priests, this humane injunction could not be, or was not, observed, and the two grades of priests hereby called into existence became the foundation of later legal developments. A far worse fate was reserved for illegitimate priests of alien divinities worshipped by Yahveh's side. These, apparently, were put to the

[1] 2 Kings xxiii. 8, 9.
[2] Deut. xviii. 6—8.

sword.[1] Death, too, seems to have been the penalty of all professional sorcerers, wizards and spirit-mongers. The decay of the Assyrian empire after the death of Asurbanipal enabled Josiah to extend his reforms beyond the borders of Judah, and we are told that he overthrew the "high places" in the cities of Samaria and slew the priests who appertained to them. By this iconoclastic campaign he probably also intended to make good his claim to include the old northern kingdom of Israel within his own realm.

Before we attempt to trace the effects of Josiah's reformation upon the religious history of his people, it is necessary to take some notice of the book upon which his policy had been based. That book was unquestionably a portion of our present Book of Deuteronomy, and may have extended, apart from certain later interpolations, from the beginning of the fifth to the end of the twenty-eighth chapter.

Deuteronomy was the product of an alliance between prophet and priest. It is probable that it was drawn up by more than one writer, and that at least one representative of either order had a share in its compilation. It represents itself to be the code of laws given by God to Moses upon Mount Horeb, and repeated by him to the people upon the borders of the promised land. Its object —hardly concealed under the mask of antiquity—was to transform the Judah of king Josiah's day into a peculiar people, holy and just, loving God and following God's law. Such was also the ideal of the prophets; and though Deuteronomy contains a fusion of prophetic and

[1] 2 Kings xxiii. 5; but cf. Stade, *Z. A. W.*, 1885, p. 292.

of priestly spirit, it is the spirit of the prophets which upon the whole prevails. But if, of the four eighth-century prophets, it is asked to whose teaching Deuteronomy most closely conforms, the answer is, to Hosea's. Hosea traced back the moral sins of his people to their abandonment of Yahveh: the entire iniquity of the nation was implied in the worship of Baal. The events of Manasseh's reign had tended to impress the same idea upon the best prophetical minds of the seventh century. It was the key-note of Jeremiah's teaching, and it is the alpha and omega of Deuteronomy. Scarcely can we now fairly and fully discern how far the idea was justified by the reality. But we do know that the idolatrous rites of the times rested upon, or included, much that was foul and immoral; witness the bloody Tophet and the houses of the sacred prostitutes which were defiled or destroyed by Josiah. The men who, in the past, had been most zealous for the pure and unalloyed worship of Yahveh, had also been most zealous for social morality, for justice, kindliness and truth; and those times of which report said that they were purest as regards religion, had also been those in which righteousness and justice had "made their lodging in the land."[1] The authors of Deuteronomy believed that right religion (as they conceived it) coloured the whole of human character: with the love of Yahveh and the desire "to walk in all his ways," to serve him with "all the heart and with all the soul," a good life, in the strictly moral sense of the word, must inevitably be combined.

Since the fundamental aim of Deuteronomy was the

[1] Isaiah i. 21.

eradication of all trace or chance of idolatry, whether as involving the service of other gods, or only that false worship of Yahveh which, to the reformers, appeared equally abominable, it was natural that the main bulk of its exhortations and ordinances should centre upon this one great object and desire. The severity of Josiah's reforms faithfully reflects the code from which they sprang. There must be no tampering with, and no pardon for, idolatry. Many of the ordinances of Deuteronomy are in this respect purely dramatic; the destruction of the Canaanites, for instance, was no longer within the range of practical politics; but doubtless the authors of the book would have desired the wholesale annihilation of any city of Judah which, after the acceptance of the code, should have re-instituted idolatry.[1] Prophetism never laid aside the touch of savage zeal which characterized its earliest manifestations. For the idolater no less, but rather more, than for the murderer, death was the only befitting sentence, and the conception of civic solidarity, as familiar to the Hebrews as to the Greeks, sufficiently explains why the guilt of some would necessarily involve the punishment of all.

To purify the worship of Yahveh from every taint of idolatry, the authors of Deuteronomy not only waged war upon all material excrescences, such as sacred pillars and poles as well as teraphim and images, which were either unworthy of the monotheistic conception of Yahveh, or common to, and hence inducive of, the worship of other gods, but, as we have seen, conceived the remarkable idea of stamping with the brand of idolatry

[1] Deut. xiii. 12—18.

every sanctuary of Yahveh outside the capital. It was a project of extraordinary boldness both in conception and execution; but the authors of Deuteronomy were clearly neither conscious of its full magnitude, nor of the difficulties which were bound to follow upon its adoption.

The practical difficulty which arose in dealing with the ousted local priests has already been alluded to. Far more serious was the prospective influence of religious centralization upon the population at large. Until the reign of Josiah, every slaughter of cattle had partaken of the character of a sacrifice, and the local altars were centres of religious feeling—not always of an elevated kind, but yet genuine so far as it went—in every town and village. But now there was to be no common worship of Yahveh except in the capital. Thither every one must journey who desired to make offering or supplication to God, and thither, whether it pleased them or not, were all to wend their way on the three great yearly festivals. The feasts of Passover, of First Fruits and of Harvest, were to be no more the occasions of merry thanksgiving and feasting in every city and hamlet throughout Judæa; men were to rejoice according to the provisions of a written law, away from their homes and from all those scenes and associations which had been, perchance, the best elements in those feasts of former times, now branded as idolatrous and illegal.

While the legislators were extremely anxious to maintain the joyous character of the three great festivals, and to encourage the common rejoicing of all the household before Yahveh, it was not likely that the majority of the population would be able to do more than fulfil the strict letter of the law in its new application: "Three times a year shall all thy males appear before Yahveh thy God." Yet though the reformers had scarcely calculated the gain and loss, history has fully vindicated their action. For the abolition of the local sanctuaries was the first step in the substitution of the synagogue for the temple, of prayer for sacrifice. Nothing was more opposed to prophetical teaching than the thought that God's favour could be won, or his wrath averted, by any multiplication of offerings. And in Deuteronomy sacrifices have the character of thank-offerings or tributes: sin-offerings are ignored. Since the magical element is eliminated, the evil effects of sacrifices are reduced to a minimum.

The single sanctuary, as Wellhausen finely observes, was also the natural sequitur of the monotheistic idea.[1] For the one God there could be but one abiding earthly seat. So far as ceremonial worship has a definite object in Deuteronomy, it is intended to subserve the idea of Yahveh's historic and peculiar relation to his people. Moreover, the secularization of animal slaughter was really a considerable gain. Though it may have left a temporary gap in the social life of Judæa, it paved the way for the introduction of a deeper sanctification of every-day life within the home itself by the fulfilment of a wider and more comprehensive law. But this is to anticipate.

If Deuteronomy was prophetist in its comparative depreciation of sacrifices, it was no less so in the large

[1] *Abriss*, p. 70.

and prominent place which it assigned to laws of justice and humanity. In this respect, as in others, it repeats the provisions of the older Book of the Covenant, and amplifies them. Justice and kindness between man and man are as much the ideal of Deuteronomy as the pure worship of Yahveh. Upon both equally the prosperity of Israel is declared to depend. And a higher motive, peculiar to this book, is repeatedly added: "Because thou wast a bondman in Egypt, therefore art thou commanded to do this thing." Even beyond the too frequently oppressed classes of the foreign settler, the widow, the orphan and the slave, the legislators' tenderness and compassion extend to the cattle at the plough and to the birds among the trees.

But the influence of the priest is distinctly felt in another branch of the Deuteronomic code, which was intended to cover the whole life of a citizen, both on its religious and on its secular side. All law was to the Israelite religious law, and as such it remained to the end. Prophets as well as priests would desire that Israel should be a holy nation, entirely devoted to its God, blameless in its relations towards him. Isaiah twice uses the word "holy" as characteristic of the regenerate Israel. As a condition of "holiness"—that is, of real dedication and consecration to Yahveh—Isaiah would certainly have insisted upon the absence of every idolatrous taint; but we can hardly imagine him attaching to the holiness which he demanded injunctions as to food and drink, or basing such commands upon a spiritual conception. To the priest, matters of ritual were naturally of high importance. In the old Book of the Covenant (if the passage be not a later insertion), the law is found: "Ye shall be holy men unto me; and flesh in the field, that is torn of beasts, ye shall not eat."[1] This priestly idea of holiness is echoed in Deuteronomy. It is connected with the desire to exclude from Israel's life everything which savours of idolatry. Israel's devotion to God must be ceremonially indicated by difference of rite and custom from the rites and customs of other races. For in antiquity, be it remembered, there was scarcely a rite or a custom which was not more or less closely and consciously connected with religion. Anxiety that Israel should avoid everything heathen and idolatrous, and anxiety that Israel should fulfil the traditional priestly ordinances of (material) holiness, are co-ordinate objects of Deuteronomy's ceremonial legislation, and doubtless in the minds of its authors they were scarcely distinguishable from one another.

It is natural that to the modern reader the most attractive portion of the original Book of Deuteronomy should be its introductory setting, from chapter v. to the end of chapter xi. Many scholars believe that the book "found" in the temple and read before Josiah did not include these preliminary chapters. For myself, I follow Kuenen and others in still adhering to the contrary view. But even if not written at the same time as chapters xii.—xxvi., they were certainly not added very long afterwards; and whether or not written by the same hands as those which drew up the more directly legislative chapters, they breathe the same spirit, and look at religion from the same point of view. An intense

[1] Exodus xxii. 31.

and eager earnestness pervades them. With frequent iteration, their author implores his people to choose the true way, and to walk in it without swerving to the right hand or to the left. The requirements of Yahveh, to be set forth in the code, are not difficult to understand or to carry out. They may be easily fulfilled when once the fundamental principle of true religion has been realized and accepted, "To fear Yahveh, and to love him with all the heart and all the soul."

Love of God is the peculiar and novel feature of the introduction to Deuteronomy. Enthusiastic himself about God, the writer expects a similar enthusiasm from Israel. Who is Israel's God? The God of the Deuteronomist is the God of the eighth-century prophets, the God before whose awful and all-embracing majesty the divine powers of other lands have faded utterly away. He is a single and self-consistent Deity, the one Yahveh, "God of gods and Lord of lords," to whom belong "the heaven and the heaven of heavens, the earth also with all that is therein."[1] And this supreme God has chosen to adopt one people as his own, and upon condition of its single-hearted devotion to himself and to his laws, to cover it with benefits which it has not deserved. Should not such an extraordinary position, so amazing a privilege, suffice to ensure a moral superiority over other nations? Should not Israel respond to the gracious blessings of its God with humility and gratitude? Should it not be transformed into a holy community, intent upon the service of God, and dedicating to that end all its strength and zeal—transformed, in more modern phrase, from a

[1] vi. 4, x. 17.

people to a church? To realize such a transformation is the purpose, as it is the ideal, of Deuteronomy.

On one point, however, the book does not reflect the highest conceptions of the prophets. It aimed at producing a holy people, worthy of its peculiar destiny as God's chosen. But here its purpose stops. There is no thought for the world beyond. There is, indeed, no vehement particularism such as we find in Ezekiel and in some of the later post-exilic literature; while the Moabite and Ammonite are excluded from the congregation of Yahveh "even to the tenth generation," the Edomite and Egyptian, on the contrary, may enter into it in the third generation; they must not be "abhorred" by the Israelites, the one because he is their brother, the other because they were strangers in his land.[1] But though Yahveh is the God of the whole earth, it does not appear to have occurred to the authors of Deuteronomy that it was the duty of Yahveh's people to spread the knowledge of him beyond the borders of Israel, or that this extended recognition, whether to be effected by Israel or not, was the ultimate justification and aim of Israel's election and privilege. Hinted at by the eighth-century prophets, this highest and only moral view of Israel's peculiar position among the nations of the world was to be taken up and worked out, some eighty years after Deuteronomy, by a great prophet of the exile.

Were the authors of the new code confident of success? Prof. Cheyne has spoken of the hopefulness of Deuteronomy which penetrates its every page.[2] I am myself

[1] xxiii. 3, 7. [2] *Jeremiah*, p. 75.

inclined to doubt whether this apparent hopefulness is not for the most part assumed. There seems to be more of the authors' own feelings in their frequent complaints against the national obstinacy. "Not for thy righteousness does Yahveh give thee this good land to possess it; for thou art a stiff-necked people." Emphatic is the appeal: "Circumcise therefore the foreskin of your heart, and be no more stiff-necked." It was rather a lack of hopefulness which prompted the reiterated assurance that the following of Yahveh's commands and the walking in his ways would alone, but would unfailingly, bring happiness and prosperity. This, again, is prophetic teaching, but it is insisted on with an intensity which brings out its perilous one-sidedness. It was not yet possible to get at the people, or to secure their willing allegiance to Yahveh's law, except by promises of material well-being or by threats of material distress. At the same time, these promises and threats were no make-believe on the part of their authors: ineradicable in the Israelite heart was the conviction that piety and prosperity, wickedness and adversity, respectively are, and ever must be, inseparable allies. But Deuteronomy had not yet reached the position, so often neglected or misunderstood, of the later Judaism. It promised happiness as the result of obedience to its laws; it declared such obedience to be easy and compatible with a joyous and gladsome life: it did not yet assert, as Judaism afterwards asserted, that obedience itself, be external circumstances what they may, involves and secures the highest happiness conceivable by man.

Such was the Book of Covenant which king Josiah

and his people accepted as the law of the state. The mere acceptance of a binding and universally acknowledged religious law was fraught with results which were, to some extent, independent of the actual enactments which it contained. It has often been pointed out that Deuteronomy tended to exalt the power of the priesthood, and to undermine and render superfluous the office of the prophet. It contemplates, indeed, a continual succession of prophets to be obeyed like Moses; but in ordinary circumstances the guide of life is clearly to be the law, and its interpreters the priests of Jerusalem. Through the abolition of the local sanctuaries, the public worship of Yahveh, the outward manifestation of religion, is conducted at the capital alone, by a *corps d'élite* among the sons of Levi; it was inevitable that the importance of this select body should gradually but surely increase both in its own eyes and in those of the people at large.

It is not possible in this place to pursue the literary development and completion of the Deuteronomic code. It must suffice to say that, shortly before or after the fall of the state in 586, there was added a further historical introduction, consisting of the first four chapters of our present book.[1] These chapters are written in the general spirit and style of Deuteronomy; and there seems, indeed, to have quickly formed itself a regular school of writers upon the Deuteronomic pattern, who looked at history and religion from the Deuteronomic point of view. During the exile these writers added some chapters at the close, and perhaps interpolated a few sections in the body of

[1] Their precise date is uncertain, nor are they wholly "aus einem Guss." Cf. Cornill, *Einleitung in das alte Testament*.

the main work. They also edited the historical records of the Monarchy and of the Judges, and supplied them with the framework and the criticisms which were for long accepted by posterity as of equal authority with the documents themselves.

The new Code was promulgated in 621, and Josiah's reign continued for some seventeen years. We have no record of the religious condition of Judah immediately after the great reformation. No complete prophecy of Jeremiah can be assigned to them; we have only the prophet's estimate of Josiah himself, as of one who did justice and judged the cause of the needy and the poor—a panegyric which we may with probability infer to have been specially applicable to the later period of his reign after the great reform.[1] Jeremiah, though not one of its authors, was certainly an admirer and advocate of Deuteronomy. The 11th chapter of his book, which as a whole reflects the condition of things in the reign of Jehoiakim, opens with the recitation of a divine command to repeat the words of "this Covenant" in the cities of Judah and in the streets of Jerusalem, and to urge men to fulfil them. It has been conjectured that "this Covenant" was no other than Deuteronomy, and that "Jeremiah undertook an itinerating mission to the people of Judah, beginning with the capital, in order to set forth the main objects of Deuteronomy, and to persuade men to live in accordance with its precepts."[2] How far the prophet was satisfied with the results of his mission, we do not know. It is, however, only too probable that the reformation, suddenly and violently

[1] Jer. xxii. 16.   [2] Cheyne, *Jeremiah*, p. 56.

effected, was for the majority merely skin-deep. It dealt with externals, and was not the genuine expression of a wide-felt need or of a spiritual movement. And yet it was more than well able to produce one result, which in the sequel shocked the moral nature of Jeremiah to its profoundest depths. The symbols of idolatry were destroyed or hidden away; the temple—the only sanctuary of Yahveh—stood out cleansed and purified of its heathen and defiling accretions; as head of the state there ruled a man who had made Yahveh's law his own, and sought to discharge his office with integrity and zeal. Might it not be assumed that the favour of Yahveh was now permanently secured? A perilous assumption both morally and politically! In morality, it led to indifference and corruption; in politics, to arrogance and defeat.

With the death of Asurbanipal, the Assyrian empire, as we have already seen, entered upon its final period of dissolution. Babylon revolted; and an Assyrian general of Babylonian birth who had been sent to quell the insurrection, put himself at its head and became the founder of a new dynasty. The Medes penetrated further and further into Assyria. Nahum, a prophet of Judah, predicted the speedy fall of the national foe. Before long, Cyaxares, king of Media, advanced to the Assyrian capital and besieged it. The invasion of Media by the Scythians compelled him temporarily to raise the siege, but about the year 609 he was once more before the walls of Nineveh. The moment seemed opportune for Necho II., the son of Psammetichus II., king of Egypt, to seize a portion of the Assyrian empire which now lay unprotected. He invaded Palestine, with the possible ulterior thought of extending once more the limits of the old Egyptian empire to the banks of the Euphrates. But Josiah was not willing to have escaped one vassalage only to fall into another. Though Necho had not entered Judæan territory, he was invading Israelite land over which Josiah was attempting to assert and extend his sovereignty. With the full confidence that he was under the protection of Yahveh, and that he was vindicating his rights, he set out against the Egyptian king. The two armies met at Megiddo, in the plain of Jezreel. The men of Judah were defeated: their monarch was slain.

Meanwhile the Egyptian victor continued his march. Laconically and without explanation, the historian records that Jehoahaz, Josiah's son, after a three months' reign at Jerusalem, was put in chains by Necho at Riblah, in the land of Hamath; while his brother Eliakim, under the name of Jehoiakim, was set up as the vassal ruler of Judah by its new over-lord, the Egyptian king. A fine of two hundred talents of silver and ten of gold was imposed by Necho, and exacted from his subjects by Jehoiakim.[1]

What was the feeling in Judah? A bitter shock of disappointment thrilled through the land. Were the promises of Deuteronomy delusory? Reformers lost heart; their cause was discredited. Reaction and idolatry were soon in the ascendant. Even a three months' reign was sufficient, according to the Book of Kings, for Jehoahaz to show leanings towards the old ways. Jehoiakim, his brother, son of Josiah though he was, followed the same policy. With him, the idolatrous tendency was combined

[1] 2 Kings xxiii. 29—35.

with an oppressive despotism, which showed itself in a passion for palace-building, though the means to pay the enforced labourers were wanting. In addition to this specific accusation, Jeremiah gives him a very bad character: "Thine eyes and thine heart are not but for thy covetousness, and for to shed innocent blood, and for oppression and for violence, to do it."[1] Thus once again was a great prophet of the age able to draw the inference and teach it, that idolatry and moral obliquity go hand in hand.

Deuteronomy was not formally abrogated; it was ignored. The local sanctuaries, with their syncretistic worship, sprang again into existence. Still worse was the effect of Josiah's death upon the reformers themselves. We have seen that, to men who had but imperfectly assimilated the moral teaching of the prophets, the loyal acceptance of Deuteronomy might only confirm them in the belief that religion was concerned with ritual rather than with morality. In this error they were encouraged by the defeat at Megiddo. Their conception of Yahveh's character tended to become lower; their confidence in the inviolability of Jerusalem, more obstinate and material. Of two things, one: either Yahveh was not the omnipotent God, as Isaiah and Micah had proclaimed, or the Egyptian hegemony was but a temporary misfortune, from which deliverance would soon be granted.

The one deduction was made and acted upon by the party of idolatry: the other, by those who would doubtless call themselves the national party, and who professed their unalterable allegiance to the national God. They

[1] Jer. xxii. 13—19.

would explain the calamities of the time either, in the old and pre-prophetic manner, upon the pitiful hypothesis that the anger of Yahveh was occasionally unmotived, or upon the less irreligious supposition that the defeat at Megiddo was a trial of their faith.[1] Both explanations would suggest the counsel of paying court to Yahveh by costlier and more frequent sacrifices, either to win back his favour or else to assure him of their own fidelity. To this party, which may easily have included several grades both morally and religiously, a majority of contemporary prophets and priests belonged. They preached an easy doctrine of comfort and consolation: Yahveh would protect his own; the temple was the guarantee of his favour. The call to repentance was either thought to be no longer necessary, or it was forgotten and ignored. In Isaiah's time too there had been prophets willing (did not their livelihood depend upon it?) to comply with the current demand for "smooth things and deceits"; the same teaching was put forward again with greater parade of orthodoxy and with more fanatical assurance. But the true voice of prophecy was not long silent. If the moral reformation, desired by the eighth-century prophets and by Jeremiah, their successor and disciple, had kept pace with the ceremonial reformation effected by Josiah—if no moral complaint of moment could have been truthfully alleged against the people whose army had been defeated at Megiddo—then, indeed, we may surmise that even the faith of Jeremiah would have received a shock not easily to be repaired or withstood. But inasmuch as the moral and spiritual results

[1] Stade, *Geschichte*, Vol. I. p. 672.

of Josiah's reformation had not answered to the prophet's early anticipations, it was possible for him to recover or maintain the wonted prophetic attitude, and to become once more the preacher of repentance and judgment. In this *rôle* we find him active during the reign of Jehoiakim. It would seem that, with a very small minority of other prophets, of whom the name of one only has come down to us, he assumed from the beginning of the new reign a position of open and strenuous opposition to the moral condition of Judah and to the religious policy of the king. He foretold the fall of the State, unless speedy repentance should intervene; but as yet he did not definitely declare the name of the enemy who should be God's instrument of destruction. Judah was the vassal of Necho, but it was not to Egypt that the prophet looked for a further and more comprehensive judgment.

Jeremiah was right. The Egyptian supremacy was not of long duration. Nineveh fell to Cyaxares in 607. Nabopolassar of Babylon, having secured himself towards the east and north by a close alliance with the Medes (his son Nebuchadrezzar was married to Amylis, daughter of Cyaxares), determined to secure for his own kingdom the Assyrian dominions of the west. He sent Nebuchadrezzar with an army against the Egyptians. Necho advanced to the Euphrates, and the battle which decided the fate of Palestine was fought out at Carchemish in 605. The Egyptians suffered a decisive defeat, and fled. Nebuchadrezzar was, however, compelled to defer an immediate advance. His father had died, and he hurried to Babylon to secure the throne. Returning to his army the following year (604—603), he gradually made his way through Syria, clearing the country as he went of all Egyptian garrisons which may have been left behind by Necho in his retreat from Carchemish. In the year 600 Nebuchadrezzar was master of all Palestine as far as the "stream of Egypt," and Jehoiakim, king of Judah, became his vassal.

It is possible that, even before Carchemish, Jeremiah had heard much of the growing power of Nabopolassar, and realized that the Babylonians were to be the instruments of doom; or he may—a very interesting possibility —have been compelled by the fervour of his faith to assume that some judgment would infallibly come, though ignorant of the quarter whence it should fall. "In the beginning of the reign of Jehoiakim," and thus probably before Carchemish, he received the divine call to proclaim the impending judgment in the most open manner and the most definite terms. He was to speak in the temple court before the assembled multitude, and at a time (perhaps on some day of festival) when many would come to worship from all the cities of Judah. The prophecy then uttered is preserved to us in a double form, shortened in the 26th chapter, which gives the scene and its result, expanded and interpolated in the 7th, and possibly also in the 8th and 9th chapters. Jeremiah here comes forward, not merely preaching war to the knife against idolatry and immorality, but re-asserting in the strongest possible form the old prophetic doctrine of the vanity of ceremonial worship and outward religion. The temple of the north had fallen through Israel's sin, and now, unless there was thorough amendment, the temple of the south, in which deluded prophets encouraged the people to put their trust, should be done to as was done to Shiloh. Stones are powerless to save; sacrifices are idle. "Thus saith Yahveh of Hosts, the God of Israel: Put your burnt-offerings unto your sacrifices, and eat the flesh. For I spake not unto your fathers, nor commanded them in the day that I brought them out of the land of Egypt, concerning burnt-offerings or sacrifices; but this thing commanded I them, saying, Obey my voice and I will be your God, and ye shall be my people, and walk ye in all the ways that I have commanded you, that it may be well unto you."[1] What does God's voice say, and what are his ways? To Jeremiah the answer was so certain as to need no telling. It is the old burden of the prophets: negatively, no idolatry; positively, "Do justice, love kindness, and walk humbly before God." But this was not the current teaching among Jeremiah's adversaries, whether prophets or priests, nor was it (it must be confessed) in strict accordance with the teaching of Deuteronomy. Had Jeremiah's estimate of that book been affected by his disappointment at its failure? In one passage in this very prophecy there is an angry and mocking allusion to a supposed law or teaching of Yahveh, by the possession of which his opponents lay claim to a superior wisdom, but it is not certain that any direct reference to Deuteronomy was intended. "How do ye say, We are wise, and the teaching of Yahveh is with us? Yea,

---

[1] Jer. vii. 21—23. Even the burnt-offerings, which were usually wholly consumed by fire, i.e. given to Yahveh, can be eaten as if they were "mere flesh." God will have none of them. The permission or command is, of course, contemptuous and sarcastic.

behold, for a lie has it wrought, the lying pen of the scribes."[1] At any rate, we have Jeremiah in the beginning of Jehoiakim's reign preaching the doctrine of the older prophets in its barest and most unequivocal form, and vehemently opposing any sort of compromise between the true religion of Yahveh and that popular religion of ceremonialism and superstition, to which many a priest and prophet, by a misreading of Deuteronomy, had yielded too ready an adhesion. We see him also rejecting the doctrine, developed from Isaiah, of the inviolability of Jerusalem, and, like Micah, proclaiming for city and for land ruin and desolation. He names no place, but he already anticipates captivity. If Jeremiah foretold a judgment before Carchemish, his convictions were all the stronger after the news of the battle had reached Jerusalem. He was not deceived by the temporary halt of the Babylonians upon Nabopolassar's death. The necessary instruments of God's righteous wrath could be no other than they; a judgment was imminent for Judah, and Nebuchadrezzar, under Yahveh, must be the man predestined to inflict it.

Before the year of Carchemish had passed, he foretold the coming doom, not only of Judah, but of the neighbouring states. It was not surprising that he incurred hatred and hostility. A summary such as this does not permit the reproduction of those two dramatic occasions, one before and one after Carchemish, in which Jeremiah went near to paying the penalty of his boldness with his life.[2] Urijah, who prophesied in a similar strain, was less fortunate. When he fled for shelter into Egypt,

[1] Jer. viii. 8. [2] Jer. xxvi. xxxvi.

DEUTERONOMY AND JEREMIAH. 203

Jehoiakim, at that time still the vassal of Necho, was able to procure his extradition and "slew him with the sword." Prof. Cheyne has suggested that when, in 601, Nebuchadrezzar advanced into Judæa, Jehoiakim's instant submission may have been partly due to the influence of Jeremiah's prophecy.[1] For three years Jehoiakim remained the "servant" of the king of Babylon (601—598); "then he turned and rebelled against him." We know little about Jeremiah's teaching in these three years of calm. For after the momentous occasion on which Baruch had read the roll of his prophecies "in the ears of all the people," and Jehudi the Ethiopian had read the same roll before the princes and the king, Jeremiah had been compelled to lead a life of concealment. The date of this reading is in the Hebrew text assigned to the year after Carchemish (604); but Graetz and Cheyne, following the Septuagint text, place it in 601, the year of Nebuchadrezzar's invasion of Judah, and the eighth of Jehoiakim's reign.[2] After the revolt the prophet seems to have been able, if not to appear in public, at any rate to issue written predictions of the inevitable and impending doom. It was doubtless at the instigation of Necho that Jehoiakim rebelled. The neighbouring states remained faithful to Babylon; and before Nebuchadrezzar himself appeared upon the scene to inflict a summary chastisement upon his rebellious vassal, bands of Syrians, Moabites and Ammonites, in conjunction with a small army of Babylonians drawn from the garrisons in Palestine, invaded

[1] *Jeremiah*, p. 146.
[2] Jer. xxxvi. 9; cf. Cheyne, in his *Commentary on Jeremiah*, ad. loc.

and ravaged Judah.¹ In the midst of this preliminary campaign Jehoiakim died (597), and was succeeded by his son Jehoiachin. Before three months were gone, Nebuchadrezzar's army had arrived before Jerusalem and commenced the siege. When the king joined his forces before the city, Jehoiachin, feeling that further resistance was hopeless, capitulated without conditions. It was the beginning of the end. A deportation upon a large scale was immediately set about. Seven thousand "men of might," one thousand craftsmen, together with the court, the officers of state and the king himself, were carried captive to Babylonia. But in addition to these and their families, there must have been many representatives of other classes, and neither the order of priests nor prophets was wanting among the exiles. As regards the capital, at any rate, the flower of its inhabitants both in wealth and education was thus removed. Over those that remained, in Jerusalem or elsewhere, Nebuchadrezzar appointed another vassal king in the person of Mattaniah, a younger son of Josiah and uncle of Jehoiachin. His name was changed to Zedekiah.

Even now the national spirit was still unbroken, and there was no disposition to live quietly, as Jeremiah advised, under the supremacy of Babylon. Nor was the religious and moral condition of the kingdom improved by the deportations of 597; and Zedekiah, a youth of twenty-one, had not the weight of character to check the rising flood of insubordination, injustice and corruption. Still some seven or eight years passed before the

¹ 2 Kings xxiv. 2.

inevitable rebellion was actually begun. Of the internal condition of Judah during these years we have valuable information from two contemporary sources, from Jeremiah in Jerusalem, and from Ezekiel in Babylonia. There seem to have been frequent communications between the two sections of Jews at home and abroad, and each section was well aware of the circumstances and feelings of the other.[1]

Though we may make some deduction for the exaggeration which was perhaps inevitable in prophetic oratory, the social morality of Judah appears to have been appallingly bad. The new rulers abused the offices they held; injustice, oppression and cruelty were rampant and unpunished. Religiously, the evil precedents of Jehoiakim's reign were still followed and even enlarged under Zedekiah. Idolatry steadily increased; to many, the capture of Jerusalem in 597, and the exile of king and nobles, could only signify the impotence of Yahveh. On the other side were the mass of those who hugged the delusion that Yahveh's righteous anger was satisfied by the judgment which had already been executed, and that deliverance from the Babylonian yoke and the return of the exiles were near at hand. To this party, as we already know, the bulk of the priestly and prophetic orders belonged. Doubtless they called themselves patriots, and there is no reason to deny them the title, even though their greatest opponent was in truth a truer patriot than they. These prophets were not all of them either vicious or deceitful. Perhaps now-a-days the tendency is to rehabilitate these so-called "false

[1] Jer. xxix.; Ezekiel viii., &c.

prophets" too easily, for the evidence of Ezekiel and Jeremiah cannot be lightly put aside. But there were clearly wide gradations of character among them, from the hypocritical charlatan to the honest if deluded enthusiast.

A specimen of the "false prophet" at his very best we still possess in Habakkuk, whose prophecies, though they belong chronologically to the reign of Jehoiakim, may be used to illustrate the subject before us.[1] Habakkuk, writing most probably between the revolt of Jehoiakim and the investment of Jerusalem, while acknowledging that the ravages of the enemy are the just punishment of Judah's sin, yet contrasts the guilt of the heathen foe with the relative "righteousness" of Judah, and confidently appeals to God for the chastisement and expulsion of the invader.[2]

A much lower type of nationalism in prophecy was represented by Hananiah, and yet he may well have been as sincere and as sure of his inspiration as Jeremiah himself. In the fourth year of Zedekiah's reign he openly predicted that within two years the Babylonian yoke would be broken, and Jehoiachin, "with all the captives of Judah," brought back again to Jerusalem. In the ears of the populace was it not natural that the message which seemed to breathe "the keener patriotism should sound the more sacred"?[3] Jeremiah himself (like Ezekiel) never doubted of the issue. Though always ready to allow that a further and more extreme

---

[1] I do not think this too strong a statement, in spite of Kuenen's warning, *Onderzoek*, Vol. II., 2nd ed., pp. 342, 393.

[2] Habakkuk i. 13—17.   [3] Jer. xxviii.

judgment might be averted, it was only upon two conditions: moral reformation, and thorough-going submission to Babylon. But the one condition he saw day by day unfulfilled, while in the maintenance of the other he did not believe. His hopes were fixed upon the exiles in Babylonia. They are "the good figs" to whom shall be given a heart to know Yahveh, and who will return unto him with their whole heart. They of Judah are the "very naughty figs," and among them shall be sent "the sword and the famine and the pestilence, till they be consumed from off the land."[1] He bids the exiles possess their souls in patience; for the time of restoration, though it will come surely, will not come soon. With remarkable sagacity he entreats them to put aside all thoughts of rebellion or of vengeance; let them settle down in the lands assigned to them; let them build houses and dwell in them, plant gardens and eat their fruit; let them seek the welfare of the cities in which they live, for in that welfare their own is involved.[2] It reflects a good deal of light upon the popular religion of the time that the men of Judah were inclined to look down upon the exiles, and say of them: "Ye are far from Yahveh; unto us is Yahveh's land given in possession."[3] Ezekiel, from whom we learn this, shares the opinion of Jeremiah: the new Israel shall be born from the captivity.

The story of Zedekiah's revolt, the siege and fall of Jerusalem in the year 586, cannot be related here. Nor can we follow the fortunes of Jeremiah during this terrible period, while he clung, in spite of persecution and

[1] Jer. xxiv.   [2] Jer. xxix.   [3] Ezekiel xi. 15.

imprisonment, to his old counsel of unconditional submission. This time there were no half-measures. The walls of Jerusalem were razed; the temple burnt; the sacred vessels taken away to Babylon. The kingdom was abolished; over a sparse and needy population, peasants rather than townsmen, "the poor of the land," Gedaliah, the son of that Ahikam who, at a critical moment, had helped to save the life of Jeremiah, and himself in all probability a supporter of Jeremiah's policy, was appointed ruler, with his seat of government, not at Jerusalem, but at Mizpah. We do not know the exact number of those who were sent to join the earlier band of exiles in Babylon—perhaps of men alone not less than ten thousand.

The fortunes of those over whom Gedaliah ruled form an interesting episode, on which, however, I cannot linger here. The attempt to revive, under sadly altered conditions, the national life, was doomed to failure: the murder of Gedaliah put an end to hopes which during his brief rule had still been cherished by some. Jeremiah, indeed, refused to abandon all hope even then, and after the rescue effected by Johanan the son of Kareah and his bands of freebooters, urged the people to "abide in the land," and to await in confidence a better time, which Yahveh the God of Israel would surely bring. Readers of Jeremiah will remember that his advice was rejected, and that the entire troop, including all the "remnant" which had been collected together at Mizpah, with the soldiers of Johanan and his brother captains, took refuge in Egypt. There, amid mournful surroundings of obstinate idolatry, his teaching spurned and misunderstood, his country waste and desolate, the curtain falls upon the great prophet's life in darkness and isolation. Neither those Jews who fled to Egypt, nor those who, after all ravages and deportations, still remained in Judah, contributed anything further to the development of their religion.[1]

Though four of our five Lamentations over the fall of Jerusalem were possibly written in Judah, and may serve as evidence "that the educated class was to some extent represented"[2] among those who were not carried into exile, the general level of religion must gradually have degenerated. The neighbouring tribes were not slow to make their way into the depopulated country, and to some extent to mix with the remaining Jews. The leaders of religious thought and the expounders of the religious literature had been deported to Babylon. To the exiles in Babylon, as Jeremiah and Ezekiel felt, the fortunes of their religion as well as their race were now entrusted.

The scene of the next Lecture will thus be laid in Babylonia. But before we take up the thread of history among the exiles, something must be said as to the degree of development which the religion had reached before the national life was thus violently interrupted.

It appeared likely that had Sennacherib captured Jerusalem in 701, and treated Judah as his father had treated Israel, the effects of national overthrow would have been the same in both cases. What had been the kind and degree of religious improvement in the hundred

[1] 2 Kings xxiv. 10—26 ; Jer. xxxix.— xliv.
[2] Cheyne, *Jeremiah*, p. 177.

210   IV. THE SEVENTH CENTURY:

and fifteen years which had elapsed between the fulfilment of Isaiah's prediction and the fulfilment of Jeremiah's? Upon the whole we may answer that it was not so much that there was any great advance upon the religious teaching of the eighth century, as that this teaching had been meanwhile widely enough accepted to consolidate and maintain the religious individuality of an exiled people. For although Jeremiah seems to have taught in isolation, it is to be borne in mind that he presented the prophetic doctrine in a peculiarly unattractive form. It was only a very few spiritual enthusiasts like himself or like Urijah who could digest more of that teaching than is reflected in Deuteronomy. But it was being more and more borne in upon widening circles of the people at large that Yahveh, Israel's God, was different in capacity and character from the gods of the heathen world, and that Israel in rank and destiny was other and higher than the surrounding nations.[1]

Of the religious level to which the best minds outside the prophetic circle had risen at the beginning of the sixth century, or, more precisely, after and through the religious awakening which followed upon the fall of Jerusalem, the Book of Lamentations (of which the third chapter, as a later addition, must be excluded) gives us a certain measure of insight.[2] Its writers are overwhelmed with

[1] Cf. Ezekiel xxv. 8.

[2] It is possible that the Lamentations were written in Babylon some while after the fall of Jerusalem. As Prof. Cheyne (*Expositor*, April, 1892, p. 258) has said, Lam. v. 20 "points rather to the *end* than to the beginning of the exile," and there are parallels between some verses in Lam. ii. and the Book of Ezekiel: cf. Cornill's *Einleitung*. But the general tone of the Lamentations seems to me to reflect no later

grief at their nation's fall: they lament the fate of "Yahveh's anointed, the breath of our nostrils," of the priests and prophets who were slain in Yahveh's sanctuary, for whose persons the fierce foe had no respect. Worst of all is the ruin of the temple, dishonoured by heathen spoilers whom Yahveh had forbidden to enter into his congregation, abhorred now by Yahveh himself. But throughout there runs the consciousness that the calamity has been sent because of transgression, for the sins of prophets and priests, who have shed the blood of the just in the midst of Jerusalem. "Yahveh is righteous; for I have rebelled against his commandments." These confessions are interspersed with wild cries of vengeance against the enemy, and especially against the neighbouring nations who exulted over Judah's fall and showed even more cruelty than the Babylonians themselves. Surely the anger of God must now be satisfied —the old thought of Jehoiakim's day and Zedekiah's. And another not unfamiliar voice is also heard, which we shall hear again in Babylonia: if Yahveh is wrathful still, it must be for iniquities of the past generations, for the sins, perhaps, of Manasseh's reign, even yet unatoned. "Our fathers have sinned and are not, and we have borne their iniquities."

Thus the Lamentations display many elements of the prophetic teaching, though in forms less pure than in the prophetical writings themselves, and mingled with alien

teaching than Jeremiah's, and I have therefore noticed them in this place: cf. also Löhr, *Die Klagelieder des Jeremias*, 1891, pp. 26, 27; Dyserinck, "De klaagliederen uit het Hebreeuwsch opnieuw vertaald," *Theol. Tijd.*, 1892, p. 359, &c.

and lower ideas. Not as yet is the whole of what the prophets have taught incorporated in the national consciousness. Most conspicuous by their absence, though this absence is sufficiently accounted for by the circumstances of the time, are allusions to the prophetic universalism and to the advent of a golden or "Messianic" age. The darkness of the present is not lit up by any steady ray of hope for the future.

There were two further reasons why the exile of 586 produced a religious result different from that which would have followed upon an exile in 700. In the first place, it was of considerable importance that the deportations did not take place all at once, but that the first colony of exiles had ten years in which to grow habituated to its anomalous religious position, before temple and state were finally destroyed. Secondly, the people took with them into their exile a considerable religious literature, in the study, development, editing and expounding of which there lay a rich store of compensation for sacrifice and temple ceremonial. Religious teachers were better equipped in 586 than they would have been in 700. The priests, in spite of the bitter accusations brought against them by Jeremiah, were many of them very different from the priests of Hosea: if they still clung to temple-worship and to much outward ceremonialism, they had also imbibed the doctrines of the one and single Yahveh and of civic morality. The exiles of Judah had thus ampler and better spiritual fare to sustain them in the foreign land than the exiles of Israel. Hence it is that some of the noblest chapters of the Old Testament were written upon alien soil.

It is a more doubtful and delicate question whether the seventh century witnessed any progress in the religion itself; whether Jeremiah taught a fuller and purer faith than Isaiah. A generation ago it was supposed that a considerable quantity of Biblical material was to be assigned to the seventh century; Job, the noble introduction to Proverbs, and many of the finest Psalms, were usually regarded as contemporary with Jeremiah. But a later criticism, which I believe to be more accurate, has relegated Job, Proverbs and the Psalter, to the post-exilic era. For seventh-century literature there remain only Deuteronomy, Nahum, Zephaniah, Habakkuk and Jeremiah. Nor are we even yet free from further limitation. By far the greatest of the seventh-century writers is Jeremiah; but his book, because of its very popularity, has been undoubtedly subjected to accretions and revisions, the exact number and extent of which it would be hard to estimate with certainty. The result is that it is difficult to ascertain with accuracy every element of Jeremiah's teaching, while many of the usual test and illustrative passages are of disputed authenticity. A single instance will make my meaning clear. In a most valuable, if too *doctrinaire*, monograph upon the theology of the Prophets, published in 1875, Prof. Duhm gives a sketch of the religious teaching of each prophet individually. He finds the central point of Jeremiah's religion in the spiritual communion (*sittlich-religiöse Gemeinschaft*) of the individual soul with God. But almost all the passages upon which Duhm relies for the proof or elaboration of his opinion are included among those which

Prof. Stade, in his "History of Israel," has noted as secondary and unauthentic![1]

There seem, however, to be two points in which some religious advance was made. In the first place, it would appear that at the close of the seventh century or at the opening of the sixth the monotheistic position had been finally achieved. Without in any way relinquishing his special function as God of Israel, Yahveh became the only divine power for earth and heaven. Jewish monotheism had passed beyond the stage of monolatry. But it was not till the end of the exile that emphasized religious use was made of the larger doctrine. Monolatry passed into monotheism gradually and half-unconsciously; other more present and pressing subjects were before the minds of the seventh-century prophets and lawgivers, to the exclusion of such a theoretical question as the impotence and unreality of other gods, not only for Israel (which had been urged before and was now urged again), but also for the heathen nations themselves. Yet as the dates of great achievements, whether in material discovery or spiritual revelation, have a peculiar interest, it is worth remarking that the prophecies of Jeremiah and the writings of the later Deuteronomists scarcely admit of any other interpretation than that their writers had reached, though they may not have fully realized, the pure monotheistic conception.

It is hardly justifiable, with Prof. Stade, to discount the evidence of such monotheistic passages either by excising them as secondary, or by explaining away their seemingly obvious meaning. Most critics suppose that

[1] *Geschichte*, Vol. I. p. 646, n. 2.

the Song of Moses was written before the fall of Jerusalem, and its language upon the point at issue is clear and decisive: "I, yea I, am He (i.e. the God), and there is no God beside me."[1] And in a famous verse in the fourth chapter of Deuteronomy, compiled probably at the end of the seventh or the beginning of the sixth century, the latent or practical monotheism of the eighth-century prophets has passed into a monotheism which is conscious and theoretic, and is pressed home to its full conclusion: "Know, therefore, this day, and consider it in thine heart, that Yahveh he is the God, in heaven above and upon the earth beneath; there is none else."[2] In this one fundamental dogma of its faith, the unity of God, nascent Judaism has here reached its goal. From that statement in the fourth chapter of Deuteronomy there was not, and there needed not to be, either advance or development.[3]

Even in Jeremiah we notice the growing identification of the heathen god with his image, which is so marked in Deutero-Isaiah. The heathen "gods" cannot "profit;" the apostasy of Israel is contrasted with the fidelity of the heathen to their idols, and yet these deities are no gods at all: "Hath any nation changed their gods, which yet are no gods? but my people have changed their glory for that which does not profit."[4]

Yahveh is the fountain of living waters; the idols

---

[1] Deut. xxxii. 39.   [2] Deut. iv. 39.

[3] Most scholars consider the Song of Moses to be prior to the Babylonian captivity. Zunz, and following him Cornill, assign it, however, to the exile; and Cornill does the like for Deut. iv. 39, pp. 38, 71.

[4] xi. 11.

are cisterns, broken cisterns, that can hold no water. Unequivocal is the impassioned exclamation of the prophet at the end of the sixteenth chapter: "O Yahveh, my strength and my fortress, and my refuge in the day of affliction, nations shall come unto thee from the ends of the earth, and shall say, Surely our fathers inherited lies, vanity and things wherein there is no profit."

Yahveh, as the only God, is the ruler and disposer of all the earth. This is indicated again and again in Jeremiah's prophecies. But, owing possibly to the exigencies of the age, the storm-and-stress period under which the prophet lived and wrote, we find but small space allotted to universalist hopes and predictions. They are not wanting, but they are neither prominent nor numerous. The development of a national religion into a religion nearly universal was reserved for the great prophet of the exile.

A second point of possible religious advance is more problematical. We saw that the prophets of the eighth century were concerned with the state as a whole rather than with the individual. They were not preachers to the individual conscience, but preachers to the nation; they tried to purge the body politic of sin, to transform it from bad to good, to eradicate public vices such as cruelty, injustice, licentiousness; their business did not lie with the souls of individual sinners, nor were they at pains to point out to every erring man how he might be freed from the bondage and oppression of sin. They assumed that man's will was free, and that repentance was within his power. Being evil, he could yet choose to be good. Thus Isaiah says: "Wash you, make you clean; cease to do evil, learn to do well." Prof. Cheyne speaks of the "imperfect moral conceptions of Isaiah" in this passage, implying that the prophet was ignorant that the necessary complement to every appeal to repentance is a prayer for God's grace whereby the desired repentance may be realized.[1] And this grace of God is conceived as operative by the help of the indwelling divine spirit within each individual soul. Such doctrines can only be formulated when religion is conceived individually, when the two terms of the reciprocal relation are God and man, and no longer God and the nation. In these matters it is above all things necessary to avoid exaggeration. One runs a danger of becoming the slave of words, and of applying abstractions to explain the manifold and multiform tendencies which are concurrent in every epoch. Are we to believe that disciples of Hosea and Isaiah in the eighth century did not pray to Yahveh that he might pardon their sins? Did they not feel personal joy in their relation as Israelites to him, and mortification at their private and individual shortcomings? Did Hosea, in his own chamber, not because he was unselfishly absorbed in the welfare of his people, but because "he had no conception of the relation of Yahveh to the individual soul apart from the nation,"[2] never commune in prayer with his God? Was not Isaiah able to discern a difference between "the righteous and the wicked in Zion," and to promise to the former salvation, and to threaten the latter with the judgment?[3] Doubtless, however, the solidarity of society was a con-

---

[1] *Jeremiah*, p. 39. [2] Cheyne, *Hosea*, p. 31.
[3] Isaiah xxix. 19, 20, viii. 16.

ception which had great influence upon religious ideas. Men not merely believed that they suffered because of their fathers' sins, or from the sins of a majority among their own contemporaries, but they seem also to have themselves felt personally sinful for the same reason. And similarly, when the nation accepted a new religious code, or when public reforms were made in national observance, individuals appear to have felt themselves "justified" by the national act, as if they too had experienced a personal share in the righteousness of the popular movement. There was thus both room and need for a growth of individualism in religion, and it would seem (although Prof. Stade denies it) that in the seventh century the highest minds did make some real progress in this direction. Kuenen believes that the thirty-second and thirty-third chapters of Isaiah may be assigned to this epoch, in which "the national representation of Yahvism gradually gave way to a more individual conception."[1]

Jeremiah himself is, however, the safest evidence of the change. His isolated position and the perpetual struggle which was going on within his own soul between fidelity to his divine calling and his natural sympathies and weaknesses, compelled him, in Wellhausen's words, to reflect almost more upon his own relation to Yahveh than upon Israel's, so that his peculiar circumstances became the means enabling him to consider more generally the relation of the individual man to God. Feeling, as he did, that his own difficult part

[1] *Onderzoek*, 2nd ed., Vol. II. p. 87. They are more probably post exilic. So Stade and Cheyne.

in life was not only ordered, but rendered possible by God, so that he was not merely driven to foretell his people's ruin, but was sustained in doing so by divine power, he was possibly led on to note God's function and operation in the process of repentance as applied to individuals. Thus we meet with exclamations such as, "Heal me, O Yahveh, and I shall be healed; save me, and I shall be saved." And, again, there is the prayer put into Ephraim's mouth: "Turn thou me, and I shall return, for thou art Yahveh my God."[1] The prophet (unlike Isaiah) does not believe that the judgment will be enough to ensure a new heart to the people which have so long walked in stubbornness. The new heart must be the gift of God. "I will give them an heart to know me that I am Yahveh;" "I will give them one heart and one way that they may fear me for ever; I will put my fear in their hearts."[2] God will meet half-way the penitents who "seek for him with all their hearts." Thus in that ideal age which Jeremiah, in the midst of the tumult of the nation's fall, no less confidently predicted than the prophets of the preceding century, if iniquity be still found in the regenerated community, its consequences shall not reach beyond the limits of the sinner. "In those days they shall say no more," runs the famous passage in the 31st chapter—relegated by Stade to a nameless prophet of the exile, but retained as Jeremiah's by Kuenen;—"the fathers have eaten sour grapes, and the children's teeth are set on edge. But every one shall die for his own iniquity:

---

[1] Jer. xvii. 14, xxxi. 18; cf. Lam. v. 21.
[2] Jer. xxxii. 39, 40, xxiv. 7.

every man that eateth sour grapes, his teeth shall be set on edge."[1] Thus the law of individual responsibility, which had been already laid down in Deuteronomy as a principle of human punishment, is to be extended in the Messianic age to the sphere of religion. Jeremiah implies that men in his own time were unable to shake off the bondage of religious solidarity; even he had not entirely risen above the idea which we meet with in the Book of Kings, that the sins of Manasseh were not fully expiated before the exile. But in the good time coming men would no longer be held responsible for their fathers' iniquities. The longer Jeremiah contemplated the bright vision of the ideal Israel of the future, the more glowing became the terms in which he described it. Yahveh will make a new covenant with Israel which will be in its very nature indissoluble. When he brought the Israelites out of Egypt, he bade them obey his voice and walk in his ways, so that they might be his people and he might be their God; but the commandment, though often repeated by prophet after prophet, was unheeded: that covenant was broken. In the new covenant, the same teaching which was then imposed from without and disregarded, will be written in the heart. This divine teaching will make the human teacher unnecessary. All former sins of the community will be forgotten; it will start afresh with the knowledge of God common to all, from the least to the greatest; and the purpose of the old covenant will be fulfilled in the new, for Israel will be Yahveh's people, and Yahveh will be Israel's God.[2]

[1] xxxi. 29, 30.   [2] xxxi. 31—34.

Such is Jeremiah's vision of the Messianic age. But no wide conclusions may be justly inferred from it as to the prophet's conception of the function of law in religion, or of the value of Deuteronomy. The new covenant does not "consciously and emphatically exclude law from the idea of the perfect religion."[1] No attack upon law in the abstract, or upon Deuteronomy in the concrete, entered here into the prophet's mind. All that he implies is that an external law would become unnecessary if its contents were written beforehand in the heart. For though the subject-matter of religion, under the new covenant as under the old, might be capable of expression in legal terms, the teaching of it would become needless, because it would be universally known. What, however, this famous passage does definitely indicate is, that its author predicted for a future—ideal, it is true, but in his belief neither impossible nor remote—the direct relation of Yahveh to every individual Israelite, "from the greatest unto the least," and a permanent divine aid by which each one might be spiritually re-born to a holy life in the knowledge of God.[1]

Of such a kind was the advance of the seventh century. It was, however, by no uniform and equable body of religious doctrine that the exiles were to maintain their separateness in foreign homes. There was still an imperfect fusion of higher and lower elements, both of which were accentuated and developed during the years of exile. Yet before the end of our journey is reached, it will be partly seen how either element contributed its quota to the gradual formation of a more coherent and articulate faith.

[1] Duhm, p. 242.   [2] Cf. Cheyne, *Jeremiah*, p. 157.

Lecture V.

THE BABYLONIAN EXILE: EZEKIEL AND THE SECOND ISAIAH.

THE history of the Hebrew religion during the exile in Babylon is the subject of this Lecture; a period lies before us unique in the world's records and issuing in unique results. A small fragment of a small people, transplanted by force from its own to an enemy's land, after remaining there for half-a-century without disintegration or coalescence with its environment, is then able to return to its own soil and resume its political life, with national and religious identity emphasized by fifty years of trial and suspense. This striking issue of the fall of the Judæan monarchy was due to the joint operation of many concurrent causes. We saw in the last Lecture that the earlier deportation took place in the year 597, eleven years before the final siege and sack of Jerusalem. Thus during the eleven years in which the central political life was still continued, the first exiles, who, if not the more numerous, were certainly the more important section of the community, had an incentive to maintain their national and religious distinctiveness—an incentive which was all the stronger, in so much as it was fortified by hopes of speedy restoration.

V. THE BABYLONIAN EXILE.

When the rebellion of Zedekiah forced Nebuchadrezzar to put an end to the turbulent little monarchy which would not recognize the political facts of the age, the chance, such as it was, of the maintenance of Israel's religion depended wholly upon the steadfastness of the exiles. To the second deportation were probably assigned lands at some distance from those allotted to the first; indeed, there were most likely several colonies of Jews dotted about the province of Babylon. Of their circumstances we know little, for the evidence is limited to a few allusions in Ezekiel and in those fragments of anonymous prophecy which date from the close of the exile. It would seem, however, that the conditions of life were upon the whole peaceful and even prosperous: the exiles owned lands and houses, and the same social organization which existed in Judæa was maintained in Babylonia. The Jewish colonies were left pretty much to themselves, and, with certain restrictions, internal autonomy was probably allowed to them. Thus the elders and judges of Judæa were also the judges and elders in Babylonia, and the social differences of rich and poor, high-born and low-born, were as familiar as at home. The old families and clans seem mostly to have lived together on their own lands.[1]

Such circumstances were, upon the whole, favourable to a rapid integration of the exiles into the body of the Babylonian empire. That the issue was so widely different was mainly due to the religion which the exiles carried with them from Judæa, and it indicates a fuller popular acceptance of prophetic teaching than might

[1] Cf. Stade, *Geschichte*, Vol. II. pp. 3—6.

have been inferred from the apparent isolation of Jeremiah. Yet the Book of Ezekiel sufficiently shows us the chaos of conflicting religious ideas current among the exiles. It is amazing how the short space of some fifty or sixty years was enough to bring into tolerable order and consistency this incoherent mass of old and new, of popular superstitions and prophetic doctrine. Both in thought and production the period of the exile was one of great religious activity, and the impulses then begun continued after the restoration both in Judæa and in Babylonia.

We saw in the last Lecture how the first deportation under Jehoiachin had not sufficed to dissipate certain deep-seated religious convictions either among the exiles or among those who remained behind, and how even the final blow did not by any means immediately avail to win over the majority to the religion of Jeremiah. For the prophets' conception of God and the religion which they taught required and presupposed a larger measure of ethical capacity than the majority possessed, and not even an event of such significance as the fall of Jerusalem, establishing though it did the truth of Jeremiah's predictions and the moral supremacy of the God in whose name he uttered them, was able to precipitate an ethical transformation.

There were many other interpretations of the fall of Jerusalem besides the interpretation of Jeremiah, and even that interpretation suggested new problems. To the idolatrous section of the community, for whom Yahveh was little other or more than Chemosh or Moloch, the sack of Yahveh's temple and the deportation of his people could only signify the impotence of a Deity who had so signally failed to protect his own. A transfer of allegiance to the gods of the conqueror would seem the most logical and prudent consequence. Moreover, even of those whose loyalty to Yahveh had been least hesitating, it was only a select few who had advanced beyond monolatry into monotheism. To most of them, convinced, as we have seen, that the temple at Jerusalem was the dwelling-place of Yahveh, its destruction must have given a paralyzing shock. Yahveh, as God of the land, could be worshipped, according to old ideas, within the land only; and though religion had greatly developed since David, the inviolability which Isaiah had so triumphantly claimed for Zion, and the Deuteronomic reform under Josiah, had both of them done something to revive in another form this waning superstition. For if Yahveh dwelt in Zion, where was he now that the temple had fallen? And even before it fell, how could he be worshipped in Babylon? Did not the Law itself forbid the sacrificial worship of Yahveh except in the sanctuary of Jerusalem? How was the religion of Yahveh to be maintained in the foreign land without its external embodiment? There was a natural temptation to satisfy the religious instinct either by worshipping Yahveh in forbidden ways or by worshipping Babylonian gods. For between Josiah's reform and the exile, even the inhabitants of the more distant country villages had not been so utterly cut off from the worship of God and from the practice of religious rites as were the exiles in Babylonia. Judæa was Yahveh's land, even though some could visit his temple but seldom; first-fruits and tithes could at any rate be sent to Jerusalem, and the produce of the soil was sanctified by that religious service. But the strange land and its produce were alike unclean, and the uncleanness would seem to attach itself to those who now perforce were driven into it. Although the Deuteronomic reform had made men accustomed to eat flesh without a sacrifice, we learn from Ezekiel that idolatry, by which he apparently means, not only the worship of other gods, but the irregular worship of Yahveh, with images and sacrifices (sometimes even human sacrifices), was not without its votaries among the exiles of the first deportation.[1]

Thus there was a choice of difficulties: driven out of Yahveh's land, men might think that the God of the vanquished nation had been vanquished too, and draw the legitimate conclusion that to such a God it was useless to maintain allegiance; or, if they wished to continue loyal to the God of their old home, they were unable to do him service, unable to translate their beliefs into acts of outward and visible ceremonial. Nor was this all. Even if Yahveh was the author of their misfortune, confusion was still rife as to his motives, and the consequences of the exile were still doubtful. A lack of moral perception, and an inadequate or partial appropriation of prophetic teaching, conduced to these perplexities.

In the first deportation, the spiritual descendants of those who in Manasseh's reign had interpreted Josiah's defeat and death as the result of Yahveh's incalculable and purposeless anger were now ready to suppose that

[1] Ezekiel xx. 31, 32; but cf. now Prof. Davidson's *Commentary*, pp. xxi, xxii (1892).

the divine indignation must have spent its force, and that Yahveh's people would soon be restored to Yahveh's land. Perhaps this belief was not wholly abandoned even after the destruction of the capital. Or, again, the conception of national and hereditary solidarity was darkened by a hitherto unheard-of terror. The "rebellious house," unable to recognize the moral canker in its own heart, was willing to admit that defeat and exile were the punishment of sin; but the sin was their fathers' and not their own. Had not even Jeremiah, the great prophet and preacher of repentance, himself declared that because of Manasseh, king of Judah, and for that which he did in Jerusalem, Yahveh would make his "people to be a shuddering unto all the kingdoms of the earth"?[1] The visitation of the sins of fathers upon children was a method of divine punishment perhaps consistent in isolated cases with divine justice: when, however, it was thought that a whole race was paying so great a penalty for the guilt of a past generation, there was an instinctive protest, suggested all the more readily by the repeated declaration of the prophets that Yahveh's justice was absolute. "Our fathers have sinned and are not," men said; "and as for us, we bear their iniquities."[2] The proverb, "The fathers have eaten sour grapes, and the children's teeth are set on edge," may erewhile have been framed to illustrate a fact which did not clash with old Israelite conceptions of Yahveh's justice; but now, after the ruin of the entire nation, it was quoted bitterly from mouth to mouth, and flung in Ezekiel's teeth when he proclaimed the righteousness of God.[3]

[1] Jer. xv. 4.   [2] Lam. v. 7; cf. Lev. xxvi. 39.   [3] Ezekiel xviii. 2.

Lastly, if the prophetic verdict was accepted, if some were ready to believe that the exile was the legitimate result not only of ancestral, but also of present and personal iniquity, the moral drawn too often overshot the mark. The prophets had said, Repent! but repentance, as some would hold, was now too late. The vital sap was gone from Israel; "the bones were dry, the hope was lost."[1] Men turned impatiently away, whether the prophet threatened or comforted. So great a calamity, indicating and implying so great a burden of sin, could not be recompensed or undone. Their transgressions lay heavy upon them, they said; they pined away in their iniquities.[2] A national resurrection was impossible: helpless despair was the only alternative to rebellious murmur and idolatrous apostasy.

Such were the diverse fragments of religious thought which the higher teachers of the exile had to cope with and correct. In the sixty years between the first deportation and the return, many tendencies of the pre-exilic religion were not only largely developed, but gradually converged towards each other so as to form a comparatively harmonious whole. And yet the harmony was at bottom rather apparent than real. It was during the exile that the two conflicting elements of later Judaism, its pure and absolute monotheism, and its intense and peculiar particularism, were both securely founded in the popular consciousness.

The fall of Jerusalem was the triumph of prophecy. From Amos to Jeremiah, the prophets had shown a marked indifference or hostility to ceremonial worship.

[1] Ezekiel xxxvii. 11.   [2] Ezekiel xxxiii. 10.

An anonymous prophet of Manasseh's reign had gone still further, and contemptuously coupled the offering of calves and rams with the sacrifice of first-born sons.[1] It might have been expected, therefore, that the development of religion in the exile would have proceeded along the same lines, and that a restored Judæan commonwealth would have attached less, rather than more, importance to an exact regulation of sacrificial worship and outward rite than was attached to it in the code of Deuteronomy. The contrary happened. We have, then, to regard the exile as a preparation both for the later Judaism, which could live religiously without sacrificial worship, and for the earlier Judaism of the second temple, in which that worship was apparently its most essential feature.

In the exile faithful worshippers of Yahveh had perforce to learn how to maintain their religious separateness without distinctive ceremonial. As a consequence, such rites as were not dependent upon the temple, and could be observed outside Judæa, acquired gradually a novel importance. Circumcision, which hitherto had been a custom, taken for granted, but without pronouncedly Yahvistic colour, and consequently ignored in Deuteronomy, came now to be regarded as a special divine ordinance distinguishing the sons of Abraham from other races of the world.

Of equal or greater importance is the new emphasis placed upon the Sabbath. Though its observance as a day of rest had been included among the ordinances of the Decalogue, there is no evidence that the violation

[1] Micah vi. 6, 7.

of it was wont to meet with special prophetic rebuke before the exile.[1] Even to Ezekiel, in whose book we find the first authentic reference in the prophetic literature to its "pollution," the Sabbath is a matter of temple ceremonial rather than of religious law extending beyond the sanctuary and Judæa.[2] But while it is not included in the catalogue of duties obligatory upon the individual, it is declared to have been instituted as a sign between Yahveh and the children of Israel that Yahveh was their God. Upon the Sabbath, in the time of the exile, it is not impossible that the first informal meetings were held for common prayer and for the recitation of older prophecies, histories and laws, which were afterwards systematized into the glorious institution of the synagogue. Feeble substitutes these irregular gatherings must have seemed to all who took part in them, and especially to the priests who may have organized and directed them, for the solemn and effective ritual of the temple. And yet the feeble substitutes were destined to destroy for ever the charm and potency of that gross worship of God, which in the view of even the best among the exiles was but temporarily suspended.

For the worship of Yahveh in his own chosen sanctuary was a precious memory to the faithful. Its value was magnified in their eyes because the chief sin of Judah and the primary cause of the exile had been the false worship of Yahveh and its association with the worship of other gods. Jeremiah had himself enunciated

[1] Jeremiah xvi. 19—27 is not authentic; cf. Kuenen, *Onderzoek*, *ad loc.* Amos viii. 5 is scarcely in point.

[2] Ezekiel xx. 12, &c.

this view with emphatic vehemence. But whereas he was able to unite a belief that the false and idolatrous worship had provoked Yahveh's utmost anger with a depreciation of outward worship in general, most of those who explained Yahveh's anger on the same lines set a very different value upon ritual observances. To them, the enormity of the false worship as measured by its punishment implied and proved the importance of the true. Priests would naturally be the foremost to draw this inference. The code of Deuteronomy stood midway between the position of Jeremiah and that of the faithful priesthood in the exile. For while it laid greater stress upon the elimination of false worship, it contained some regulations for the conduct of the true, and these regulations were now part and parcel of an acknowledged and accepted law.

An intense conviction that a false worship of Yahveh and an idolatrous worship of other gods had been the capital offence of Israel made itself felt in every department of religious activity during the exile period. And in this conviction there was thus almost necessarily involved a concurrent exaltation of the true worship as an integral and important element in the religion of Yahveh.

We may trace both these tendencies in the editings of the older historical records. That long chronicle of Israelite history which is contained in the books of Judges, Samuel and Kings, was reduced to its present shape by writers of the Deuteronomic school. Part of their work was done between Josiah's death and the fall of the monarchy, but it was carried on and almost completed during the exile. It is unnecessary for our present purpose to distinguish the pre-exilic from the exilic additions, inasmuch as the same spirit pervades them all. These books did not indeed escape further additions and interpretations in the post-exilic period; but their main character, the framework in which the facts are arranged and the uniform lesson they are made to teach, were the product of the periods immediately before, and either during, or soon after, the exile.

The most noteworthy feature in these writers' conception of their nation's past is its pessimism. From the death of Joshua to the exile of Jehoiachin, the history of Israel has been one long scene of apostasy and ingratitude.[1] The sweeping judgment of Hosea and Jeremiah on their people's past is systematized and even exaggerated by the historical editors. From them is derived that impression of perpetually recurring idolatry, interspersed by intervals of repentance after chastisement and deliverance, which the whole period from Joshua's death to the foundation of the monarchy is made to present. From them proceeds that emphasized insistance that the desire for a king was equivalent to the rejection of Yahveh.[2] For Israel was no longer a nation as other nations were, it was a religious community with a religious mission to fulfil. The moral which the history, thus interpreted and coloured, is intended to convey is that God had always been just and gracious, Israel always disobedient

[1] Judges ii. 11—19, x. 6—16, &c.; 2 Kings xvii. 7, &c.
[2] 1 Sam. viii. 7.

and intractable. After the establishment of the monarchy, David for a short period realized the ideal. There was no idolatry; the worship of Yahveh was centralized at Jerusalem. The law of Moses was thus at last obeyed, for the reign of David had now become, both popularly and religiously, the standard in accordance with which all men prayed that God would fulfil his promises: political power, religious purity, both integral elements of the Messianic hope, were then for one brief period united together. At David's death the descent began. The ingrained desire for idolatry and idolatrous worship showed itself anew; and this, the distinctive sin of Israel and Judah, continuing with fitful intermissions from age to age, compelled Yahveh to root them up out of the land which they had defiled.

Thus the judgment passed upon Israel is always dominated by a single tendency. Whereas the prophets had combined the charge of idolatry with the charge of immorality, the historians dwelt exclusively upon the former. Even Hosea, however much he puts Baal-worship at the head and front of Israel's offending, makes God declare that he will avenge the blood of Jezreel upon the house of Jehu. The historian, on the contrary, at the end of the narrative of Jehu's bloody purgation, makes God promise to the destroyer of Baal the possession of the throne for four generations, because "he had been zealous in doing that which was right in the eyes of Yahveh."[1] This is the point of view of Deuteronomy pushed to a one-sided extreme. And thus we see how,

[1] Hosea i. 4; 2 Kings x. 30.

in the exile, when the external worship of Yahveh was at an end, its importance grew with the very fact of its cessation.[1]

As it was with the writers or adapters of history, so it was with the collectors of laws. Whether the historical editors were priests or laymen, we cannot tell: the code-makers of the exile undoubtedly belonged to priestly circles. We do not know whether the priests of Jerusalem already possessed written rules for the temple service and the ceremonial rites connected with their office. It is, however, improbable that these existed in any considerable number. The teaching of the priesthood was oral and traditional, maintained by custom and practice. In the exile, however, the need would arise for the preservation by written record of the true priestly tradition. When the promise of restoration should be fulfilled, and the temple rebuilt, it could be only from a written code that the priests of that brighter age would learn to serve Yahveh's altar correctly, or teach the layman his ritual duties.

Thus the priests began to codify the traditions of their order, and these rules were destined to become part of an accepted divine law, with an authority equal to that of Deuteronomy. For many customs of the temple were of unknown antiquity, and it was implied in Deutero-

[1] Cf. Chavannes, *La Religion dans la Bible*, Vol. I. p. 273. His attack upon the Deuteronomistic school seems, however, to be somewhat exaggerated. Can we assume that these writers had no interest in morality? Did not the true worship of Yahveh involve civic justice and neighbourly compassion?

nomy, though it was denied by Jeremiah, that such customs were as ancient and as authoritative as the moral ordinances of the Decalogue and the Book of the Covenant. Ezekiel accepts this point of view and enforces it, and it is not subsequently contested. Remains of such earlier codifications of pre-exilic practice are preserved to us as portions of a larger whole which, though its birthplace was Babylonia, was not composed till after the return from the exile, and cannot, therefore, come before us till the next Lecture. But this larger whole borrowed most of these remnants at second-hand from a minor code, which was itself the product of separate collections. Though the language of this code, especially in one famous chapter, resembles that of Ezekiel, from whom some of its ideas are borrowed, its general conceptions are parallel rather than imitative, and it may, therefore, though somewhat out of the chronological order, be noticed by us here.

Originally it is supposed to have included considerable portions of Leviticus xvii.—xxvi., together possibly with some other of the older priestly sections in Leviticus and Numbers. It was put, like Deuteronomy, into the mouth of Moses; for the colophon to the code, appended to the concluding exhortation in Leviticus xxvi., boldly states: "These are the statutes and judgments and laws, which Yahveh made between him and the children of Israel in mount Sinai by the hand of Moses." The perilous example of Deuteronomy was thus literally followed. As the compiler of this code lays great and repeated stress upon the kindred ideas of purity and sanctity, defilement and profanation, it has received from Prof. Klostermann the commonly accepted surname of the Law of Holiness.[1]

It is characteristic of the priest that the conception of sanctity extends both to ceremonial worship and moral integrity, and is applied equally to persons and to things. The Law of Holiness includes that short collection of moral ordinances which culminates in the famous injunction, "Thou shalt love thy neighbour as thyself."[2] Yet the love of neighbour and stranger, and the honouring of mother and father, are no more and no less elements of holiness than the smallest ceremonial observance. Israel, as Yahveh's people, must keep itself free from uncleanness of every kind, that the land may not be defiled and Yahveh's name profaned. Sin is impurity; it is thus regarded less as the guilt of the individual, the secret taint of his own heart, than as the pollution which affects the land and community of Yahveh.[3] This priestly conception is also strongly emphasized by the prophet Ezekiel, though he unites with it a marked individualism. Its close connection with ceremonial worship, and the importance which it implicitly assigns to that worship, are both indubitable.

Thus in two directions of exilic activity there is a growing attention paid to the ritual service of Yahveh, in spite, or rather because, of the absence of temple-worship. We have now to trace it in a third direction of greater interest and peculiarity, because it is combined with elements which had hitherto been free from

---

[1] For the Law of Holiness, cf. the *Introductions to the O. T.*, by Cornill, Driver and Kuenen.

[2] Lev. xix. 18.   [3] Cf. Lev. xviii. 25, xx. 3, 7.

priestly influences, and is expressed for us in the writings of an extraordinary man. We have seen in the Book of Deuteronomy the effects of a priestly and prophetic alliance; we have now in the Book of Ezekiel to observe the seer who, unlike his elder contemporary Jeremiah, when he became a prophet, remained a priest. But Ezekiel is too great a teacher, and occupies too important a place in the history of Israelite religion, to be used to illustrate a single tendency. That must only appear in its proper time and place in the general survey of his doctrine.

Though the fall of Jerusalem and of the monarchy was the triumph of prophecy, it was also in a certain sense its dissolution. Prophecy had grown up as a religious factor of Israelite life in close conjunction with the state. Its message had been directed to the people; its import was national. The main burden of that message was national judgment for national guilt. It is true that with the announcement of the judgment there was ever associated the promise of restoration. But this concerned the future and not the present; while it was the necessary complement of Yahveh's righteousness, it was the threat, and not the promise, which the prophets' contemporaries had to receive as Yahveh's message to themselves. But when the threat had been fulfilled, when the temple lay in ruins, and the people were exiled, the prophet's occupation was gone. Changed circumstances demanded a different quality of teaching. What was necessary now was so to transform the character of the exiles, that the promised restoration, the advent of the golden age, might not be too long delayed. The judgment had come;

men lived in it. The work before religious teachers now was to help Yahveh to the earlier fulfilment of his word. That side of the prophets' teaching which had before, as it were, filled up the gaps and intervals of their more public and definitive utterances—their labour as religious teachers, in the more modern sense of the word—came now prominently to the front. But since the office of teacher could be discharged by the priest as well as by the layman, and seeing that there now existed many priests who had absorbed and adopted some fundamental doctrines of the prophets, priests could resume their old place as the natural instructors of the community.

There was also another reason which helped to bring about the decay of prophecy. That reason was the law of Deuteronomy, now being supplemented by the priestly codifications. The teaching of Yahveh was becoming fixed in written codes; it was no longer the business of the teacher to listen in his own heart for the fresh inspiration of God, and to proclaim it before the world as Yahveh's message and bidding; his duty was to apply his spiritual insight and capacity to the ancient and authentic law of God, which in its origin and its fixity stood above the individual and determined his words.

Till the close of the exile, when the imminent deliverance once more let loose the spirit of prophecy, though of a prophecy very different from that of the monarchy, we hear of no other prophet but Ezekiel. There lived, indeed, among the exiles prophets who were to Ezekiel as Hananiah was to Jeremiah, but of the true line Ezekiel is the only known representative. It is, moreover, to be noticed that his prophetic call took place before the final siege and capture of Jerusalem, and that a main feature of his distinctly prophetic work was to predict the fall of the capital and the ruin of the monarchy.

Ezekiel resembles the prophets of the pre-exilic period in that his utterances included the same object as theirs—the announcement of a judgment. And he is still so dominated by this fundamental prophetic idea, that against the sinners among the exiles he can only fulminate the old threats, though in what the judgment upon them is to consist he does not indicate, and cannot have been himself aware.

The commanding figure of Ezekiel stands thus on the border-land between old and new, and unites the triple functions of prophet, priest and lawgiver. For the codes to which reference has just been made proceeded from circles in which Ezekiel had been the moving spirit, and their authors were perhaps stirred, or at least influenced, by his example. Many a point in the teaching of post-exilic Judaism may be traced back to Ezekiel as to its fountain-source. This may explain why Ezekiel has come in for so much of that vigorous and hostile criticism meted out by Christian scholars to Judaism. The full extreme of depreciation to which this criticism can extend is best instanced in Prof. Duhm's interesting book on the Theology of the Prophets.

To Duhm, Ezekiel is a dogmatic supernaturalist, in whom human sympathy and original inspiration are alike wanting. In his book there is not from end to end one single new idea of religious or ethical value. He materialized the prophetic conception of holiness; he changed the ideals of the prophets into laws and dogmas. His God imposes upon men an infinite series of isolated commands, which strangle all moral liberty. Adopting for his lower ends the language of the prophets, he speaks of a "new spirit" and a "heart of flesh;" but what is meant is a rigid and mechanical obedience to external enactments, not any inward freedom from sin in the true and Christian sense. In Ezekiel's new Jerusalem we have no longer anything to do with prophetical religion; we already breathe the air of Judaism and the Talmud.[1]

We saw how at the first exile, in the reign of Jehoiachin in the year 597, the *élite* of the Jewish state in all its orders was deported to Babylonia. Among the ministers of the Jerusalem temple, the aristocracy of the priesthood, the sons of Zadok, was Ezekiel. He was probably old enough at the time of the exile to have already officiated at Yahveh's altar, and he may have remembered as a boy the last years of Josiah's reign, in which the reform of Deuteronomy was in full effect, and the worship at the central sanctuary undefiled by semblance of idolatry. Ezekiel was a priest in the fullest sense of the word. Pure of heart, passionately attached to his God, and to his God's service, he probably lived and moved in the ideas and habits of his order. His zeal and affection for temple ceremonial and the altar of Yahveh are found reflected, in softer moods and phases, in many a hymn among the Psalter. But to Ezekiel, brought up in the priestly division of the Deuteronomic school, and clinging with all his might to that half-prophetic and half-priestly conception of Israel's sin

[1] Duhm, *Theologie der Propheten*, pp. 252—263.

and Israel's duty which has already come before us, this affection, upon Josiah's death, would soon be transformed into sombre passion. The past and the future of his people may already have been food for solemn reflection to the young man's mind, when he was taken from his chosen home and work, and transported with his fellow-exiles to "Tel-abib, by the river Chebar, in the land of the Chaldæans." There, without losing his special priestly proclivities, he was yet free to take a less narrow survey of his people's needs. In the leisure of the exile he could study and consider the teachings of the prophets, as well as those of his friends and kinsmen, the priests. He was drawn to replace his interrupted work at the altar by work for his God and for his people of another and a higher kind.

The same sins which had caused the captivity were still prevalent among the community at Tel-abib, and both at home and abroad the wrath of Yahveh was yet, and rightly, unappeased. False hopes were rife among the exiles; nor would they be able to give heed to the exhortations of their teachers till a doom, similar to, but more terrible than that which had befallen the Judah of Jehoiachin, befell the Judah of Zedekiah. Till Jerusalem had succumbed, there could be no prospect of repentance and restoration. By thoughts such as these we may imagine Ezekiel to have been drawn towards the office of teacher and prophet. In the fifth year of the exile, B.C. 592, six years before the final capture of Jerusalem, he felt able to begin his task, and "the word of Yahveh came unto him, and the hand of Yahveh was upon him." How long he lived afterwards is not precisely known; his vision of the new Jerusalem is dated in the twenty-fifth year of the exile, that is B.C. 572, and a note appended to one of the earlier prophecies is dated two years subsequently. Ezekiel must therefore have outlived the fall of the Judæan kingdom by at least fifteen years. From a literary point of view, the book of his prophecies stands alone in the Old Testament. It consists of an ordered series of discourses collected and arranged in their present form by the prophet himself. Though the text has been very badly preserved, and in the later chapters occasionally tampered with, there are no such interpolations or appended chapters of a later age as we meet with in Isaiah and Jeremiah; Ezekiel wrote and, as it would seem, arranged his own book from its beginning to its end.

Like Isaiah and Jeremiah before him, Ezekiel represents his call to the prophetic office as having been accompanied by a vision. But Ezekiel's visions are more frequent than those of the two older prophets, as well as more specialized and prolonged. Besides the inaugural vision by the river Chebar, there are three others, in two of which the *locale* is Jerusalem, whither Ezekiel is carried by the spirit, or the hand, of Yahveh.[1] It is very difficult to make out—nor is the inquiry of much profit—how far there was, or was meant to be, any actual spiritual experience of the prophet corresponding, even roughly, to the literary form as written down by him subsequent to the event. It is clear that whatever Ezekiel may have believed himself to have heard and seen in the visions must have been smaller and vaguer

[1] viii.—xi., xl.—xlviii., xxxvii.

than their detailed and elaborate reproduction in the present book of his prophecies. For the entire scheme of the new Jerusalem, the exact measurements of temple, city and land, the prescriptions for priests, Levites and prince, are all represented as having been supernaturally repeated to, or witnessed by, Ezekiel in the course of a single vision. Similarly, the description of the sins of the old Jerusalem before its destruction is set in the framework of a vision, in which historic personages are actually introduced, of whom one is said to have suddenly expired during Ezekiel's recitation of a prescribed prediction of the coming judgment.[1] Lastly, the inaugural vision contains that minute description of a strange theophany, in which Yahveh is represented in human shape upon a chariot formed of mysterious "living creatures"—the whole suggested to the prophet's imagination by a mixture of old memories of Phœnician symbolism in the Jerusalem temple with Babylonian sculpture perhaps before his eyes at Tel-abib. Parallel, too, with this tendency to give visionary setting to thoughts which he believed were sent to him by Yahveh, are the symbolic actions, more frequent in Ezekiel than in any other prophet. These, far more certainly than the visions, may be regarded as pictorial illustrations or metaphorical aids to the more vivid realization of his meaning.[2]

Ezekiel's book, as he apparently arranged it, is divided into two parts, of which the first deals with Judah's present and past, the second with its future and the

[1] xi. 13.
[2] Cf. Kuenen, *Onderzoek*, Vol. II., 2nd ed., p. 271 (with notes 11, 12, 13) and p. 282.

future of its neighbours. By far the greater portion of the first part consists of prophecies of the fall of Jerusalem. That fall was a necessary antecedent, in Ezekiel's eyes, to repentance and restoration. Indirectly, therefore, these prophecies concern the exiles, but their direct subject is the Judah of Palestine, and not the community in Babylonia. Similar in kind to the contemporary predictions of Jeremiah, they place the false worship of Yahveh and the various idolatries before the reader with a more ceaseless iteration and less frequent reference to moral obliquity. As in the case of Jeremiah, the earlier prophecies of Ezekiel, when they were collected after the fall of Jerusalem, received here and there the stamp and revision of fulfilment. But no more than Jeremiah's are they to be regarded as mere *vaticinia post eventum*.

While Ezekiel in comparatively few passages deals directly with his fellow-exiles of Tel-abib, we know from his own mouth that his prophetic mission was specially for them. The reason of this curious divergence between the space allotted to the Judah at home and to the Judah abroad, his own peculiar charge, is found in the fact that his unwritten and unrecorded labour was devoted to the "saving of souls" among the exiles. For there are several indications that a good deal of Ezekiel's most important work among the exiles in Babylonia lay outside the set and formal prophecies which are now collected in his book, resembling rather the duties of a religious teacher in modern times, and not capable of being expressed or elaborated in written words. He was appointed as a watchman to the house of Israel, to warn the wicked of the consequences of his wickedness, and the righteous who turned from his righteousness of the consequences of his backsliding. Such is the brief summary of his mission in the third chapter, but we cannot rightly understand it or measure its range without taking some other passages, as well as the general religious condition of the exiles, into our consideration.

We saw that there existed two extremes of religious opinion among the exiled Jews. There was, on the one hand, much complaint of Yahveh's injustice towards his own people, the still unshaken belief either that Israel had a claim on its God through its own merits, or that it was now suffering for the old and outworn sins of bygone generations; on the other hand, there was the willing confession of national iniquity, but accompanied by moral lethargy and religious despair. Ezekiel's duty, therefore, as a preacher of penitence and conversion, was to inspire both contrition and confidence. His business was to create a true religious hopefulness in the mercy of God, and a true religious humility as to the merits of man. This dual doctrine does not indeed appear in dogmatic or complete shape in Ezekiel's pages; while emphasizing one side of it, he often seems to ignore the other, and both sides need expansion and correction. But at the same time the deeply religious doctrine of humility combined with hope, which has played so great a part in one form or another both in Judaism and Christianity, owes its origin to Ezekiel.

Before we see how he applies it, it is necessary to point out that to Ezekiel this doctrine of humility and hope is but the converse of another doctrine of equal, if not greater, importance to the prophet's mind—the justification of God. Ezekiel conceived himself as sent with a religious mission to the house of Israel, but that he so conceived himself was due to his consuming jealousy for Israel's God. Like Elijah of old, he was very jealous for Yahveh, the God of Hosts, and was filled with the idea that God's honour was involved in the fortunes of Israel. Ezekiel regarded himself as Yahveh's champion. Hence his tremendous earnestness, and his power, far greater than Jeremiah's, of almost entirely suppressing his own personality in the discharge of his office.

It is commonly said that the Yahveh of Ezekiel represents a religious retrogression from the Yahveh of Isaiah or Jeremiah. Yahveh, to Ezekiel, is a Deity august, majestic and terrible. An infinite distance separates him from man. He is just to the very letter, but he is without tenderness and compassion. The God of Deuteronomy is loved: the God of Ezekiel is feared. Ezekiel's Yahveh is the prototype of the Allah of Islam.

If we impartially examine Ezekiel's conception of God, we shall find it to be a fusion of new and old. The prophet seems to share, or at least freely uses, the old and strange idea that God actually dwelt in the temple of Jerusalem, and in the restored community of the golden age would dwell there again for ever. Yet his defined earthly residence did not prevent Yahveh from having complete cognizance of what was passing in other places and in all human hearts. Together, moreover, with this circumscribed and semi-pagan conception, Ezekiel's Yahveh was also very properly separated from man by all that difference which must and does distinguish the human from the divine. The prophet is addressed by Yahveh as "son of man:" the creature must recognize his frailty and his dependence upon God. In special divine manifestations Ezekiel employs angels instead of, or together with, Yahveh as the interpreters of God's will. But all this exaltation of God's infinitude is of real religious value, and expresses one true aspect of the relation between Deity and man. It did not lead to any obscuration, either in Ezekiel or in the later Judaism—for every charge which is made against the Yahveh of Ezekiel is repeated with interest against the God of Judaism—of the other side of this relation, that, in spite of difference in kind and in degree, there can be real communion between man and God.

Yahveh is not more difficult to serve for Ezekiel than for Isaiah: he makes no greater demands upon his worshippers than the Yahveh of Jeremiah. The endless series of isolated commands exists only in Prof. Duhm's imagination. For Ezekiel, God is not farther off in his dealings with Israel than for any of his predecessors. Within the hearts of the regenerate Israelites the divine spirit is the bond of union and communion between them and God. Ezekiel's fear of God is the reverence of the freeman, not the terror of the slave. That this reverence need not degenerate into terror, is one of the prophet's most fundamental teachings. "I delight not in the death of the wicked; I have no pleasure in the death of him that dieth." The really unsatisfactory feature about Ezekiel's conception of God—though that, too, contains an important religious truth, and is re-echoed by many another teacher—is his one-sided insistance upon Yahveh's honour.

Solicitude for God's honour seems at first sight, and in some respects really is, vainly officious; it betokens an idle anxiety not to run counter to the designs of Providence. To Ezekiel, Israel and Yahveh are inseparables. When Israel through its sinfulness compelled Yahveh to leave his earthly dwelling-place and expel his people from its land, it disturbed a relation which for God's sake, as well as for Israel's, must ultimately be restored. The world exists for the glory of Yahveh, and the goal of history is not reached till, in Ezekiel's favourite words, it is known and understood of Gentile as well as Jew, though in a very different sense and with very different results by one than by the other, that "I am Yahveh." We can understand how the blessedness of man may be regarded as the glory of God, and how in man's labour for his fellow-man he may be stimulated to do his best by the idea that he is working for God's cause; but it is a false loyalty when, as in Ezekiel, the object of God's own management of human history, as regards the great majority of his creatures, is not that they may be reconciled to him—converted from their evil ways to lead a life of goodness and content—but that he may have the empty satisfaction of their acknowledgment, in the midst and by the means of desolation and carnage, that he is indeed a very mighty and powerful God.[1] It is remarkable that the great judgment upon the nations is not to accompany, but to succeed, the re-establishment of Israel in its own

---

[1] Prof. Davidson is inclined to give a larger and better interpretation to the "knowledge of Yahveh" as acquired by the nations. See his *Commentary*, p. xxxviii.

land. Its sole object, therefore, is the further and complete vindication of Yahveh's honour. At the cost of innumerable lives, the heathen are to learn that the catastrophe of Israel's exile was wholly due to Israel's sin. So only can Yahveh's omnipotence be brought home to them. It is Yahveh who stirs up Gog and his huge army to slay them with supernatural horrors upon Israelite soil. After their destruction the "Messianic" age continues undisturbed: "from that day and forward" Israel and the nations will both know Yahveh as in his relations to either he respectively is, the one as omnipotent and compassionate, the other as omnipotent and malign.[1] In later Apocalyptic developments, Ezekiel's fantastic idea of Gog's invasion after the Israelite restoration was expanded into a universal or last judgment, which was to form the end of temporal or even earthly history and the introduction to a new era.

A more detailed consideration of the judgment upon Gog and his confederates may here be neglected. For Ezekiel is far more attractive and valuable in his own special mission as a preacher of repentance—grounded on and conditioned by humility and hope—than as a theologian mapping out the purposes of God in the history of man. His justification of God's dealings with Israel only interests us now as the theoretic background for his doctrine of Israel's relation and duty towards Yahveh in the present and the future. As such only I would consider it here.

Like the Deuteronomistic editors of the historical records, Ezekiel has nothing but condemnation for Israel's

[1] xxxix. 22; cf. the whole of xxxviii. and xxxix.

past. He even extends the series of its apostasies still further back, and asserts that as the Israelites were given up to Egyptian idolatries when God made himself known to them as Yahveh, so did they perpetually rebel against him and follow their abominations from that time onwards.[1] Why this idolatrous and rebellious nation was chosen by Yahveh to be his human bride, is not definitely explained. But the choice and covenant once made, God's holy name was bound up with the history of Israel. Hence arose a terrible dilemma. Though Israel's sin was Yahveh's dishonour, the destruction of Israel would be a greater dishonour still, an open profanation before all the world, who knew that Israel was the people of Yahveh. No punishment short of ruin and divorce would be adequate for Israel's persistent guilt; but over against the Scylla of unsatisfied vengeance there stood the Charybdis of violated honour. Israel enjoys the benefit of this divine antinomy. God himself must make them capable of being pardoned and restored; he himself must free them from the sin, out of which they are unwilling or unable to emancipate themselves; he must give them a new heart, and put a new spirit within them, that they may walk in God's statutes and execute his will.[2]

This is Ezekiel's theodicy. The nation has nothing to complain of; it owed everything to God in the past, and will owe everything to him in the future. Wholly unmerited were the past benefits; wholly justified was the present punishment; wholly undeserved would be the future restoration. The theodicy seems framed to

[1] xvi., xxiii.   [2] xxxvi. 21—37.

suit the needs of those who heard it. For its human moral consists in shame and hope, in contrition and humility. And these contrasted qualities in their combination are equivalent to repentance. Thus Ezekiel's theodicy fits into and connects itself with his religious doctrine upon its directly human side, as expressed in his work as a shepherd of souls among the exiles at Tel-abib. Both led him on to his marked and even exaggerated individualism.

In the fall of the state a common calamity, whether banishment or death, had befallen alike good and bad.[1] It was only prophetic exaggeration which could assert that among the exiles in the first deportation there were not many faithful worshippers of Yahveh devoted to the law of Deuteronomy. What other explanation of their present misfortune could be found than that they suffered for their fathers' sins? It was not merely an undiscerning wilfulness which might employ the adage of the "sour grapes:" a reasoned despair might do the same.

In traversing the truth of this proverb, Ezekiel makes no attempt to deny its applicability to former events. That perhaps was impossible. He deals with the present and the future, and carefully ignores the past. God's message now is that the soul which sins shall die. By this is meant that the "judgment" of God shall overtake the sinner, while the righteous shall escape. Or, put reversely, there shall be a certain retribution for the wicked, and for the righteous assured "life." Not according to the proverb of the sour grapes, in which past

[1] With momentary inconsistency, Ezekiel in one solitary passage admits and even emphasizes the fact, xxi. 8, 9 (Heb.), R.V. 3, 4.

generations had seen no injustice, but against which the generation of the exiles, while still believing it, protested, is the method of God's retributive relation with man. God's ways are equal. "The son shall not bear the iniquity of the father, neither shall the father bear the iniquity of the son: the righteousness of the righteous shall be upon him, and the wickedness of the wicked shall be upon him."[1] Individualism is pushed even further. Experience shows that the man who is "righteous" to-day is not always righteous on the morrow. Nor, again, is there any reason why the sinner should not repent and become righteous. The descent from righteousness to sin, and the ascent from sin to righteousness, are alike possible within the limits of a single life. In these cases the law of retribution is modified to meet the altered circumstances: the sinner, who was once righteous, shall be punished; the righteous, who was once sinful, shall "live."

Ezekiel does not clearly define his meaning, and probably there were two somewhat inconsistent notions concurrently in his mind: on the one hand, the simple moral idea that "it is never too late to mend" (there being always pardon for the repentant sinner); on the other, the more theological idea that in any general divine judgment, the verdict upon every man would be determined according to his moral condition at the moment, no matter what had been his previous history.

It is evident that Ezekiel's individualistic doctrine is still very inadequate. Men are not either entirely righteous or entirely sinful: nor do they pass at a bound

[1] xviii. 20.

from the one condition to the other. A more developed theory would perhaps point out that the new heart and the new spirit, which Ezekiel here urges the exiles to "make" unto themselves, and elsewhere alleges to be the gift of God, must be in truth both God's gift and man's achievement.[1] Again, judged by experience, the doctrine—for Ezekiel is limited to an earthly life—is untrue; it is a mere transference of the doctrine of retribution from nations and communities to isolated and individual men. It assumes that as God judges and deals with nations, so he judges and deals with individuals—an assumption which is not borne out by facts. But it was a step of enormous value in the direction of personal religion, and towards a better theory of the relation of man to God. For though it is true that the son does bear the iniquity of his father, it is not true that he so bears it as a direct punishment from God. The denial of the fact was a necessary preliminary to the formulation of a doctrine which should admit the fact, and yet find room for it in the justice of God. Ezekiel broke for ever with the false notion of divine vengeance transmitted from generation to generation, and from the equally false and despairing idea that repentance is beyond human power. There was no need, so Ezekiel told his fellow-exiles, that they should "pine away in their iniquities:" "Cast away from you all your transgressions, whereby ye have transgressed: and make you a new heart and a new spirit: for why will ye die, O house of Israel. For I have no pleasure in the death of him

---

[1] Cf. xviii. 31, with xi. 19, xxxvi. 26.

that dieth, saith the Lord Yahveh: wherefore turn yourselves and live."[1]

Jeremiah has already made us familiar with the sins which Ezekiel lays to the charge of his contemporaries both in Judæa and Babylonia. The exilic prophet, to whose heart, as we have seen, the pure worship of the one Yahveh was very near and dear, lays greater stress on liturgical delinquencies than Jeremiah, and far more than Isaiah. Yet he by no means ignores offences against morality, and in the "catalogue of sins in Jerusalem,"[2] the old iniquities, against which the eighth-century prophets so repeatedly protested, re-appear one by one. Each section of the population is charged with those particular vices which are the exact opposite of the virtues properly belonging to it: the princes, with bloodshed, injustice and blackmailing; the prophets, with deceitful and lying messages from Yahveh; the priests, with making and teaching no distinction between holy and profane, the unclean and the clean. Among the sins with which he reproaches the city generally, are unchastity, bribery, usury and contempt of parents; while its guilt on the moral and the ceremonial side is summed up in the two typical crimes, bloodshed and image-making.[3]

Ezekiel's best German commentator says of him that "he as markedly makes the right cultus the main and most important factor in religion, as the real prophets found its essence in the moral commands of Yahveh."[4]

[1] xviii. 31, 32.
[2] The heading of the Authorized Version in chapter xxii.
[3] xxii. 6—12, 25—29.   [4] Smend's *Ezekiel*, p. 308 (1880).

This statement seems to confuse Ezekiel's conception of religion for the individual with his picture of the restored Jerusalem. It is deduced from the fact that in the last nine chapters of Ezekiel's book, in which he lays down his scheme of the new Judah and its capital with minute regulations for temple and worship, there is scarcely comprised a single moral injunction. But it would be very surprising if ethical mandates were found in such an incongruous connection. From a priestly point of view, and with a love for temple ceremonial not shared by Isaiah or Amos, Ezekiel is here sketching out a plan by which, in the Israel of the golden age, every semblance of idolatry may be avoided, and Yahveh may dwell once more within his chosen home. The temple is to be the visible emblem of Yahveh's presence, the centre of the commonwealth and its salient glory. Only once, in fixing the possession of the prince in the newly-appointed territory, and his duties as temporal guardian of the temple, does Ezekiel's angry recollection of the unworthy past turn him from his subject, and induce him to insert a parenthetical and irrelevant reference to the maintenance of "justice and judgment" in the princely office.[1] Are these nine chapters too much to devote to the external organization of temple and land? The old customs and laws had been inadequate to prevent pollution and defilement: Ezekiel would provide against their recurrence, and suggest the means for the permanent display of the divine presence in all its glory. Did he therefore imagine that every individual in Israel would merely concern himself with temple ceremonial, and have no other duties

[1] xlv. 9.

in life but those of worship and ritual purity? Is it true that for Ezekiel the whole life of the people in the "Messianic" age is to be merged in the service of the temple? Those who affirm this can only do so by an arbitrary separation of the last nine chapters from the rest of Ezekiel's book. For what are the duties of the individual as given twice over in two prominent chapters, which from another point of view have already come before us? What are those statutes of life, the doing of which would be the mark of that new heart and spirit which repentance and God's grace should win for Israel at the last? They include the avoidance of idolatry; but otherwise they are exclusively ethical. Even the Sabbath is not mentioned. What must I do to be saved? Ezekiel answers: Serve Yahveh only; be just, be pitiful, be chaste. Is this a low and external inventory of the statutes of life? Is it mere formalism and outward ceremonial? In what does it differ, except by the great addition of chastity, from the old prophetic requirement, "to do justly, and to love kindness, and to walk humbly before God"? Yes, say Ezekiel's critics; it differs in one important particular, and this difference alters the character of the whole. Ezekiel is the father of Judaism, and the destroyer of the prophetic religion precisely in this, that he is a legalist. That is no true morality which is an affair of "statutes and judgments." If you are just and chaste and pitiful, because God's statutes and judgments bid you be so, then your pity, chastity and justice are, as it would seem, of small account.

This is not the place to consider the accuracy of an opinion which, in a more generalized form, will come before us hereafter. The author of Deuteronomy was able to couple the requirement to fear Yahveh and to love him with all the heart and with all the soul, with the requirement to keep Yahveh's commandments and statutes. Jeremiah, who foretells a new covenant under which God will write his law in the hearts of Israel, is also able to think of this "law" as consisting of "statutes and testimonies." But it is perfectly true that Ezekiel more habitually conceives the will of God as expressed for man in "statutes and judgments," by which phrase he was doubtless alluding partly to the law of Deuteronomy, and partly to his own oral teaching and to that of former exponents of Yahveh's religion. In so far he is a legalist, and in this, as in other things, maintains his place and vindicates his importance as a bridge between old and new.

It may be noted, however, that in two significant respects he differs from the maturer legalism of the Rabbis. The catalogue of "statutes and judgments," "which if a man do he shall live by them," is exclusively moral: it is the teaching of the prophets expressed in legal terms. In so far the later legalism would appear to fall below the level of Ezekiel. But in another respect it was, as we shall hereafter see, greatly superior. To Ezekiel, the aim of the community is the glory of Yahveh; but this aim is not effected through the individual, but by a complicated system of temple ceremonial, a magical process of purifications and sacrifices, which, in their purpose and result, stand over and above the people for whose sakes they are nominally undertaken. Yahveh's honour on the one hand, old and heathen conceptions of the priesthood on the other, combine to produce this isolation of outward and public religion from the religion of the individual. In the later Judaism this chasm is bridged over. Rites and ceremonies become absorbed in the law of the layman, and the sanctification of Yahveh's name, while still an end in itself, is effected by the lives of his worshippers. Though externalities become part and parcel of the law of God, they spring from a motive, to be disclosed hereafter, which greatly modifies their character and lessens their capability for harm.

Yet in his legalism as in his individualism Ezekiel points the way. He was also more than a fingerpost, more than a mere expression of tendencies in the air. Though partly the product of his environment, his originality cannot be questioned.[1] At a critical moment he gathered together the still serviceable, but isolated, elements of religious thought which were current in his day, and wove them into something like an ordered and articulated whole. Not that Ezekiel is by any means always consistent. He is too much concerned with actual life for that—too busy with his practical mission. He is no dogmatic theologian of the school, but a man who, with a few firmly cherished theological principles at his command, was above all things intent upon

[1] One side of his premonitory work I have been compelled to leave untouched. His temple vision is a forerunner of the priestly legislation now embodied in the Pentateuch. Ezekiel's last nine chapters have been said to supply the key to the great Pentateuchal puzzle. When dealing with the priestly code, it may be necessary to refer to one or two points in Ezekiel's scheme (such as his distinction between Zadokites and Levites in the service of the altar) which may help to explain the later legislation.

the actual needs of the community among which he worked. And so he broke their false pride and showed them where their true hope lay; he admonished and he comforted, rebuked and consoled, by turns. Old ideals and old explanations had crumbled or were crumbling away: Ezekiel transformed them. Into old doctrine he infused a new vitality, and the result was a doctrine which was both old and new. Prophet as he was, he yet paved the way for the legalism and individualism of the later Judaism; and thus—what is more surprising still—priest though he was, and priestly as were his aims, he paved the way for a religion in which the priest was superseded.

The latest date mentioned by Ezekiel brings us down to 570, sixteen years after the fall of Jerusalem. Nothing had occurred to break the peace of the Babylonian empire. As year followed year, the Jewish exiles would gradually settle down to their altered life, and a new generation grow up which had never seen or could not remember its forefathers' home. The various parties would maintain their differences, or even increase them, and new parties would perhaps also arise. Not all who worshipped Yahveh faithfully would still be yearning for a return to Palestine; some would abandon the expectation, or, like modern orthodox Jews, regard it as a pious aspiration unrelated to their own lives. Prayer was gradually becoming a valuable substitute for sacrifice. But in other circles, and especially among the exiled priests, the lost worship was still passionately desired; and doubtless for the majority, who had not yet identified ideals with illusions, a change in the political sky would wake again the dormant longing for the fulfilment of the old promises.

Meanwhile, for some years after the voice of the great prophet-priest had ceased, there was no movement or likelihood of change. Nebuchadrezzar died in 562, but the strength of the empire was not visibly diminished during the reigns of his two successors, Evil-Merodach and Neriglossor. In 556, thirty years after the fall of Jerusalem, the throne of Babylon was seized by a leader or figure-head of a successful conspiracy, Nabonnedos, who was not a member of the founder's race. Two years before, his future conqueror and successor, Cyrus the Achæmenid, had ascended the throne of Ansan (Elam) and of Persia. Persia had been wont to recognize the supremacy of Media. Cyrus was soon strong enough to assume an independent attitude, and Astyages was powerless to prevent it. His soldiers revolted, and Cyrus, in 549, became master of Media. It was now evident that a new candidate had arisen for the sovereignty of Asia. But since the death of Nebuchadrezzar, the reins of government in Babylonia had fallen into feeble hands. Nabonnedos, a pious antiquarian, was no soldier. The danger was soon recognized. In 547, an alliance was formed between Babylon, Egypt, Lydia and Sparta, against the growing menace of Cyrus' power. It is unnecessary to follow the victorious course of the Persian king in detail. It is enough to recall how Cyrus, turning first against Lydia, soon made himself master of Sardis and the kingdom of Crœsus. A breathing space of seven years was neglected by Nabonnedos. His religious policy and vacillation had made him widely unpopular, and when Cyrus opened the campaign in 539, a single battle sufficed to decide the issue. One city after another opened its gates, and Babylon itself followed suit. In 538, Cyrus entered the capital in triumph, and received, as it would appear, on all hands an enthusiastic welcome. The Persian king was greeted by the ministers of the native gods themselves as the monarch of Babylon. It was a great and bloodless victory.

The patriotic feeling of the Jewish exiles had already been aroused by the report of Cyrus' conquest of Media. Old hopes revived; and as patriotism and religion were still inseparable, these hopes were quickly clothed in religious vesture, and re-acted upon religious impulses. Prophecy had slumbered since Ezekiel. There was no important message from Yahveh. There were no signs of the time needing interpretation. But now a new period had begun. Since the onset of the Assyrians, the Israelites had been accustomed to hear from their teachers that the great movements and conquests of the ruling Asiatic nations intimately concerned themselves, and were even providentially ordered or supervised by Yahveh for the sake of Israel. But hitherto, although Assyrians, Scythians, Chaldæans might have been stirred up to their invasions for Israel's sake, the result to be produced was uniformly punitive and calamitous. Now, however, the worst had happened; the judgment had fallen; Israel and Judah were exiles from their land. And yet Yahveh's promise was that the judgment should prove but a temporary purgation, not permanent ruin. Now that Asia was once more in trepidation, and the hurly-burly of change had begun anew, the tumult, if it had any bearing upon the fortunes of Judah, could only betoken redemption and deliverance. If the early successes of Cyrus foreshadowed the fall of Babylon, that fall must be the herald of Israel's restoration, a prelude to the golden age.

Prophecy, then, awoke from its lethargy; but it was a prophecy inevitably different from that of Isaiah or even of Ezekiel. It was, as a rule, coarser-fibred, more ordinarily patriotic, less ethical, and consequently, in the higher sense, less religious. The men who anticipated and foretold the future in the pre-exilic age had announced a coming judgment upon national depravity: religious faith was raised to a sublime pitch to recognize in the triumph of the invader the overruling providence of God. Now it was otherwise. Faith was still needed. The conquest of Lydia was quite different from the conquest of Babylon; nor was there any apparent likelihood, even if Babylon should succumb, that a new master would rehabilitate the exiles' fortunes, or allow the re-establishment of their commonwealth in Judæa. During the seven years' pause after the capture of Sardis in 546, the hopes of many would begin to flag, and the visions of deliverance be pronounced rash and premature. Before 539 faith was necessary to recognize in Cyrus the certain destroyer of Babylon and the deliverer of Judah. Yet it was a faith very different from that which made Jeremiah recognize in Nebuchadrezzar the instrument of Yahveh's wrath. It was the faith of patriotism raised to a white heat by religion. Ethical elements might easily be wanting in it; fierce revenge, the hate of the captive for his captor, would form a prominent part.

Though in general the lot of the exiles cannot have been hard, there must have been individual cases of oppression and cruelty. Thus the hope of national deliverance would be merged in a vision of triumph over the fallen foe.

It would not have been prudent for any eager exile to speak too publicly of the events which, as their shadow fell before them, the eye of faith enabled him to foresee. But many a whisper would pass from mouth to mouth, and many a broadsheet of prophecy would circulate from hand to hand. Such fragments of prediction must probably have been composed in considerable numbers between 546 and 539; even after the restoration the type was by no means exhausted, for the glowing anticipations, whether for their own nation or for their oppressors, were far from being fulfilled by the events which immediately preceded and succeeded the fall of Babylon.

In the collection of prophecies now preserved to us in the Old Testament, we have, however, only two independent fragments of this kind which can with certainty be attributed to this period. They are now comprised in the first half of Isaiah xxi., and in the thirteenth and fourteenth chapters (xxi. 1—10, xiii. 2—xiv. 1—23). The second includes that splendid song of triumph over fallen Babylon, with the description of its monarch's reception in Hades, the Authorized Version's rendering of which contains the famous hexameter, "How art thou fallen from heaven, O Lucifer, son of the morning!"[1] It is full of the spirit of mockery and revenge. Babylon is the type of wickedness and pride; the day of Yahveh is

[1] xiv. 12.

at hand, the hour of retribution and of doom. The fall and punishment of Babylon occupies almost the entire space: only three verses out of forty-four deal with Israel and its restoration. In them, although a higher note is touched, the predominant feeling is markedly particularist. The peoples shall bring back Israel to its own land, "and the house of Israel shall possess them in Yahveh's land for bondmen and for bondmaids: they shall take them captives whose captives they were, and they shall rule over their oppressors." It is true the thought was not without excuse:

> "Who shall blame,
> When the slaves enslave, the oppressed ones o'er
> The oppressor triumph for evermore!"

But the religious genius of Israel was not limited to visions such as these. In one master-mind, at any rate, the approach of Cyrus gave the impulse to a wider doctrine and a grander theodicy. Like Ezekiel, though for other reasons, this prophet stands on another plane from the prophets of the monarchy. He exercised a wide influence upon both contemporaries and posterity. Disciples imitated his thought and method so closely, that it is not easy to distinguish their writings from his; while, what is of far deeper significance, some of his doctrines sank deep into the national consciousness, fashioning and moulding the religious ideas of men who, in many other respects, held opinions different from his own. The fusion was not always happy; its result not always homogeneous or consistent. But this was not the fault of the exilic teacher.

The name of this prophet is unknown. His writings,

or perhaps one should more correctly say some of his writings, are preserved among the last twenty-seven chapters of the Book of Isaiah. Since the beginning of this century, when it was first noticed that these chapters have nothing to do with the Isaiah of the eighth century, it has been commonly supposed that they all date from the close of the exile and proceed from a single hand. Recent criticism, however, has thrown grave doubts upon this unity of authorship and plan. To me, following Prof. Cheyne's lead, it seems hardly safe to attribute to the unknown writer—called, for convenience' sake, the Second or Deutero-Isaiah—more than nineteen out of the twenty-seven chapters. These nineteen are chapters xl.—lv. and chapters lx.—lxii.[1]

Like the other and lower "prophets" who, after the early successes of Cyrus, began to predict the approaching annihilation of Babylon, Deutero-Isaiah is primarily concerned with promise and not with judgment. He begins where the pre-exilic prophets left off. They closed their threats with a word of consolation: he opens his work with the famous apostrophe, "Comfort ye, comfort ye." God's righteousness, which erewhile could only be made manifest in judgment, must now be expressed in salvation. The fall of Babylon, not the fall of Jerusalem, is to be the seal of Yahveh's truth, the signal token of his fidelity to his own nature and to his own

[1] See art. "Isaiah," by Prof. Cheyne, in *Encyc. Britt.*, 9th ed., 1881; and "Critical Problems of the Second Part of Isaiah," *Jewish Quarterly Review*, July and October, 1891. Cf. also Kuenen's *Onderzoek*, Vol. II., 2nd ed.; and Marti, *Der Prophet Sacharja*, 1892, p. 40, n. 1. [To these references must now be added the very important new commentary on the whole book of Isaiah by Prof. Duhm, 1892.]

word. Yet Deutero-Isaiah shows notable differences from those of his contemporaries whose main thought was revenge. Though the fall of Babylon is the condition precedent, the prophet is far more deeply concerned with its results. The deliverance of Israel and the world-wide issues of that deliverance are his proper theme. For since Israel's restoration was to be a far bigger thing than the mere re-establishment of a single people in its own land, Deutero-Isaiah combined with his message of redemption a great amount of distinctive doctrine, explanatory of the Author, the meaning and the consequences of those great events which were shortly to come to pass. Nor, again, was Deutero-Isaiah so carried away by patriotic exaltation as not to realize that Israel by no means deserved the possession of that wealth of external and internal prosperity which, for God's own purposes, was yet to be its share. Though the spiritual change must now be brought about by other causes than judgment, change was still needed, for there still was much in Israel to deplore and reprehend. But in his statement of that which required change and merited reprehension, Deutero-Isaiah once more shows his originality.

The pre-exilic prophets, together with Ezekiel, were never weary of protesting against those national delinquencies which consisted in idolatry and the violation of the moral law. Deutero-Isaiah declaims against idolatry, which was still, after fifty years of exile, not wholly eradicated; but he is conspicuously silent about the moral law. He summons his contemporaries, not to repentance, but to faith. He chides them for their unbelief, for their weakness of capacity to recognize either the nature or the power of God. Ezekiel, in his labours as shepherd of souls among the exiles at Tel-Abib, attempted to help the regeneration, which God alone could ultimately effect in the mass, by urging men forward on the path of virtue and good works: Deutero-Isaiah, in ascribing, like Ezekiel, the completed work of spiritual regeneration to God, seeks to help and hasten the divine operation by stimulating faith. A man who believes in Yahveh, upon this prophet's lines, is necessarily regenerate. In a highly suggestive passage, Prof. Duhm has for this reason compared Deutero-Isaiah to St. Paul.[1]

This great teacher of the exile is thus intensely theological. He moves in the region of the ideal, and his language, even when dealing with actualities, present or to be, is liable to shade away into metaphor and symbol. He is often argumentative in his manner; theories and ratiocinations abound; his style is literary, and both matter and form indicate that his work was from the first addressed to the reader, and was not intended for oral delivery. The nineteen chapters, assigned to him by Prof. Cheyne, were, however, not necessarily written at one time or as a complete whole. While all of them were probably written between Cyrus' conquest of Lydia in 546 and his advance into Babylonia in 539, the first nine, which have many marks in common, were probably composed before the remaining ten. But this latter section, unlike xl.—xlviii., has no unity, and may be the aggregate product of three or four separate broad-sheets.

The primary object of Deutero-Isaiah was to foretell

[1] *Theologie der Propheten*, p. 291.

the sure deliverance of the exiles after the fall of Babylon by the agency of Cyrus. In the first nine chapters Cyrus is almost as important a figure in the prophetic landscape as Israel. In the Persian king's achievements could be discerned the finger of God himself, while their completion would synchronize with the full revelation of the divine glory.

That revelation was to form the theological correlative of Israel's deliverance from Babylon, and it may thus be regarded as the second object of the prophet's message. Both objects imply or presume, as a third element in a manifold whole, the conversion of the heathen nations to the knowledge and worship of the true God. These are the three constituents of the coming time of which the early victories of Cyrus were the earnest.

We may fairly assume that the prophet was not himself led by the advent of Cyrus to reach that lofty conception of Yahveh which he asks his reader to gather from the onset of the Persian king. Deutero-Isaiah, we may infer, was a monotheist before he heard of Cyrus, and thus it is that in his rhetorical fashion he combines in a twofold manner his conception of Deity with the news of Cyrus' successes. There is the thought that Yahveh, who caused all other things, also wrought this; and there is the opposite reflection that Yahveh, who wrought this, must be the cause of all other things.

Deutero-Isaiah cannot justly be regarded as the first exponent of that unqualified and absolute monotheism which from his time became and remained the fundamental dogma of Judaism. In the last Lecture we saw how an earlier writer had proclaimed the doctrine that

"Yahveh is God in heaven above and upon the earth beneath; there is none else." But Deutero-Isaiah was the first to emphasize and make use of this plenary and unconditional monotheism. And as an integral portion, or as the inevitable consequence, of his monotheistic doctrine, he adopts a novel attitude towards idolatry.

Yahveh is the only God. Israelite and Gentile must both acknowledge this truth. Deutero-Isaiah writes for the former, but in his theoretic passages he frequently has the latter also in his mind. The prophet speaks usually in Yahveh's name.[1] "I, Yahveh, am the first, and with the last I am he; before me no God was formed, neither after me shall there be; I, I am Yahveh, and beside me there is no deliverer; I am Yahveh, and there is none else; beside me there is no God." In proving his thesis of God's unity and uniqueness, the prophet employs two main arguments, one of them taken from the world of nature, the other from the history of man. The argument from nature is based upon the idea, now first put forward as a religious dogma, that Yahveh is the Creator of the universe. It cannot be said that Isaiah or Jeremiah did not believe in the world's creation by Yahveh, but they made no religious use of the belief, and in so far it was not consciously apprehended and realized. Deutero-Isaiah, on the contrary, applies the argument habitually. Yahveh is the uncreated Creator: such only can be the Maker of the visible world. Identifying the heathen gods with their idols, the argument from creation pleads the impossibility of that, which is itself the product of a product, having been the Author

[1] xli. 4, xlviii. 12, xliii. 10, 11, xliv. 6.

of all the universe of things. Some divine power must have made the world: who, if not Yahveh? "Lift up your eyes on high, and see. Who has created these? He who brings out their host by number, and calls them all by name." Yahveh is the God who "created the heavens, and stretched them forth, that spread forth the earth with the things that spring out of it, that gives breath to the people upon it and spirit to them that walk through it," "Yahveh the Maker of all things."[1]

The argument from human history would be more correctly termed the argument from Israelite history, were it not that, even more than the doctrine of creation, it was intended to convince and confound not only hesitating Israel, but the whole ignorant Gentile world. Yahveh, the Creator of the heavens and the earth, is as much the God of Israel as he was to Amos and Isaiah. He chose Israel for his own purposes, and through all the changing fortunes of its history, Yahveh's will has been the one determining cause in punishment and blessing. The signs of his rule have been the messages of the prophets.

It is in full harmony with his marked theological tendency that the element in prophecy which strikes Deutero-Isaiah most vividly, and of which he makes the greatest use, is the element of prediction. The personal and ethical features disappear. To Jeremiah, the most essential function of the prophets, who, since the day on which Israel came out of Egypt, have been sent by Yahveh continually, was to bid men "turn them from their evil way and from the evil of their doings."

[1] xl. 26, xlii. 5, xliv. 24.

To Deutero-Isaiah, the essential point is the conformity of their predictions with the historic issues which they foretold. The captivity had been predicted; could the votaries of any heathen god furnish a parallel? But besides the captivity, there had been predicted also a subsequent event, greater and more wonderful still —big with vital consequences to all humanity—and this greater event was now being accomplished before the eyes of all. The prophets had spoken of Israel's restoration from the land of its exile, and Cyrus was the chosen instrument of Yahveh to justify that crowning feat and consummation of prophecy. In one sense, therefore, Cyrus was foretold; in another, inasmuch as the method and scope of the deliverance had not previously been revealed, he forms an element of that new evangel which Deutero-Isaiah is commissioned to deliver. In so far as the fall of Babylon was foretold, and since Cyrus is to bring about its fall, the Persian king makes Yahveh manifest to those who are as yet ignorant of the true God. The victories of Cyrus confound the idolators.[1]

To appreciate Deutero-Isaiah's polemic against idolatry aright, we have to remember the country in which he wrote, and the scenes which were passing before his eyes. Babylon, city and land, was the home of magnificent idolatry, and nowhere was there a wider popular identification of the image with the god. Our prophet may have witnessed the in-bringing of the Accadian idols to Babylon to protect the capital from the imminent cata-

[1] Cf. xl. 2—29, xliii. 8—19, xliv. 6—9, xlv. 6, 21—25, &c. &c.

strophe.¹ Though this strange event happened after the publication of his first prophetic pamphlet, it is sufficiently suggestive of the temper of the population and of the time, and it indicates that his sarcastic descriptions of idol manufacture may well have been drawn from life. This complete identification of the material idol with the worshipped god is as novel as the prophet's doctrine of creation. To Deutero-Isaiah, idolatry is not merely sinful for the Israelite as a transgression of the command, "Thou shalt have no other gods beside Me;" it is also theoretically and intrinsically absurd—absurd for the Gentile as for the Jew. A log of wood of which part is used for fuel, and part is wrought into a god—what sort of deity is this that a man should bow down to it and say, "Rescue me, for thou art my god"? The folly is so transparent that the prophet can only regard it as an inexplicable self-delusion. "A deceived heart has led him astray, so that he cannot rescue himself and say, Is there not a lie in my right hand?"²

Idolatry is therefore absurd, and with the coming of Cyrus its days are numbered. For the victories of Cyrus and the redemption of Israel are to fulfil the word which has gone forth from Yahveh, the oath which by himself he has sworn, that unto him every knee shall bow.³ This final *dénoûment* of the world's drama is to be partly brought about by the agency of Israel. To understand it, the prophet's conception of Israel and of its mission must first itself be understood. That conception is not always the same or wholly self-consistent. Its

---

[1] Cf. Tiele, *Babylonisch-Assyrische Geschichte*, p. 475.
[2] xliv. 9—20.   [3] xlv. 23.

highest features are the most important in the history of our subject, as they are also the newest and most characteristic.

To Yahveh's omnipotence in the world of external nature corresponds his omnipotence in the world of man, and his emergence from the limitations of the patron deity was impressed upon the prophet's mind no less by the one than by the other. All history is Yahveh's province: the whole habitable world—for the earth was created for man to dwell in it—the theatre of his conscious and rational dominion. The universalist tendencies of the eighth-century prophecy were taken up and enlarged by this nameless prophet of the exile. To him in his noblest mood—in this widely differing from the particularist Ezekiel—the nations are ends in themselves and have an independent value of their own. They are not mere foils to set off the higher glory of Israel and of Yahveh. There is comparatively but little triumph over the fall of Babylon; there is only one doubtful allusion to any violent judgment to be inflicted upon the nations generally before the full establishment of the Messianic age.[1]

In consonance with this wider view of God's providence is the prophet's attitude towards Cyrus. It is true that he was called and crowned with victory for the sake of Israel, Yahveh's elect, and in so far he is a tool in God's hands, like Nebuchadrezzar to Jeremiah, who entitled that monarch also "the servant of Yahveh." But in reality a far higher position is assigned to Cyrus by the later writer. That the reason of this was due

[1] xlv. 20.

T

to Cyrus' religion is very doubtful. Of that, whether monotheistic or not, the prophet was probably in ignorance. It is rather that Cyrus is at once the instrument and the symbol of the conversion of humanity to the worship of the true God. He is Yahveh's anointed and friend, even his beloved one, who has been sent forth on his career of victory, that he and all men after him may know and acknowledge that "from the rising of the sun unto the setting thereof" there is none but Yahveh.[1] It was not wonderful that the prediction of so exalted a position entrusted to a heathen king aroused arrogant disbelief among Jews who were eager that the deliverer should be miraculously raised up from among their own ranks.

Yet in spite of this increased toleration for the Gentile world, Yahveh is still primarily the God of Israel. To Israel were sent the prophets of old time: to Israel is addressed Yahveh's message now. Israel shares in the exaltation of its God: Yahveh's government embraces the world, but its centre is Jerusalem.

To Ezekiel, as we have seen, the main object of Israel's and the whole purpose of the heathen nations' existence were to subserve and express the earthly glory of Yahveh. As regards Israel, this conception was partly due to Ezekiel's pessimistic estimate of both its past and its present, so that its deliverance from captivity could only be accomplished because it was necessary for God's own private and personal ends. Deutero-Isaiah does not lose sight of this motive altogether; as a whole, Israel is not worthy of the coming salvation, and the exile—the fur-

[1] xlv. 1, xliv. 28 (Kuenen, *Hibb. Lectures*, p. 132), xlviii. 14, xlv. 6.

nace of affliction—has not produced the purgation which might reasonably have been looked for. It is still true: "For mine own sake, for mine own sake, will I do it, for else how would my name be desecrated? and my glory I will not give to another."[1] Yet the human motive for God's redemptive action is even more prominent, partly for the sake of Israel and partly for the Gentiles'.

The estimate of Israel is less pessimistic than in Ezekiel. There have been in the past, and there were in the present, pious and faithful Israelites, worthy of Yahveh's love. It was God's love for Israel, a love unextinguishable and everlasting, which induced him to choose it for his people. Israel has a threefold mission— to itself, to the world, and to God. But the three aspects belong to one whole: God glorifies himself by means of Israel, but Israel is glorified with God.[2]

How can Israel have a mission to itself? With all its sins in the past, and all its sins—of misdeed and misbelief—in the present, Israel, as a whole, is incapable of fulfilling the work for which it has been "called." And yet that work is upon the eve of its accomplishment. Ezekiel avoids the dilemma by his prediction of a new spirit. Deutero-Isaiah, too, teaches a similar doctrine. "I, even I, blot out thy rebellions for mine own sake, and thy sins I will not remember."[3] But by his less pessimistic estimate of his ancestors and contemporaries, he is able to suggest another solution of the problem. The better elements in Israel have preserved it in the past and preserve it still. Without the faithfulness of the few, the many would have utterly deserted Yahveh,

[1] xlviii. 11.   [2] xliv. 23, xlv. 25, lx. 9.   [3] xliii. 25.

and Israel's name been blotted out. Nor is their work yet over. They must leaven the mass, and fulfil the mission of Israel to the world at large. This thought supplies the key to the conception of the Servant. The name is sometimes applied to Israel as a whole, and sometimes to an ideal Israel, distinguished from, and even opposed to, the Israel of the present and of the flesh.

Primarily, Israel is Yahveh's servant, loved of Yahveh with a peculiar love.[1] The partiality of the patron deity is still not entirely superseded. Even in Deutero-Isaiah Yahveh gives nations for Israel's ransom, peoples in its stead.[2] Before God and the world, Israel as a whole is still the privileged servant, but as regards its proper function and peculiar work, Israel as a whole has become incapable of discharging them. It is only by the ideal Israel that Israel's mission can be successfully carried out. The Servant in this sense is a conception arrived at by selecting all the noblest traits in the best spirits of Israel's past history and in some of the prophet's own contemporaries, and uniting them together in a typical and highly idealized personification.[3]

The actual Israel is the opposite of the ideal Israel. Yet through the ministry of the Servant the ideal and actual Israel will ultimately become one. The actual Israel is blind to God's work and deaf to God's word, while the function of the ideal Israel is to spread abroad

[1] xli. 8, 9, xliv. 1, 2, xlix. 3.   [2] xliii. 3, 4.

[3] In Prof. Duhm's new Commentary a new and divergent interpretation is given of the Servant passages, the chief of which, i.e. xlii. 1—4, xlix. 1—6, l. 4—9, lii. 13—liii. 12, are supposed to have an independent origin, and to have been written, not by Deutero-Isaiah, but by a later and post-exilic author.

the knowledge of God. One picture of the ideal Servant is too characteristic to be omitted even in a rapid sketch like the present, and although it is so familiar to us all: "Behold! my servant, whom I uphold, mine elect, in whom my soul is well pleased; I have put my spirit upon him; he shall cause religion (literally "law") to go forth to the nations. He shall not cry nor clamour, nor cause his voice to be heard in the street; a crushed reed he shall not break, and a dimly burning wick he shall not quench; truthfully shall he cause religion to go forth. He shall not burn dimly, neither shall his spirit be crushed, till he have set religion in the earth, and for his teaching the countries wait." For Yahveh has appointed him "for a light of the nations; to open blind eyes, and to bring out captives from the prison," that God's "salvation may reach unto the end of the earth."[1]

Here, and in one other corresponding passage, the prophet rises to the conception of an Israel chosen for the nations' sake, and preaching the great doctrine of the one and only God to all the world. By this conception Israel's election loses its particularist sting, and becomes a means to an universalist end. Israel's special endowment is the religious truth which has been revealed to it; but now, in the fulness of time, that truth, through Israel, is to be shared with the Gentile. The coast lands and isles—for such appears to be the fuller connotation of the word translated "countries" by Prof. Cheyne, and "islands" in the Authorized Version—are already waiting for Israel's teaching. By a strange flight of poetic imagination, the prophet conceives the distant

[1] xlii. 1—7; cf. xlix. 1—9.

coasts and islands of Asia Minor, which the news of Cyrus' Lydian war may have brought within his ken, as weary of their ineffectual idolatries, and longing—like the shiver of nature before the dawn—for the light which was soon to irradiate their darkness.

In other passages Deutero-Isaiah represents the conversion of the nations as the direct work of Yahveh, or as a deduction drawn by themselves from the facts of Israel's deliverance and restoration. The striking conception of Israel as the chosen instrument and mediator of that conversion only occurs twice; but, from the solemn emphasis of the language, it can have been no random flight of thought, although obviously there did not yet exist even the vaguest surmise how this doctrine, now first formed and taught, should be realized in fact.

Indeed, the prophet is perfectly conscious of the seeming absurdity of his prediction. Israel is now despised by all, abject and abhorred. Those who are the truest Israelites, who come nearest to the ideal, are despised the most—despised and ill-treated. It is likely enough that any fitful Babylonian persecution fell most heavily upon the more patriotic section of the Israelite exiles. Oppression, forced labour, imprisonment and even death, may occasionally have been their lot. But these faithful ones would not only be specially subject to the insults of the foreigner, but also to the disregard and contempt of many among their own people. After the final victory of Babylon, Gentile and Jew will alike recognize their error. The latter will perceive that it has been the neglected few who, through their fidelity to Yahveh, have made the national redemption a moral possibility.

Upon the basis of these facts and expectations, the prophet, in the memorable fifty-third chapter, which, with the possible help of older material, was perhaps inserted in its present somewhat incongruous position "as an after-thought," has suggested a new theodicy and a novel *rationale* of the imminent deliverance.[1] He had opened his message with the statement that the punishment already received had adequately atoned for the sins of the past; he had also enunciated the theory that any iniquity of the present which still constituted a bar to redemption must be wiped away by God's grace; and now, in addition to these hypotheses, he goes on to teach that the greater and yet undeserved sufferings of the few may have been endured by them and accepted by God in full satisfaction for the sins of the nation as a whole. By the stripes and death of the Servant, Israel was preserved; to this agency a regenerate people would ascribe alike its temporal and spiritual redemption. As with the theory of "the new spirit" in Jeremiah and Ezekiel, this teaching is not put forward as a general truth; it holds good only for a particular class of people under particular circumstances. It was left for other and later teachers to show that both the one doctrine and the other—God's share in the conquest of sin, and the conception of suffering as "a conscious voluntary sacrifice"—were truths of universal validity.

As regards the second doctrine, Deutero-Isaiah lays the main stress, not on the Servant's voluntary endurance of suffering for the sake of the nation, but upon God's acceptance of it in lieu of a further punishment

[1] Cheyne, *The Prophecies of Isaiah*, 4th ed., 1886, Vol. II. p. 53.

of the whole people. This is a remnant of a sacrificial theory which the teaching of the prophets themselves had already been sufficient to explode, and from which later Judaism has made itself satisfactorily free.[1]

By the character of the Servant's work in the past— in other words, and without idealization, by the fidelity of a zealous minority in every age—he has been prepared for the work which lies before him in the future. But that work he will then carry out under very different conditions—at one with his own people, and sharing with them in their glory. After Babylon has fallen, he will no longer be despised, but triumphant—no longer disregarded, but acknowledged by all as the appointed servant of God. Then "kings shall see and rise up; princes, they shall bow down; because of Yahveh, in that he is faithful, and of the Holy One of Israel, in that he chose thee."[2] And finally, after the deliverance has been effected, and the exiles have settled in their own land, Israel and the Servant become one and the same. For the redemption of which Cyrus is the instrument will be spiritual as well as material. God by his grace helps on to a victorious issue the Servant's work. Thus the prophet bids the exiles seek God, because in that very hour he is near, and will let himself be found.[3]

[1] In reading over and correcting the proof-sheets of the present Lecture, Mr. Carpenter pencilled to the above paragraph the following note, which I have ventured to transcribe: "No doubt this idea is present: but it always seems to me that 'the main stress' is on the purifying effect which the Servant's sufferings—when really understood—will have upon his own countrymen. The key to the meaning of liii. 4—6 lies surely in verse 11."

[2] xlix. 7.   [3] lv. 6.

Ezekiel had urged his listeners to make them a new heart, and he had also promised this "new heart" as the gift of God. Deutero-Isaiah combines demand with promise, declaring, "Seek ye a new heart, and it shall be given you."

It is, therefore, a regenerate Israel which is to be restored to its ancient home. How does the prophet conceive the new Jerusalem which is to rise up out of the ashes of the old? No plan is formulated, such as Ezekiel's, for its religious organization. Nothing is said of the details of worship, though an altar and sacrifices are implied, just as churches or synagogues might be implied as necessary features of a religious society in any prophetic writer of our own time. But as the false worship of the pre-exilic period is forgotten or ignored by Deutero-Isaiah in the pressure of the present and in the greatness of his tidings, so in depicting the glories of the new Jerusalem he has nothing to say about safeguards against the violation of Yahveh's holiness, in the elaboration of which the priestly spirit of Ezekiel saw such value and found such pleasure. There is a significant silence about the law, whether of Deuteronomy or of the priests. Israel is not rigidly separated, as in Ezekiel, from the profane world, but the Gentiles partake freely of the spiritual nourishment which is dispensed at Jerusalem. But the old particularism still partially remains. For in the chapters which deal with the redeemed community—it is scarcely a nation any more, nor is there any allusion to an earthly king—the Gentiles are regarded mainly from the point of view of increasing the wealth and glory of Israel by the services and tribute which they willingly pay to it.[1] Yet Israel is the world's centre, not through any merit of its own, but because of the religious truth which has been committed to it. Jerusalem is the world's capital because Yahveh dwells there.

In spite of his monotheism, the prophet does not hesitate to retain the old conception of Deity inhabiting a particular place, and revealing himself there in visible effulgence of supernatural light. God is not, as in Ezekiel, located absolutely within the temple; Deutero-Isaiah's idea apparently was that he would be poised in a cloud of radiant light above Jerusalem. Yet how far all this is pure metaphor and symbolism, and how far literal, it is very difficult to determine, and perhaps the prophet himself could scarcely have told us. There is no other writer in the Hebrew Scriptures whose language so frequently passes and re-passes from the material to the spiritual, or who hovers so habitually upon the confines of either.

The full range of the prophet's vivid imagination is employed to depict both the spiritual and material beatitudes of Israel's future. Its population is increased; its land is extended; its riches are multiplied a thousand-fold. And this good fortune is to continue for ever. Compared with the eternity of the golden age, God's wrath was but for a moment; the new covenant of peace, which is sealed in the hour of deliverance, will be absolute and everlasting. For there will be no further need of judgment. Internal regeneration will correspond to external magnificence. "All thy children shall be dis-

[1] lx.—lxii.

ciples of Yahveh, and great shall be their peace." "I will make peace thy government, and righteousness thy magistrates. Violence shall no more be heard of in thy land, desolation nor destruction in thy boarders: and thou shalt call thy walls Salvation and thy gates Renown. The sun shall be no more thy light by day; neither for brightness shall the moon give light unto thee: but Yahveh shall be unto thee an everlasting light, and thy God thy glory."[1]

Soon after these glowing words were written, Cyrus, the friend and anointed of Yahveh, took the first step towards their accomplishment.

Cyrus entered Babylon in the year 538, forty-eight years after the capture of Jerusalem. He was welcomed, as I have already mentioned, by both priests and nobles. Contrary to the anticipations of the other Jewish prophets and of Deutero-Isaiah himself, no punishment was inflicted upon the conquered people; the capital was not plundered. Cyrus, far from putting an end to heathenism, gave himself out as protector of the native religion, "publicly ascribing his successes to the favour of the gods of Babylon, offering daily sacrifices on their altars, and restoring and embellishing their thrones."[2] This was part of his policy of general conciliation: another instance of it was his permission to the Jewish exiles to return to their own land. How this was secured we cannot exactly tell. The Jews, at any rate, according to Cyrus' own words, were not the only body of exiles upon whom a similar favour was conferred. To whatever quarter

[1] liv. 13, lx. 17—19.
[2] Hay Hunter, *After the Exile*, Vol. I. p. 30.

of his empire such exiles returned, they would form an important bulwark of Persian rule, and help to strengthen the stability of his dominions. It is very doubtful whether any other grounds than those of state-craft need be assumed for the favour of Cyrus towards the exiled Jews.[1]

Arrangements for the departure occupied a year. In 537, 42,360 exiles, including men, women and children, started for Palestine. The sacred vessels of the temple, which Nebuchadrezzar had removed to Babylon, were given back to them. Those who stayed behind were probably more numerous than those who went. A more complete restoration would doubtless have presented insuperable difficulties.

The selection of those who should go and of those who should stay does not seem to have been left to individual choice. It was certainly not only the zealous who went, or only the indifferent who stayed. The selection was a national concern, and it is probable that representatives of every family among the exiles were now sent back to Judæa. Within each separate family there may have been some opportunities for individual choice, though even here the determining motives would not have been only indifference or zeal. This dual aspect of the composition of the first settlement, that it was supposed to represent the entire Israelite nation, and at the same time was in close connection with those who remained behind in Babylon, is partly indicated by the fact that

---

[1] The edict of Cyrus in Ezra i. 1—4 is unauthentic. Cf. Stade, *Geschichte*, Vol. II. pp. 93, 99; and for the inscriptions of Cyrus, Cheyne, *Isaiah*, Vol. I. pp. 304—306, Vol. II. pp. 288—294.

they who formed it now called themselves "the men of the people of Israel," and now the *Gola*, "the men of the captivity."

For nearly a hundred years after the return, a true history of Judaism would have not more to do with the life of the settlers in Palestine than with those who remained loyal to religion and race even in their Babylonian homes. The Judaism of the future did not receive some of its most distinctive features until the union of these two streams of Jewish life in the days of Ezra and Nehemiah.

Lecture VI.

THE RESTORATION AND THE PRIESTLY LAW.

WITH eager outlook into the future the Jewish exiles set forth from Babylon upon their homeward journey. Not less hopefully, and with no feebler interest, did the mass of those who perforce remained behind watch for news of the restored Jerusalem. Some forty-two thousand souls were charged with the inspiring duty of renovation and retrieval. In them and through them prophecy must be fulfilled. They, " the sons of the captivity," are also "the people of Israel," now at last proudly conscious of their peculiar status and mission.[1]

The classes of which the troop of home-comers was composed need examination. A list drawn up not very long after the re-settlement in Judæa has fortunately been incorporated in more than one later history, and in the absence of other contemporary and authentic evidence for the first seventeen years of restoration, it constitutes a record of great importance, meriting the patient care which divers scholars have bestowed on it.[2]

In this list there are enumerated, first the lay, and

[1] E.g. Ezra vi. 16.

[2] Ezra ii.; Nehemiah vii.; cf. Smend, *Die Listen der Bücher Ezra und Nehemia*, 1881.

then the sacerdotal elements, and in it, for the first time in an historical document, there is made that distinction between Priest and Levite which was wholly unknown to the authors of Deuteronomy. For in Deuteronomy "Levite" and "Priest" are interchangeable terms, and the full designation of the ministrants at the altar is that of "Levitical priests." The origin of the distinction, which is full-blown in the list of the home-comers from Babylon, has already come under notice. It was half-practical, half-theoretical. Josiah's reformation had resulted in establishing a wide difference between the legitimate Levitical priests of Jerusalem, descendants in the main, either really or by repute, of Zadok, the priest of David, and the irregular Levitical priests of the high-places, now rigorously interdicted and demolished by the high-handed enthusiasm of the young king. This result the authors of Deuteronomy had foreseen, and they had attempted to provide against it. But they were unable to secure for the discredited priests of the high-places equal recognition with the priests of the Jerusalem temple, the dignity and importance of which their own code had so enormously enhanced. Such rustic priests as were brought, or migrated, to Jerusalem could only attain to the position of servitors to the Zadokites. This relative inferiority was subsequently legalized in the priestly code and based upon Mosaic authority, but it was arrived at as an outcome of the hard logic of facts between Josiah's reformation and the downfall of the state. Indeed, the elaborated hierarchy of the later code might never have found its place there, had not the great prophet of the early exile adopted and even accentuated the actual condition of things in the temple services as he himself, before the first crash came, had known and loved them. In his ideal temple of the Messianic age, his own order, the Zadokites, are to be the only priests; the Levites who "went astray from Yahveh after their idols" should "be keepers of the charge of the house," but should not draw nigh unto God "to do the office of a priest."[1]

Though Ezekiel made too marked a distinction between the purity of the priests of the capital and the idolatry of the priests of the "high-places," his partiality had important issues. But his desires were not completely realized. What conflicts and negotiations took place from the time of Ezekiel to the triumph of Cyrus it is impossible to say, but the upshot was that some Levites who were not Zadokites, priests of the high-places and not of Jerusalem, were admitted into the legitimate priesthood. There is reason to believe that this compromise, which of course did not satisfy the claims of those Levites who were still excluded, had been arrived at before, possibly only shortly before, the return of the first colony of settlers in 537. The number of priests, according to each recension of the list, amounts to the same large total, 4289. So high a figure—unless recklessly exaggerated—even if it include women and children, seems best accounted for upon the hypothesis that other Levites had already been admitted to the priesthood in addition to the so-called sons of Zadok. That the remaining Levites were far from acquiescing in the prospect offered to them may be inferred from the very

[1] Ezekiel xliv. 10—14.

small number who took part in the homeward journey. To the 4289 priests the 74 Levites offer a marked and significant contrast. The singers, porters and Nethinim, are not yet incorporated among the Levites; in the list they follow as separate classes of temple servitors.[1] Thus some "Priests" and many "Levites" remained in Babylonia; and it is important to bear this fact in mind, inasmuch as the reformation of 444 was organized and brought about by new sacerdotal and legal influences fresh from the land of exile. When that period is reached, it will be seen how great a change had taken place in the character of the "Levites," from what it must have been in the age of Ezekiel, perhaps even from what it was in the age of Zerubbabel.

It was a first disappointment in a long series which was to come, that over the homeward-bound exiles an alien govenor was appointed. In one of his latest essays Kuenen has accepted Stade's view that the Sheshbazzar, who is described in the Book of Ezra as the first governor of Judæa, is not Zerubbabel under a Persian disguise, but must be regarded as an independent Persian functionary, who was specially nominated by Cyrus for adjusting and supervising so delicate a matter as the re-settlement of the exiles in lands by no means destitute of inhabitants.[2] Under him there seems to have been a council

---

[1] Cf. Stade, *Geschichte*, Vol. II. p. 106, &c.; Kuenen, *De geschiedenis der priesten van Jahwe en de ouderdom der priesterlijke wet* (*Theol. Tijd.*, 1890, pp. 1—42); Vogelstein, *Der Kampf zwischen Priestern und Leviten seit den Tagen Ezechiels*, 1889.

[2] Stade, *Geschichte*, Vol. II. pp. 100, 101; Kuenen, *De chronologie van het perzische tijdvak der Joodsche geschiedenis*, 1890, p. 11 (283).

of twelve Judæans, of whom the most important were Zerubbabel, the grandson of Jehoiachin, the representative of the royal house and of many a Messianic hope, and Joshùa, grandson of Seraiah, "the chief-priest" of the Jerusalem temple in Zedekiah's day, who had been slain by Nebuchadrezzar "at Riblah in the land of Hamath."[1]

Before long, Joshua exchanged his old title of "chief-priest," which naturally accrued to him, for that of high or great priest, under which name his successors for six centuries were destined to be known. Whether the change of name betokened an immediate increase of dignity and power is not certain. It is perhaps going too far to say that the very office of high-priest was created—for reasons which are still hypothetical—in the interval between the return in 537 and the exhortations of the two prophets Haggai and Zechariah in 520. For the pre-exilic "chief-priest" must also have been a personage of distinction and importance. The increased influence of the high-priest depended upon more general considerations, the change of appellation pointing rather to augmented power in the future, than indicating a radical and immediate aggrandizement.

What proportion of the former kingdom of Judæa was occupied by the restored exiles at the first settlement is a difficult question, which happily does not directly concern us here. A far more important point, if only we could get definite information about it, is the relation of the home-comers to the inhabitants whom they found in possession, as well as to their nearest neighbours—

[1] 2 Kings xxv. 18—21.

people, moreover (and here lay the difficulty), of whom some were kindred, some alien and some mixed. Can we guess at the attitude which the returning exiles would be likely to assume? Only vaguely. The two great prophets of the captivity, Ezekiel and Deutero-Isaiah, would clearly have ranged themselves upon opposite sides. Ezekiel would have denounced semi-heathen associations; Deutero-Isaiah would have hailed in closer relations with the remnant of Judah and Israel, and with the half-pagan, half-converted foreigners, a first practical realization of his universalistic dreams. Whether the latter prophet was still alive we do not know; but the list seems to indicate that even in Babylon the priestly spirit of Ezekiel was paramount in the counsels of the exiles.[1] There must have been some among the exiles who had more or less perfectly absorbed Deutero-Isaiah's teachings—not only his higher monotheism, but his wider conception of Israel's mission to the Gentile world. Echoes of his teaching may still be heard in subsequent prophetical and lyrical literature. But the historical records—such as they are—of the first hundred years after the return (before the curtain falls for a time upon external Jewish history) were drawn up by men of different views, so that it is impossible to learn from them what was the real strength and influence of their opponents. Or, rather, it is impossible to discern whether, besides the baser opponents, whom they stigmatize with not unjustifiable scorn, there were many others whose opposition proceeded from purer motives and rested upon a nobler basis of prophetic universalism.

[1] Ezra ii. 59, 62, 63.

Nor must we forget that it was far easier for Deutero-Isaiah and his disciples to contemplate in Babylonia a mission of Israel to the Gentiles and a close alliance with converted heathens, than for anything of the sort to be enacted upon Judæan soil. The advocates of separatism and exclusiveness had many arguments upon their side. Ritual strictness was beginning to be associated with religious purity—so much had been effected by the union of the two streams of prophecy and sacerdotalism in the person and teaching of Ezekiel; nor is there any reason to doubt that with religious purity there was very frequently associated a fairly high degree of moral earnestness and integrity. Before the settlement in Judæa had lasted many years, it also became evident that universalism might prove an open door to religious laxity and easy-going indifference. The more difficult cause was the cause of particularism, and the difficulty of a cause tends to increase its apparent probity and disinterestedness.

The people with whom a *modus vivendi* of one kind or another had to be effected were, as has been said, partly kindred and partly alien. In Judæa itself there were living descendants of the old native population which had been left behind by Nebuchadrezzar in 586 and subsequently had not joined in the migration into Egypt after the murder of Gedaliah. Some of these may have been admitted into the ranks of the "sons of the captivity," but many had probably intermarried with heathen intruders; while the majority, not having passed through the purgation of the exile, were on a lower level of moral and religious development. Idolatrous tendencies were possibly prevalent among them.

Were the home-comers to lose their hard-won freedom from idolatry by association and intermarriage with such as these? Northwards there lay a larger problem. Here, again, the population was mixed, and included descendants of the "ten tribes," and of the foreign settlers introduced by the Assyrian conquerors. Whether these two elements were clearly separate or separable, so that either could be distinguished from a third 'element arising from intermarriages between them, may well be doubted.

Though the men subsequently called "Samaritans," and composed partly of Israelite and partly of alien blood, worshipped Yahveh as their national God, they worshipped him in all probability less purely and with less understanding than the returned exiles. It is easily intelligible that the latter should not have desired to sully their religious purity by too close an alliance; and such apprehensions, which subsequent events proved to be by no means unjustified, must be allowed their full weight in an attempted judgment upon the action of the restored community, while it must at the same time be fully remembered that lower jealousies and petty exclusiveness may also have come into play.

So far, then, as we can gather, the leaders of the community observed at first a repellent or negative attitude towards their neighbours. As soon as the exiles had arrived at Jerusalem, a treasury for the temple was established and offerings to it were freely made.[1] The next

[1] Ezra ii. 68, 69.

thing would naturally have been to set to work upon the rebuilding of the sanctuary. An altar for sacrifices was, indeed, erected; but the author of Chronicles, who was also the compiler and editor of the Books of Ezra and Nehemiah and wrote more than two centuries after Cyrus, appears to have been in error when he describes the temple building as having been begun "in the second year of their coming unto the house of God at Jerusalem." Sheshbazzar, the Persian governor, may have formally laid the foundation-stone, but, if so, the work was not further carried on, and for some sixteen years it remained in abeyance.[1]

What caused this delay? There was probably a concurrence both of external and internal reasons. The Chronicler attributes the suspension of the work to the aroused hostility of the northern neighbours. They (the adversaries of Judah and Benjamin, as he proleptically calls them) "came to Zerubbabel, and to the heads of the fathers' houses, and said unto them, Let us build with you: for we seek your God as ye do; and we do sacrifice unto him since the days of Esar-Haddon, king of Assur, who brought us up hither. But Zerubbabel and Jeshua and the rest of the heads of the fathers' houses, said unto them, Ye have nothing to do with us to build an house unto our God," thus refusing them any share in the work.[2] Stade disbelieves this statement: the more cautious Kuenen, however, thinks we may accept it as substantially accurate.[3] If so, it would

---

[1] Ezra iii.; Haggai i.; cf. Stade, *Geschichte*, Vol. II. pp. 115—117; Kuenen, *Onderzoek*, Vol. I. p. 501, &c.

[2] Ezra iv. 1—5.   [3] Kuenen, *Onderzoek*, Vol. I. p. 505.

supply an adequate explanation for the strange delay. To the enmity and opposition of the neighbours thus early aroused, and used for the hindrance of an undertaking in which they were not allowed to share, there may also be added some internal reasons to which Schrader and Stade have drawn attention.[1] A natural desire to secure their own individual possessions and to spend leisure and money upon these, combined with bad harvests and comparative poverty, may have helped to make men think that for the present an altar of sacrifice was sufficient for their religious needs. If Cyrus had really promised to rebuild the temple at his own expense, the promise had not been fulfilled. Perhaps, too, the very fact that outward circumstance was still sordid and insecure may have helped to confirm the hesitation. Both indifference and scrupulosity might strengthen the feeling that the time for building Yahveh's house had not arrived, seeing that his wrath was still not wholly overcome.[2]

Thus there is no bright picture to be given of that restoration, the coming and character of which had been portrayed in such glowing colours. And now upon a community, disappointed and ill at ease, the curtain falls for some sixteen years, to rise again in the second year of king Darius, 520 B.C.

That interval was not calculated to raise the hopes or fire the enthusiasm of those who had already begun to contrast their own experience with the anticipations of

[1] Schrader, *Ueber die Dauer des zweiten Tempelbaus* (*Theol. Studien und Kritiken*, 1867, p. 460, &c.).

[2] Stade, Vol. II. pp. 120, 121.

the exilic prophets. Of all that Deutero-Isaiah or even Ezekiel had predicted, nothing had yet been realized. How was this to be accounted for? Had God cancelled his promise or forgotten his word? Similar disappointments in the pre-exilic period, both after Hezekiah's reform and at the death of Josiah, had been tolerably intelligible. Not long after the deliverance from Assyria and Hezekiah's reform, Manasseh had begun his reign of idolatrous reaction; and even when Josiah died, it might be said that his people were still tainted with vestiges of idolatry, and that the sins of Manasseh were unatoned. But now it had been distinctly stated by one prophet at the beginning of the exile, and by another prophet at its close, that past sin was pardoned, and that a new heart would be granted by the grace of God. On the return from Babylon, an era which should redound to Yahveh's glory no less than to his people's prosperity would infallibly begin. Apart even from the promise of the new heart, there were no great sins to explain a deferment of the predicted glories. There was no open and public idolatry as in the pre-exilic period; and yet it could not be said that the impoverished and dependent community did credit to the glory of its God.

This analysis of current difficulties indicates at the same time the insufficiencies of the religious point of view. A solution was to be effected, and a higher religious level attained, mainly—though this will seem a paradox to many—by the agency of the Law. As yet there was but little religious individualism—little joy in the Law for its own sake and without reference to consequences. Religious teachers could not yet urge men to find their own personal satisfaction in the service of God, because religion was still too much bound up with the community as a whole. Above all, there was as yet no clear conception of a future life, nor even of a bodily resurrection, with which to explain and to endure the trials and perplexities of earth.

Meanwhile the course of Persian history had not run smoothly since the death of Cyrus in 529. The levies of men and supplies for Cambyses' Egyptian expedition must have caused distress in Judæa. Then came the revolt of Pseudo-Smerdis, and the confusions and rebellions which ensued before Darius was seated firmly on the throne were scarcely over in the second year of his reign. Was it the excitement caused by these events, the hope of independence to which they naturally gave rise, which brought about a revival of the old prophetism? For our next contemporary sources are the writings of the two prophets, Haggai and Zechariah. These men renewed for the last time the form of prophecy to which we have been used in the pre-exilic period: their names and personalities, and the circumstances under which they wrote, are exactly known. In this respect they join on to Jeremiah and Ezekiel, whereas Deutero-Isaiah, with all his greatness, belongs to the class of anonymous writers represented afterwards by the apocalyptic theologians who try to hide their own lack of conscious inspiration under a mask of assumed antiquity.

Critics have often noticed a decay of freshness and originality in the writings of Haggai and Zechariah. Contrasted with Amos and Hosea they show a falling-off in creative power. But true though this may be, we must beware of attributing it to the inferior religious capacity of the post-exilic period. One form of religious expression was to be exchanged for others. Circumstances were no longer favourable to prophecy; the prophet, as we know him before the exile, needed for his sphere of action a corrupt community, and an intense antithesis between the evil many and the faithful few. The lessons of prophecy had been well-nigh exhausted by the teachers of the Assyrian and pre-exilic age. They were preserved in writing, and could be referred to by new teachers. Such a reference is actually made by Zechariah.[1]

One difference—and that a great one—had certainly resulted from the introduction of the Deuteronomic code. When the older prophets had drawn their accustomed antitheses between the spirit and the letter, or between ethical and ceremonial religion, they had denounced a ritual which was half-idolatrous in character, and which, though the outgrowth of sacred custom, was sanctioned by no recognized and authoritative law. Such antitheses were no longer permissible: the public and outward service of Yahveh had been purged of idolatrous elements, and the manner in which it was carried on was regulated more and more by rules and prescripts accepted on all hands as the Word of God. Again, in the olden times, after every allowance has been made for exaggeration, there evidently existed a frequent and glaring association of moral laxity with ceremonial exactitude: in the days of Zerubbabel and Joshua, on the other hand, as in the days of Ezra and Nehemiah, moral and ceremonial strict-

[1] Zech. i. 4, 6, vii. 7.

ness must often have gone hand-in-hand.¹ A problem of the post-exilic period was to create new vehicles of expression for the religious spirit: we shall subsequently see in what various ways the problem was solved.

The prophecies of Haggai and Zechariah both date from the year 520. Changes had taken place since the early days of restoration. Joshua was now high-priest. Zerubbabel, royal prince though he was, had been entrusted with the position of governor—a bid, perhaps, for the loyalty of the Jewish community, which in the troubled days of the Persian empire was not without its value.²

Haggai is mainly concerned with the rebuilding of the temple. Untouched as the work still was sixteen years after the return, *that* was now the sin which prevented the coming of the Messianic age. The prophet's denunciations took effect: the work was begun. And now Haggai's tone changed from threat to promise, from rebuke to encouragement. He ventured upon a perilous time-prediction. "It is but a little while," and the house which was then rising from its ruins should be filled with glory; from the day on which its foundations were laid, God would bless his people. Yet more: political independence and the overthrow of Persian rule were at hand: "the strength of the kingdoms of the nations" shall be destroyed, and Zerubbabel, Yahveh's servant, shall be as a signet-ring upon Yahveh's hand—an allusion, as clear as the prophet dared to make it, to the re-establishment of the monarchy.³

[1] Of course not always; cf. for the earlier period Zech. vii. and viii., and for a later (? Nehemian) period, Isaiah lviii.
[2] Haggai i. 1. [3] Haggai ii. 6—23; Stade, Vol. II. pp. 124—127.

Just as the work of rebuilding was begun, Zechariah entered upon his prophetical career. In addition to the peculiar form of his prophecies—the visions and interpreting angels, of which more in the sequel—there are some other points in the eight chapters of his book worthy of immediate notice. For although in the main his prophecies run parallel to those of Haggai, he has special characteristics of his own, and in one important feature resembles the pre-exilic type more closely than his contemporary.

Like Haggai, he is persuaded that the Messianic age is near. But he attributes its delay to other causes besides the neglect of the temple. The moral condition of the restored exiles was not what might have been expected from those who could remember the fate, and the reasons for the fate, which had overtaken their ancestors: there was still need to plead the cause of justice, honesty and compassion. As in Ezekiel, we find in Zechariah the two correlative aspects of spiritual reformation; it is enforced as the bounden duty of man; it is promised as the free gift of God.[1]

In depicting the Messianic age, Zechariah shows greater freedom and variety than Haggai. Joshua, the high-priest, occupies a more exalted place. Zerubbabel is to finish the temple and to sit upon his fathers' throne, Joshua the priest will stand at his right hand, and the counsel of peace will be between them.[2] Jerusalem will be filled with outward glory and spiritual blessedness; for

---

[1] viii. 16, 17, iii. 4, v. 5—11.

[2] vi. 13, partly according to the LXX. Cf. Cheyne, *Origin of the Psalter*, pp. 21 and 36; Stade, Vol. II. p. 126, n. 1.

God shall dwell once more in her midst, and she shall be called a city of truth and the holy mountain of Yahveh. The universalist hopes of older prophets are not forgotten. A judgment upon the heathen there will surely be, but nevertheless—so the prophet concludes his collected utterances—"It shall yet come to pass that there shall come *ples, and the inhabitants of many cities: and the inhabitants of one city shall go to another, saying, Let us go speedily to entreat the favour of Yahveh, and to seek Yahveh of Hosts: I will go also. Yea, many peoples and strong nations shall come to seek Yahveh of Hosts in Jerusalem, and to entreat the favour of Yahveh. Thus saith Yahveh of Hosts: In those days it shall come to pass that ten men shall take hold, out of all the languages of the nations, shall even take hold of the skirt of him that is a Jew, saying, We will go with you, for we have heard that God is with you."[1]

In this prophecy of a time when many nations shall "join themselves to Yahveh and be to him for a people," as in his noble contrast between fasting and morality, Zechariah breathes the spirit, if he does not echo the words, of the Babylonian Isaiah. Not unworthily is the list of historical prophets closed with him.

A difficulty—perhaps instigated by the hostile neighbours—occurred in the early stages of the rebuilding of the temple. The governor of the West Euphratic provinces inquired as to the authority under which the Jews had ventured to commence the work. Appeal was made to Darius, when the original permit of Cyrus was happily discovered at Ekbatana, and the order given that

[1] viii. 20—23.

the building should be suffered to continue. In four years, that is, in 516, the sanctuary was finished, and the dedication was celebrated "with joy."[1]

Perhaps some of the earliest hymns included in our existing Psalter were written to celebrate its completion; for the glorious Accession psalms, which tell of "the enthronement upon Zion of the Divine King,"—songs which are a lyrical echo of Deutero-Isaiah's prophecies,— are possibly to be ascribed to this period. Yahveh has now entered upon his world-wide Kingship, and the nations are bidden to ascribe to him who is their Judge and King, as well as Israel's, the glory which is his due. Nature and humanity are alike to bring their tribute of praise and thankfulness.[2] But once more the high anticipations of prophets and poets were doomed to disappointment. Darius secured for the Persian empire a new lease of prosperous existence: there was no question of Zerubbabel ascending the throne of his ancestors; and, so far as we know, the experiment of a Davidic governor was not repeated.

The consequence was that, as Yahveh showed no disposition to help his people, the leaders of the community turned again to the advancement of their own interests and to purely secular aims. In the uncertainty which still hangs over the date of Malachi—whether, namely, that little book precedes or succeeds Ezra—the main feature of the time about which we can speak with confidence was the prevalence of mixed marriages. Several causes contributed to these alliances, but the main cause

---

[1] Ezra v. 6—vi. 16.
[2] Cf. Cheyne, *Origin of Psalter*, p. 71.

was doubtless social and political: the semi-Israelites of the north, and the half-Judæan, half-alien settlers elsewhere, were many of them rich and prosperous, and a closer union with them would confer, from a secular point of view, considerable advantages.

At the same time it must be remembered that the memoirs and chronicles of the time were composed by fierce opponents of the mixed marriages. A genuine desire on the part of the half-breeds to become full members of Yahveh's communion, and a genuine desire on the part of some Jews to put the universalist aspirations of the prophets into practice, may also have been coincident motives in the attempted amalgamation. But modern historians are right in pointing out that even if many of these marriages were contracted from nobler motives than the opposite party allowed or even understood, they were nevertheless a great danger to the community as a whole, and likely, if suffered to continue unchecked, to bring back the religious condition of the people to a pre-exilic level. For neither the inward nor the outward religion of that time was firmly enough established to assimilate, without debasement or retrogression, a large influx of elements from a lower religious plane.

In this doubtful and difficult position the community remained for nearly sixty years after the completion of the temple. Historic accounts of this period there are none: whether any Biblical writings are to be ascribed to it is very doubtful. What has just been said is, therefore, deduced from the records of the following period, and more especially from the memoirs of the man who was to inaugurate a new era. For the curtain rises upon the opening of a new reformation, more decisive and more lasting than the reformation of Deuteronomy.

It comes from Babylon. Here, for the eighty years which had elapsed since the restoration under Cyrus, a large Jewish colony had continued to live and thrive under conditions and circumstances very different from those which their brethren were experiencing in Judæa. They, too, must have felt some disappointment in the perpetual postponement of the Messianic age; but they had gradually grown more accustomed to a lack of national and political independence, and could more naturally let their Jewish feelings find vent in purely religious directions. From their vantage-ground of distance they were keen critics, doubtless, of the faults displayed by the community in Palestine, and thus they may have been more easily able to attribute the failure of the prophecies to the errors and shortcomings of their kindred rather than to the anger, neglect or incapacity of the national God. They were not exposed to the same disintegrating influences which surrounded the settlers in Judæa; but though they had no temptation to intermarry and coalesce with the native populations of Babylonia and Persia, they were not uninfluenced by their associations. Eighty more years of life in or near the chief cities of a great empire made them keener and better educated.[1] At the same time they had become not less, but more, attached to their peculiar tenets and distinctive rites, for they had learned to realize their value and significance. General conceptions such as

[1] Smend, *Listen*, p. 5, n. 2.

those of holiness, and of Israel's abnormal position in the world at large, were more vividly realized, and even shed a strange and purifying light upon ceremonies of older date and of unknown origin.

We have especially to notice the legal work of Priests and Levites, who became, as it would seem, more and more exclusively, the spiritual leaders of the community in Babylonia during the eighty years between the restoration under Zerubbabel and the reformation under Ezra. Of prophets we hear nothing. It was indicated above that a very small proportion of Levites took part in the first settlement. Yet it would appear as if the Levites in Babylon, wholly forgetting the semi-idolatrous associations and memories of the past, became, as much as the Zadokite priests, students of the legal traditions of Yahveh's worship, and no less keen than they for strictness of ceremonial observance. Attempts at reconciliation were forthcoming, and these were ultimately to be successful. For without abandoning the vantage-ground of superiority which Josiah's reformation and Ezekiel's teaching had given them, the Zadokites were content to represent the position of the Levites, not as a punishment, but as a privilege of Mosaic ordinance. This further compromise—over and above the inclusion of "Ithamarite" Levites as fully qualified priests—was embodied in the law-book which Ezra, as we shall shortly see, brought with him from Babylonia to Jerusalem.

Ezra's mission and his fortunes in Jerusalem were recorded by him in memoirs, of which, unhappily, only fragments have been preserved to us. Thus there is a good deal in his history and in the reformation which was ultimately effected by the co-operation of Nehemiah, which must remain doubtful. Some things upon indubitable evidence we know; but much more, which would be needed to make the picture complete and intelligible in all its parts, must remain unknown.

Ezra set out on his journey to Jerusalem in the seventh year of Artaxerxes I., 458 B.C. Who then was Ezra, and what precisely were his objects and intentions? He was a Zadokite, closely related to the high-priest's family. But by later historians he is given another name than priest. Not only by the Chronicler, but also by an earlier writer, he is called indifferently Ezra the priest and Ezra the scribe or *sopher*. Here the word "scribe" has already its later religious significance, which it scarcely possessed in the days of Ezra himself: the Chronicler expands it into "a scribe skilful in the law of Moses;" while Artaxerxes' commissory letter—itself, however, of uncertain authenticity and date—speaks of Ezra as "the priest, the scribe of the law of the God of heaven."[1] That Ezra brought a book of law with him is certain. He was not the author of that book, though he may possibly have had some share in its revision and enlargement. In his day there could scarcely have been a clear distinction between priest and scribe: that is to say, there were as yet probably no scribes who were not either priests or Levites. It was not till the letter of the Law was thoroughly fixed, and existed as a supreme and authoritative religious power, that an order of scribes could grow up dissociated from, and even antagonistic to, the priesthood.

[1] Ezra x. 10, 16; Neh. viii. 1, 2, 4, 9, xiii. 13; Ezra vii. 6, 21.

Whether Ezra had received any summons from friends of his own line of thought in Jerusalem is doubtful. Seeing that communications passed not infrequently between the two sections of the community, it would *a priori* have seemed probable that Ezra's journey was induced by news of the mournful condition of affairs in the home country. But the precise point which was most bitter and hateful to Ezra and the men of his school —the prevalence of mixed marriages—seems to have come upon him soon after his arrival as an unheard-of and appalling novelty. In the rescript of Artaxerxes, Ezra is described as sent by the king and his counsellors "to inquire concerning Judah and Jerusalem according to the law of thy God which is in thine hand," and valuable subsidies are given him for the better provision of the temple services, as well as important privileges for its priests and servitors.[1] This letter of Artaxerxes is, however, clearly coloured from the Jewish point of view. It is even doubtful whether its compiler had ever seen the original decree.

But in the stress which it lays upon the temple services the letter seems accurately to reflect the truth. For the main object of Ezra's coming with the law of God in his hand is plainly indicated at the outset of his own memoirs: " Blessed be Yahveh, God of our fathers, who has put such a thing as this in the king's heart, *to beautify the house of Yahveh which is in Jerusalem.*"[2] Ezra's further action was prompted by the condition of things which he found existing in the capital. His original aim

[1] Ezra vii. 14—25. [2] vii. 27.

was a thorough re-organization of the entire ceremonial worship upon the basis of a new code.

Ezra took with him a considerable band of associates. Exclusive of women and children, 1068 persons were counted up at the place of departure. But in spite of the compromises, both practical and theoretical, between Zadokites and Levites, none of the latter had volunteered to take part in the fortunes of the new colony. Zadokite though he was, this abstention of the Levites grieved Ezra keenly; and when, after special effort and entreaty, thirty-eight Levites were persuaded to undertake the journey, he regarded their consent as a special indication of the divine favour. And now follows a curious incident. Ezra was unwilling to ask the king for any escort for himself and his fellow-travellers; he had used the customary phrases of religious piety in speaking to Artaxerxes of the power and benevolence of his God, and he was unwilling that the effect should be weakened, or an obvious retort put into the Persian courtiers' mouths, by any confession of fear. Yet the perils of the road were many. So Ezra proclaimed a fast, and God was earnestly besought to grant a prosperous journey. When Jerusalem was reached without let or hindrance upon the road, not a man in all the company but would believe that the supplication had been heard. Their courage was raised for the execution of the ritual reform which they had set out from Babylon to accomplish. The treasure was weighed out and deposited in the temple; a large sacrifice was offered up. Then the king's commission was delivered to certain Persian officials, and their help was sought and obtained for the support of the community and of the "house of God."[1]

But all further progress in the "beautifying" of the temple, or in the introduction of the more developed priestly law, was stopped by the news of the mixed marriages. Ezra's horror on learning that the whole community, from its temporal and spiritual chiefs downwards, was tainted with this pollution, knew no bounds. He broke forth into open lamentation. It is noticeable that the peculiar character of the mixed marriages did not pass muster even as an extenuating circumstance. They are described as purely heathen; and the fact that many of the "strange wives" must have been of semi-Israelite descent and had very possibly worshipped from infancy the God of Israel, is studiously ignored. At the close of Ezra's prayer his memoirs are broken off, and from a later authority which now takes their place we have only a fragment remaining, so that much obscurity hangs over the issues of these deplorable disclosures.[2] Ezra and his associates, together with the stricter party in Jerusalem, were enabled to carry the people with them. A proclamation was issued summoning the whole manhood of Judah to a solemn convocation at the capital. On the twentieth day of the ninth month—that is, in December—this strange assembly actually met. All the people sat in the "open space before the temple, trembling because of this matter and for the great rain." It must have been an extraordinary spectacle. No miracle was expected: no royal compulsion had driven them to the spot: it was a spontaneous expression of the hold

[1] Ezra viii. 1—36   [2] Ezra ix. (close of the memoirs).

which religion had obtained over their minds. The full measure of the difference between Israel before and after the captivity is revealed to us in this gathering. Ezra urged an immediate expulsion of the foreign wives. But a more prudent course was adopted. A commission of investigation was appointed to draw up a list of the transgressors. This work occupied the commission, of which Ezra was naturally the head, for three months, and the narrative breaks off with what is, presumably, a copy of the list which was then submitted to the people and its rulers. Yet this list only contains 113 names, made up of 17 priests, 10 Levites, and 86 laymen. Are we to suppose that it only enumerates the notable families who had intermarried with the "peoples of the land"? Would so much indignation and dismay have been evoked if the mixed marriages had been confined to so small a number?[1]

Meanwhile a misplaced chapter of Ezra gives the clue to the sudden suspension of the narrative. Things went badly with the reforming party between the attempted dissolution of the mixed marriages and the arrival of Nehemiah. Popular enthusiasm had perhaps infected a certain number of the supposed transgressors. From pressure or conviction, some of the tabooed marriages were annulled and the "strange" wives expelled. In other cases, doubtless, the husbands followed their wives into exile, and helped to kindle a flame of anger and revenge among the neighbouring communities, whose daughters had been exposed to indignity.

Both within and without Jerusalem there was opposi-

[1] Ezra x.; cf. Kuenen, *De Chronologie*, &c., p. 45, &c.

tion to the new reform. Ezra, consequently, seems to have thought the further development of his plans impracticable until he had secured Jerusalem from hostile attack. He attempted, therefore, to rebuild its walls and to make it a fortified city as of old. But he had reckoned without his hosts. Once more the Persian officials were induced to take up the enemies' cause, and this time with better effect. The fortification of the city, although not devised with insidious intent, might easily be regarded as a step towards rebellion. Artaxerxes accordingly gave orders that the work should be stopped, and with the help and to the satisfaction of the hostile neighbours, the walls were broken down, so that the outward condition of the capital was more miserable than before. Ezra's influence was destroyed, and very possibly several of the men who had followed their wives into exile may now have returned with them to Jerusalem.[1]

After twelve or thirteen years' interval of suspense and degradation, Ezra's party received unexpected aid from Persia. The reformation which the priest had been unable to complete was taken up and brought to a permanent and victorious issue by a distinguished layman. Nehemiah, the cup-bearer of Artaxerxes, is reasonably coupled with Ezra as the joint restorer of the enfeebled community and the joint founder of Judaism. His story must be read in detail in his own memoirs, of which a large part has been happily preserved for us, as well as in the modern histories of Israel. There is a vein of egotism in his character, but on the whole he deserves

[1] Ezra iv. 6—23; cf. Stade, Vol. II. pp. 158—162.

admiration for his devoted zeal and integrity. He was a courtier of high rank, but he was nevertheless with all his heart and soul a Jew, and in theory and practice an adherent of the strict separatist party, the best spirits in which were also men of that civic integrity inculcated by the prophets.

The first motive of his expedition was the rebuilding of the walls of Jerusalem—the removal of the "affliction and reproach" under which the community was labouring, with the ramparts of its capital broken down and the "gates thereof burned with fire." How, appointed by Artaxerxes governor of Jerusalem, he fulfilled his main mission, in spite of intense and often treacherous opposition from enemies both without and within the city, cannot be repeated here, but two points must not be passed over. Firstly, the particularist policy of Ezra was ratified and confirmed by the new governor. The Jews are the servants of the God of heaven: as for the outsiders, they have "no portion, nor right, nor memorial in Jerusalem."[1] Secondly, the prophets of the time were opposed to Nehemiah, and apparently in league with the hostile neighbours.[2]

While the party which had baffled Ezra was not strong enough to resist the force and *prestige* of a governor appointed by the great king, active and insidious correspondence was carried on between Nehemiah's enemies within and without Jerusalem. But the new governor was not to be turned from his purpose, nor entrapped by clumsily managed plots. He reminds us of the Maccabees in his fine combination of unshaken confidence in God

[1] Neh. ii. 20.   [2] vi. 7—14.

THE PRIESTLY LAW. 313

with a wary promptitude for the successful execution of his plans. His language, when an armed attack was expected, is thoroughly Maccabean: "Be ye not afraid of them," he urged the builders; "remember Yahveh who is great and revered, and fight for your brethren, your sons and your daughters, your wives and your houses."[1] This is something better than the "sword of Yahveh and of Gideon." It implies, even as the fierceness of the covenanters implied, the inspiring consciousness of a holy cause.

After fifty-two days of unremitting labour, during great part of which Nehemiah and his immediate followers never left their posts nor put off their clothes, the work was finished: the walls were built and the gates set up. The successful conclusion of Nehemiah's primary object was immediately celebrated by a joyful dedication, in which Ezra, who now suddenly re-appears upon the scene, is recorded to have taken part.[2]

But the ceremony of dedicating the walls was to be quickly followed by a ceremony of far deeper import. We know nothing of what must have passed between Nehemiah and Ezra after the arrival of the former at Jerusalem; yet we know that Nehemiah would be heart and soul with Ezra in the desire to establish the temple ceremonial and the whole outward worship of Yahveh upon a more adequate and honourable basis. They would think alike, too, in desiring to prevent the pollution of Yahveh's name and service by lax observance, or by any

[1] iv. 14 (iv. 8, Heb.).
[2] Cf. Stade, Vol. II. pp. 173—175; Kuenen, *Onderzoek*, Vol. I. p. 498; *De Chronologie*, p. 30.

want of ritual purity. Seeing that these two connected objects were to be attained, according to Ezra's judgment, by the introduction of that new law (in addition to the already acknowledged law of Deuteronomy) which he had brought with him from Babylonia, the sympathizing governor must have been willing and anxious to put all facilities in Ezra's way for making that yet unpublished code known to, and accepted by, the community. There could be no better opportunity for this delicate and difficult task than a day immediately after the dedication of the walls, when the people were already raised to a high pitch of religious enthusiasm, and when a large number of the country population was still present at Jerusalem. Thus it would seem that the ceremony of dedication followed at once on the conclusion of the building, upon the 25th day of Elul, and that the introduction of the law was arranged for the first day of the following month—Tishri, 444 B.C.[1]

Neither from Ezra's nor Nehemiah's memoirs are we allowed to hear the story. In the ill-arranged Book of Nehemiah, we are suddenly brought, as it were, face to face with the imposing scene, in the following words from the hand of a later historian: "And all the people gathered themselves together as one man into the broad space that was before the water-gate; and they spake unto Ezra the scribe to bring the book of the law of Moses, which Yahveh had commanded to Israel." Then Ezra brought the law and read therein.[2]

But before we follow further the story of this reading and of its effects, it is necessary to consider what manner

[1] Cf. Stade, Vol. II. p. 176.   [2] Neh. viii. 1—4.

of book it was which was thus openly set forth to the people, and what may yet be learnt of its history and origin.

The greater portion of it is undoubtedly still preserved to us in large sections of the Pentateuch and Joshua. Speaking very roughly, and including additions made subsequently to the proclamation under Ezra in 444, it embraces some eleven chapters in Genesis, some nineteen in Exodus, the whole of Leviticus, and twenty-eight chapters of Numbers.[1] If you were to print these eighty-five chapters together, they would not make a continuous whole, neither would they form a "book" in the ordinary acceptation of the word. The reasons are manifold. The Pentateuch, as we now possess it, is a fusion of these eighty-five chapters with the two far older narratives of the pre-prophetic or early prophetic period, and with the law of Deuteronomy. That fusion was effected in the generations succeeding Ezra. But when the eighty-five priestly chapters were dovetailed with the other sixty-eight (omitting Deuteronomy), neither portion of the conglomerate was unimpaired by the process. But this is only one reason out of three for the fragmentary appearance of the eighty-five chapters if printed by themselves. Another is, that additions were made to

[1] For the Book of Genesis the English reader will find the Priestly and Prophetic portions most easily and conveniently distinguished in Mr. Fripp's excellent little volume, *The Composition of the Book of Genesis* (London : Nutt, 1892), of which the small size must not lead any one to ignore the immense amount of patient labour and detailed investigation which has been given by the author to what most people would consider somewhat tedious and unattractive work.

the "book" subsequently to Ezra. And the third and most important is, that in the form in which Ezra read it aloud to that famous assembly at Jerusalem, it was already an interpolated book, without any claim to artistic unity.

In spite of this double series of interpolations, these eighty-five chapters of the Pentateuch and the corresponding fragments in Joshua have a unity of another kind—a unity of character. All of them, whether historical or legal, are written from a sacerdotal point of view, and reflect the characteristic conceptions of the priest. The writers are Israelites; still more, they are Israelites who have absorbed some main elements of prophetic teaching, and who start from the platform of monotheism. But the prevailing instincts of the priest all the ancient world over are also theirs: they correspond clearly to their type. In this respect it will have to be observed how the aims, and still more the ideas, of the authors of the priestly code differed from the later legalists, who yet were in the unfortunate predicament of having to accept a law, full of priestly narrownesses and survivals, as the pure and undiluted word of God.

The interpolations which had been introduced into the central portion of our eighty-five chapters are mainly earlier than that central portion itself. They consist of those codifications of pre-exilic laws and customs of which mention was made in the last Lecture. These collections, however, of which the most important is the law of holiness in Leviticus xvii.—xxvi., appear in our present Pentateuch in an enlarged and edited form, and it is a moot question how far these editings may be the work of the author of the "central portion," or of another but kindred mind.

Meanwhile, the central portion, which thus stands between the earlier codifications and the later post-Nehemian additions, is that part of the whole on which our attention may be chiefly fixed, for it, as it were, determined the tone of all the subsequent accretions. Wherever these do not clearly differ from its general spirit, they can be quoted in illustration.

This central portion, then, which perhaps originally did not include much more than half of the present eighty-five priestly chapters in the first four Pentateuchal books, was not a lengthy work and was not intended for specialists.[1] It may have been written about 500 B.C.; but whatever the exact date, its origin lies between Zechariah and Ezra (520—458). Its object was to present a picture of Israel's sacred institutions as they should be, and as the author doubtless hoped that by means of his book they would become. On the precedent of older models, this desired ideal is represented as having been originally prescribed by God through Moses and realized in the distant past. It is cast in the form of a history extending from the creation of the world to the Israelite settlement in Canaan. Besides his general priestly proclivities, the author has a special and peculiar delight in dry genealogies, exact dates and precise measurements. How far these details have any sort of traditional basis is very doubtful.

[1] Cf. Wurster, *Zur Charakteristik und Geschichte des Priestercodex und Heiligkeitsgesetzes*, Z.A.W., 1884, pp. 112—133.

Israel's sacred institutions centre round the temple and its service, and the main portion of the book is thus devoted to the relation how that service of the temple, which, for the Mosaic age, has to be modified into a moveable tabernacle, was organized and established. What ought to and was to be is described under the disguise of an inauguration of a supposed Mosaic original, while almost every recorded incident in the history has its ceremonial or institutional bearing.

A full analysis of the book and of its supplements must naturally be sought elsewhere. Here it is only proper and needful to dwell upon its general character, and upon the nature of its more salient religious conceptions.

It may at once be noticed that, both in its original form and as introduced by Ezra, the book primarily concerns the community and not the individual. Ultimately the Law became a means of religious satisfaction, and a veritable link between God and man, so that the multiplicity of its enactments was regarded as a privilege, leading those who were fortunate enough to know and follow them to a higher religious level and to their temporal and eternal bliss. This, however, is a later point of view; it is the legalist's conception and not the priest's. The business of the priest is to make a holy community, among whom God may dwell. We have already met this strange idea in Ezekiel; it is the central conception of the priestly code. The laws are not primarily intended to secure man's happiness, but God's satisfaction. Human prosperity is not, as in Deuteronomy, either the bribe or the goal; the prevailing motive is the glory of God. Extravagant as the conception is, there is something grand and spiritual about it. To the community is assigned a purely religious end: political aims are ignored, for the people lives for God's sake and not for its own. Push the conception one stage further back, and with a revival of far earlier ideas, the land as Yahveh's dwelling-place becomes more important than the people which inhabit it: the necessity, for example, of exacting blood for blood lies in the fact that the stain of blood which defiles the land can only be wiped out by the blood of him that shed it, while the mischief of defilement is the pollution of the chosen residence of Yahveh.[1]

In Babylon the Jewish priests seem to have lost touch with the political aspirations of their people. Dreams of world-wide rule under a beneficent king harmonized rather with prophetic modes of thought than with priestly visions. The priest's Messianic age is one in which the holiness of Israel is preserved inviolate, and God dwells secure in a sanctuary, officered and directed according to his will. Nothing is said in the priestly code of a possible king; the pre-exilic monarchy was a thing of the remote past, and the hopes which in Judæa had been associated with Zerubbabel seem to have found no echo in Babylonia. Above the high-priest no lay ruler is indicated: indeed, the hierarchy, which the author of the "central portion" contemplates, scarcely admits, as it wholly ignores, any secular officers by its side. With the general life of the community the priest who has no aim beyond holiness has nothing to do. Perhaps it did not even interest him.

[1] Numbers xxxv. 33, 34.

His business is purely religious, and the centre of his thoughts is Yahveh. Priestly as his conception is both of God and of religion, it must be allowed that in his own way God and religion are both very near and dear to him. As with Ezekiel, so also with the authors of the priestly code, the charge has been brought against them that their conception of God is distant and transcendental. But this charge labours under the same inaccuracy. Because their God was a different Deity from the God of the prophets, or from the God of Jesus, or from the God of modern Jews and Christians, he was not therefore necessarily a God less near and dear to them. He was perpetually in their thoughts, and they conceived him as dwelling in their temple: the life of the community was consecrated to his service for his sake as much as, if not more than for its own.

There is certainly a fusion in their conception of God between old heathen notions and prophetic ideas: this fusion is characteristic of the entire priestly law. Gross anthropomorphisms are carefully avoided, but God still comes down from heaven to earth, talks with Moses face to face, and is revealed in theophanies of cloud and fire.[1] God's wrath is still aroused—albeit no longer from unknown causes—by accidental or trivial violations of his sanctity; and the priestly writers, apparently in all good faith, really believed that there might still be an almost mechanical explosion of divine anger on account of offences wholly removed from the sphere of morality, but trenching upon the maintenance of Yahveh's honour.[2]

[1] E.g. Genesis xvii. 3, 22; Exod. xxxiv. 34; Lev. ix. 23, &c.
[2] E.g. Lev. x. 1—6; Exod. xxx. 33; Numbers i. 53.

For the service of the sanctuary, as it is the chief end of the national existence, so is it invested also with peculiar dangers, and any deviation from the laws laid down for its regulation would be followed by terrible results.

Why Israel has been chosen by God is not clearly stated. It is an ultimate fact of religion, to be accepted without explanation. "Ye shall be holy unto me: for I, Yahveh your God, am holy, and have severed you from other peoples that ye should be mine."[1] But as through Israel Yahveh is glorified to all mankind, the acknowledgment of Yahveh's glory may be said to be the final cause both of Israel's election and of the world's history. In this point priestdom and prophecy are at one; yet it may well be questioned whether the constituent elements of Yahveh's glory would have seemed the same to Isaiah as to the authors of the priestly code. Meanwhile, in Israel, God has appointed a certain method by which he will be served, and certain rites by which he will be approached and propitiated. It must be remembered that the Yahveh of the exilic priest is the God of the spirits of all flesh, and the Creator, by divine fiat, of heaven and earth. And yet this sole and unique God is to be domiciled in some mysterious way or other—for what the exact conception was can never be precisely recalled—within a human shrine.

No wonder, then, that the absurd disproportion of the two terms, the God and his dwelling-place, should tend in some degree to exaggerate the old priestly fears of the result of divine contact with earthly things and beings. Hence a large proportion of the rites and cere-

[1] Lev. xx. 26.

monies in the priestly code is directly concerned with the removal of all possible sins and defilements which may either be inconsistent with the presence of God within his sanctuary, or convert it into an occasion of appalling consequences to his chosen people. They do not carry their efficacy in themselves, but owe it to the divine decree. All of them—including sacrifices—are supposed to have started into existence together, perfect and ready-made. Before the Mosaic legislation, for example, nobody had ever dreamed of such a thing as sacrifice, at least none of the well-regulated ancestors of the Israelites from Noah and Abraham downwards. But the rites and ceremonies which God does choose are naturally those which lay ready to the author's hand in tradition and pre-exilic practice. Some of them embody superstitious ideas of extremest antiquity, and are strangely pagan in their very form and enactment, yet out of all the heathen sting is removed through their adoption and promulgation by Yahveh.[1] That marriage of heathen practice to monotheistic use is one of the oddest and saddest features of the whole priestly code.

God, then, to the main author of the priestly legislation, should live in the very centre of Israel. A single sanctuary needs no longer to be fought for as in the days of Josiah: it is everywhere assumed. The divine majesty at the centre is hedged round by a double ring of servitors, and the Israelites themselves, as the third ring, make the distance yet wider between the centre and the profane world without.

In the matter of priests and Levites the new code

[1] E.g. Lev. xiv. 53; Numbers v. 17, &c., xix. 2.

THE PRIESTLY LAW. 323

suggests a compromise. The priests are no longer to be identified with the Zadokites, as in Ezekiel: they are the sons of Aaron. Besides those who fell victims to the divine wrath, Aaron had two other sons, Eleazar and Ithamar.[1] Eleazar is the ancestor of Zadok: all other Levitical priests who could manage to pass the magic circle might be enrolled as sons of Ithamar. The other descendants of Levi, outside the family of Aaron, are not admitted to the rights and privileges of the priesthood; yet their lower position is no longer represented, as in Ezekiel, as due to any fault of their own, but as a divine arrangement from the beginning. The Levite, as the second-grade servitor of the sanctuary, is also a privileged person, of superior holiness to the common Israelite; nor is the law, which is careful to secure a good revenue to the priest, neglectful of the material interests of the Levite.[2]

Since the priest's heart is bound up with his sanctuary, almost all his code is directly or indirectly concerned with it. "To the author of the priestly legislation, the interests of the altar and of its ministers are the chief matters of moment—not religion and morality. Purity of skin and of dishes is more important than purity of heart."[3] Such is the verdict of a most distinguished scholar to whom all Biblical students are deeply indebted; but it is, nevertheless, inaccurate and one-sided. Morality was not indifferent to our legislating priests; but it was not, if

[1] Numbers iii. 1—4.
[2] Numbers iii. 6, &c., xviii. 21—24, &c.
[3] Reuss, *Die Geschichte der heiligen Schriften alten Testamentes*, § 379, p. 489 (2nd ed., 1890).

one may say so, upon their agenda-paper. Their business was the regulation of the cultus. That was susceptible of, as it required, minute direction and enactment: the laws of morality were simpler, and had been sufficiently laid down in earlier codes. If it be asked whether the priestly conception of holiness did not include morality, or whether an outrage on morality was not also conceived as an outrage upon sanctity, the answer would certainly be affirmative; but it has to be borne in mind that a violation of morality could but seldom be even partially atoned for by sacrifice, and that it therefore fell outside the priestly sphere. Touches here and there show us, however, that our priests were not indifferent to morality. Virtue and vice were antecedent to sacrifice and ritual. Noah was righteous, and walked with God when all the world was filled with violence. The maxim for Abraham's conduct is not unworthy of a prophet: "Walk before me, and be thou perfect."[1]

But the thorough priestliness of our authors makes them naturally full of conceptions which are very alien to ourselves. A localization of Deity carried with it grave risk of materialism. It gave a new lease of life to the old heathen idea that a man could be nearer to God in one place than in another; and that this idea was now associated with a single and supreme Deity made it but the more incongruous. And it also furbished up and strengthened the strange, unprophetic notion—which was to lead to far-reaching and extraordinary consequences—that one class of men might be "nearer" to God than another, or that the Deity could

[1] Gen. vi. 9—11, xvii. 1.

only be approached by some external mediator or intercessor.

That famous command of the earlier code of sanctity, "Ye shall be holy, for I, Yahveh, your God am holy," may be taken as watchword and key-note for one whole side of the priestly legislation. That God may dwell in the chosen sanctuary and radiate his glory unobscured, everything in Israel from circumference to centre must be holy; and the nearer to the centre (the nearer, in other words, to God), the higher must be the degree of holiness required, the more elaborate the rules and precautions in order to realize and maintain it.

Now the conception of holiness familiar to an Israelite priest of even the sixth or fifth century retained many characteristics of its original connotation in primitive religions. What those characteristics were, and how they arose and came to be, anybody can now learn by reading Professor Robertson Smith's delightful book, *The Religion of the Semites*.[1] "Holy" may be roughly regarded as a general term to describe the peculiar condition of a person or thing, as it is or as it should be, which has any relation to or connection with deity. It has primarily "nothing to do with morality and purity of life." Even when the term had become partially moralized, the old ideas still maintained themselves among the priesthood. Thus holiness to the Israelite priest was outward as well as inward, physical as well as spiritual, material as well as moral. Moreover, in his actual legislation, that portion of holiness which he could specially deal with by precept and rule was the material, the phy-

[1] Cf. especially pp. 132—149 (Lecture IV.), and pp. 427—437.

sical and the outward. In the command, "Ye shall be holy, for I, Yahveh, your God am holy," the idea of ethical sanctity is included, but it was only the violation of physical sanctity which could be fully rectified by ceremonial ordinance, and which therefore lay entirely within the reach and compass of the code. If, then, to touch a dead mouse impairs a man's holiness, and God's desire is that all Israel should be holy (each class in its own degree), it is, in the first place, clear that that which injures the holiness of the community, be it done voluntarily or involuntarily, be it moral transgression or ritual mishap, is in all cases alike an offence against Deity. Thus sin (in our sense of the word) tends to be looked at, not from the prophetic point of view as a social and public obliquity, nor from the later point of view of some sages and psalmists as a pollution of the individual soul, but in harmony with the general aim and object of the priestly authors, as a breach of purity, a disturbance of that undefiled condition of the land and its inhabitants under which alone God can continue to dwell among his people and in his sanctuary. The code is, indeed, *more* concerned with involuntary than with voluntary offences, for—with some small exceptions—it is only the first class of which the pollution can be overcome by ceremonial means.

In this respect we see clearly to what large extent the priest, while maintaining many of his own peculiar points of view, had yet shared in and absorbed the higher religious teaching of the prophets. There is no longer any idea of influencing God by sacrifice beyond and above the range of its influence as divinely decreed.

A deliberate moral iniquity is not to be obliterated by sacrifices. It must be punished under the penal law or forgiven by repentance, and for the individual there is no other means of atonement. It is the blot upon the community entailed by individual guilt which is otherwise provided for. Under the atoning efficacy of sin and trespass-offering there fall for the individual only involuntary offences, whether moral or ritual, and such voluntary offences of either class which are (1) not done with deliberate intent to insult the majesty of God, or (2), being confessed by the doer, are not punishable under the ordinary civic law. In certain cases where restitution is possible, it must precede the atoning sacrifice.[1]

While, however, a distinction is carefully drawn between intentional and unintentional wrong-doing, between intentional transgression of ritual or moral commands there is none. The laws of God are all on the same level: he who, by malice aforethought and with deliberate intent, gathers sticks upon the sabbath, is no less worthy of the gravest punishment, and has committed no less a sin, than he who robs his neighbour or commits adultery. We have evidence here, on the one hand, of the intense danger of ascribing any merely ceremonial practice to the commandment of God, and, on the other hand, of the equal danger of dragging God down into the sphere and conditions of man. Directly the platform of the older prophets is abandoned—that nothing but the moral law is the law of God—you run the risk of setting up a whole series of acts utterly unconnected

[1] Cf. Dillmann's *Commentary* on Lev. iv.—vi.

with morality upon the same level as itself. So, too, with the other mistake committed in the priestly code. Since God is conceived as dwelling in a human sanctuary, his own holiness, as well as the sanctity which he requires from man, becomes materialized, and can be violated by acts outside that moral law in the breach of which alone any insult to the divine majesty can properly be supposed to consist.

Again, if many elements in the priestly conception of "holiness" have their roots deep down in a distant past when religion and morality were but imperfectly allied, and superstitious fear was closely connected with religious ceremonial, this is still more the case with the conception of "uncleanness." Here, also, what uncleanness originally meant, and how it gradually became separated off from the idea of holiness, may be profitably studied in Prof. R. Smith's book. In the priestly legislation, as God enjoins holiness and forbids uncleanness, that which is unclean, be it person or thing, is in a condition more or less offensive to God, and if to him offensive, then sinful. Where, perhaps, to our modern eyes, this conception of uncleanness produces in the priestly code the strangest use of the term "sin," is that, in accordance with ancient and once widely prevalent superstitions, certain purely natural processes or accidents are regarded as polluting, and consequently as sinful.[1] Thus

[1] Would that the Judæan priests could have risen to the discriminating judgment shown in the great saying attributed to Theano, most frequently called the wife, sometimes the daughter, of Pythagoras (Zeller, *Philosophie der Griechen*, Vol. I. 4th ed., p. 288, n. 1): Θεανὼ ἐρωτηθεῖσα ποσταία γυνὴ ἀπ' ἀνδρὸς καθαρεύει, Ἀπὸ μὲν τοῦ ἰδίου, εἶπε, παραχρῆμα· ἀπὸ δὲ τοῦ ἀλλοτρίου, οὐδέποτε. Stob. *Flor.* 74, 53;

if you touch a human corpse, you must be "purged from sin."[1] Leprosy, which seemed a divine plague, and such maladies and contingencies as are related to the mysterious powers and functions of life and generation, entail a sin-offering after their cessation or cure. A woman after child-birth must bring the same. Strangest of all is the rite to be used if "leprosy" breaks out upon the walls of a house. Here the house has to be atoned for by animal blood, just as if it were a human being. The externalization of holiness may be said in this rite to reach its climax.[2]

At the basis of the enactments concerning public ceremonial lie the same fundamental conceptions of holiness and sin. All is looked at from God's point of view rather than man's; the individual is more than ever sunk in the community. And the community is no longer a people, but a church: the function of Israel is the glorification of God. Thus the institution of sacrifice in the

---

Diogenes Laertius, viii. 1, 43. I am indebted for the reference to L. Schmidt's charming book, *Die Ethik der alten Griechen*, Vol. I. p. 133 (1882).

[1] Numbers xix. 12. On the method and original meaning of such purifications, cf. *Religion of the Semites*, pp. 404—407.

[2] Lev. xii. 6, xiv. 18, 33—53, xv. 15—30. For the last passage in Leviticus, cf. Frazer, *The Golden Bough*, Vol. II. pp. 238—243; and generally, R. Smith, *Religion of the Semites*, pp. 427—437; and from a particular point of view, Schwally, *Das Leben nach dem Tode* (1892), p. 85. I have purposely omitted from these necessarily very brief and fragmentary remarks that phase of "uncleanness" which results, as it were, from an excess of holiness, or from having had to do with specially holy things. In such cases, the common origin of both uncleanness and holiness in "taboo" seems particularly clear: cf. *Religion of the Semites*, pp. 332, 405, 431, 432; *Golden Bough*, Vol. I. pp. 167—171.

priestly code becomes something very different from the aspect which it wore in the old pre-exilic days, or even in Deuteronomy. That difference can easily be interpreted entirely to the disadvantage of the new code; but great care must be taken in such comparisons and antitheses, else one might find it hard to explain the passionate and spiritual attachment to the temple and its services in the post-Nehemian period. If the spontaneous and natural character of the old pre-exilic worship seems to have given way to a fixed and mechanical system of sacrificial exercises, one must remember that these exercises were not necessarily or usually regarded as a burden, but, like the law itself, as a glorious manifestation of Yahveh's intimate relations with Israel, and as the chosen means of man's communion with God. Higher religious feelings soon began to clothe and vivify the sacrificial system of the priestly code than were ever suggested or aroused by the sacrifices before the exile, whether at Jerusalem or in all the high places of Judæa.

In the pre-exilic period the most frequent and characteristic offerings were those which kept closest to their ancient form—namely, the sacrificial meal. We have seen how, originally, the slaughtering and eating of flesh was always accompanied by, or rather was identical with, sacrifice. The most familiar sacrifices were those in which the offerer himself shared in their consumption. Such offerings, whether they were casual or connected with the three yearly festivals, were in either case expressions of joy and festivity, and belonged to that portion of religious ceremonial which was common to the religion of Yahveh with other cognate religions.

Deuteronomy had neither modified the character of the sacrifices, nor regulated them minutely: the great change which it introduced—its complete break with the past—was the secularization of slaughter, and the prohibition of all sacrifices except at the central sanctuary. But it was this change which paved the way for the arrangements and conceptions of the priestly code. Here the individual is not exactly left out in the cold; the manner of his sacrifice is, indeed, minutely regulated; but the real interest of the code lies in the public offerings of the whole community. So long as the individual makes his sin-offering whenever it is required, and thus, so far as in him lies, prevents any pollution resting upon Israel, the priestly legislators do not appear to be further concerned about him. Apart from the whole, he is a mere fragment of that collective religious entity which absorbs the life of its constituent atoms.

After the exile the temple of Jerusalem effectually became what Deuteronomy had first sought to make it, the sole place of worship for the whole nation. But it became much more. It was the place in which the religion of Yahveh was outwardly expressed. Such a visible symbolism could not be left to the varying taste of individual worshippers; it needed distinct and defined regulation, independent of chance and permanent in form. Collective or public sacrifices were not unknown in the pre-exilic period. In the later monarchy, at any rate, daily sacrifices were offered up in the temple, and paid for by the king. But the temple of Jerusalem, even after Deuteronomy, was still in great measure the sanctuary, not of the nation, but of the capital and the king. Ezekiel had first suggested its local severance from the palace, and by the time when the priestly code was written, the connection of the temple with the monarchy had faded away. The code desired to make it, what in fact it had partly become, the centre of the national life, just as its highest officer was to be the foremost man in Israel.

God, for whose sake Israel exists, has ordered a certain manner of divine worship. This worship, therefore, forms the most important feature in Israel's life, and the expense of it becomes a national charge. The two main kinds of communal sacrifices are the burnt-offering and the sin-offering.[1] Burnt-offerings, given in their entirety to God, were the fit sacrifices for a people as a whole; they were also the most solemn and mysterious, and not without peculiar propitiatory force.[2] Upon new moons and the three annual feasts national sin-offerings were added, and to these sacrifices was specially devoted a new festival, or rather a new fast-day, which gradually acquired enormous importance and celebrity. The priestly legislation maintained the three old yearly festivals of Passover, Pentecost and Tabernacles, although it modified their character and the method of their celebration. Among them, however, it somewhat strangely intercalated two new days of "holy convocation" and abstention from labour—in this, as in other innovations, owing the general conception to Ezekiel.

[1] On the origin, growth and meaning of these two forms of sacrifice, cf. R. Smith, *Religion of the Semites*, pp. 219, 220, 329—333, 382, &c.
[2] Cf. e.g. Lev. i. 4.

The first day of the seventh month—the old New Year of the pre-exilic period—is to be specially hallowed over and above the new moons of other months, while upon its tenth day "whatsoever soul shall not be afflicted shall be cut off from among his people."[1] The rites to be observed at the sanctuary upon this Atonement-day are elaborately described in the sixteenth chapter of Leviticus. For our purposes the unity of that chapter need not be questioned, though it would seem that it is a conglomerate of two or more independent elements, and that the atonement of the people and the atonement of the sanctuary were not originally part and parcel of the same law.[2]

The atonement of the sanctuary is a curious example of the confusion in the priestly authors' minds upon the subject of sin. It assumes that sin, under the form of impurity, can propagate itself from person to things, which things, if devoted to sacred uses, need all the more urgently a ritual purification.[3] Since it is God who

[1] Lev. xxii. 23—32.
[2] See Stade, *Geschichte*, Vol. II. p. 258 ; Benzinger, *Das Gesetz über den grossen Versöhnungstag* (*Z. A. W.*, 1889, pp. 65—89); Schmoller, *Das Wesen der Sühne in der alttestamentlichen Opfertora* (*Theol. Studien und Kritiken*), 1891, pp. 205—288.
[3] Cf. *Religion of the Semites*, p. 389. The language used above is, I think, accurate. In the sprinkling of the blood on the day of Atonement, which "cleanses the altar, and makes it holy from all the uncleanness of the children of Israel," Prof. R. Smith tells us that "an older and merely physical conception of the ritual breaks through, which has nothing to do with the forgiveness of sin ; for uncleanness in the Levitical ritual is not an ethical conception." But nevertheless it would really seem as if the material sanctuary could be made "unclean" through all offences alike, whether physical or moral, so

orders the ritual and chooses that it shall produce the required effect, the process, which would otherwise savour of magic, is rendered harmless.

More important for us is the atonement of the people. It is unnecessary to consider closely the curious rite of sending a goat into the wilderness to Azazel, an evil spirit or demon, strange and unexampled as it is that a superstition of this unmonotheistic kind should have been incorporated into so late a code. More germane to our central purpose is the effect of the whole ceremonial: "On that day shall atonement be made for you to cleanse you: ye shall be clean from all your sins before Yahveh." "It shall be an everlasting statute for you, that atonement shall be made for the children of Israel for all their sins once a year." Here the cleansing power, which Ezekiel himself had attributed in symbolical language to the redeeming Spirit of God acting in the heart of man, is apparently ascribed to a solemn yearly ceremonial. There is no doubt that this institution was likely to lead, and did lead, to many fresh superstitions. By the letter of the law it was seemingly implied that the guilt of all sins, of what kind soever, be they ritual or moral, voluntary or involuntary, would be wiped out and atoned for by the ceremony of the Atonement-day.[1]

that one is justified in speaking of a "confusion in the priestly authors' minds upon the subject of sin." For the atonement of the holy place is made (Lev. xvi. 16) "because of the uncleannesses of the children of Israel, and because of their transgressions, even all their sins." The expression "all their sins" throws together, I imagine, both ceremonial and moral wrongdoing into a single, undistinguished heap.

[1] To avoid misunderstanding, it should perhaps be noted here that the official *Rabbinic* teaching restricted the atoning virtue of the day

By a process of ingenious combination, some scholars have argued that only unintentional sins were included in this annual forgiveness.¹ Nothing in the sixteenth chapter of Leviticus, however, would warrant such a distinction. "All sins," without exception, and including, therefore, those which are committed with "a high hand" presumptuously, are to be atoned for in the great tenth day of the seventh month.² The truer explanation

to sins committed against God. Sins committed against man, which are of course also an offence against God, can only be forgiven on and by the Atonement-day, after the sinner has made his peace with, or given satisfaction to, the man against whom he has sinned. To him, moreover, who says, "I will sin and the Day will bring me atonement, the Day brings no atonement:" Yoma, viii. 9. I may be permitted to add here that Prof. R. Smith is in error when he says, that "even in the theology of the Rabbins penitence atones only for light offences, all grave offences demanding also a material prestation" (*Religion of the Semites*, p. 413). The passage in the Mishnah (Yoma, viii. 8) to which he refers, says, "Repentance atones for light offences then and there" (i.e. God pardons them immediately); "with regard to heavy offences, repentance makes them hang in the balance until the Day comes and atones for them." Here, first of all, nothing is said of "material prestations." The atoning efficacy lies in the Day itself, the functions of which continue the same even after the destruction of the Temple and the complete cessation of sacrifices. Secondly, no more is implied than that there is a *formal* suspension of forgiveness between the repentance and the Day. Practically, forgiveness is assured by repentance; formally, it is suspended till the actual Day arrives. Otherwise, what would there be left for the Day to do? No teachers, as we shall subsequently learn, exalted the place and power of repentance more than the Rabbis. There was no sin for which in their eyes a true repentance could not obtain forgiveness from God.

¹ Cf. Kuenen, *Religion of Israel*, Vol. II. p. 272.

² Nor do I think that the "Mishnic interpretation," adopted apparently by Prof. R. Smith (*Religion of the Semites*, p. 388), can have been in the mind of the author or authors of Lev. xvi. It is neither

of this seemingly immoral arrangement must rather, I imagine, be sought for in those fundamental characteristics of the priestly code which have already come before us. The Atonement-day is instituted for the community, not for the individual. And it is instituted because Yahveh dwells, and that he may continue to dwell, within the land of Israel. All sins, whether moral or ritual, whether intentional or involuntary, even if legally punished or ritually atoned for, may be supposed to leave behind them within the community a certain sediment of impurity. But a far graver taint would be entailed by "sins" which had escaped notice, or by those for which no propitiation had been made. In the first case, while the individuals would be morally guiltless, the error committed must yet be supposed to have its natural and necessary effect in a slight, but yet real, impairment of the national sanctity; in the other, while the secret doom of divine excommunication would yet hang heavy over the individual offender, the propitiatory rites of the Atonement-day would suffice to clear the "congregation" as a whole. Such an annual ceremony, then, may have seemed necessary in order to reduce the defilements of Israel to a minimum, and to prevent Yahveh's wrath breaking forth with the violent reaction of outraged holiness upon a comparatively innocent people. For God's localization in Jerusalem, which ought to be Israel's dearest privilege, would then become its most menacing danger. Thus,

said nor implied that the Atonement-day is only intended to "purge away the guilt of all sins, committed during the year, that had not been already expiated by penitence, or by the special piacula appointed for particular offences."

for God's sake—for his own purpose of glorification through Israel—as well as for his people's, it was advisable that all possible means should be taken to enable the close relationship between Deity and man to continue undisturbed. The logical circle—that the atoning ceremonies were ordered by God to produce their effect upon himself—was necessarily unperceived by the priestly mind.

Public worship and its belongings exhaust by far the greater part of the priestly legislation. This limitation is, as we have seen, only natural, considering the aims and ideals of the legislators. It is curious, however, that their code, together with the older code of Deuteronomy, should have formed a law which was to be independent of temple and of land, and which proved capable of being preserved and maintained in wholly alien and even adverse conditions. Three of the main causes which brought about this result were strengthened by, though they did not originate in, the priestly code. The three ordinances which could be, and had been, observed outside Palestine were those concerned with food, the sabbath and circumcision. A prohibition of many "unclean" animals and birds had been included in Deuteronomy, and was repeated in the later code: it was of essentially priestly character, and fell within the compass of that personal and individual holiness which was required from every unit in order that the whole people might be the fitting instrument of the divine glory. Circumcision, ignored, perhaps studiously, in Deuteronomy, is in the priestly code referred back to Abraham for its date of institution, and is described as an everlasting covenant. It is the passport of admission to the Passover service, which without it is forbidden to the foreigner. In its conception and treatment of the sabbath, the priestly code shows the influence of Ezekiel and the exile. For Ezekiel had been the first teacher to include a violation of the sabbath among Israel's sins, while the exile had necessarily tended to augment the religious importance of a ceremony which could be observed abroad as well as at home. The priests' sabbath is very different from the sabbath of the Book of the Covenant or Deuteronomy. There the sabbath was instituted for man's sake: here—and this is the true opposition—it is instituted for God's sake. It is connected with the creation; God himself, after fashioning the universe in six days, rests upon and sanctifies the seventh. In its desire to link every religious observance directly with its divine source, the code falls into an unwonted anthropomorphism. The sabbaths are Yahveh's sabbaths, and their observance is the observance of a perpetual sign that "ye may know that I am Yahveh that doth sanctify you."[1] Thus the social character of the sabbath is ignored: it becomes purely religious. Meanwhile the severity of its observance was greatly increased; for the more rigorous the injunction—the more absolute the rest—the more visible becomes the sign, and the more perfect the sanctification. Let no stick be gathered, or no light be lit, that the purity of the divine day may suffer no defilement from the hand of man.[2]

When the law of the priest became the law of the

[1] Exodus xxxi. 13.
[2] Numbers xv. 32—36; Exodus xxxv. 3.

scribe, the observance of the sabbath was not relaxed, but, on the contrary, more and more rigidly maintained and strengthened; and by critics generally the obvious crudities of the priests' sabbath are laid to the charge of, and made to characterize, the sabbath of the Pharisees. It certainly would seem as if the priestly code had crushed out the human and joyous elements which must have predominated in the sabbath of the pre-exilic period and of the Deuteronomic law. And yet, whether it square with certain theological and preconceived opinions or not, the fact remains that the severe and law-surrounded sabbath of the priests, passing over in these respects unchanged into the religion of the Scribes and Pharisees, was from the earliest Rabbinic age down to the present hour a day of the keenest and purest joy—a day beloved and hailed by rich and poor, old and young alike—a day, finally, of high religious satisfaction and of true communion with God.

It has been said that the main object of the priestly code was to provide for the visible expression of God's glory through the worship of a people divinely chosen for that peculiar end. Yet the God who elected Israel, so that he might dwell within Israel's sanctuary, is the only God and the Creator of all. One is, therefore, induced to ask, what, according to the priestly legislation, is the relation of Israel and Israel's God to the peoples of the outer world?

At the first blush the universalism of Deutero-Isaiah seems wholly absent. In its concern for God's glory and the proper ministration of his sanctuary, the priestly code forgets God's creatures outside Israel, and ignores their claims upon his care. Yet it is not inspired by any fanatical hatred of the heathen, such as was born of struggle and persecution in the Maccabean era: and it is equally free from any irreligious pride in Israel's peculiar position and privilege as the possessor of the divine sanctuary. On the one hand, Israel must keep clear of all alliances with the heathen which might jeopardize its religious purity. This feeling is indicated in the stories of the patriarchs. Again, where any foreign tribe has injured, or is likely to injure, that necessary purity of Israel's religious practice and faith, the letter of the priestly law seems to require that such an offending nation must be exterminated; human blood is of less consequence than the holiness of Israel, for the holiness of Israel is a condition precedent to the glory of God. The "paper" slaughter of the Midianites shows the relentless consistency of the priestly mind.[1] And yet, on the other hand, the priestly code incorporates the older laws for the just and tender treatment of the foreign settler; and some sections of it emphatically insist upon a single ordinance both for Israel and for the stranger. No hindrance was to be put in the way of the "stranger" being incorporated by the rite of circumcision into the very body of Israel, and, as it would seem, such new members were to have all the privileges of Israelites by blood. Distinctions drawn by Deuteronomy between different nations, and as to the particular generation at which their descendants might be received into the community, do not re-appear in the priestly code.

Possibly these more generous regulations have also

[1] Numb. xxxi. 1—24.

another meaning. There seems to shine through them the fundamental object of the whole legislation. For good or for evil the strangers were permanent elements in the commonwealth, and had as such to be reckoned with in any legal code which was to be practically enforced. The problem was, therefore, how they might least impair the holiness of the community and the glory of God. By enabling the foreigner to join the Israelite community and to participate in its worship, or by demanding from him, if he remained outside, the observance of certain fundamental rites, that object would best be gained.[1] There is thus a mixture of motives; but in the result the position of the non-Israelite according to the new law is very favourable; perfect equality is, moreover, easily attained. It cannot be denied that the code, partly for his own sake and partly for God's, held out under certain fundamental conditions the right hand of fellowship to any stranger who might choose to grasp it: in this respect its authors may be said to have advanced beyond Deuteronomy, and to have partially translated into their own language and practice the universalist ideas of the Babylonian Isaiah.

"We cannot but own"—to use Prof. Kuenen's words —"that they were grand and beautiful designs which the lawgiver (of the priestly code) had in view. He formed broadly the idea of a holy people dedicated to Yahveh, and tried to realize it on a large scale."[2] To him, and to the men of his school, religion was the one absorbing

[1] He probably had to observe the sabbath and to abstain from incest and idolatry and from drinking blood.

[2] *Religion of Israel*, Vol. II. p. 285.

interest of life which had driven all other interests out of the field. From one point of view, there can be nothing higher than a whole community giving up its life to the glory of God. But the danger and the mistake of the priestly code arose when it mapped out the sphere wherein that service of God was to be rendered. The service of man is the only safe practical expression of the service of God. Any other expression of it leads to evils, be it the evil of asceticism, of ritualism, or of selfish pride. The code devised a field for religion outside the field of morality, and destroyed that close union between them which had been taught by the Prophets.

Jeremiah had denied that sacrifices were an integral portion of God's law, but they formed the chief subject of the new legislation. Religion was manifested in ritual, and therefore ritual assumed an exaggerated importance. In this sense the law was distinctly anti-prophetic. God's vengeance was threatened for the most trivial ritual offences; because directly ritual becomes the expression of religion, there is no difference of value between one ordinance and another. The sense of proportion becomes wholly lost. No better example can be found of the extraordinary distortion of judgment that results from making ritual, equally with or even more than morality, the manifestation of religion, than the legend of the campaign against Midian. By the express command of God, all the captives, except the virgins reserved as concubines and slaves, are put to the sword; adults and children are treated alike. But while all this is done in obedience to a divine mandate, contact with the corpses defiles; and thus all who have been engaged in the massacre must purge themselves from sin before they may enter the camp wherein is the sanctuary and presence of Yahveh.[1] While the painful incongruity between this moral callousness to bloodshed and this intense zeal for ritual purity forces itself at once upon the attention of the modern reader, it was clearly unperceived by and imperceptible to the narrator. In the calm judicial tone of the story we have to deal with no living national hatred; its origin and tenour lie simply in a distorted religious vision.

There was the further danger that the authors of the code would defeat their own ends by excess of detail. A frequent repetition of the sin-offering was likely to bring the ordinance into disrepute, if not into actual contempt. It lost its effect by repetition. "The lawgiver," as Prof. Kuenen remarks, "has overshot his mark." Where the sin-offering was offered without any consciousness of sin, the rite would tend to degenerate "into a mechanical, spiritless act."[2] Again, certain ritual offences, such as eating the flesh of animals which had died a natural death, were probably known to be of not infrequent occurrence; while others, as for example, touching the carcase of such animals, could scarcely be avoided. The code enacts that whoever does these things shall wash his clothes and be unclean until the evening.[3] Thus, as Prof. Kuenen points out, there seems to be no reason why the offence should not be committed, if men were willing to put up with temporary uncleanness and perform subsequent ablutions. By its "minute precepts

---

[1] Numbers xxxi. 1—24.   [2] *Religion of Israel*, Vol. II. p. 269.
[3] Lev. xi. 39, 40, xvii. 15.

and distinctions," the priestly law "weakened the sublimity of the precept, 'Be holy, for I, Yahveh, am holy;' it threatened to weaken the fear of pollution by multiplying the cases in which uncleanness results."[1]

How far these effects were actually produced, and how far they were successfully avoided, it will partly fall within our province to consider in a subsequent Lecture. It will then be seen that when the law of the priests became the law of the scribes, its character was gradually modified. It then became a law, not merely for the community, but also for the individual, and religion was once more, as in the old pre-exilic days—but in a far higher and nobler manner—a personal affair, which could bring to every one who lived within its range and fell under its influence a keen, spiritual satisfaction.

Meanwhile it is easy, and even tempting, to contrast the spontaneity of the older cultus with the statutory character of religion in the priestly code. No one has portrayed, because nobody could portray, this contrast more incisively than Wellhausen; and even his own foot-note of qualification does not remove the impression from the reader's mind that the religion of the new code was less religious than was the popular religion of the pre-legal periods. Its whole cultus, he says, "is nothing more than an exercise in piety (*Gottseligkeit*), which has simply been so enjoined once for all without its being to any one's advantage."[2] Yet as an exercise in piety the

---

[1] *Religion of Israel*, Vol. II. p. 270.

[2] *Prolegomena zur Geschichte Israels*, p. 82, n. 1 (*History of Israel*, E. T., pp. 78, 79, n. 1), and 497, 499.

cultus was the indispensable stepping-stone to the law as personal joy. The "monotonous seriousness" of the priestly code does not seem to have been felt by those who practised its enactments and witnessed its worship. The "ascetic religious exercises" led to a religion which is markedly unascetic; the "shell" of cultus which the priestly code displayed was in real life soon filled with a new "soul," more pure, more religious and scarcely less joyous than the old "soul," which, according to Wellhausen, had fled when spontaneity and nature were succeeded by statute and technique. For somehow or other, as we may gather for a certainty from the Psalter, statute and technique, while they effectually did away with lawless licence, foul sensuality, or the unrestrained and secular jollity of feasts—half-sacrifices, half-picnics—made free passage and play for the exercise of emotions more unequivocally religious. Even the cultus of the priestly code, apart from the law as a whole, provided food for the religious spirit, however hard the fact may be for us to comprehend. Many a pious worshipper would have spoken of its "high service" with solemn rapture. Many in the post-Nehemian age would have said that it "dissolved them into ecstasies, and brought all heaven before their eyes."

Of such a mixed nature, then, in itself, and pregnant with results both good and bad beyond anything that its authors could have desired or thought of, was the code which from his raised platform Ezra the priest read out before the people upon that memorable September day. From early morning until noon was occupied with the reading, which was interpreted by a running commentary or homiletic paraphrase from certain Levites appointed for the task.[1] It is noticeable that the Levites take so prominent a part in the introduction of the law: the rigour of the reforming party was objected to by a considerable section of the Jerusalem priesthood, however much the interests of their order were safeguarded by the new code.

And now there is a repetition of the same religious emotion which was evoked by the great assembly thirteen years previously. When the law has thus been publicly recited and explained, and when the people recognized that so much of what could but seem to them the authentic words of Moses and the direct command of God had been hitherto a dead letter, neglected and disobeyed, they broke forth into weeping and lamentation. We hear nothing of such an outbreak in the otherwise closely parallel story of Josiah's reform in 621, and of the reading of the Deuteronomic code. What an immense religious development lay between the two ceremonies! To these weeping men and women, religion is, after all, a real thing and no mere external rule. The way in which Nehemiah and his colleagues check this outburst of genuine repentance is also significant, and points forward to later characteristics. "This day," they argue, "is holy unto Yahveh; eat, drink, be merry, and send portions unto the poor."[2] For cheerfulness and charity were two main qualities which sprang from the possession of the law.

That holy rejoicing in which the first reading culmi-

---

[1] Neh. viii. 7 (see Variorum Reference Bible).
[2] Neh. viii. 9, 10.

nated was continued at the Feast of Tabernacles, celebrated according to the new prescriptions of the priestly code for eight days instead of seven. For the twenty-fourth day of the month a special fast was appointed. After the people had assembled, "with fasting and sackcloth and earth upon their heads," there seems to have taken place a fresh purgation of foreign elements from the holy community. Repeated reading from the law follows, and the Levites are again prominent.[1] Ezra then makes a long speech, in which he gives an historic retrospect of Israel's past, confessing that it has been one long story of rebellion and ingratitude.[2] If the sins of the past are not even yet atoned for, neither is the present free from its own iniquity.[3] Hence the yoke of the foreigner still presses heavily. In this confession the old ideas of solidarity re-appear in a modified form. Israel, both of the past and of the present, constitutes a single whole, and the generations which compose it are linked one with another in a common guilt. The past merges into the present, and is inextricably commingled with it. And throughout the ages this attitude has been maintained by Judaism: martyrs and saints have, century after century, repeated the memorable words: "Thou art just in all that has befallen us: for thou hast acted faithfully, but we have acted wickedly."

It was thought desirable to close the fast by drawing up a covenant, sealed and signed by the chief laymen, priests and Levites, pledging the community to the

[1] Neh. ix. 1—5.   [2] Neh. ix. 6 (LXX.).
[3] Neh. ix. 32—37.

maintenance of the law.¹ An indication of future trouble was the significant absence of the high-priest's name. In this written document, besides the general promise to "walk in God's law which was given by Moses, God's servant," two special points of great importance were included. Of these, one was that the purity of the race should be rigorously maintained. The priestly code had only indirectly alluded to this delicate subject; it was, therefore, specifically added in the covenant that "they would not give their daughters unto the peoples of the land," nor take the daughters of the latter for their sons. The second point concerned the due observance of the sabbath, the festivals and the sabbatical year. As we can gather from Nehemiah's expressions upon his second visit to Jerusalem, the strict observance of the sabbath was not enforced without much opposition and difficulty; a presentiment of this, and a sense of the contrast between the sabbath as then observed and the sabbath as the priestly code depicted it, may have suggested the expediency of some special mention of this fundamental law.

Over and above the formal covenant, various by-laws were drawn up and agreed to for the due maintenance of the temple services, and the people pledged themselves to an accurate fulfilment of the prescriptions of the code as to first-fruits, firstlings and tithes.²

At this point our record suddenly fails us; we are left to guess how far Nehemiah in the remainder of his governorship was able to enforce the terms of the covenant and the by-laws, and what was the exact measure and nature of the opposition which he encountered. It

[1] Neh. ix. 38, x. 31.   [2] Neh. x. 32–39.

is, however, sufficiently clear that the new reform and the new code were not accepted without a struggle. The governor's strong hand was needed to repress murmurings, and to prevent dislike of the new régime passing into open disregard. Twelve years after his arrival in Jerusalem (433), Nehemiah was compelled to return to his post at the court of Artaxerxes. After a period of unknown duration, he obtained fresh leave of absence, and revisited Jerusalem (whether as governor is uncertain, but at all events invested with considerable powers), only to find that the great reform was in a fair way towards general dissolution.

In one scanty but yet precious chapter—a fragment clearly of Nehemiah's fuller memoirs—is contained all that the chronicler, or an earlier compiler, has allowed us to hear of Nehemiah's second visit.[1] On the evils which he was then straightway called upon to combat, we may, perhaps, find some supplementary light thrown in the anonymous pamphlet which passes as the Book of Malachi, and which may possibly belong to the interval between Nehemiah's first and second visit to Jerusalem.

There were two main sources of opposition. The neighbouring communities had still their friends within Jerusalem, and especially among the priests. It would seem as if mixed marriages had again become frequent, and even led to the divorce of native Judæan wives.[2] Connected with this growing laxity was an indisposition to observe the sabbath with the strictness required by the law.

But, secondly, there was special trouble from the

[1] Neh. xiii. 4—31.   [2] Malachi ii. 11—16.

priesthood. The old quarrel between priests and Levites was unappeased, and the former seem to have regarded the new code as too favourable to the latter. The richer priests were less dependent on the temple dues, and neglected the services. Laymen made their profit out of these quarrels, and no longer paid into the sanctuary their tithes and heave-offerings. In spite of the introduction of the law, the yoke of the foreigner was still unbroken, and men once more began to say, "It is vain to serve God."[1]

There must also have been a small third party which was discontented with the religion of the law and with its particularist tendencies from nobler motives than those of personal ease or religious indifference. Echoes from the voices of this party, who held that Ezra's code was an insufficient realization of prophetic aspirations, are still to be detected in the Bible. It is, however, safer to consider these fragments of universalism hereafter, and not to fix them too definitely to the interval between the proclamation of the law and Nehemiah's second visit. Nevertheless we may infer from them with comparative certainty that the hired and degenerate prophets who attempted, in conjunction with Tobiah and Sanballat, to wreck the work of Nehemiah even in its early stages, were not his only opponents, but that these included others whose motives and purposes were disinterested and of high religious value.

Meanwhile Nehemiah upon his return to Jerusalem acted with his usual vigour. He took effective measures to secure that "the portions of the Levites" should be

[1] Malachi i. 13, iii. 8, 14.

faithfully paid over to them, and the desecration of the sabbath summarily discontinued.

Of momentous importance for the future of Judaism was his action towards the priesthood. Corruption, from Nehemiah's point of view, had infected the high-priestly family itself. Eliashib, the high-priest, now allied by marriage to Nehemiah's old enemy Tobiah, had allotted him a large apartment within the precincts of the temple. A grandson of Eliashib had married the daughter of Sanballat the Horonite, and was living with her in Jerusalem. Nehemiah acted with a high hand: his brief record speaks of no opposition; but opposition, and that a violent one, there must have been. Supported by all the rigorists, and armed with the authority of Artaxerxes, Nehemiah carried the day, and expelled his chief enemies from Jerusalem. His words are significant, and when taken in conjunction with a statement of a later author, imply far more than explicitly they say. Out of Tobiah's chamber Nehemiah " cast forth all the household stuff," and ordered a general purification of all the chambers in the temple-courts. As to the grandson of Eliashib—to quote Nehemiah's own words—" I chased him from me." And then there follows a prayer in which the use of the plural pronoun lets us guess that the expulsion then effected was not limited to Eliashib's grandson: "Remember *them*, O my God, for *their* defilement of the priesthood, and of the covenant of the priesthood and of the Levites. And I purified the people (literally, "them") of all foreigners."[1]

Now Josephus, in relating the foundation of the Sama-

[1] Neh. xiii. 28, 29, 30.

ritan schism and of the rival sanctuary upon Mount
Gerizim, tells a story which bears a strong resemblance
to this passage in the authentic memoirs of Nehemiah.
In spite of the difference of date, for which Josephus is
responsible, we are able definitely to connect the two
narratives. Eliashib's grandson may be identified with
the Manasseh of Josephus, while the name of his wife,
Sanballat's daughter, was Nicaso. From Josephus we
learn the important fact that there was at this time—that
is, on the expulsion of Manasseh from Jerusalem—"a great
disturbance among the people, because many of the priests
and Levites were entangled in such (i.e. foreign) marriages. All these revolted to Manasseh;" while, by the
help of Sanballat, a new temple was erected near Shechem,
upon Mount Gerizim.[1] Hither probably flocked many
laymen as well as priests to whom the reforms of Nehemiah were distasteful, and who found their position in
the capital insecure. By enforced expulsion and voluntary secession, Judæa was thus purged of the more dangerous opponents to the new reformation.

Its more disinterested opponents remained: these would
not have been willing to go the length of setting up a
rival temple under foreign protection. Their voices were
not wholly silenced; rather were they able, by accepting
the law, to help to preserve the universalist aspirations
of the older prophets. When the law ceased to be chal-
lenged, nascent Judaism was able to make some advances
in the way which Deutero-Isaiah had pointed out. The
final victory of Nehemiah opened up the era of post-exilic

---

[1] Josephus, *Antiquities*, xi. 7, 2, and 8, 2—4; cf. Stade, *Geschichte*,
Vol. II. pp. 188—191.

progress : proselytism began and spread, till fresh dangers from without checked its diffusion. Together with the law, other spiritual manifestations took their rise and flourished. The priest as a factor in religion becomes of less importance : beside and overshadowing him there step upon the stage the figures of the Psalmist, the Wise man and the Scribe. Specifically Jewish history in the long interval between Nehemiah (430—176) and the Maccabean era, so far as outward events are concerned, is almost wholly wanting. Judæa is but one province out of many, whether of the Persian empire or of the Ptolemaic and Seleucid kingdoms. But the internal history can still be roughly traced. Thus while there is no record of outward events in the Old Testament after the second visit of Nehemiah, the prophetic and poetical books contain the products of at least three centuries of internal religious movement, sometimes advancing, sometimes receding. It is for this reason that our history of the Hebrew religion as recorded in the Old Testament cannot terminate with the victory of Nehemiah, but must classify and arrange the various religious voices, and the different steps and stages of development, which the literature of the three succeeding centuries may still enable us to recognize and distinguish. To this work the three final Lectures of this series will be devoted.

It may be convenient to add here the Priestly Sections of our present Pentateuch, in the sense defined upon p. 315, according to Prof.

354 VI. THE RESTORATION AND THE PRIESTLY LAW.

Driver's analysis (*Introduction to the Literature of the Old Testament*, 4th ed., 1892, p. 150):

Genesis: i. 1—ii. 4 a; v. 1—28, 30—32; vi. 9—22; vii. 6, 7—9 (in parts), 11, 13—16 a, 18—21, 24; viii. 1—2 a, 3 b—5, 13 a, 14—19; ix. 1—17, 28—29; x. 1—7, 20, 22—23, 31—32; xi. 10—27, 31—32; xii. 4 b—5; xiii. 6, 11 b—12 a; xvi. 1 a, 3, 15—16; xvii.; xix. 29; xxi. 1 b, 2 b—5; xxiii.; xxv. 7—11 a, 12—17, 19—20, 26 b; xxvi. 34, 35; xxvii. 46—xxviii. 9; xxix. 24, 29; xxxi. 18 b; xxxiii. 18 a; xxxiv. 1—2 a, 4, 6, 8—10, 13—18, 20, 24, 25 (partly), 27—29; xxxv. 9—13, 15, 22 b—29; xxxvi. (in the main); xxxvii. 1—2 a; xli. 4 b; xlvi. 6—27; xlvii. 5—6 a (LXX.), 7—11, 27 b—28; xlviii. 3—6, 7?; xlix. 1 a, 28 b—33; l. 12—13.

Exodus: i. 1—7, 13—14; ii. 23 b—25; vi. 2—vii. 13, 19—20 a, 21 b—22; viii. 5—7, 15 b—19; ix. 8—12; xii. 1—20, 28, 37 a, 40—51; xiii. 1—2, 20; xiv. 1—4, 8—9, 15—18, 21 a, 21 c—23, 26—27 a, 28 a, 29; xvi. 1—3, 6—24, 31—36; xvii. 1 a; xix. 1—2 a; xxiv. 15—18 a; xxv. 1—xxxi. 18 a; xxxiv. 29—35; xxxv.—xl.

Leviticus: i.—xvi. (xvii.—xxvi.) xxvii.

Numbers: i. 1—x. 28; xiii. 1—17 a, 21, 25—26 a (to *Paran*), 32 a; xiv. 1—2 (in the main), 5—7, 10, 26—38 (in the main); xv.; xvi. 1 a, 2 b—7 a (7 b—11) (16—17), 18—24, 27 a, 32 b, 35 (36—40), 41—50; xvii.—xix.; xx. 1 a (to *month*), 2, 3 b, 6, 12—13, 22—29; xxi. 4 a (to *Hor*), 10—11; xxii. 1; xxv. 6—18; xxvi.—xxxi.; xxxii. 18—19, 28—32 (traces in 1—17, 20—27); xxxiii.—xxxvi.

Deuteronomy: xxxii. 48—52; xxxiv. 1 a, 8—9.

LECTURE VII.

FROM NEHEMIAH TO THE MACCABEES: EXTERNAL INFLUENCES AND INTERNAL ORGANIZATION.

OLD Testament history closes with the age of Nehemiah. But Old Testament literature flourishes for three hundred years more. In other words, while the Bible tells us nothing directly of the external events which happened, and of the men who were conspicuous in the Jewish community after the second visit of Nehemiah to Jerusalem, a considerable portion of its literature must be assigned to the three centuries which elapsed between the times of Nehemiah and the times of the Maccabees.

Nor is this inconvenient disparity between the bareness of outward history and the largeness of literary material —material, be it also remembered, which is wholly anonymous—compensated by any records outside the Old Testament itself. Josephus and the classical historians help us, indeed, to some extent; but, in comparison with what we still desiderate, their help is small. The consequence is, that from Nehemiah to the uprising of the Maccabees—a period of some 270 years—the lives and even the names of but very few men are known to us who influenced the course of religious development.

Moreover, the whole external history of the Jews between these two dates is almost blank. Judæa, as a province of Palestine and Cœle-Syria, shared the fortunes of the larger wholes of which it formed a part. It was involved in the general stream of history, but had no independent political life before the persecutions of Antiochus Epiphanes. -Till the Persian kingdom was overthrown, the Jews remained its subjects: incorporated then in Alexander's empire, their land after his death became a subject of contention between the Egyptian Ptolemies and the Syrian Seleucids.

The Persian period lasted for about a hundred years beyond the age of Nehemiah (432—332), and a further century and a half elapsed between Alexander and the accession of Antiochus Epiphanes (332—176). But the particular dates of the post-exilic literature are not yet so satisfactorily ascertained as to enable us to distinguish accurately between the products of the Persian and of the Greek periods. Although, therefore, the two centuries and a half between Nehemiah and the Maccabean revolt naturally separate into those two divisions, it is not possible to devote this Lecture to the age of the Persian domination, and the next to the age of Hellenism. The steps on the road we have to traverse are hard to trace. An average pious Jew of the year 176 B.C. was in a different stage of religious development from an average pious Jew of the year 432; but it is not easy to say precisely in what the religious difference consisted, and it is excessively difficult to say by what degrees and stages the development was brought about.

The date of the latest book now included in the Old

Testament cannot be fixed with certainty. But we may make our way forwards upon the hypothesis that the whole of the present canon was in existence by about the year 130 before the Christian era. The object of the last three Lectures of the present series is to carry the story of Israel's religious development down to about the same period. It is obvious that ending there we shall end *in mediis rebus*, and it may seem as if the story ought to be pursued at least 130 years further. For to most people the history of Judaism as a religion ends when its mission, as it would seem, was taken up and enlarged by Christianity. From this point of view, what is chiefly needed is an exact picture of every side and phase of the Jewish religion in the days of Jesus and of Paul, so as to explain, partly as simple development, partly as opposition and revolt, and partly as new departure, the better religion which superseded it.

Simple and valuable as this method is, it can nevertheless for many reasons not be followed here. In the first place, the religious history of the century and a half between the first Maccabees and the birth of Christ is so important and complicated, that its adequate presentation would need a series of Lectures to itself.

But, secondly, from the Jewish point of view, and possibly from the point of view of an historian neither Jew nor Christian, the religious development of Judaism was as unfinished at the age of Christ as it was in the age of Judas the Maccabee. Judaism was then advancing towards the full establishment of that phase of its history which is known as Rabbinism. But both for good or for evil, and probably for the former more than for the latter, the Rabbinic phase of Judaism was not fully established till at least two hundred years after Christ. To judge Rabbinism by the religious condition of the Jews at the time of Christ is historically inaccurate.

A Jew, moreover, to whatever section of modern Judaism he may belong, is clearly unable to treat the post-exilic religion of Israel in the light of Christian teleology. That is why, according to Prof. H. Schultz, none but Christians can ever understand the Old Testament.[1] A judge of perfect impartiality would possibly deny this capacity to both Jew and Christian alike. At any rate, the effect of viewing post-exilic religious history in the light of this particular teleology is not purely explanatory. As we shall see in the sequel, it colours facts and distorts them. For Christian theologians still too habitually look at the later Judaism through Pauline spectacles. And no one who estimates Rabbinism in its earlier phases from the point of view of its greatest antagonist can ever estimate it correctly.

In abandoning a Christian teleology, no attempt must be made to substitute another in its place. To estimate the post-exilic religion of Israel from Nehemiah to the Maccabees from the point of view of modern Judaism, would be not less open to objection than to look at it as a preparation for Christianity. And from a wider point of view, as Christianity and Judaism are both living forces, changing their character from age to age, all teleologies alike become increasingly inadequate. The absolute religion is a figment of the philosopher or the partizan.

[1] *Alttestamentliche Theologie*, 4th ed., p. 54.

Our course in this Lecture, after a sketch of the outward events of the Persian and Greek period, and an indication of the Biblical literature which probably belongs to each, will be first of all to point out the general position of Judaism with reference to the outer world. The influence of Persia and of Hellenism will then be considered—the former quite briefly, for reasons to be then assigned; the latter, as more general and diffused, at greater length. To the influences from without may succeed the internal framework. That framework consisted in the main of two heterogeneous elements, a building and a book, the Sanctuary and the Scriptures. The temple with its priests, the holy writings with their scribes and students, will occupy our attention for the remainder of the Lecture.

First, then, we have to prelude the religious history of the time with a very short survey of the historical events of the Persian and Greek periods from the days of Nehemiah to the accession of Antiochus Epiphanes.

The reign of Artaxerxes I. Longimanus (465—425) and that of Darius II. Ochus (424—405) seem to have comprised no events of special importance for Judæa. Egypt was able, in the latter years of Darius' reign, to secure its independence, and Persia apparently did not attempt to re-conquer it till after his death. Egyptian wars were always troublesome for the Jews: some of them were compelled to serve in the Persian army, and their land was subject to the forced contributions and painful experiences of a border country, through which detachments of Persian soldiery would march towards their Egyptian campaigns.¹ Darius was succeeded by his son Artaxerxes II. Mnemon (405—359), upon whom there followed Artaxerxes III. Ochus (359—338). In the reigns of the second and third Artaxerxes, Persian rule seems to have changed for the worse; growing severity and growing weakness went hand-in-hand. Artaxerxes II. established or extended the worship of the goddess Anaitis under material forms in various parts of the empire, and not only thereby "compromised the purity of Mazda-worship," but possibly also showed some religious persecution towards those who refused to accept a new divinity at the king's decree.² Berosus, from whom we hear of this development of Anaitis worship, mentions Damascus as one of the places where her image was set up and ordered to be adored.³ The danger, therefore, was brought near to Judæa. Wars with Egypt continued; and, according to Diodorus, the year 365 B.C. was signalized by a wide insurrection of the "inhabitants of the sea-coasts of Asia" against the Persians. It was headed by Ariobarzanes, the satrap of Phrygia, and the confederates included "the Syrians and Phœnicians and almost all that bordered upon the sea."⁴ Did the Jews, willingly or under compulsion, join this revolt? It is by no means impossible, and at any rate they must have suffered in its suppression and in the general agitation

[1] Even in Ezra's time, cf. Neh. ix. 37.
[2] Cheyne, *Origin of the Psalter*, p. 293.
[3] The passage is quoted by Graetz, *Geschichte der Juden*, Vol. II. ii. p. 413.
[4] Diodorus Siculus, xv. 90, 3.

of the time. A second revolt against Artaxerxes Ochus was more serious. The Jews took part in it, and paid dearly for their temerity. Ochus was a vigorous ruler, who attempted, although in vain, to stem the gradual dissolution of his empire. The revolt began about the year 358, and was not finally quelled till 350. Diodorus alludes to the insurrection of the Phœnicians, and describes at length the dramatic conquest of Sidon.[1] From some late, but apparently well-informed authorities, we gather that Ochus, in the same campaign in which Phœnicia and Egypt were subdued, captured Jerusalem and deported many Jews, "some to Hyrcania by the Caspian Sea, others to Babylonia." This event was great enough, Prof. Cheyne thinks, to be rightly called "the third of Israel's great captivities."[2]

Between this unsuccessful insurrection and the invasion of Alexander, we know nothing of what happened to Judæa. The Jewish historian Josephus mentions one solitary and painful incident for the whole period of Persian rule after the age of Nehemiah. It appears that after the death of Joiada the high-priest,[3] his younger son Joshua, relying upon the friendship and promises of Bagoses, the general of "another Artaxerxes," attempted to secure for himself the high-priestly dignity to the exclusion of the legitimate claims of the elder brother, Jochanan. In the course of a quarrel, Jochanan slew

[1] Diodorus, xvi. 40, 4 to 45, 6.

[2] Cheyne, *Psalter*, pp. 53, 61; and *Jewish Quarterly Review*, Vol. IV. pp. 107—110; Graetz, *Geschichte*, Vol. II. ii. p. 309; and *J. Q. R.* Vol. III. pp. 208—219.

[3] Neh. xii. 10, xiii. 28.

Joshua within the very precincts of the temple. Bagoses was not slow to use his opportunity. He is said to have laid upon the Jews, as a punishment, a special tax of fifty drachmæ for every sacrificed lamb. This oppression continued, according to Josephus, for seven years.[1]

Empty as these hundred years thus are of great names and deeds, considerable portions of Old Testament literature must nevertheless be assigned to them. Half the Psalter, large sections of the Book of Proverbs, the idyll of Ruth, and—of the prophetical writings—the Books of Joel and Jonah, with several chapters now embedded in the Books of Isaiah and Zechariah, were all perhaps the product of the Persian period.

It is impossible to enter here upon the stories connected with Alexander and the Jews. That he showed them favour and granted them peculiar privileges is, however, certain.[2] At his death in 323, Laomedon became satrap of Syria, but only retained it for three years; for in 320, Ptolemy Lagi, the satrap of Egypt, invaded and conquered Syria. The Jews remained faithful to Laomedon, and Ptolemy, who captured Jerusalem by an attack upon the Sabbath when no opposition was offered to the enemy, deported a number of them to Egypt.[3] Here, however, his enmity ceased. The Jews settled in Alexandria were treated with marked favour; and as regards Judæa itself, Ptolemy, like the majority of his

---

[1] Josephus, *Antiquities*, xi. 7, 1.

[2] Cf. Graetz, *Geschichte*, Vol. II. ii. pp. 224, 225; H. Bois, *Alexandre le grand et les juifs*, in *Revue de théologie et de philosophie*, 1890, pp. 557—580; 1891, pp. 78—98.

[3] Josephus, *Antiquities*, xii. 1.

successors and of the Syrian kings, appears to have followed the policy of Alexander. By this calculated capture of Jerusalem on the Sabbath, as compared with the violation of the sacred day witnessed by Nehemiah, we can measure the advance which the strict observance of the law had made in the life and hearts of the people. The year 320 marks also the beginning of a troublous period, during which Syria, including Palestine, was the convenient cause of constant strife between the Ptolemies, Antigonus or his son Demetrius, and the Seleucids.

Judæa remained in the hands of Ptolemy for five years, when Antigonus, upon the death of Eumenes and the formation of the new coalition against himself, invaded and conquered Syria in 315. The victory of Gaza in 312 brought the province once more under Egyptian control; but after the battle of Myus, in which Demetrius retrieved the disaster of Gaza, it was evacuated by Ptolemy, and the peace of 311 left it for nine years in the undisturbed possession of Antigonus. Graetz has shown it to be probable that Ptolemy, in his retreat from Syria in 312, included Jerusalem among the cities the fortifications of which he then destroyed.[1]

A complicated series of events, in which the position of Jerusalem and Judæa is not clearly defined, opens with the year 302. The campaign, which ended at Ipsus with the death of Antigonus, had been preceded by a short incursion of Ptolemy into southern Syria. He reduced its cities; but upon a false rumour that Antigonus had overthrown the confederate army of Lysimachus and Seleucus, retired upon his own king-

[1] Graetz, *Geschichte*, Vol. II. ii. p. 230, n. 1; Diodorus, xix. 93. 7.

dom, leaving garrisons in the "cities which he had taken in Cœle-Syria."[1] Thus in 302 Jerusalem appears for the third time to have fallen into the hands of Ptolemy. If it did so, however, it must probably within the next few years have been re-captured by the enterprising and indomitable Demetrius. For a casual notice of Eusebius alludes to his destruction of the city of Samaria in the year 297 or 296, and Droysen argues that his occupation of Samaria would necessarily imply the possession of Cœle-Syria.[2] Within two years that province, including Judæa, was to have yet another master in the person of Seleucus, whose renewed conflicts with Demetrius, after the temporary peace of 299, ended in the acquisition of Cœle-Syria about the year 294.[3] Seleucus vied with Ptolemy in friendship towards the Jews. He induced (or compelled) a number of them to settle in his new capital, Antioch, and in other cities of his foundation, where considerable privileges were granted them.[4] These privileges, we may assume, consisted for the most part in the establishment of their own tribunals, the free exercise of their religious customs, and in the suspension or alteration of any local law which interfered with or ran counter to them. Whether, either in Syria or in Egypt, it included a citizenship equal to that of the Macedonian conquerors, is disputed.

For fourteen years Judæa continued, with the rest of Cœle-Syria, as a province of the kingdom of Seleucus.

[1] Diodorus, xx. 113, 1.
[2] Droysen, *Geschichte des Hellenismus*, 2nd ed., Vol. II. ii. p. 243.
[3] Droysen, Vol. II. ii. p. 255, n. 2, p. 258, n. 2.
[4] Josephus, *Antiquities*, xii. 3, 1; *Contra Apionem*, Vol. II. 4.

Then, in 280, Ptolemy II. Philadelphus "took advantage of the confusion caused by Seleucus' murder to seize Cœle-Syria and Phœnicia."[1] For over seventy years afterwards Judæa appears to have enjoyed a profound peace. Graetz has shown it to be most improbable that it was affected by the invasion of Antiochus III. in 220.[2] It did not fall into his hands till the next war with Egypt, which began in 204. A Syrian party, for reasons which are not wholly clear, had formed itself in Jerusalem, and the city appears to have been acquired by Antiochus without difficulty.[3] Meanwhile, about 202, Scopas, the Ætolian, was sent by the ministers of the young king Ptolemy Epiphanes to recover Cœle-Syria: he occupied Jerusalem and left a garrison in the citadel. But after the battle of Panion (200), in which Scopas was utterly routed by Antiochus, Jerusalem once more fell into the hands of the latter. Josephus expressly notes that the Jews of their own accord went over to him, received him willingly into Jerusalem, and helped him to subdue the citadel.[4] Antiochus rewarded the Jews with special gifts and privileges. Judæa henceforth, till the time of the Maccabean revolt, remained a province of Syria. Its condition was tolerably prosperous, and at least undisturbed by external foes or rival potentates during the remainder of Antiochus' reign, as well

[1] Mahaffy, *Alexander's Empire*, p. 120.
[2] Graetz, *Geschichte*, Vol. II. ii. p. 250.
[3] Daniel xi. 14; Ewald, *History of Israel* (E. T.), Vol. V. p. 283, n. 6; Graetz, Vol. II. ii. p. 262, n. 2.
[4] Josephus, *Antiquities*, xii. 3, 3.

as during that of his son and successor, Seleucus Philopator (187—176).

Of the internal history till the close of Philopator's reign, we know hardly anything. The one incident which Josephus records is the story of Joseph, son of Tobias, and of his son Hyrkanus.[1] The names of the high-priests are also preserved; and Josephus, combined with some passages in Sirach and the second Book of Maccabees, and with a few early Rabbinical fragments, helps to make two or three of them something like distinct personalities. Joseph, as we shall see, represents the evil effects of Hellenism on the Jewish character. His long administration as tax-gatherer of southern Syria had a great influence upon Judæa generally. He brought the Jews, says Josephus, "out of poverty and insignificance to a relatively high pitch of prosperity." The twenty-two years in which he farmed the taxes are assigned by Prof. Graetz to B. C. 230—208. Josephus speaks of "seditions" among the people after his death "because of his sons." The opposition between the elder ones and Hyrkanus had apparently a deeper cause than a mere family quarrel. It was connected with the rival parties who either favoured the existing Egyptian domination, or desired its overthrow in the interests of Antiochus. If Hyrkanus was for Egypt, his brothers were for Syria; they belonged moreover to the Hellenistic party which was rapidly forming itself in Jerusalem. The high-priest Onias III., who succeeded Simon II. shortly after the incorporation of Judæa into the Seleucid king-

[1] *Antiquities*, xii. 4.

dom, was opposed to the Hellenists; and the movement which began with the journey of Simon, the temple overseer, to Apollonius, the Syrian governor of Cœle-Syria, and with the subsequent despatch of Heliodorus to the temple of Jerusalem upon his unsuccessful mission of plunder, culminated in the events which were partly the cause for the persecutions of Antiochus Epiphanes.[1] With that persecution a new era begins.

To the one hundred and fifty-six years which lie between the conquest of Syria by Alexander and the accession of Antiochus Epiphanes, the varied literature which was subsequently to form the canon of the Old Testament owes something, though perhaps less than to the Persian period which preceded them. The Book of Chronicles was then compiled, and the Psalter enriched with many of its most beautiful hymns of prayer and praise. Not improbably also the earlier chapters of Proverbs and the Book of Job must also be brought down as late as the opening years of the Grecian period.[2] Ecclesiastes, third and saddest of the "Wisdom" writings of the Old Testament, almost unquestionably belongs to it.

There were two opposite forces at work in the Judaism of the post-Nehemian age—an impulse to separation and particularism, and an impulse to inclusion and absorption. The Jews were placed in a peculiar religious relation to the outer world. They had reached the stage of absolute monotheism, and reached it, not by the gradual diffusion of philosophic thought among the cultivated classes, but by the purification and development of their own national

[1] 2 Maccabees iii. 4—40.
[2] Cf. Cornill, *Einleitung in das Alte Testament*, 1891.

religion. For Yahveh as the only God was Yahveh still; in a peculiar and partial sense, God of the Jews. His glory was bound up with Israel's; so that even if the Jews did not deserve, it was necessary for Yahveh's honour that in the end they should receive, a better fate than other peoples. But even apart from this, and from all lower religious promptings, there was another obstacle to the diffusion of universalism. It was well-nigh impossible for the Jews to regard the gods of other nations as manifestations or expressions of the one and undivided Divine Essence.[1] They saw no incongruity between national worship and monotheistic dogma, such as a philosophic Hellene could perceive between his own personal belief and the popular cultus of Zeus. Their own popular cultus was true and divinely ordained, and consequently the possible service of other gods was for them an intolerable profanation. It was based upon the worship of the divine in material forms; and too often there were connected with it rites which the unsophisticated Jew, with his growing hold upon the virtue of chastity, regarded as a scarcely less flagrant abomination. And just in proportion as religion, in the guise of ceremonial, pervaded all life and all its daily occurrences, so did intercourse with the Gentile become difficult and polluting to the Jew. To the cultured Greek, such an attitude could only be construed as evidence of folly or misanthropy. The monotheistic basis of Judaism would generally escape him: he would only see in it one more national cult, no better and less attractive than all the rest. A radical

[1] It is to my mind still doubtful whether even Malachi i. 11 can properly be so interpreted.

opposition between one worship and another seemed to the Greek of the Hellenistic era an absurdity. All were in one sense almost equally false, and in another sense almost equally true. To this tolerant syncretism, the Jew, unprepared as he was to appreciate its philosophic basis, could only offer unwavering opposition. He was bound to maintain his distinctiveness amid an idolatrous and unbelieving world.

But with this impulse towards separatism and isolation, there went an opposite impulse towards inclusion and absorption. This must have been equally unintelligible both to the ordinary heathen and to the cultivated Hellene. Yahveh, though God of the Jews, was also God of the world, and if his glory was bound up with Israel's, it also required for its fullest earthly diffusion that he should be acknowledged as only God by all mankind. The ideals of Deutero-Isaiah were not wholly forgotten. In the interests of Yahveh the heathen must be won over to his service. This theocratic impulse towards enlargement had been, and still was, represented, both in prophecy and apocalypse, as the Gentile acknowledgment of Yahveh after the vengeance of the judgment-day. But in ordinary times, when the judgment-day sank into the background, it became apparent that human means must be taken for the accomplishment of the desired end. For its own renown, let Israel labour to spread the knowledge of their Deity and their Law.

It was motives such as these which produced the proselytizing tendency of the later Judaism. That tendency became, as it would seem, clearly marked towards the close of the Persian period. Exclusiveness had been the policy of Nehemiah and Ezra—exclusiveness even towards men who, of semi-Israelite birth themselves, genuinely desired a religious union. No sooner, however, was the Law securely established than efforts were made to bring over to official Judaism the descendants of the very people who had been rejected before. Psalmist, scribe and historian all bear witness to this new impulse. It met naturally with some opposition, and questions arose as to the relation of the new-comers to the Jews of pure blood, which were answered now in a larger and now in a narrower sense; but it is incorrect to represent the strict adherents of the Law as always opposed to the proselytizing tendency. It was only through a misgiving lest a large influx of proselytes should lead to religious laxity that some of the later Rabbis discouraged their reception; what the general feeling of the earlier scribes was, is well indicated in the derisive rebuke of Jesus, which, however exaggerated, has surely its element of truth.[1] In following the traces of the proselytizing tendency in the pre-Maccabean era within the Old Testament itself, while the age of the Diadochoi was undoubtedly the more favourable to proselytism, it is impossible to draw a clear line of cleavage between the Persian and the Greek periods.

Prof. Stade is of opinion that the author of Chronicles (about 250 B.C.), throwing the events of his own days into antiquity and giving them an historical setting, alludes to some ineffectual efforts which were made to win back to Judaism the now self-sufficient and fully organized community of the Samaritans. But

[1] Matt. xxiii. 15.

further north, the mixed inhabitants of Galilee were gradually and successfully won over to Judaism; while even at an earlier date, Israelites or half-breeds who dwelt within Judæan territory, or who had immigrated thither from the north, were readily accepted as proselytes.[1] They are described as having separated themselves from the uncleanness of the peoples of the land to seek Yahveh, the God of Israel.[2] In the latest portions of the priestly code, inserted after Nehemiah, the legal equality of native and stranger is strongly emphasized. The exquisite idyll of Ruth was possibly written as a polemical pamphlet in the days of Ezra. Its object is to show that marriages even with foreigners of full blood need have no evil influence upon religion, seeing that the alien woman may soon learn to be as Jewish as native Jewesses themselves. I am more inclined to place its date somewhat later, at a time when such arguments could be more coolly stated than in the heated antagonisms of Ezra's age. Does the story of Jonah typify Israel's unwillingness to cause the light to shine unto the Gentiles? At any rate, its obvious tendency is to show that Yahveh's interest is not limited to Israel, and that the nations are to feel, not only his retributive justice, but also his complementary qualities of pity and loving-kindness. Universalist passages were also inserted in older prophecies. Such probably is the beautiful fragment which now constitutes the opening of Isaiah's

[1] Stade, *Geschichte*, Vol. II. pp. 198, 199; 2 Chron. xv. 9, xxx. 5—25.
[2] Ezra, vi. 21; Neh. x. 29.

second, and of Micah's fourth chapter.¹ Such, too, is a noble passage in Isaiah lvi. Here the stranger, who has joined himself to Yahveh, is yet introduced complaining, "Yahveh has utterly separated me from his people." This seems to imply that, in spite of the letter of the Law, certain legal differences were being suggested or had even been established between proselytes and Jews. The author of the prophecy comforts the new-comers with the assurance : "The sons of the stranger that join themselves to Yahveh to minister to him and to love his name, to be his servants, every one that keepeth the sabbath from polluting it, and taketh hold of my covenant; even them will I bring to my holy mountain and make them joyful in my house of prayer : their burnt-offerings and their sacrifices shall be accepted upon mine altar ; for mine house shall be called an house of prayer for all the peoples."² That same combination of real universalism with marked affection for Jerusalem and its temple is also found in several passages of the Psalter.

¹ Isaiah ii. 2—4; Micah iv. 1—4. This prophecy is usually regarded as a quotation from an older contemporary or predecessor of Isaiah and Micah. It is more probably a post-exilic interpolation. Cf. for a high appreciation of its doctrine, Steinthal, *Zu Bibel und Religionsphilosophie* (1890), p. 77. "Höheres als jenes Fragment gibt's auf Erden nicht."

² Cf. Cheyne, *Psalter*, p. 294, and *Jewish Quarterly Review*, Vol. III. p. 602; Duhm, *Isaiah, ad loc.*, who characteristically belittles the passage, its author and *das Judenthum* in general. As to their exact date, it is quite possible that these eight verses, which surely have no connection with what precedes or follows them, may be contemporary with Ezra. But the writer is opposed to Ezra's particularism, not, as Duhm thinks, *in der Hauptsache mit ihm einverstanden.*

Some of these date probably from the opening of the Grecian era. Others perhaps are earlier.[1] The Persian government does not appear to have pressed heavily upon Judæa, though things changed for the worse with the reign of Artaxerxes Mnemon and the revolt of 365. To measure the influence of Persia upon the internal development of Judaism is difficult, and leads at once to questions still debated and unsettled. There was no spiritual unity pervading the different portions of the Persian empire, such as Alexander sought to create in his own kingdom through the medium of a common culture. It is, however, acknowledged that some specifically Zoroastrian beliefs ultimately filtered into Judaism, and were gradually assimilated. Many Jews still lived in Babylonia, where they would be more directly subject to Persian influences. The frequent communications which passed and re-passed between Judæa and the various settlements of the Diaspora could carry fructifying germs of Zoroastrian doctrine from east to west, and secure for them a final acceptance in the official religion of Jerusalem. Zoroastrian influences towards the growth of angelology, and also, as it would seem, towards the doctrine of a future life, will be noticed in the next Lecture. More generally, however, one would like to know whether the pure religion of Zoroaster had any wider result in making the Jews discern that God's light had shone upon mankind through other windows than theirs, or whether it tended in any degree to lessen the religious gulf which seemed to mark them off from the heathen world beyond. But such questions, fascina-

[1] Cf. Psalms lxxxvii., lxvii., lxvi. 5, xxii. 28, lxv. 3.

ting as they are, must, in all probability, remain for ever unanswered.

Of the general influence of Hellenism, not only in Egypt but also in Palestine, we can know far more; but even here it is of the two extremes of attraction and repulsion that we know the most, and we must trust chiefly to inference for an estimate of that fusion of Hellenism and Judaism which was gradually gaining strength and making way among a large middle party during the hundred and fifty years between the overthrow of the Persian empire and the accession of Antiochus Epiphanes.

Alexander the Great's policy of treating the Jews with marked toleration was pursued by the Diadochoi. It was both useful and easy to secure their loyalty. As political independence grew more and more inconceivable, religious autonomy became the practicable prize, the full guarantee of which was sufficient to win their gratitude. Thus in the intervals during which the land was spared from the soldiery of the Ptolemies or the Seleucids, Judæa enjoyed periods of repose, in which religious thought was not driven to harp perpetually on enemies and misfortunes, but could also make some quiet progress in depth and many-sidedness. Judæa was soon surrounded by a fringe of Hellenistic cities, and in many of them Jews resided who were in constant communication with Jerusalem. The knowledge of Greek language and Greek customs grew apace; and with it probably, at least among a few, the knowledge of some elements of Greek thought and philosophy.

To extremists at either end, Hellenism was chiefly

attractive or repellent through those of its elements which were in themselves unseemly and in their effects disintegrating and injurious. For if on its higher side it soared to the purest heights of philosophy, on the lower side it opened the door to wantonness and debauchery. There was a phase of later Hellenism which was loose in sexual relations and supple in deceit. It cannot be forgotten that even the highest Greek culture tolerated that nameless vice which was no less loathsome to the Jews of Alexander's age than to ourselves. And, lastly, even the philosophic thought of Hellenism made no protest against the popular polytheistic idolatry, but used its terms and practised its rites. To many a simple and pious Jew, Hellenism could only have seemed to be one polytheism the more—a polytheism more dangerous and more immoral than those with which Israel had previously been confronted.

Upon men of feeble religion and nerveless morality, or on those who, for whatever reason, found the life of the Law tiresome and unattractive, Hellenism laid powerful and corruptive hold. Its moral influence may be gathered from the story of Joseph the son of Tobias, in whom and whose family, Holtzmann, somewhat unfairly, discovers "the first historic example of that bad type of Judaism which makes this blessed people of God in the eyes of many people, not without reason, contemptible to the present day."[1] For if the sons of Tobias are the first historic instances of this hateful type, it is because in them Hellenistic veneer had spoilt Judæan simplicity. Other examples of the type may also have been due to

[1] Stade, *Geschichte*, Vol. II. p. 287.

the too rapid absorption of the evil elements in an alien civilization.

The growth of the Hellenistic party, with its aping of Greek customs in direct violation of the law, is indicated in the opening chapter of the first Book of Maccabees. It culminated in the establishment of a Greek gymnasium at Jerusalem, and in an attempted obscuration of the physical mark of difference between Gentile and Jew. Concurrently with these revolutionary Hellenizers, who probably consisted for the most part of the more aristocratic sections of the people, there grew up naturally a party of vigorous reaction. The antagonism between the two came gradually to a head, and the persecution of Antiochus was heralded, and partly caused, by increasing internal dissensions in Jerusalem and Judæa. Of the conservative opposition, the leaders of which were known as the *Chassidim*, the pious or devoted ones *par excellence*,[1] we find evidence in the Psalter. In the 1st and 119th Psalms, which pretty certainly belong to this period, the Hellenizers are described as "transgressors," "sinners," "scoffers" and men of "pride."[2] With them are contrasted the righteous, whose delight is in the law of Yahveh. Along with the wealth introduced, according to Josephus, by the successful machinations of Joseph the son of Tobias, there came luxury, and with luxury there followed debauchery and sexual license. May not then the "strange woman" of the opening chapters of Proverbs, against whose seductions the Wise Man so repeatedly warns his disciples, be in all probability a product of the Grecian age? It is, however, noticeable

[1] 1 Macc. ii. 42.   [2] Cheyne, *Psalter*, pp. 51, 241, &c.

that there is no evidence in the pre-Maccabean era of any direct idolatry. Monotheism was too deeply rooted. It was on the social side only that Hellenism proved attractive. Even marked Hellenizers drew the line at sacrificing to a heathen god.[1]

In the presence of moral and religious dangers like these, strict upholders of the national religion became stricter still. It would seem probable that the conception of a hedge to the law—the erection of an outer circle of legal fortifications to make the inner citadel of the written law more secure—may owe its origin to the Greek period, in which the spirit of Hellenism, not yet developed into persecution, had nevertheless already become an active religious danger.

But before things had reached this pass, Hellenism had exercised, even upon Palestinian Judaism, a modifying influence, without directly interfering either with men's attachment to their native religion, or even, except incidentally, with the sovereignty of the Law. "In addition to Hellenizers of pronounced anti-national and heathen disposition, such as Jason, Menelaus and Alkimus, the age also produced men who, in spite of their knowledge of Grecian literature and their pleasure in Grecian studies, were yet attached with immovable fidelity to their people and their faith."[2] Although this phase of Palestinian Judaism was transient, it is necessary to mark its traces, because these are not wanting even in the Old Testament itself. Hellenistic environment suggested or stimulated the impulse to expansion and universalism.

[1] 2 Macc. iv. 19.
[2] Freudenthal, *Hellenistische Studien*, p. 128.

"A persuasive presentation of true religion," says Prof. Cheyne, "only became possible in the Hellenistic age."[1] Some Jews perhaps entered also into the Hellenistic dream of a single culture for all the world, but with the knowledge of Yahveh for its foundation and its crown. Might not Israel even yet "blossom and bud and fill the face of the world with fruit"?[2]

It has already been observed that of the universalistic passages in post-exilic writings, some of the most marked belong to the Hellenistic period. A more direct influence of Hellenism may probably be traced in the Wisdom literature. There is no reason why a reflective or even speculative mood as to religious doctrines should not have naturally ensued on the final overthrow of idolatry and the general acceptance of a single official religion in theory and practice. But it has been cogently suggested that such a tendency, though it may have begun in the Persian period, would have been furthered and stimulated in an Hellenistic atmosphere. The Old Testament contains no clear evidence that any specific doctrines or forms of Greek philosophy were known to Jewish writers in Palestine; nor do the remains of Palestinian Greek literature of the pre-Maccabean or Maccabean era prove conclusively that any fusion, such as was even then going on in Egypt between Greek and Hebrew thought, was being attempted in Judæa. The allegorical method which explained away various crudities or difficulties in the sacred histories, as it explained away the immoralities of Homer, was a product of Alexandria, and

[1] Cheyne, *Psalter*, p. 295.
[2] Isaiah xxv. 11 (early Greek period).

there are no instances of its having been used on Judæan soil.

Yet the Essenes of a later age may warn us not to be too sure that between the unthinking Hellenizers on the one hand and the rigid conservatives upon the other, a syncretistic process was not going on even in Judæa. Hellenism must have tended to detach a certain section of the scribes or wise men from the study of the written law to more general teaching in religion and ethics. At the extreme wing of such a section would stand the lonely figure of Ecclesiastes. His date is probably about 200 B. C. The loosening of the religious bond, the wider outlook, the critical awakening, the falling-off in attractiveness and satisfying power of the old doctrines and practices, which Hellenistic influences effected, led in him to no aping of foreign customs, but to a mournful Epicureanism which the additions of his editors have not been able to disguise.[1] He has lost his interest in religion: for it fails to satisfy the wants of the human heart or to still its questionings, which, again and again repeated, are always left without an answer. He still believes in God, and he would still counsel men to get wisdom and practise it; but the object of wisdom is personal happiness, and sensual pleasure is a part of it. Ecclesiastes, however, is within the Bible a wholly isolated thinker. Attractive as his book may be, it stands outside the line of religious development.

But this is not the case with the author, if he falls

[2] Cf. the paragraph on Ecclesiastes in Schwally, *Das Leben nach dem Tode* (1892), pp. 104—106, and especially p. 106, n. 1, with the reference to Paul Haupt's most ingenious essay.

within this period, of the nine introductory chapters of Proverbs. He too, it has been urged, had felt the influence of Hellenistic thought, of which we can trace the product in his work. Later on I shall attempt to show that the function of Wisdom in the Proverbs generally, and its implicit identification with goodness and religion, are not necessarily to be regarded as even the indirect creation of Hellenism. But when, in the eighth chapter, Wisdom is described as the artist or master-workman who, fashioned by God before the world, was ever by him in his creative work, "his daily delight, sporting before him continually," it is fair to argue that we can hardly refuse to admit the intrusion of distinctively Greek ideas.[1] But touched though he be by an alien culture, the writer's Judaism is still real and ardent. His religion gives him moral stability as well as spiritual satisfaction. And the incipient philosopher has not lost his hold upon orthodoxy. He still can say: "Honour Yahveh with thy substance, and with the first-fruits of all thine increase."[2] And as he, elsewhere so seemingly detached from all specifically national and ceremonial elements, is still obviously a Jew, so on the other hand is Sirach, who repeatedly enforces the claims of the Law and identifies it with Wisdom, able to accept and assimilate for his ideal sage a variety of general culture which was certainly not without a tincture of Hellenism.

[1] viii. 30, 31. This contention has been well put by Holtzmann in Stade, *Geschichte*, Vol. II. pp. 296, 297; cf. also Reuss, *Die Geschichte der heiligen Schriften alten Testaments*, § 403, p. 521; and Cornill, *Einleitung*, p. 225.

[2] Prov. iii. 9.

His book, written about twenty years before the accession of Antiochus, and therefore within the Old Testament period, stands at a parting of the ways. He is concerned to warn his readers against a wisdom which is contrary to religion: "Inquire not into the things too hard for thee, and what is above thy strength examine not. Consider that which has been commanded thee, for thou hast no need of the secret things."[1] He believes that "many have been led astray by their own imaginings;" days of visitation are at hand in which the wise man will beware of transgression.[2] Some were clearly inclined to taste forbidden fruit under the plea of gathering experience. Sirach replies: "The knowledge of wickedness is not wisdom," for "in all wisdom there is observance of the Law." He even ventures on the statement, obvious to us, but unusual in the whole course of scribe-teaching from Proverbs to the Rabbis: "He that has small understanding and fears God is better than one that has much wisdom and transgresses the Law." For there is a spurious wisdom which is an "abomination."[3] But at the same time the picture of the ideal wise man drawn by Sirach shows that, while the Law was the foundation of his wisdom, it was by no means its only source. Hellenistic is Sirach's emphasis upon leisure as the condition of wisdom. "The wisdom of a scribe comes by opportunity of leisure: he that has little business

[1] iii. 20, 21, ed. Fritzsche (A.V. iii. 21, 22); cf. Psalm cxxxi.
[2] iii. 23 (A.V. 24), xviii. 26 (A.V. 27); cf. Mr. Ball's note on this second passage in the new "Variorum Reference" edition of the Apocrypha (1892).
[3] xix. 18—22 (A.V. 20—24).

can become wise."[1] For the wise man has much to do before he attains his goal. "He that gives his mind to the law of the most High will seek the wisdom of all the ancients, and be occupied with the prophecies. He will give heed to the sayings of renowned men; and where subtle parables are, he will be there also. He will seek out the secret things of similitudes, and be occupied with riddling parables. He will stand among great men, and appear before princes; he will travel through strange countries; for he will make trial of good and evil among men."[2] While, therefore, the ideal sage of Sirach is faithful to the Law, his intellectual horizon is not limited by his native Scriptures. Though the new culture has its peculiar dangers, it is not of necessity an evil.

What would have been the final outcome of all these streams of tendency if the violence of Antiochus Epiphanes had not supervened, we can hardly say. Hekatæus of Abdera, in a passage where the Greek historian seems to speak and not the Jewish interpolater, asserts that through the long period in which they were subject to foreign princes, especially during the Persian and Macedonian supremacies, the Jews were so much mingled with other races that the hold which many of their national usages had upon them was considerably weakened.[3] Hekatæus was a contemporary of the first Ptolemy, and may have written his history about 300—at an early phase, therefore, of the Hellenistic movement.

[1] xxxviii. 24.   [2] xxxix. 1—5; cf. xxxi. 10, 11.

[3] Müller, *Fragmenta Hist. Græcorum*, Vol. II. p. 393 (Diodorus Siculus, ed. Müller, Vol. II. p. 580); cf. Schürer, *Geschichte*, Vol. II. p. 818 (E. T. Div. ii. Vol. III. p. 305).

Prof. Schürer thinks (and who is better qualified to offer an opinion than he?) that "had the Hellenizing process been allowed to take its course in quiet, Palestinian Judaism would also probably have gradually acquired a form in which it would have been hardly recognizable. It would have become even much more syncretistic than the Judaism of Philo." For the events which preceded the Maccabean revolt make it, as he thinks, probable that the Hellenizing party had already obtained the upper hand. The *Chassidim* would have dwindled down into a sect. But the persecution of Antiochus broke the spell, and Judaism was saved. "For not only the rigid Chassidim, but the great mass of the people, stood up in battle for their ancient faith." Hellenism was overcome, and as an influence on the regular development of Judaism, was, in Judæa at any rate, of no further account.[1]

Having said thus much of external influences, it is time to turn now to the internal framework, the Temple and the Scriptures.

The introduction of Ezra's law had mainly been brought about for the sake of the better and more permanent establishment of the public worship, and of such subsidiary ceremonials as were dependent on it. Ezra's interests were bound up with those of the temple. Though a scribe, he was also a priest, and his work as scribe was conditioned by his ideals as priest. The law which he introduced had grown up in the school of

---

[1] Schürer, *Geschichte*, Vol. I. p. 147 (E. T. Div. i. Vol. I. p. 198). The Hellenistic development of Judaism outside Judæa, of which the chief seat was Alexandria, falls beyond the scope and purpose of the present Lectures.

Ezekiel, and its object, as we know, was more collective than individual. To the priests the cultus was the fixed expression of Yahveh's will, the token of his presence within the community of Israel. It was emphatically an end in itself: as the false and idolatrous worship of the monarchy had caused the punishment of exile, so the perpetual maintenance of true worship would secure for a faithful people the favour of its God. Both for Israel and for the world, the relation of God to his chosen people—nay, his very existence and reality—were symbolized and evidenced in the temple service and in that which appertained to it. It was performed for God's glory as much as for Israel's safety. Like the Roman Catholic Mass, it was a perpetual divine manifestation.

A literary expression of this conception of the temple and its worship is the Book of Chronicles, including the editorial portions of Ezra and Nehemiah.[1] Written about 300 or 250 B.C., its object was to give a fresh narrative of the history of the Judæan monarchy in the light of the author's own religious opinions. These by no means tally exactly with the general religious opinions of his time. By Hellenism the writer was entirely unaffected. He was a Levite, and a main purpose of his narrative was the glorification of the temple and its worship. In re-writing the pre-exilic history, he supposes that the priestly law must have always been the authoritative code of nation and king. Thus David is made to organize the entire temple service as so pious a monarch ought to have organized it if the Pentateuch had been his guide, and as, therefore, the author of Chronicles

[1] Cf. Kuenen, *Onderzoek*, 2nd ed., Vol. I. pp. 515, &c.

doubtless sincerely believed that it actually was organized in the Davidic age. The temple is the centre of Israel's life and the object of its existence. This Levitical conception of national purpose and temple ceremonial was not only opposed by a few chosen spirits who revived the old antagonism of the prophets between substance and form, but was also largely modified by various movements of religious thought. Judaism had really, though unconsciously, passed beyond the priestly limit, and was transforming the mere outward cultus into something purer and more spiritual. With the animal sacrifices, ordained by the letter of the law, praise and prayer became closely associated, and the theory of God's presence within the temple helped to evoke some of the noblest religious sentiments out of apparently most unpromising material.[1] Spiritual communion with God and the pure joy of a felt nearness to him were born from participation in the temple service. To go to Jerusalem became a high religious satisfaction; to take part in statutory ceremonial evoked feelings which could not be created by statute. The literary evidence of these facts, which seem so curious for us to-day, is to be found in the Psalter, now commonly described as the religious hymn-book of the second temple. Its exact relation to the fixed temple psalmody is not easy to ascertain. We know that the position of the temple singers increased in importance during the Persian period. In Nehemiah's time they were not included among the Levites, and were probably reckoned low in the social scale. But by the age of the Chronicler—at the opening

[1] Cf. Wellhausen, *Abriss*, p. 89.

of the Grecian period—they were already an integral portion of the Levites, of whose duties sacred song formed no unimportant part. Some of the psalms in our present collection may have been composed by them; others, by hymn-writers outside their ranks, but for temple use; while others again, though written independently, were perhaps adopted by the Levites for the same purpose. But however this may be, the fact remains that some of our noblest and most spiritual psalms owe their origin to the temple and its worship.

Yet close as is the connection between psalter and sanctuary, a few psalms show a marked antagonism to the sacrificial system, and join on, in this respect, not to the *Torah* of the priests, but to the preaching of the prophets.[1] Others accentuate, not the beauty of the temple, but the all-sufficiency of the written Word. The psalmist's religion may be truly said to have been wider than that of priest or sage. He was less a specialist than either of these, and is thus our best authority for the post-exilic religion. For the psalmist, if one may so individualize the many authors of the Psalter, is the spokesman of the national piety in its noblest and purest form. His book marks the religious level up to which prophet, priest and sage had educated the national consciousness. It is the reflection of all these in turn, but of all with a special *nuance*, and often with a spiritual development or application, peculiarly its own. By their patriotic devotion to their people, in whose name they so often speak, and by their frequent combination of prophetic principles with warm attachment to the puri-

[1] Cf. Psalms xl., l., li.

fied forms in which religion was outwardly clothed, the psalmists represent a certain fusion between prophet and priest, as well as between prophet and scribe. Various elements of religion, such as the conception of God and of man's communion with him, the ideas of sin and atonement, were all affected by the temple. That its influence did not become more powerful still was due to the counter influence of the law. For when the law became an end in itself, as distinct from the temple, for the sake of which so much of it had originally been introduced—when the scribe became a separate personality from the priest, with whom he had been originally identical—the ceremonial of the temple was subordinated to the overmastering conception of the law. The cultus was henceforth but a portion of the law, to be minutely maintained no doubt, but maintained because the law ordained it. God's glory and Israel's were realized, not in the temple-worship, but in the fulfilment of the law of which that worship was but a part. Because the majesty of the law overshadowed the temple, Judaism was able to survive when the temple had been destroyed.

Yet throughout the Persian and Greek period the temple-worship retained outwardly its dignity and importance. The temple was the only material possession of unquestioned value of which the Jewish nation could boast; it was the one thing for which Judæa was famous in the outside world.[1] Its renown was reflected on its people. In post-exilic times it was a really national place of worship. Before the exile its services and sacrifices had been maintained by the king; now it was a

[2] Cf. the fragment in Polybius, xvi. 39.

national concern, and, as it would seem, the people willingly paid the heavy taxes in money and kind which the establishment of the temple necessitated. The institution of the twenty-four watches (*Mishmaroth*), which falls within Old Testament times, shows how it was attempted to give to the temple services a thoroughly representative character. Like priests and Levites the entire people was divided into twenty-four classes, of which one was supposed to be present each week in Jerusalem at the daily sacrifice. As a matter of fact, as it was clearly not possible for a whole class to muster at the temple, it appears to have been customary for a small selection of them to go to Jerusalem, while for the remainder there were special services in their own synagogues. In this way the temple ceremonial was linked on to that new institution of the synagogue which was ultimately to supply its place.[1]

The book of Ecclesiasticus, written some fifteen or twenty years before the accession of Antiochus Epiphanes, shows the impression made upon the mind of a representative Jew of that period by the magnificence of the temple ritual.[2] At the same time, while bidding the reader to "fear Yahveh and honour his priest; to love him that made thee with all thy strength, and to forsake not his ministers,"[3] Sirach is easily able to appropriate and retain the prophetic teaching: "He that shows gratitude brings an offering, and he that gives alms sacrifices a thank-offering." The preceding verse shows

---

[1] Schürer, *Geschichte*, Vol. II. pp. 225, 226 (E. T. Div. ii. Vol. I. p. 175).

[2] l. 1—24.   [3] vii. 30, 31.

how he came to say this: the law had put sacrifice into its proper place. For "he that keeps the law brings many offerings; he that takes heed to the commandments offers a thank-offering."[1] Yet man must not appear empty before God; for, whatever may seem to be the inutility of sacrifice, "*all these things are to be done because of the commandment.*" Here is the influence of the law fully dominant over the influence of the priest.

But the written law, though incomparably the most important, was yet only a portion of that collection of sacred Scriptures which constituted the second great factor in the religion of the post-exilic period. These Scriptures consisted first and foremost of the Pentateuch; next, of the histories of Joshua, Judges, Samuel and Kings; and lastly, of a collection of prophetic literature still in a more or less floating condition, and capable therefore of editorial expansion, but already possessed of a definitely sacred character. The Judaism of the second temple became gradually the religion of a book. More especially the influence of the law constantly tended to transform and overcome the hierarchic and priestly character which, in the days of Ezra, the religion seemed destined to assume. Through the law and its teachers was created a religious individualism, the growth of which is a feature to be borne in mind in the history of post-exilic piety. On the theoretic side this result was partly achieved by making the fulfilment of the law an end in itself for every individual; on the practical side, by those re-unions for Scripture reading and prayer which became the better substitute for the beloved

[1] xxxii. 1—5 (A.V. xxxv. 1—5); cf. xxxi. 18—20.

local sanctuaries of pre-exilic days, and which were destined to supersede the material worship of the temple.

We cannot trace the origin of the synagogue. It is possible, as we have already seen, that even in the exile there were meetings on sabbaths and fast-days for religious teaching and exhortation. But in the form in which they occur in Josephus and the New Testament, the synagogues can only have been a consequence of the law, so that they were probably instituted and gradually developed after the age of Ezra. Two concurrent objects were achieved by them. In the first place, they were places of assembly for the recitation and exposition of the law and the prophets; secondly, they were places for communal and public prayer, in which religious unity and self-consciousness could be expressed and maintained apart from the temple. By the Maccabean age they had become numerous, so that the Syrian enemy aiming at the total destruction of Judaism not only profanes the sanctuary, but "burns up all the synagogues of God in the land."[1]

The synagogal service in those early pre-Maccabean days cannot be precisely determined, but it probably already included a practical confession of faith in God and his word—contained in the *Shema* and in two appended passages[2]—a section from the law continuous from week to week, so that the whole was read through in a cycle of three years; a reading from the prophets—not fixed,

---

[1] Ps. lxxiv. 8.

[2] Deut. vi. 4—9, xi. 13—22; Numb. xv. 37—41. Mr. Schechter informs me that the two last passages were perhaps added at a later period.

but left to the choice of the individual and only customary on sabbaths; together with a few short prayers. This last portion was expanded afterwards into the wellknown eighteen benedictions, called either *Tefillah*, as the prayer *par excellence*, or *Amidah*, because the congregation stood during their recitation. It is generally assumed that the three first and the three last of these benedictions, in a somewhat simpler and shorter form than that in which they are found in Jewish prayer-books to-day, were already in existence before the Maccabean era.[1]

It is not difficult to see that an institution such as the synagogue must have had an enormous effect upon religious life. It actively helped to individualize religion, and to bring it home to the hearts and understanding of all. Through the influence of the law and the synagogue, religion was gradually emancipated from the narrow interests to which the hierarchy was inclined to limit it; without losing its particularism, it yet became more human, less fixed to a single locality, less riveted to temple and state. This effect of the law was also helped forward by the exigencies of circumstance: the wide Jewish diaspora was compelled to shape for itself a daily religion independent of Palestine. The law supplied a noticeable defect in the religion of Nehemiah's day by creating a new spiritual satisfaction, and consequently a new spiritual motive. It was here aided by the novel doctrine of a future life and a bodily resurrection, the growth of which must be traced in the next Lecture. And the two together suggested a fresh theodicy.

[1] Cf. Schürer, *Geschichte*, Vol. II. pp. 376—386 (E. T. Div. ii. Vol. II. pp. 75—89).

Temple and law imply for their maintenance priest and scribe. In these two personalities the religious and political organization of the Jewish people in the post-exilic period is practically comprised. Already in the age of Zechariah the high-priest occupied a position of nearly equal importance with Zerubbabel, the representative of the Davidic line. In the age of Nehemiah the high-priest and his family showed, in the eyes of the rigorists, a deplorable religious laxity. After the introduction of the law the general tendency remained as before. The high-priest was as much chief officer of state as official representative of the national religion. Such a position was peculiarly liable to moral corruption. Even for the Persian period the odious story of Bagoses shows how mean intrigue and open violence were not unknown in the high-priest's family. But as the office was hereditary, it acquired stability and influence, while the family of David sank into the background and into comparative insignificance. Together with the richer laymen, the upper priesthood formed an aristocratic body of conservative instincts, likely to look at religious matters from a semi-political point of view. Their leader, the high-priest, stood at the head of a senate, first authenticated for the age of Antiochus III., and composed partly of priests and partly of laymen.[1] In the late Maccabean period, when the scribes had become a powerful party in the state, they too won places upon this council or Synedrion.

The numbers of the priests are not easy to determine. Whereas the lists in Ezra and Nehemiah mention 4289

[1] Josephus, *Antiquities*, xii. 3, 3.

for the return under Zerubbabel, Pseudo-Hekatæus, as quoted by Josephus, states that in his time their numbers were only 1500.[1] As only comparatively few were wealthy and influential, this difference between the rich priests of the capital and the poorer priests who lived mainly in the country may perhaps partly account for the origin and development of the scribe. Not to be neglected also in the history of this difficult process are the Levites. Prof. Schürer has conjectured that the small numbers who returned with Zerubbabel and Ezra were substantially increased by descendants of other old Levitical, or in the pre-exilic sense priestly, families who had not been deported to Babylon.[2] However this may be, we may fairly assume that their numbers at the opening of the Hellenistic period exceeded a thousand. It was noticed in the last Lecture how prominent a position was assigned to certain Levites at the first reading of the law at the reform of Ezra and Nehemiah. There are traces that this special predilection was continued,[3] and many Levites may have found in the teaching of the law a nobler recompence for their inferior position in the sanctuary.

In the ranks of the hierarchy we thus find two main divisions. There was an upper class, who were men of politics as well as of religion, and associated with them there must have been many, both among priests and Levites, who found employment in the routine business of the temple and sufficient satisfaction in its discharge.

[1] *Contra Apionem*, i. 22.
[2] *Geschichte*, Vol. II. p. 189 (E. T. Div. ii. Vol. I. p. 227).
[3] Cf. 2 Chron. xxxv. 3, xvii. 7; 1 Chron. xxiii. 4.

But over and above these, though separated from them by no hard and fast line, were others who were seldom occupied at Jerusalem, or who, for one reason or another, found the material duties of the temple insufficient for their religious needs. Such persons, possessed of adequate leisure, because free from the necessity of devoting all their time to the satisfaction of bodily wants, were well fitted for the posts of teachers, interpreters and students of the law and the sacred Scriptures generally. Can the growth of this class and of the various forms which it assumed, until one particular form predominated, be traced back to its beginnings?

Unfortunately not. The Pharisees of the later Maccabean era, progenitors of the Scribes and Rabbis of the New Testament, appear in the field of history on a sudden, but how they emerged from the priesthood of Ezra and Nehemiah history has left unrecorded. We start with a code introduced by priests, and in accordance with priestly ideals. Of this code they were the authors, custodians and interpreters. By the time of John Hyrkanus (135—105), the stories in Josephus respecting his conflicts with the Pharisees, whose leaders were the men known later as Scribes and Rabbis, show that the law was taught, interpreted and developed no longer by priests, but by men outside their ranks and often opposed to them in religious practice and belief.[1] This great change, fraught with momentous consequences for Judaism, had resulted partly from the growing worldliness of the upper sections of the priesthood, and partly from the growing affection of the people for the law itself. Priestly

[1] *Antiquities*, xiii. 10.

as so much of it seems and is, it yet sank deeper and deeper into the hearts of the people. Soon after Ezra, as we shall shortly learn, its two main portions, the priestly code and the Book of Deuteronomy, to which the older histories of the patriarchal and Mosaic age had been attached, were welded together into a single whole. Discrepancies between different parts of the law, or between the law and other portions of sacred Scripture, were almost completely overlooked. Prophets and historians seemed only to interpret and accentuate it. For the final advent of the Messianic age, the fulfilment of the law appeared more and more assuredly to be the preparation decreed by the will of God and indicated in his sacred Word.

Thus the need of teachers in the law and the Scriptures arose quite naturally out of their increasing popularity. And as the law, both in the wider and the narrower sense, passed out of priestly control, because the community as a whole had gradually become more unselfishly interested in it than the official hierarchy, the people began to raise up teachers out of its own ranks. To such purely lay teachers must be added those priests and Levites (chiefly at the lower end of the social scale) who, as compared with the upper priesthood of the capital, belonged by birth rather than by sentiment to their respective orders. For there was never any rigid separation, or fixed wall of partition, between priest and scribe. Even in later times a priest might be a scribe, and at least one high-priest is famous as a lover of the law.

In the Persian period, the scribe as such, apart from the priest, is scarcely known by name. Prof. Schürer's opinion is that "in the first centuries after the exile till well down into the Greek period, the priests maintained their superiority." And again: "At the time of Ezra, priest and scribe are practically identical. From the beginning of the Greek period they become more and more distinct."[1]

Within the Old Testament itself there are still many remains of the literary activity of the earlier scribes. Many will be surprised to learn that the products of one branch of this activity must be sought for in the Wisdom literature, and more especially in the Book of Proverbs. The post-exilic origin of Proverbs and Job, while still largely disputed, is gradually gaining ground.[2] Yet if insuperable difficulties seem to prevent our assigning these books to the period of the monarchy, or even of the exile, it might seem that the difficulties are scarcely diminished by dating them after Nehemiah. For if the lay scribes owed their origin to an independent study of law and Scriptures, how can the Book of Proverbs, which appears to be the outcome of a merely general

[1] *Geschichte*, Vol. II. pp. 175, 320 (E. T. Div. ii. Vol. I. p. 208, Vol. II. p. 9).

[2] See, for example, Cornill, *Einleitung in das alte Testament;* Cheyne, in *Expositor*, 1892, pp. 244—251. I would also venture to refer to my own article, "Notes upon the Date and Religious Value of the Proverbs," in *Jewish Quarterly Review*, Vol. II. pp. 430—453. It should, as Mr. Carpenter has pointed out to me, have been more distinctly stated that while the general religious tone of the whole, and most of the specifically religious adages individually, must be set down to the credit of the post-exilic period, many "of the maxims of social and personal experience may really be of very high antiquity." The various separate collections, which we can partly still distinguish in x.—xxxi., may undoubtedly "have taken up elements of great age."

teaching, almost more ethical than religious, be rightly assigned to them? In Proverbs there is scarcely a single reference to specific enactments of the law; and it is not only the priest, but also Israel itself, with all its hopes and aspirations, which is conspicuous by its absence. The history of the past and the ideals of the future—the warnings and anticipations of the prophets—are all equally ignored.

Two explanations have been put forward of these curious phenomena. The first is that the whole Book of Proverbs, as well as the Book of Job, must be assigned to the Greek period, more especially to that era of comparative prosperity and calm under the rule of the Ptolemæan kings (280—200). The peculiar characteristics of Proverbs, above referred to, will then be partly due to an epoch the tokens of which have been described as the "reconciliation and commingling of Judaism and Hellenism with one another."[1] But as it seems scarcely safe to put more than the nine introductory chapters as late as Alexander or the Ptolemies, another explanation must be attempted.

The compilation and editing of the larger portion of Proverbs might be retained for the Persian period on the hypothesis that the book represents only a single phase of the early scribe teaching, and that the study of the Scriptures made itself felt in more directions than one. We do not sufficiently bear in mind the great variety and many-sided development of the post-exilic religion before the time of the Maccabean persecution. That event was a turning-point in the history

[1] Stade, *Geschichte*, Vol. II. p. 296.

of Judaism. Till then, at any rate, life under the law did not necessarily produce that narrowness of mind and mood, that absorbing interest in ceremonialism and legal observance, and that rigid and overmastering particularism, which it is too customary to ascribe to it. If Proverbs and Job, to say nothing of the Psalter, are all post-exilic, critics will have to unlearn the usual assumption that the law in itself necessarily tended to stifle every wide and liberal religious impulse, and to drive all who paid it allegiance into the narrow groove of letter-worship and formalism.

But further we have to ask, How are we to account for that conception of religion and morality under the form of Wisdom, which such books as Proverbs and Ecclesiasticus show to have become common and customary in the Persian and Hellenistic periods? It was, I think, a by-product of the law which, regarded as a thing to be learned, naturally implied the possession of wisdom in him who had learned it. Human wisdom, the wisdom of adages and proverbs, had been as familiar to the Jews as to other eastern nations. It was the wisdom of Edom.[1] It was the wisdom of king Solomon, in which he excelled "the children of the East-country and all the wisdom of Egypt."[2] But before the exile this secular wisdom had not been much thought of by the religious teachers of Israel. Too often the wise men had taken up an antagonistic attitude to prophetic doctrine. Too often they were but wise in their own conceit, and their wisdom was of no avail in the hour of need. But the law of Deuteronomy was to give Israel a material for wisdom

[1] Jer. xlix. 9; Ob. 8.   [2] 1 Kings v. 10 (E.V. iv. 30).

which should surpass the wisdom of the nations. In a late chapter of Deuteronomy the claim is put forward that true wisdom is the prerogative of religious faith. The "judgments and statutes," given through Moses to Israel, constitute Israel's wisdom and understanding in the sight of the nations. They, therefore, and the "things which thine eyes have seen"—in other words, the records of the past—must be taught from generation to generation.[1]

But there had also been a semi-intellectual element in the religious vocabulary of the prophets: they had expressed religious excellences intellectually. Thus Hosea's formula for the highest religious desideratum is "the knowledge of God." In the ideal age depicted by Jeremiah teaching becomes unnecessary, for all will "know" their God: Deutero-Isaiah, speaking of the same future, which seemed to him so near, and addressing Jerusalem, declares that "all thy children shall be disciples of Yahveh." A prophecy usually attributed to Isaiah, but just possibly of the Persian period, specializes the spirit of Yahveh which shall rest upon the coming Messiah, "as the Spirit of wisdom and understanding, the Spirit of counsel and might, the Spirit of knowledge and fear of Yahveh." The fool, even in the oldest Israelite terminology, is identified with the wicked.[2]

What sort of "teaching" went on in the exile, and what relation it bore to the study of the law in priestly circles, we hardly know. That deputation which Ezra sent to the Levites to urge them to join him in the

[1] Deut. iv. 6, 7.
[2] Hosea iv. 6, iv. 1, 6; Jer. xxxi. 24; Isaiah liv. 13, xi. 2.

expedition to Judæa, consisted of nine "chief men" and two "teachers."¹ In the public reading of the law some fourteen years later, thirteen Levites explain the wording and "give the sense."² When we pass to the time of the Chronicler, at the opening of the Hellenistic age, we find him attributing to Jehoshaphat a commission of divers persons "to teach the people in all the cities of Judah." This commission consists of five nobles (the object of whose presence does not seem apparent), nine Levites, and two priests. With them they have the book of the law of Yahveh. Thus here again we find the Levites prominent as teachers. In another passage the Chronicler speaks of the Levites as those "who taught all Israel."³

This teaching which the law required and fostered could clearly not have been limited to ceremomial. The ethical elements of the law needed equal or even greater attention. When once the idea was reached that the total sum of religious truth and doctrine—the teaching of the prophets as well as of the law—constituted Israel's peculiar wisdom, it was natural that the early scribes and students of the Scriptures should apply these truths in detail, according to the old manner of gnomic teaching, to the life of their own time. "Wisdom" assumed a religious form; and in place of the old sages of the opposition, we have now orthodox sages of the law, who, teaching on the basis of the religion both of prophet and priest, incline now to one side and now to another, but are unconscious of any bygone conflict between the two.

[1] Ezra viii. 16. [2] Neh. viii. 7.
[3] 2 Chron. xvii. 7, xxxv. 3.

Circumstances, moreover, were favourable to such quiet, general instruction. The post-Nehemian age, till the time when Hellenism became first a seductive danger and then a tyrannical persecution, was one of comparative calm in the history of Judaism. Idolatry was overcome: the law was accepted as the basis of outward worship: the Persian and early Greek rule, if not without its occasional troubles, was yet free upon the whole from conflict and persecution. Hence the possibility for reflectiveness and even for speculation. It was a fit opportunity for systematic teaching—not for the spasmodic and semi-political teaching of the prophets, but for the ethical and individualistic teaching of the sage. That teaching, of which much of our present Book of Proverbs may well be a partial product, rests on the basis both of the prophets and of the law, though it seldom alludes to either. It reflects in some measure the doctrine both of lawgiver and prophet, though it is in itself non-prophetic and non-priestly. It treats morality as a matter of discipline, instruction and rule—and in this respect it follows the law; it sets morality above ritual, and finds the content of religion in the fear of God and a good life—and in this respect it follows the prophets. Thus the Wisdom literature lay, as it were, between law and prophecy, but on either side of it there were going on at the same time two other activities of Scripture students. On the one hand, there was the priest-scribe who expanded and edited the law; on the other, there was the prophet-scribe who expanded and edited the prophets.

Of the priest-scribe's work, the greater part falls probably in the half-century immediately after Ezra. Additions were made in the first instance to Ezra's own code, which, as we saw, was already a conglomerate when Ezra introduced it. Some of these additions were made in order to give sanction and authority to the ritual changes and developments of the day; of these, the two most obvious and interesting are the law of the extra evening burnt-offering, and the law of the yearly poll-tax of half-a-shekel, neither of which can have existed in Ezra's code.[1] Sometimes the additions are little more than repetition or amplification, of which the most remarkable is found in the last six chapters of Exodus. Here "a very short original account of the execution of the commands (respecting the erection of the Tabernacle) of Exodus xxv. sqq. was gradually elaborated, till at last it was brought into the form of the instructions themselves."[2] Sometimes, too, additions were made to the narratives; of these, a famous one, which is rather modification than addition, was made in the interest of the priests and to the detriment of the Levites, thus showing that the quarrel between the two orders continued for some time beyond the age of Ezra.[3] Of the priestly chapters in our present Pentateuch, about a quarter may perhaps be considered as later than the original "priestly code." It is hardly possible to say how much of this quarter was already in existence before Ezra's time, and how much was added afterwards. A more important work of the priest-scribe was the combination of the priestly law with Deuteronomy and the

---

[1] Cf. Kuenen, *Hexateuch*, p. 307, &c.   [2] Ibid. p. 73.

[3] Ibid. pp. 95, 334. Vogelstein, *Der Kampf zwischen Priestern und Leviten*, 1889, pp. 48—55.

older sacred history of the patriarchal and Mosaic ages. This combination, with the subsequent or contemporaneous separation of the chapters we now call Joshua from the law itself, formed the final stage in the history of the Pentateuch. In this last redaction, the priestly code —itself half-narrative, half-legal—was used as basis, so that but little of it was probably lost. And although some of the older narratives had to be shortened or omitted, inasmuch as the same events could not as a rule be related twice, it is probable that we still possess the larger portion of the earlier documents. When the Chronicler speaks of the Book of the Law of Yahveh, there can be little doubt that he means the Pentateuch in its present form. For when he wrote, in the first century of the Grecian period, the long work of redaction was drawing to its close. But even after the Greek translation of the Pentateuch, about the middle of the third century, some few short glosses were added in the Hebrew text; and with regard especially to the last six chapters of Exodus, the Hebrew text of which differs so widely from the Septuagint, we cannot be sure that they existed in their present form in all authorized copies before about 200 B.C.

This long-continued editorial manipulation of the Pentateuchal texts was only possible because of the great scarcity of copies: in the Persian period, at any rate, the mass of the people knew the law by oral teaching and recitation rather than by having read it themselves. The authorized copies of the law would be those which were held or issued by the priests and scribes of the capital. Any interpolation would be regarded by those who heard it for the first time as a piece of ancient Torah, hitherto passed over, perhaps hitherto unrecorded. It seems impossible to acquit the interpolators of the post-Nehemian age of all blame, but the different ideas about books and their integrity and authorship then prevailing must never be lost sight of. The men who added to Ezra's law, and combined it with the older records, probably believed those records to be documents of great antiquity, and, for the most part, of Mosaic origin; but it does not seem to have occurred to them that there was any objection to incorporating the new laws of their own time in the older code. To strengthen didactic effect they saw nothing wrong in adding a trait or a touch here and there, in expanding a narrative, or even in inserting an extra story. The law, in the long period of its oral growth and transmission, had been gradually increased and modified from age to age; yet each accretion had been good Torah in its turn, and found its place in the swelling store of legal tradition. When the oral Torah gave place to the written code, the same custom for a time prevailed, the same tendency towards expansion and addition as time and circumstance might demand. Editorial necessities, too, made themselves felt; narratives from different sources had to be dovetailed into each other; laws from various collections incorporated into a single whole. The authority of the code as a fixed and immutable body of law, given at one definite point of time in the past, and standing above and outside all subsequent tradition, could only begin to assert itself when the dovetailing process was finished, and the number of written copies had immensely multiplied. Then, as the knowledge of its very words was more widely diffused, the divinity of the law became gradually a hard-and-fast dogma, culminating at last in the belief that every letter had its own meaning, and the whole book its pre-existence in heaven.

A similar liberty of treatment was applied to the text of the Prophets. By the time of Ezra there already existed a considerable mass of generally accredited prophetical Scripture, most of which was of known authorship. Nevertheless, even these prophecies were undoubtedly pruned and added to, though the exact extent of these processes, which have been of late emphasized by Prof. Stade, it will be scarcely possible to discover. The Septuagint enables us to put our finger on one instance in which the text was changed because the event foretold had not come to pass.[1] It is probable that this is not the only case. The additions are somewhat easier to determine. They are of several kinds and of different lengths, consisting sometimes only of a few verses, sometimes of an entire paragraph. Or, again, independent "prophecies," written on some special occasion and circulated, like Deutero-Isaiah's, as separate broad-sheets, were afterwards inserted in larger collections, such as the scrolls of Isaiah or Zechariah, and invested thereby with the authority and durability of the older writings into which they were incorporated. Or, lastly, such separate prophecies may have been inserted *ab initio* in the older prophet's scroll, and never intended for independent circulation. This expansion and editing of the

[1] Zech. vi. 11—13, with the commentators and Stade, *Geschichte*, Vol. II. p. 126.

prophetical records extended probably into the Grecian period.

Its authors were prompted by various motives, but in almost all cases they were not the same motives as those which animated either the prophets of the pre-exilic periods, or even Haggai and Zechariah. The older prophets had been teachers; their editors were not. Teaching was conducted by the law and by that regular instruction of the scribes which has already come before us. The transition from genuine prophecy to editorial expansion is not therefore to be regarded as a mark of religious deterioration or sterility, as is so often and so strongly urged. Religious and ethical teaching, as well as religious spontaneity, found their vent in other channels. Such passages as Isaiah lviii., the famous homily on the distinction between the outward and the spiritual fast, are exceptional. In only one instance, moreover, do we find a separate post-exilic prophecy by a man whose name is given, and whose work is in consequence independently preserved. All other additions, with that exception—the Book of Joel—are anonymous.

The main object of these additions—both of the shorter interpolations and of the inserted or appended chapters—is to foretell and to depict the Messianic age in one or other of the various forms in which it was then conceived. A few of these additions are universalist, like the fragment in the second chapter of Isaiah, treating of Jerusalem as the world's spiritual metropolis; but the tendency of the great majority of them is national. Israel is by no means free from sin; but as compared with the heathen overlord and oppressor, Israel is righteous, its

enemies wicked. Most of these expansions of prophecy—
Isaiah xi. 10—16, xxiv.—xxvii., xxxii., xxxiii., lxiii.—
lxvi.; Jeremiah l., li.; Zechariah xii.—xiv., to instance
some of the longer passages—were designed for comfort,
and not for reproof. If sin was acknowledged, it was
either the sin of a particular party within the community,
or a somewhat vague and indefinite sinfulness in which
the writer felt himself equally involved. In both cases
the real object was, not to rebuke sin, but to announce
its disappearance either by a miraculous dispensation of
divine grace or through a judgment-process which, as
the immediate harbinger of the Messianic age, should be
partial for Israel, but wider for its foes. What provoked
these semi-prophetic utterances was, as of old, some
external event, foreboding change; but in the movement
was seen, not judgment upon guilty Israel, but judgment
upon the guiltier nations. That is why these expansions,
ending as they did in the apocalyptic literature, lie rather
outside the general religious life, and were not relatively
anything like so important as their present place in the
canon might suggest.[1] When the Syrian revolt began
under Ochus, when Alexander destroyed the empire of
Persia, when the Diadochoi fought against each other
and Judæa was often visited by war and distress, national
hopes revived, and men wondered whether the time of
deliverance, the golden age of peace and plenty predicted
by the seers of old, was not at hand. Such were the
times in which these late pieces of prophecy were composed.

[1] Cf. a few, but very important words of Kuenen in *Theol. Tijd.*,
1891, p. 508.

One book now included in the twelve minor Prophets hardly falls within the same category as the accretions to Isaiah and Zechariah or as the prophecy of Joel. This is the Book of Jonah, which is rather a romance with a moral than an ordinary prophecy. It links the work of the prophet-scribe with the work of Scripture students in other fields. It used an historic figure of olden times, but from the first, in all probability, was not meant to be accepted as a record of antiquity. Allied to it are the book of Ruth, which we have already seen to be a story with a purpose of the early post-Nehemian period, and among the Apocryphal writings the books of Judith and Tobit. The use of the traditional figure of Job, and the historic figure of Solomon, in the books of Job and Ecclesiastes, is closely similar. And this same artifice of fictitious antiquity, applied for very various purposes to the above-mentioned works, was in the book of Daniel applied differently again. Here in the midst of the Maccabean uprising and the persecutions of Antiochus, an unknown writer seeks to comfort his distressed fellow-countrymen by throwing his picture of the past and the present and his hopes for the future into the form of predictions uttered by a prophet of the captivity. With these predictions he combines a variety of romantic incidents and marvels, all tending to quicken the constancy and strengthen the faith of the persecuted and struggling Jews. He thus follows the precedents of Jonah and Ruth, but expands or improves upon his models in a manner which afterwards found wide imitation and development.

In these different literary productions of the post-exilic

period, we see that the long interval between Ezra and Judas the Maccabee was full of religious fervour and vitality. The spirit of religion expressed itself in a variety of ways. What manifold thought and activity there must have been in an age which edited the Law and expanded the Prophets, which produced the Psalter and the Proverbs, the books of Job and Ecclesiastes, Joel on the one hand, Jonah on the other, Chronicles and Ruth! What fresh inspiration and true religious zeal in an age which created the synagogue and its early ritual to serve as a complement to, and afterwards to take the place of, temple and sacrifice! And all this, be it remembered, in an age when ancient prophecy had ceased, when the letter of the law had succeeded to the free spirit which mocks at forms. How many the prejudices which should be corrected in this newer, more critical and more truthful view of the post-exilic age! We used to be told that the rule of the law, which began with Ezra, inaugurated a period of gradual sterilization and decay. More and more the legal yoke was supposed to crush out inspiration and originality; a mediocre and depressing uniformity was believed to take the place of the fresh and breezy variety of pre-exilic days, when, amid much wild disorder and many strange aberrations, there was yet room and opportunity for an Amos and a Jeremiah; instead of prophecy, there is the letter which kills; a chilling external legality causes the level of true religion to sink lower and lower, till the measure of its worthlessness becomes full, and the time for the new teaching is at hand.

It is now no longer possible to represent the post-exilic period in such a light as this. But prejudices die hard; and the antagonism to the Law and to its religion, which still reigns supreme in the greater number of Christian theologians, is trying to find a way out of an obvious difficulty. The imperfections of the post-exilic literature and religion are explained as direct results of the Law; its excellences are a dying protest against its stifling dominion. Thus the Psalter, albeit it has been the beloved possession of Judaism ever since the days of the Maccabees, is yet a reaction of old Israelite piety against Judaism, a proof that the religious genius of Israel could not be quenched even by Ezra and the Pharisees! That old Israelite piety, which was expressed erewhile in superstition and idolatry, is awakened once more, and lo! its outcome is the Psalter.[1] In the last Lecture I shall consider the truth of this supposed divorce between the Law and true religion. Meanwhile it remains to point out a general explanation for the great variety of religious thoughts and impulses which characterizes the post-exilic period.

The religion of Ezra and his succecsors was an unconscious combination of two incompatibles. Though the two ingredients were blended in very various proportions—hence the diversity in the effects produced—neither was ever wholly wanting. Uncompromising monotheism on the one hand; a single nation and a national ceremonial upon the other; the incongruity is apparent. The conception of Deity did not square with the religious cultus; the idea had outgrown its embodiment. Or, again, it might be said that idea and embo-

[1] So Cornill, *Einleitung*, p. 214.

diment sprang from different sources. The first was prophetic and original, peculiar to the genius or inspiration of the highest spirits in Israel; the second was popular, customary, heathen. But it was inevitable that idea and embodiment should re-act upon each other, the idea sometimes transfiguring the embodiment, the embodiment sometimes detracting from the purity of the idea. It was the embodiment which enabled lower beliefs, such as the peculiar relation of God to a particular place, to live on side by side with higher doctrine by which they had in principle been overcome. Hence the prophetic conception of a single spiritual God, Creator of heaven and earth, and the living self-conscious ideal of righteousness and beneficence, was wedded to a religious practice which implied that abstention from certain foods or the exercise of ablutory purifications could bring men nearer to the holy God.

But another reason why the idea was unable to dispense with the old embodiment, or to create a new one better fitted to itself, was the fact that the idea, original as it was, was built up upon the basis of a popular religion. From an historical point of view this connection was necessary for the ultimate result. For if the prophets had spoken of the one God, and not of the one Yahveh, then, as in Greece, they might have given us a monotheistic philosophy, but not that wider and more potent good, a monotheistic religion.

In the Hellenistic period, the two main elements in the Jewish religion were being severally developed in antagonism with each other. The attraction of Hellenism tended to soften down or eliminate the national forms;

the repulsion against Hellenism tended to accentuate them. It is not possible to enter into the details, whether external or internal, of the Syrian persecution and the Maccabean revolt. With them began a new era, of which the mixed issues lie outside Old Testament limits. Not that the literature of the Old Testament fails us even now. For some forty years at least after the accession of Antiochus it still continues. More than one psalm yet preserved to us was written during the days of persecution and conflict, and some, too, echo the days of victory and triumph. When the darkness was deepest, the Book of Daniel was written to cheer the Maccabean warriors; while the fierce passions evoked by the struggle are revealed to us in the Book of Esther. But the new religious parties and tendencies produced by the revolt and its consequences belong to the history of Rabbinism or to the origins of Christianity, not to the history of the Old Testament.

Yet one point, in conclusion, before we turn to examine the religious content of the post-exilic literature of the Bible. The Maccabean revolt drove out Hellenism, and prepared the way for the full development of Rabbinism. It left the Law triumphant and supreme. After Antiochus' ill-starred persecution, we no longer find that rich variety of religious literature and tendency which marks the period between Ezra and the Maccabees. The worship of the Law and the domination of Scripture set their seals upon all forms of literary productiveness, and thus in certain respects there is a family likeness in them all. Nationalism, particularism, legalism, are now all-powerful, and their influence is all-pervading. All this would

INTERNAL ORGANIZATION. 413

seem to indicate retrogression, and in one direction it actually does so. Let no one, however, suppose that it indicates stagnation, sterility or decay. Above all, let no one suppose that it indicates a lower level of personal religion in the heart of each individual believer. For the religious fervour which marks much of the literature of the pre-Maccabean period was no less, but even more, a characteristic of the Judaism which succeeded it. Religion has never been a purer joy and a deeper satisfaction, God has never been more truly loved and more nobly served, than among those who followed the full-blown particularism of the Rabbis. Under the influence of Hellenism and in the waning of the national idea, God, to the author of Ecclesiastes, had become distant. It was the Law and the national idea which brought God near. In orthodox Judaism the Law supplied the place of the person of Christ in orthodox Christianity. It was the almost living link between the human and the divine.

Lecture VIII.

FROM NEHEMIAH TO THE MACCABEES: GOD AND ISRAEL.

In roughest outline I sought to sketch out in the last Lecture the environment and organization of the Jewish religion during the three hundred years between Nehemiah and Simon the Maccabee. I attempted to gauge the successive influences of Persian and Hellenistic supremacy, and of Hellenistic if not of Persian thought, upon the development of Palestinian Judaism. Internally, the Temple and the Law were shown to be the two great facts round which so much of the religious life clustered, and by which it was so markedly determined. The temple and its priests, with all their variety of priestly ideas and regulations; the law and its wise men and scribes, with all their wide diffusion of teaching and precept—these were the two constituent, though heterogeneous elements, which may be regarded either as the sheath and casing of the religion, or more accurately as the sources from which its life was drawn. It was pointed out also that law and temple were not antithetic, but that, unfortunately, the greater portion of the law to the study of which the scribes consecrated their lives, and for which they sought the undivided allegiance of their race, was priestly in its thought and priestly in the rites which it enjoined. Some attempt must now be made to present, at least in its main features, the actual content of that religion, the framework of which has been thus, however imperfectly, described. It is mainly by the help of the Old Testament that this must be accomplished. But though we are confined within Old Testament limits, the literature of that book, as we have seen, still continues for three centuries after the reformation of Nehemiah. The classes of post-exilic literature within the Old Testament, and of the men who produced it, have been already indicated. In our fragmentary sketch of the religious organization, the figures of the Levitical historian, of the editors and expanders of the prophetical books, of the apocalyptic seers, of the psalmists and of the sages, branching off into the Rabbi on the one side and the isolated philosopher on the other, have already come before us. What was the religion which all these various teachers, thinkers, singers, were contributing to form?

By putting the question in that shape, I indicate, at the risk of some misinterpretation, the tendency and aim of our inquiry. I indicate also the lines on which the inquiry must be conducted. Time and opportunity are wanting to delineate fully the separate "religions" of the Psalter, of the Wisdom books, of the Apocalyptic writings. It is obvious that each possesses its own distinctive peculiarity. But these varieties can only be alluded to incidentally. The main object must be to elicit what was common and generic to them all, and was adopted and further developed in the subsequent and post-biblical periods.

Moreover this necessary limitation determines the point of view from which I approach the subject. It is not the point of view from which the post-exilic period is usually regarded, and it may well be argued that it is not the point of view which meets the requirements of universal history. Its comparative novelty may be its best defence. To most people, the main interest of the post-exilic period lies in the fact that it was the seed-bed of Christianity. From that point of view, divers elements in the body of religious doctrine receive an importance which they neither possessed at the time nor acquired afterwards in the history of Judaism. Thus the question how far even Palestinian Judaism admitted any distinctions in the different aspects of the Divine Being— how far, for example, the divine spirit was hypostatized —is clearly of great interest and value in tracing the genesis of Christian doctrine; but it was a very subordinate matter both in the religion of the time and in post-biblical Judaism. Again, while the whole influence of the Law upon religious life and conceptions is of universal importance, the Epistles of St. Paul and the origins of Christianity are more picturesquely explained by dwelling upon what was evil in that influence rather than upon what was good. The Messianic idea was of importance in the history both of Judaism and of Christianity, but of far greater importance for the latter than for the former: the Messianic king, at any rate, as distinguished from the general and wider conception of the Messianic age, was of comparative insignificance in the

VIII. GOD AND ISRAEL.

Jewish religion both before the Maccabees and after them.[1]

In the general sketch of post-exilic religion here to be attempted, it will be advisable to keep two qualifications of interest concurrently in view. In other words, the chief stress and detail must be reserved for those points which were of most importance in post-biblical Judaism, or which are essential elements in an unsectarian Theism of to-day.

In dealing with the religious material still preserved to us in the extant literature of these three hundred years, one is compelled to arrange and divide it in certain categories and classes, and in doing so, to incur a considerable risk. People are apt to forget the chronological sequence, and the historic relation of one idea or doctrine to another; they are also apt to ignore the background of life and circumstance, out of which the ideas, to some extent at least, arose, by which they were nourished, and with which they were in a hundred different ways intermingled and entwined. The history of a religion tends to be lost in a chapter of theology. Then, again, the material itself is likely to be arranged upon some modern plan; and this, too, may help to turn what should be only a simple narrative into a delineation of abstract dogmas and beliefs. These dangers of a method which it yet seemed in this place impossible to avoid,

[1] I do not of course mean that his figure disappears. As Mr. Carpenter reminds me, "though absent from Daniel and only obscurely present in Enoch, the Messianic king is prominent enough in the Psalms of Solomon." Maimonides made the belief in his advent a dogma of the synagogue; but as compared with his position in Christianity, the statement in the text may, I think, be regarded as accurate.

were briefly but luminously pointed out in one of the latest of Professor Kuenen's essays.[1] In the history of no religion are they more real than in that of Judaism. Perhaps if we recognize this beforehand, we may be the better able to escape them.

Both in biblical and post-biblical times, Judaism was far more deeply concerned with practice than with doctrine. Upon the theoretical side, religious imagination exercised an unfettered play; there was no crystallization into dogma, no formal delimitation of creed. Judaism remained for a long while very simple, and withal very incoherent. Its doctrines were inarticulate, almost chaotic; its conception of God was full of contradictions. It needed accommodation and re-adjustment as soon as it came in contact with, and claimed to satisfy, a philosophically trained intelligence. But it was fully able to quicken and to satisfy the religious aspirations of ordinary men. We can see now that one part of their religion was inconsistent with another; but unperceived inconsistencies did not prevent their religious ideas from becoming and producing for them all that less jarring and incongruous doctrines can produce or become for ourselves.

It was a childlike religion, and occasionally it tended to become not merely childlike, but childish. But since simplicity and inconsistency have their own peculiar advantages, it proved itself a religion not only admirably suited to the every-day moralities of common life, but also pre-eminently capable of evoking that constancy and

[1] " Voor en na de vestiging van het Christendom :" *Theol. Tijd.*, 1891, pp. 509, 510.

heroism which alone could have preserved its adherents through so many weary centuries of suffering and persecution. Was it mere defect or partly a merit that the religious exponents of the second temple tended more and more to empty Jewish life of all legitimate intellectual and spiritual interests except the interests of religion? On the one hand, religion became all in all to the average man: his habitual occupations were steeped in and surrounded by religious precepts and reminders. But the loss, on the other hand, was correspondingly, or more than correspondingly, large. The typical Jew had no interest in politics, in literature (other than the religious literature of the past), in philosophy, or in art. He was content to be governed from without, if the government left him free to regulate his life and the life of his community according to the precepts of the law. Hellenism had shown him a glimpse of a wide world beyond. But when Hellenism became identified with apostasy and persecution, the Jew shut himself up more uncompromisingly than ever within the narrow compass of his law. This voluntary withdrawal from every other exercise of the human spirit naturally produced an injurious effect upon religion. It tended to make it small and petty. Judaism lost all that invigorating influence which accrues to religion from the general life of the world, and from the reaction of politics, art and philosophy, upon religious doctrine and practice. By a certain internal tendency and natural inclination, as well as by the pressure of external force, it became as it were a backwater outside the broad stream of human development.

Is it possible to sum up in a few sentences, which may serve as text for a following commentary, the simple religion of an average pious Israelite in the post-exilic period? His faith clustered round three comprehensive words: God, Israel, and the Law. There is a uniqueness about each: one Law, one People, one God. The Jewish peasant was herein on a level with—nay, even above the level of—the most educated Greek philosopher; he believed in one God, incorporeal, invisible, whose likeness it was ludicrous and impious to symbolize or typify in any human form. Yet of God's nature he could hardly have told you more than the prophets; he believed him to be good, just and holy—all-wise, all-knowing, all-powerful—endowed with no more than a father's severity, but with more than a father's love, towards Israel, his son. Therefore our pious Israelite feared and loved the God under whose protection and government he lived; he observed gratefully the precepts of that perfect and divine law which God had been pleased to bestow, as a privilege and glory, upon Israel, the chosen people. He led a quiet and industrious life, while ethically and socially his religion tended to make him chaste, cheerful and compassionate. But those upon whom he spent his charity—a charity of service and sympathy, not merely of almsgiving, the charity of equals among each other, not merely of the richer to the poorer—were his fellow-Israelites who observed God's law: outside them he could not recognize brotherhood, but only unclean apostates and oppressors, the enemies of Israel and of God. Like the pious Christian of to-day, he also expected a reward, if not in "heaven," then upon the earth at a day of resurrection; but it would be as unjust to him as to the modern Christian to say that the expectation or desire of the reward was the motive of his well-doing and of his observance of the law. To the idea of resurrection was closely attached the advent of the Messianic age, implying the deliverance of Israel from the domination of the foreigner, with all the other excellences and glories predicted by the prophets of old. This Messianic hope was something more than a mere pious belief. It had a certain influence on the individual's daily life; for he was one unit out of the many units which made up Israel. He was a portion of the whole, and as such he could help or hinder. Israel was benefited by his good deeds and by his faithful and punctilious observance of the holy law: it was injured by his sin. He, to however small an extent, could hasten or could retard the coming of the golden age.

It is a religion of this simple kind which has to be here depicted. In this Lecture I shall deal with the conception of God and his relation to Israel: in the concluding Lecture, with the Law.

The impulse given by Moses had reached its goal. The single but patron Deity of Israel had been developed into the only divine Power in heaven or on earth. Yahveh had become God. The people of Judæa was practically as monotheistic as the people of England to-day. Other celestial beings were supposed to exist, but they were strictly subordinated to the one, true God. In this respect the work of the prophets had been brought to a final and triumphant conclusion.

But while Yahveh had become God, God still remained

Yahveh. Though he had become the unlimited and uncontrolled Ruler of the universe, he still remained God of Israel. Though the world was his creation, Israel was still his peculiar people. Though heaven and earth could not contain him, he dwelt in Zion. The post-exilic religion was coloured and determined by these contrarieties—contrarieties to us so apparent, by the Jews so unperceived. Let us notice in broad outlines at the outset the good and bad results of thus retaining the national Deity within the conception of the universal God.

Its evil influence is tolerably obvious, and has repeatedly been emphasized. Religion, unable to emancipate itself from national presumptions and embodiment, could not attain to a working theory of the relation and nearness of God to the individual man, unqualified by distinctions of race. Its good influence is less generally recognized. It seems strange that good should have sprung from what was, after all, a narrow and prejudiced limitation. Yet some of the most valuable and essential elements in "personal" religion were secured and realized through the fact that, to the individual Israelite, God was still Yahveh, the God of the Jews. In the religion of every-day life, that limitation brought God near to him; it made him feel the influence of God within his heart as well as in the outer world; it made him certain that God was a loving Father interested in the welfare—in the material and spiritual welfare—of his Israelite sons.

The nature of God was not defined. An infiltration of Greek philosophy was perhaps needed before the statement could be directly made, "God is spirit." Yet the opposition between the composite nature of man and the pure spirituality of God was as familiar to the Jews as to ourselves; and to the average Jew it probably implied pretty much the same as it implies to the average Englishman. But while every material representation of Deity was rigorously forbidden—and thus even the popular imagination did not probably picture its God in the likeness of man (in this, unlike and superior to the popular imagination of mediæval Europe)—the God of the post-exilic period and of Judaism generally was very "personal" and "transcendent." God was transcendent, however, not as being distant and unapproachable, but because the conception of him was so very simple and childlike; partly also he remained transcendent because of the mere weight and mass of scriptural authority. In this point, as in several others, Judaism was overburdened with the letter and the supposed literal truth of a collection of holy writings, many ideas in which it had entirely outgrown, but which, unfortunately, were more and more regarded as infallibly accurate and verbally inspired.

If the "transcendence" of Deity was not a result, neither was it a cause of any distance or separation between God and the world. But in the current estimates of Judaism, God's transcendence is closely connected with this supposed separation, while both are combined with his exaggerated and limiting personality. Let us seek to get these alleged defects clearly before us, and then, from the actual facts of the case—from the relation of God to nature, to Israel and to the individual Israelite, as well as from the divine character as it was generally conceived in post-exilic Judaism—we shall be able to judge how much, or how little, the allegations are justified by the reality.

While in the period after Ezra it is allowed that the cruder anthropomorphisms of the pre-exilic religion have been overcome, it is asserted that God remained as much as ever a "magnified and non-natural" personality, on the mere human model, with all its imperfections removed and all its excellences indefinitely increased. He ruled the world from without: his spirit was not conceived as immanent either in nature or in man. In its influence upon personal religion this is thought to have resulted in a lack of inwardness and spirituality. A Dutch theologian has recently declared that the absence of any mystic element is a thoroughly characteristic feature of the purest Judaism.[1] Only an elect spirit here and there could conceive of God as unlimited by conditions of space, and yet as dwelling with the contrite and the humble. For the many, with Yahveh's withdrawal from Palestine to heaven—his habitual dwelling-place in the post-exilic period—he had become estranged from the hearts of men.

Elohim or God is still more remote and unapproachable than Yahveh. "God is in heaven," says the Preacher; "thou art upon earth: therefore let thy words be few."[2] Such a doctrine is regarded as the legitimate outcome of a purifying process unchecked by any counterbalancing theory of God's revelation or immanence in man. God can, indeed, help the human sufferer if he pleases; but

[1] Chavannes, *La Religion dans la Bible*, Vol. I. p. 393.
[2] Ecclesiastes v. 2.

his help is more and more believed to be evidenced in miracle, rather than conditioned by that indwelling and divine spirit which is the permanent link and source of communion between Deity and man.

Now let us pass from the theory to the facts upon which it is based. It is true that God was usually conceived as dwelling in heaven, although he was also frequently supposed to be present in an undefined sense in the temple at Jerusalem. He was often called the "God of heaven." But this conception had no such unfortunate consequences as might be logically deduced from it. "Heaven" was gradually becoming emptied of its purely local signification. Its religious usage was no more prejudicial to the idea of God's nearness than it is to ourselves. We, as well as the Jews of the post-exilic period, address God by a common title, of which the word "heaven" forms a part, but which seems rather to link us with God than to separate us from him. "Our Father which art in heaven" is not generally supposed, at any rate, to be the formula of supplication to a distant God. It is almost ludicrous when the mournful utterances of a single and isolated pessimist like the author of Ecclesiastes are taken as conclusive illustrations of the post-exilic religion.

In his relation to nature, God was conceived not merely as its creator but also as its constant sustainer. Such is the evidence of the Psalter. It is true that a definite and articulate theory of God's spiritual immanence in the external world was never finally established, nor was there more than an approach to the idea of changeless laws of nature, themselves expressions of divine will. But nature was certainly not regarded as a lifeless product turned once and for all out of the craftsman's hands. Nature, animate and inanimate, was the object of God's perpetual care, and testified to his glory and his wisdom. Prof. Toy has rightly noticed that God's close connection with nature is brought out in a marked manner in the later literature. "He watches over and controls the sustenance and life of all plants and animals, and directs immediately all natural phenomena." He points out also that "this ascription of tenderness to the divine feeling for nature was the result of belief in the universal divine providence, unchecked by narrow national feeling. The Jews (clinging to the old tribal feeling) found it hard to conceive of the God of Israel as thinking kindly of Israel's enemies; but there was no such feeling of hostility towards beasts and birds, mountains and seas, trees and flowers."[1]

Just as the marked transcendence of God over nature did not have the effect of separating nature from God, so also God's immediate rule and control over all natural processes did not suggest any such metaphysical and theological puzzles as were suggested by his government in the affairs of man. Nature's waste and cruelty, its apparent wilfulness and callousness, the nature "red in in tooth and claw with ravine" which "shrieks" against faith in a loving God—these aspects of the world without do not seem to have occurred to the Jews of the post-

[1] Toy, *Judaism and Christianity*, 1890, pp. 80, 81. This limitation is of course not peculiarly Jewish. As Mr. Schechter has suggested to me, while St. Francis spoke of his "brother wolf" and of his "little sisters the doves," he would hardly have spoken of his brother Turk, heretic or Jew.

exilic period. Nor were they troubled by the problems of dualism—an "infinite" God outside nature, an "infinite" nature beyond God. None of the religious difficulties which seem to us to flow so obviously from the conception of an external God can be illustrated in them. They obtained all the good results of an emphatic insistance upon the divine personality, and practically none of the evil.

The same happy inconsistency is apparent in their ideas of God's relation to man. It is true that they had no elaborate theory of the divine within the human, which in one form or another constitutes the perennial charm of mediæval mysticism, whether Jewish, Christian or Mohammedan. It needed the genius or inspiration of St. Paul to make the triumphant assertion: "In him we live and move and have our being;" but the ordinary religious uses and applications of the statement were already familiar to the men who wrote the Proverbs and the Psalms. For the theory of Paul, which with its touch of mysticism is so attractive, is but the proof of his previous statement that God is near to "every one of us," and that he can be found by man. That he was "near," if not to all mankind, at least to every Israelite, the Jews were firmly convinced. It may be safely said that, with the solitary exception of Ecclesiastes, no portion of the post-exilic literature reveals or teaches a God who, for the purposes and feelings of personal religion, is distant from the individual Israelite. For what does God's nearness practically mean? It means, I suppose, firstly, that God knows and is cognizant of man's actions and thoughts. He is not merely omniscient because he cannot help knowing everything, but because he cares to know all about his human children. It means, secondly, that God enters into ethical relations with man, that he helps those who seek goodness to find it. In the Chronicler's words, God both tries the heart and has pleasure in uprightness. If men seek him, he will be found of them; he will establish their hearts unto himself that they may keep his commandments.[1] Or again, in the sayings of the sages: "Sheol and Abaddon are before Yahveh: how much more the hearts of the children of men. God loves him that follows after righteousness. Whom Yahveh loves, he chastens, even as a father the son in whom he delights."[2] God may be in heaven, but "the prayer of the humble pierces the clouds."[3] Thus even the Wisdom literature knows no distant God. Thirdly, God's nearness means that he is ready to forgive the penitent, and that man can be conscious of a real communion with him. God's nearness in this sense is repeatedly illustrated in the Psalms. If, indeed, the Psalter, that monument of post-exilic piety from Ezra to the Maccabees, taught a distant God, eighteen centuries of Christian piety would not have been able to use it as a medium of religious edification. The truth seems to lie between the ordinary Jewish view, which would deny to Jesus and Paul any development or improvement of the old Jewish conceptions of God, and the critical Christian view, which delights to misuse the words of later Jewish literature as a foil to the teaching of the Gospels and

---

[1] 1 Chron. xxviii. 9, xxix. 17, 18.
[2] Prov. iii. 12, xv. 9, 11.
[3] Sirach xxxii. 17 (ed. Fritzsche), A.V. xxxv. 17.

the Epistles. For the real means—as we shall shortly see more fully, and have already noticed incidentally— by which later Judaism triumphed over the religious dangers of a one-sided exaggeration of the divine transcendence, while they were thoroughly effective, were yet national and particularist. Jesus and Paul triumphed over them by a more general method, by bringing into more habitual and emphatic prominence the other and complementary aspects of Deity, the immanence of the divine spirit in the souls of men and the universal fatherhood of God.

It has further been alleged that the greater prominence of angels in the post-exilic literature is due to an anxious and deistic tendency to keep God as much as possible away from any direct intervention in human affairs. There is no doubt that, from a variety of causes, angels, both good and bad, play a greater part after the return from Babylon than they had played hitherto. Ignored in the religion of the prophets or external to their essential teaching, the various divine agencies were now, under the developed and yet popular monotheism of the time, transformed into God's ministers and servants. The gods of the nations, so far as they retained any reality, went through the same change. The stars, to the Jews no less than to the Greeks animate beings, became a portion of the heavenly host which attended Yahveh on high. Through the medium of the Persian religion, Jewish angelology was greatly extended. Its doctrine of evil angels will come before us again. Meanwhile it may be noted that in two late Psalms, in Maccabean Daniel, and in a few other places, the idea is expressed that God has assigned the direction of the different nations of the world to patron angels.[1] In one passage in the Book of Daniel, Israel is also entrusted to a guardian angel who fights for its cause, whereas elsewhere we find the notion that Israel has been reserved by Yahveh for his own direct control.[2] A divine judgment upon the angelic patrons of the heathen is occasionally threatened; while in Daniel and in Tobit a few angels have already received proper names.[3]

Yet upon the whole the doctrine of angels had for a long while but little influence upon actual religious life. We find them frequently mentioned in the apocalyptic literature, and even as early as the prophet Zechariah. There was a natural disinclination to bring the Godhead down into human conditions, and for supernatural conversations angels formed a convenient substitute for God. Such a use was quite compatible with a full sense of personal communion with God in every-day life. Though the angels, once introduced and particularized, paved the way for much foolish speculation and superstition, even these, as the New Testament sufficiently shows, could easily subsist with a high conception of Deity. In the Psalms and the Wisdom literature, which reflect the actual daily religion and religious teaching of the post-exilic period from Ezra to the Maccabees, we hear very little of angels, except as the ministrants and servitors of

---

[1] Ps. lviii. and lxxxii.; Dan. x. 13, 20; Ecclesiasticus xvii. 17; Deut. xxxii. 8, LXX.

[2] Dan. xii. 1, as against the passage in Eccles. and LXX. of Deut. referred to in last note.

[3] Is. xxiv. 21; Dan. viii. 16.

God. But if they were derivatively connected with the transcendence of God in its influence upon the religious life, it is precisely here where we ought to find them most prominently. If angels were not needed to bridge the gulf between man and God, what was the actual means of access from the one to the other? It has been said that it was reserved for Christianity to make fuller and more articulate use of the theory of the holy Spirit, both as dwelling in man and as uniting him with God. In Talmudic Judaism, while the omnipresence of God in nature and man is emphatically asserted in the doctrine of the Shechinah, the use of this term implied no definite theory of relation between the several aspects of the Divine Being, and seems to be little more than the chosen appellation of God in his close connection with all created existence and more especially with Israel. But though the doctrine of the Spirit remained inchoate and indistinct, it is not wholly wanting. The Spirit is occasionally referred to in the Psalter as the vital principle to which all things owe their being and their life. One Psalmist links the goodness of God's Spirit to his prayer that God may teach him to do his will, while another asks that God's holy Spirit may not be taken from him. The omnipresence of God in a third is identified with the ubiquity of his Spirit.[1] Man's spirit by its high capacity is proved to be akin to God's. "It is a spirit in man and the breath of the Almighty that gives understanding." For "the spirit of man is the lamp of

[1] Ps. cxliii., li. and cxxxix.

Yahveh," a lamp which Yahveh has given. Through God's light, man sees light too.[1]

Nevertheless, little use was made of such doctrines. Instead of bringing God near to themselves, or proving the communion between him and them by any theory equally applicable to all mankind, Jewish teachers laid stress upon the special relation of God to his chosen people—upon that peculiar revelation of himself which had been vouchsafed to Israel, and to Israel alone, in God's perfect and immutable law. The tragedy of post-exilic Judaism, if I may say so, is precisely this—that its tenderest and most devotional elements were inseparably associated with its emphasized nationalism. Its strength was concentrated upon its weakest side. Yet this paradoxical and disconcerting contradiction must not lead us to think that the higher elements were absent. We must not under-estimate their value or misjudge their quality, because the medium of their expression was unsympathetic or inadequate.

This caution is very necessary in dealing with God's relation to Israel. For what, from the outside, may often seem pride or particularism, was from the inside no less frequently a source of religious edification and practical piety. In considering that relation, while its injurious results must not be ignored, its good results—especially in their bearing upon the divine "nearness"—must none the less be borne in mind.

On the theoretical side, the influence of God's close relation to Israel in bringing him near to the individual

[1] Job xxxii. 8; Prov. xx. 27; Ps. xxxvi. 10.

VIII. GOD AND ISRAEL.

Israelite, is well illustrated by his supposed residence within the temple.

In this belief, old pre-exilic notions still continue. God's omnipresence is indeed occasionally alluded to;[1] but the greater need for the Israelites was to be convinced that he was near to *them*, and this was partially achieved by associating his dwelling-place in heaven with his dwelling-place in Israel. God's presence in the temple is frequently asserted in the Psalter; and the sanctuary was an unfailing resource for arousing or heightening a keen religious ardour. The most passionate passages in the Psalter—those which show the greatest craving after God and the deepest feeling of close communion with him—are inseparably connected with the material temple upon the hill of Zion. It was absence from the temple which provoked the famous outburst: "As the hart pants after the water-brooks, so pants my soul after thee, O God." It was in the temple that the author of the 73rd Psalm felt the riddles of the world oppress him no longer, so that he soared to the full heights of his mystic communion with God.

When the temple was destroyed, other and less material links between Israel and God had already attained sufficient recognition and strength to enable Judaism to dispense with the sanctuary and its services without religious loss. The law provided all that the temple had provided, and more besides. It was the tangible and yet spiritual guarantee of God's permanent covenant with his people.

Meanwhile, over and above temple and law, the simple

---

[1] In the Rabbinic literature, frequently.

belief that God loved Israel, and stood committed to that love both by his promises in the past and by the revelation of his purpose in the course of history, amply sufficed to determine his relation with the individual Israelite as typified in that of father to son, rather than in that either of master to slave, or of ruler to subject. For it was God's relation to Israel, as applied to the individual, which transformed a theoretic monotheism into a practical and personal religion. Unfortunately, it was God's covenant with Israel which mainly regulated and determined his relation to the outer world. The nearer he was to Israel, the further he was removed from the foreigner. Thus when Israel as a whole was contrasted or compared with the heathen who knew not Yahveh, its peculiar covenant with God became a prolific source of religious prejudice and illusion.

For in God's relation to Israel the old conception of a patron deity still survived, and being forced into false harmony with the monotheistic point of view, became infinitely more dangerous. God still ruled the world in the interests of Israel, and religious thought had again and again to consider how the facts of the present, which perpetually came into conflict with this dogma, might yet be explained upon the hypothesis of its truth. The growth of the doctrine of a resurrection and of a future life solved the difficulty here, as it solved a parallel difficulty in the life of the individual. At the day of resurrection the heathen enemies of Israel might either be excluded from the new and more glorious existence, or they might be condemned to terrific and supernatural punishments. Never was there more absolute identification between the cause of a nation and the cause of God: never was the self-deception which partly caused, and partly followed, the identification more thorough-going and sincere.

The divine partiality for Israel was explained in various ways. The nations were regarded as the conscious and designed enemies of God. For the enemies of Israel must be enemies of Israel's God. Israel, on the contrary, was righteous, the beloved of Yahveh. This theory was definitely and permanently established by the persecution of Antiochus Epiphanes. Israel, indeed, was not sinless; but by the side of the ingrained godlessness of the heathen, it might be so regarded. Thus God dealt on one method with the heathen, on another with Israel. The present sufferings of Israel were conceived as trials which purified and enlightened; they were the chastisements of a father, ever ready to welcome his repentant son with forgiveness and affection. The future sufferings of the heathen oppressors were to be punishments for punishment's sake; their object was not improvement, but vengeance.[1] For the brighter the light which shone upon Israel by its possession of the law, the deeper the shadow which was spread over the godless world beyond.

But not only did Israel deserve and not only must Israel therefore receive the divine favour, in the future if not in the present, by reason of its superior righteousness, its knowledge of the true God and its faithful obedience to his law, but God himself was pledged for

[1] E.g. 2 Macc. vi. 12—16, vii. 32—34; Wisdom of Solomon, xi. 10 (but cf. also xii. 20—22).

his own sake to secure Israel's ultimate triumph and prosperity. God's honour was at stake: God's glory would be manifested in the glory of his chosen people. In the Maccabean struggles, Israel felt that its heroic fidelity to the law was offered up as a sacrifice to the cause of God. "For thy sake, for thy sake," was the passionate cry, "are we killed all the day long."[1] And therefore for his own sake let God put an end to suffering and persecution. If sins still prevent salvation, then, "cancel our sins, for thy name's sake." Thus the prayer in the Book of Daniel, which has been adopted into the Jewish liturgy, closes with the urgent appeal: "O Yahveh, hear; O Yahveh, forgive; O Yahveh, hearken and do: defer not for thine own sake, O my God: for thy city and thy people are called by thy name."[2] God is sincerely besought to work deliverance, not for Israel's glory, but for his own. "Not unto us, O Yahveh, not unto us, but unto thy name give glory, for thy lovingkindness and for thy truth's sake."[3]

In one sense the post-exilic writers knew that God was self-sufficient. He needed from man no material gift.[4] Sacrifices were prescribed rites on prescribed occasions. They were regarded no longer as in themselves pleasant to, or operative upon, God. But God was nevertheless conceived as sympathetically interested in Israel. As the exilic redactor of Judges had said that Yahveh's "soul was grieved for the misery of Israel," so a prophecy in Isaiah, belonging to the late Persian period,

---

[1] Ps. xliv. 23. [2] Dan. ix. 19.
[3] Ps. cxv. 1 (also Maccabean). [4] E.g. Ps. l. 8—15.

declares that in all their distresses "he was distressed."[1] God loves Israel with all the emotion of a human love. But his purpose in choosing Israel, both for his own sake and for man's, was never again conceived with the breadth and largeness of view which was the signal characteristic of the Babylonian Isaiah. The goal of history was the triumph of Israel, and in that triumph the conversion of the nations occupied a limited and secondary space. If after the struggles and judgments which ushered in and accompanied the glories of the Messianic age, the nations survived at all, they would survive mainly for Israel's welfare as its servitors and dependents, and for the enhancement of God's glory by their acknowledgment of his exclusive divinity. They would not be converted for their own sakes, but for Israel's and for Yahveh's. This, at any rate, was the more general and prevailing view, though instances of a better universalism are, I believe, by no means wanting within the wide compass of the Rabbinical literature.

Into the details of the Messianic hope it is unnecessary to enter. Its essential element on the material side was the re-establishment of Israel's national independence,

[1] Judges x. 16; Isaiah lxiii. 9. But the variant reading of the LXX. in the latter passage makes it probable, as Prof. Duhm has ably shown, that we should render with a slightly modified text, "No messenger, no angel—his own countenance saved them," &c. The same emendation was made independently by Grätz (*Emendationes in plerosque sacrae scripturae veteris testamenti libros*, 1892, p. 35), and by Oort (*Theol. Tijd.*, "Kritische aanteekingen op Jezaja 40—66," 1891, p. 475). But even if the Massoretic text rests on corruption or misunderstanding, it has its own theological value, and the statement above may stand. The idea which the text embodies was much dwelt upon and developed in Rabbinical literature, e.g. Mechilta, 16 a.

coupled always with unalloyed prosperity and sometimes with world-wide dominion. On the spiritual side it implied the rule of righteousness and purity, the destruction of sin, the full triumph of the law and of the law's religion, together with the more or less complete incorporation of the heathen into the kingdom of God. Whether as vassals or as allies, the survivors of every nation would recognize no other God than Yahveh. The Messianic king, who wins the victory over the final efforts of the hostile heathen and inaugurates the golden age, is not in himself its most important feature. He is rather the emblem of the era, and sometimes, as in the Book of Daniel, his figure is absent. Moreover, the whole Messianic doctrine underwent far-reaching modifications when embodied into, or confounded with, the dogma of the resurrection and of a "world to come."

Of the growth of that dogma or belief something must be said later on: here it may be noticed, first, that in its earlier form, as in the Book of Daniel, resurrection and Messianic age synchronize with each other; secondly, that the expectation of a personal share, by means of a bodily revival, in the Messianic glories, gave to the Messianic hope itself an added vitality, influencing the religious life of every day. Indeed, the hope of a personal resurrection naturally became even more powerful as a motive of religious action than the re-establishment of the national kingdom. As a further stage, this hope detached itself from the Messianic idea, and developed into an independent religious solace and stimulus of permanent and predominating power.

The general effect of God's favouritism towards Israel

was twofold. It conduced, as Professor Toy has remarked, "to religious vigour and to religious pride."[1] On the one hand, it made God very near and dear to every individual Israelite. God's love was vouchsafed to him, not as a man, but as a unit in Israel. He felt that the divine "loving-kindness and truth" belonged through the community to himself. If in many of the Psalms the "I" who speaks is really the personified Israel, the personification was natural and easy because the writer felt himself one with his people—one, at any rate, with that godly party among his people which alone embodied and represented the veritable Israel. His joys and sufferings were theirs; and if Israel was a people near to God, that nearness was appropriated and realized by the individual believer. But, on the other hand, the contrast between "righteous" Israel and the "ungodly" heathen generated not merely a deep-seated particularism, but also a marked sense of religious superiority. Though this sense of superiority was only relative to the heathen, it must occasionally have tended to produce even in the individual a certain proud self-righteousness. On the whole, however, it is a remarkable fact that the intense conviction of God's nearness to Israel, as well as the frank identification of the cause of Israel with the cause of God, did not prevent a high average of true religious humility within the community itself. That praise of humility which is familiar to us in the Psalms, the Proverbs and many prophetical passages, did not close with the Old Testament. It is equally frequent and

---

[1] Toy, *Judaism and Christianity*, p. 78.

emphatic in the Rabbinical literature.¹ Within the community it pervaded the religious atmosphere more and more. It may be that the Hebrew word '*Anav*, which we usually render humble, should be more properly translated by "submissive to God's will;" but it is certain that the virtue which the adjective (together with its cognates, "the broken heart," the "contrite and lowly spirit") describes, came more and more fully to include in its implications all that we ordinarily mean by religious humility. Jesus simply enlarged on an announcement of the Psalmist, and quoted his very words when he said, "Blessed are the humble, for they shall inherit the earth."² Humility, by the Jews acquired, as one may roughly say, during the Babylonian exile, was never afterwards forgotten, but rather developed, strengthened and purified by subsequent experience. To this fact I shall have to recur in the next Lecture. If Israel was righteous in comparison with the heathen (and of religious conceit in this national sense the Jews, like every other religious body, were indubitably guilty), before God, measured by an absolute standard as we should say, Israel's righteousness was nought. Then the sense of human frailty and sinfulness (of which more in the next Lecture) was immediately felt. Nor was it a mock or inadequate humility which suggested the words in that very ancient prayer, still retained and daily recited in the Jewish Morning Service: "What are we? what is our life? what is our piety? what our righteousness?"

[1] Cf. Aboth, iv. 4; Sotah, 4 *b*, 5 *a* and *b*; Mechilta, 72 *a*, &c.
[2] Ps. xxxvii. 11.

VIII. GOD AND ISRAEL.

Man's only justifiable vaunt lies in his capacity for the conscious service of God.[1]

[1] Cf. Rahlfs, *'Ani und 'Anav in den Psalmen*, 1892; Authorized Daily Prayer-book of the United Hebrew Congregations of the British Empire, pp. 7, 267; Steinthal's essay on *Demut* in his *Zu Bibel und Religionsphilosophie*, 1890, pp. 166—179. It is true that Prof. Duhm, in his comment on Isaiah lvii. 15, "I dwell with him also that is of a contrite and humble spirit," says that these expressions denote primarily the physical condition of the Jewish community before the coming of Nehemiah; and secondarily the spiritual depression which was caused thereby, and which evoked among those who were faithful to the law a zealous seeking after God by prayer and confession and ascetic exercises, producing thus that humility which makes the *'ani* pious (lxvi. 2). "It is perfectly obvious that this temporal humility," continues Prof. Duhm, "this spiritual condition, which springs as little from any real need of the heart as physical self-abasement is the normal condition of those who are faithful to the law, has very little indeed in common with Christian humility." I believe this criticism is inexact and unfair even for the particular passage in Isaiah: it would be certainly wholly inaccurate if it were meant to apply to the "humility" of the nomistic Rabbis. And yet one cannot but have an uncomfortable suspicion that such an extension of meaning is more than half implied. Cf. the notes on Isaiah lix. 21 and lxvi. 2. So far as I understand the matter, the humility which Jesus accounted blissful in the first beatitude was both verbally and essentially identical with the humility which was held in equal honour in Jewish "legalism." In another note (on Isaiah xlix. 23), Prof. Duhm speaks of *der gottlose Hochmuth des späteren Judenthums*. Does Prof. Duhm forget, or does he purposely remember, that Judaism is a living religion which numbers many millions of adherents? Surely these sweeping and violent assertions are as injudicious as they are one-sided. They lead to obvious recriminations, equally well-founded and equally exaggerated. In view of the intolerant attitude of Christianity towards those beyond its pale, and of one section of Christianity towards another, a Jewish writer might easily speak of *der gottlose Hochmuth des späteren Christenthums* or *Protestantismus*, and easily justify the saying. And yet there was such a thing as Christian humility, and so too there was such a thing as *jüdische Demut*.

In its conception of the divine character and attributes, post-exilic Judaism absorbed and appropriated the teachings of the prophets, and in applying them to the individual, softened and refined them. To the prophets of old, the most present attribute of the moralized Deity was naturally his righteousness; to the individual Israelite of the second temple, the most present attribute was as naturally his loving-kindness. As on the theoretic side the epigrammatic summary of the Divine nature in the simple words, " God is Spirit," is first found in the work of a genius who united in himself some of the highest thoughts of both Greece and Judæa, so on the practical side the comprehensive and illuminating dictum, "God is Love," is not found in any work of purely Hebrew origin. Yet if the Jew did not say God is love, he felt and said that God is loving,[1] although in the word he used there was an historic and often half-conscious reference to God's love for Israel as the basis and source of his love for the individual Israelite.

The unreasoned and mysterious wrath of the pre-exilic Yahveh was no longer an object of dread. For if the calamitous condition of Israel sometimes seemed to show that God's anger was roused against his people, his anger was not conceived as causeless. It was because God had set Israel's iniquities before him, its secret sins in the light of his countenance. But even this gloomy mood was only occasional, and rarer still was the conception that God's wrath has driven his people deeper and deeper into the slough of iniquity.[2] For the permanent and every-day religion of Judaism, no scriptural passage

[1] E.g. Ps. cxlv. 17. [2] Ps. xc. 8; Is. lxiv. 5—7.

VIII. GOD AND ISRAEL. 443

better illustrates the prevailing doctrine and belief about God's character and his dealings with the individual Israelite than the 103rd Psalm. There, to use our modern phraseology, which is not that of the Psalmists, God's mercy is described as exceeding his justice. Hence it was that God could be conceived as man's Teacher, Shepherd, Father; his Rock and his Shelter, under whose wings he can take refuge. Hence it was that God's loving-kindness seemed better than life itself, and that communion with him was fulness of joy. A one-sided belief in a mere God of justice (in our sense of the word) could never have produced the Psalter. It needed a God who was conceived as "righteous in all his ways and loving in all his works," "full of pity and compassion, long-suffering and of great loving-kindness."

This divine beneficence was in quiet times capable of being extended to mankind at large. "Yahveh is good to all."[1] In the Greek and pre-Maccabean period the tendency undoubtedly existed to make God's providence co-extensive with humanity. Even Sirach, who on the whole is strongly nationalist, can say, "The loving-kindness of man is towards his neighbour: the loving-kindness of God is towards all flesh."[2] The universal charity of God is the moral of Jonah. But in the main the more emotional aspects of the divine goodness seem limited to Israel—partly because outsiders are regarded either as Israel's enemies, or as an unclean multitude, ignorant of the law—partly because the noblest and gentlest attributes of God were originally suggested by his peculiar relations to Israel.

[1] Ps. cxlv. 9. [2] Ecclesiasticus xviii. 12.

God's dealings with man were never reduced to any congruent system. The various ideas upon the subject which we find expressed in the post-exilic literature—often mutually self-contradictory—and the difficulties and doubts to which these contradictions gave rise, are due to the different sources from which the ideas originated. Deep-rooted in the Hebrew mind was the belief that suffering was the divine retribution for sin. As strongly held was the converse of the same proposition, that God, being just, punishes sin and rewards goodness. These maxims were fundamental principles of the prophetic teaching, though by the prophets they had been applied, not to individuals, but to communities. For man's deserts, the prophets, speaking generally, knew no higher law of God's dealing than that of measure for measure. If this law was modified in the case of Israel, the explanation was found less in God's mercy toward Israel, but rather in God's fear that adequate punishment might cross or hinder his own purposes and the earthly diffusion of his glory. Taken over by post-exilic teachers, these various' views were then applied to the individual. They were even emphasized and exaggerated. Correspondences were sought and discovered between human action and the divine award. Such and such calamities must be the result of such and such sins. Of this unworthy method of explaining the varying fortunes of humanity there, are several instances in the Rabbinical literature.[1] The law of the physical

[1] Cf. Aboth, v. 11, 12; still worse is Sabbath, ii. 6. One wonders how such a fantastic idea could have been framed, still more how the passage which embodies it could have been incorporated in the Prayerbook.

world, that action and reaction are equal and opposite, was supposed to be the law of the spiritual world, and a one-sided enthusiasm of religious partizanship, whereby the internal foe was as much God's enemy as the heathen oppressor, strengthened men's belief in its validity. This is the law, which, whatever its date, is clearly and forcibly expressed in the 18th Psalm: " With the merciful thou showest thyself merciful; with the upright thou showest thyself upright; with the pure thou showest thyself pure; and with the froward thou showest thyself perverse."[1]

On the other hand, this doctrine of accurate correspondence between retribution and desert was gradually modified by four other conceptions, which were really exclusive of it as an all-embracing dogma, though they were not consciously so regarded. The first of these four we have already noticed. It was the predominance of the divine mercy over the measure-for-measure rule. The second was the growth of the idea that suffering was educational and disciplinary. The third was the discovery, as an end in itself, parallel with and superior to material prosperity, of spiritual satisfaction in communion with God and in the performance of his law. This discovery secured to the individual a happiness which was largely independent of circumstances, inasmuch as the acts and feelings involved were their own reward. The fourth, and most far-reaching of all, was the intro-

[1] This Psalm is assigned by Cheyne (as a solitary exception) to the pre-exilic period, to the age of Josiah. Stade, on the other hand, thinks it may be even later than the Persian period: *Geschichte*, Vol. II. p. 222.

duction of the belief in a resurrection and a future life. This last conception took the sting out of earthly misfortune, and diminished the importance assigned hitherto to earthly prosperity.

Yet even with all these newer and modifying conceptions, the doctrine of divine retribution was still strongly maintained. For Jewish thinkers did not recognize any indirect influence of God in human affairs. God's rule was direct and immediate.[1] It was not that the Jews saw no difference between material and spiritual evil, or that they were unable to cozen their minds into believing that apparent evils were mere blessings in disguise. But the difficulty arose because an ethical explanation was thought to be necessary and discoverable in every individual instance. Deformity and disease, for example, are ills to which flesh is heir. If an innocent child suffers from an incurable disease, what can the explanation be? We should not dare to say that such a child was expiating his parents' sins, nor should we

---

[1] Cf. the superb passage in Luria (Act v.):

"My own East!
How nearer God we were! He glows above
With scarce an intervention, presses close
And palpitatingly, his soul o'er ours!
We feel him, nor by painful reason know!
The everlasting minute of creation
Is felt there; now it is, as it was then;
All changes at his instantaneous will,
Not by the operation of a law
Whose maker is elsewhere at other work.
His hand is still engaged upon his world—
Man's praise can forward it, man's prayer suspend
For is not God all-mighty?"

say that his calamity was a discipline specially sent by God for his moral improvement; but to the Hebrew, with his immediate reference of all effects to the direct causation of God, one of these explanations was almost inevitable.[1]

But it was especially in the past history of Israel that the finger of God was held to be discernible in every incident. In the present, both for the individual and the community, the general decision of the religious spirit to bow in resignation before the inscrutable will of God tended to overcome the desire for explanation of God's decrees. But Israel's vicissitudes in the past were intended for Israel's instruction in the future. In the past, when prophets had warned and foretold, and when God had interfered by miracle alike in blessing and in punishment, the methods of God's rule must lie more obviously open to the intelligence of men. Israel's history was holy; for the nearer the nation stood to its God, the more direct must be his intervening providence for punishment, discipline or reward.

The most uncompromising champion of the doctrine of divine retribution as applied to the sacred history of the past is the Levitical author of Chronicles. Everywhere we discern God's hand directing the fortunes of his people according to the strictest letter of a retributive law. Consciously or unconsciously, he shapes the facts to suit

---

[1] It may be noticed that in the famous passage, John ix. 1—7, of which so much use is made, the explanation of the man's blindness is purely relative to the occasion. The object and explanation of his blindness were that Jesus might cure him of it, and thus make manifest the works of God.

the theory.¹ For the pre-exilic history of Israel was the great lesson-book to the Jews of the second temple, and the Chronicler knew no higher or better lesson than that obedience to God's law ensured prosperity, while disobedience ensured punishment and calamity. And not only was the vivid illustration of this doctrine regarded as of ethical and religious value for human conduct, but it was used to justify the ways of God to man, and amid the perplexities of the present, to prove by a methodized survey of the past that the justice of God had been always triumphantly vindicated. The work of the Chronicler is in truth a great historical theodicy, conceived on wrong principles to our minds, and with defective distinction between ritual form and moral substance, but a theodicy notwithstanding, intended to further and to strengthen a religious ideal as it had shaped itself in the author's mind.

It must be carefully noted that this tendency of the Chronicler was not the permanent and necessary outcome of the Law. Christian historians have shown a similar desire to read direct interventions of God into human affairs. Thus M. Boissier says of Paul Orosius: "To show clearly the excellent order which God has implanted in the world and the rigorous justice which he exercises, every action, good or bad, must be immediately rewarded or punished. Unfortunately, that is what does not always happen. The facts frequently contradicted the pious system of Orosius, but he has his explanations ready, and thanks to his subtle arguments, whatever

[1] Cf. Stade, *Geschichte*, Vol. II. p. 228; Driver, *Introduction*, p. 494, &c. &c.

turn events may take, Providence seems always to come off with flying colours."[1] Is the history of Orosius to be regarded as the constant and necessary outcome of Christianity? As little must the Book of Chronicles be used to illustrate more than a single tendency in postexilic Judaism, which in the religion of every-day life was held in check by those other tendencies which have already been briefly named.

A perpetual reference of all incidents of national and individual life to the direct causation of God—to a causation, moreover, which was supposed to work on such simple lines as retribution and discipline, temptation or reward—while it usually deepened the reality of religious faith and accentuated the fervour of religious life, afforded at other times a stimulus to doubt. God's universal and ceaseless activity was not merely a joy, it might be also a harrowing mystery. In seeking to explain life's riddles, the inquiring spirit, confined as it was for the greater portion of the Biblical period to the life on earth, often failed in its search.

Prosperity seems to have misled men less frequently than calamity. Upon the whole, the Jews did not get so very much of it. There is little evidence to show that

[1] *La fin du paganisme*, Vol. II. p. 462. St. Augustine, in the twenty-first book of the *De Civitate Dei*, in which he earnestly argues that the fires of hell, to which the far greater portion of the human race is irrevocably condemned, are eternal and material, is even anxious to maintain the doctrine of proportionate retribution and the "justice" of God among the everlasting torments of the damned. "Nequaquam tamen negandum est, etiam ipsum æternum ignem pro diversitate meritorum quamvis malorum aliis leviorem, aliis futurum esse graviorem, sive ipsius vis atque ardor pro poena digna cujusque varietur, sive ipse æqualiter ardeat, sed non æquali molestia sentiatur" (xxi. 16).

2 G

prosperity was regarded as a sure token of righteousness, however frequently calamity might be interpreted as the implication of sin. Self-righteousness, as a sense of communal innocence and only derivatively of individual well-doing, was suggested by the contrast between Israel and the heathen, or by the exact fulfilment of the law. Individual prosperity did not suffice: gratitude for divine beneficence was too sincere. Personal happiness was rather attributed to the overflowing goodness of God than to the merited excellence of man. On this side the doctrine of measure-for-measure in the present and to the individual was never logically applied.

Suffering and calamity—national trouble most of all—exercised the religious thought of the time more sorely. And to the individual the most significant sorrow was that which came to him as a unit in Israel. It was this suffering which seemed the strangest, or rather it was this suffering which needed explanation (of whatever kind) most urgently, as being most directly connected with the big purposes, and as issuing immediately from the holy will, of Israel's God. And in addition to the sufferings of the righteous, there was the correlative difficulty of the prosperity of the bad. The two together constitute the problem of Job. Till late in the post-exilic period, when the doctrine of a future life produced a new theodicy, the old view that the bad would ultimately be punished and have an evil end, while the good would ultimately be rewarded, was still, in spite of all its manifest crudities, obstinately maintained. We find it repeated over and over again in the Psalter, in the Proverbs and in Sirach. Contrariwise, grave calamities

VIII. GOD AND ISRAEL. 451

betokened grave offences. This position, which is that of Job's friends, was never definitely abandoned for good and all. Alongside it, however, the theory that suffering was disciplinary for the good, while prosperity only egged on the wicked to more overwhelming destruction, was steadily developed. Suffering made the good better; prosperity made the wicked worse. Thus God's chastisement should be submitted to as a merciful training. No man is wholly sinless: the growing seriousness of the age saw in youth a time of light-hearted error, while in the heavy trials of manhood it recognized a heaven-sent opportunity for turning wholly to God. "It is good for me that I have been afflicted; that I might learn thy statutes."[1] In that process of learning there was no finality. In the midst of trouble the righteous would "hold on his way, and he that has clean hands wax stronger and stronger."[2] The Talmudic saying, "Him whom God loves he crushes with suffering," puts the climax upon this direction of post-exilic thought.[3]

Or again, according to the main lesson of Job, it came to be realized that the bestowal of weal or woe cannot be explained in accordance with the ordinary methods of retributive justice. Suffering might be regarded as a means of increasing man's trust in God, a test of his capacity to serve God for nought. "It is not in our power," said R. Jannai, "to explain either the prosperity of the wicked or the afflictions of the righteous."[4] No feelings rooted themselves more deeply in Judaism than

---

[1] Ps. cxix. 71. The national "I" does not exclude a personal reference.
[2] Job xvii. 9.   [3] Berachoth, 5 a.   [4] Aboth, iv. 19.

those of absolute faith in God and unconditional resignation to his will. The famous utterance of Job became one of the main principles which enabled the Jews, through a thousand martyrdoms and persecutions, to be true to their religion in spite of every temptation to abandon it: "Shall we receive good at the hand of God, and shall we not receive evil?"

As regards outward good and outward evil, Judaism tended to steer a middle course. The official religion never inclined towards asceticism, or to a depreciation of external good fortune and a philosophic contempt for external calamity. But the influence of the law made itself felt in two directions. First, like such gnomic poets of Greece as Solon and Theognis, its interpreters laid great stress upon moderation and self-control. True happiness was said to consist in a mean, whereby man was removed alike from the temptations of poverty and of wealth.[1] But, secondly, the law suggested and gave birth to inward and spiritual pleasures, which tended to make outward joys and outward sorrows of only secondary significance. The observance of the law was no longer, as in the days of Deuteronomy, a means to an end; it was its own end. Hence the temptation to secure increase of pleasure or exemption from pain by transgressing it was proportionally reduced. In times of persecution the official religion had trained men to the temper of mind indicated in the Book of Daniel: "If it please God, he will deliver us; but if not, then also we will not transgress the law."[2]

The doctrine of evil angels or demons had little influ-

[1] E.g. Prov. xxx. 8.   [2] Dan. iii. 18.

ence in the modification of any theory of divine retribution or in the development of a fixed theodicy. In popular superstition the notion of demonic possession became important outside the Biblical period, but it scarcely affected seriously the higher and official religion. It was independent of the fundamental doctrines of Judaism; it was an ugly excrescence which did no permanent injury to the essential faith. It could ultimately pass away without leaving any serious traces behind it upon the religion as a whole, and it may, therefore, in this place be safely neglected. More important was the strange figure of Satan. His past history and origin are disputed and obscure. Found thrice in the Old Testament, he has been explained, now as an adaptation of the Persian Ahriman or Angro-mainyus; now as a revival or resuscitation of an old Israelite demon, akin to the satyrs of the desert mentioned in Leviticus and the Book of Isaiah; and quite recently as an independent creation of the prophet Zechariah. Twice his name is used with the article, and once without. With the article, "*the* Satan," in English about equivalent to "the adversary," suggests at once an office and function rather than a mere personal name. Whatever his origin, his first appearance in literature is in the Book of Zechariah, where the prophet in a literary vision depicts him as opposing the heavenly purification of Joshua, the high-priest. By this opposition, the Satan is perhaps meant to personify the principle of uncompromising and sleepless justice, avouching that Israel's sins were even yet inadequately atoned for. In accordance with the higher principle of divine grace or forgiveness, he is rebuked into silence.

In the Book of Job the conception is extended.[1] The Satan is there represented as one of the angels or "sons of God" who form the court of the divine king; but in his relation to man he not only remembers sin, but also provokes it. Job's integrity irritates him; by the permitted infliction of suffering he tempts Job to renounce God. In the Book of Chronicles, where Satan—and here without the article, as if the descriptive appellation had now become a proper name—appears for the third time, he takes the place of God in the older narrative of Samuel at the temptation of David to number the people. The motiveless wrath of Yahveh, familiar to the pre-prophetic age, had become ethically and religiously impossible. The Chronicler therefore substitutes Satan, but no further use is made of him.[2] So in Job, Satan is merely brought into the pictorial introduction, but plays no part in the dialogue.

Of infinitely more important effect, and of permanent and far-reaching influence, upon the doctrine of retribution, and upon the estimate of earthly woe and earthly bliss, was the growth of a doctrine of resurrection and of personal immortality.

The origin and growth of this belief, which, in one form or another, seems to us so inseparably connected with a belief in God, are difficult to trace. In the age

---

[1] Cf. Marti, in *Theologische Studien und Kritiken*, 1892, pp. 207—245. He attempts to prove that Satan is the free creation of Zechariah, and also, as I am glad to find, that Job is later than Zechariah.

[2] 1 Chron. xxi. 1; 2 Sam. xxiv. 1.

of Ezra there is apparently no hint of it: in the age of the Maccabees it is a common, though not even yet universally accepted dogma. Its rise must thus be referred to the three centuries which elapsed between the composition of Ezra's memoirs and the composition of the apocalyptic Daniel. It is wonderful that the highest spirits in Israel were able for so many years to place boundless confidence in God, uncheered by any hope of happiness and fuller enlightenment beyond the grave. A lack of individualism and a suppression of self in the community accounts for something, but undaunted faith in God accounts for more. Standing upon the confines of the wider hope, we may not improperly recall, in the noble words of Delizsch, the grandeur of that more limited faith of which the barriers were now being removed. "This is just the heroic feature in the faith of the Old Testament, that in the midst of the riddles of this life, and face to face with the impenetrable darkness resting on the life beyond, it throws itself without reserve into the arms of God."[1] But the words "Old Testament" in this passage tend to produce a misconception in the reader's mind. He might gather from them that while the Old Testament outlook was limited to the present life and was bounded by death, the belief in resurrection and immortality was the creation of the New. That supposition is false. Within the Old Testament period, and even within Old Testament literature, the gloom of Sheol begins to lighten; while between the Maccabean age and the birth of Christ, the "larger hope" had become a permanent dogma of Judaism.

[1] In his Commentary on Ps. xxxix. 8.

The appearance and establishment of this dogma in the Jewish religion were probably due to a variety of causes, partly native and partly foreign. The former were mainly connected with the Messianic belief and the growth of individualism. The metaphor of national resurrection was not unfamiliar; as the desire waxed stronger among the units of Israel that they too might individually share in the glories of the coming age, the parallel expectations of neighbouring nations and creeds helped to transform this national metaphor into a literal belief as applied to the righteous dead. This transformation was the easier, inasmuch as death was never believed to cause absolute annihilation: the self still continued a joyless and shadowy existence in Sheol. Again, as the problems of life pressed more and more heavily upon the perplexed spirit of man, the suggestion—encouraged by influences from without—might gradually dawn upon the soul, whether possibly the unequal distribution of God's justice might not be remedied in another life. These influences from without, of which mention has parenthetically been made, can only have been two—the influence of Persia and the influence of Greece. Prof. Cheyne, with great learning and equal skill, has lately expounded the view that for Palestinian Judaism the outer influence was almost exclusively Persian. The immortality of the soul, which is so important an element in Platonic philosophy, was adopted by the Hellenized Jews of Egypt; while the Palestinian Jews were stimulated by the Zoroastrian doctrines of resurrection and judgment after death. Perhaps, however, the influence of Greece should not be wholly excluded. For while the author of Ecclesiastes alludes to the doctrine of spiritual immortality only to reject it, the very allusion would seem to argue that the notion had already been mooted in the Palestinian society of his day. But it is certainly an exaggeration to maintain that the resurrection of the body was only the Jewish method of expressing the immortality of the soul.

The first, or at all events the first clear, conception of any life after death for the individual, apart from and beyond the worthless life of Sheol, was that of a bodily resurrection at the Messianic era. Within the Old Testament the two instances of this conception are both found in apocalyptic writings; it would seem as if in this form the hope had first suggested itself to the exalted and pictorial imaginations of enthusiastic visionaries. In those four grand but mysterious chapters in Isaiah,[1] the date of which has been assigned either to the late Persian, or more probably to the Greek, though pre-Maccabean period, an earthly immortality is predicted for the contemporaries of the approaching millennium; at that time —already anticipated in the writer's imagination—God would "swallow up death for ever." Moreover, the departed believers, the pious dead of Israel, are conceived as being allowed to share, by miraculous interposition of God, in the Messianic glory: "Let thy dead men live: let my dead bodies arise: awake and sing ye that dwell in the dust; for thy dew is the dew of lights, and earth shall produce the shades."[2] In Maccabean Daniel, while the resurrection is also connected with the Messianic era, and has earth for its scene, the idea is extended by the

[1] xxiv.—xxvii.   [2] xxv. 8, xxvi. 19.

conception of a wider judgment—wider at least for Israel—upon good and bad alike. Both are raised out of Sheol, to receive a recompence according to their works. "Many of those that sleep in the dust of the earth shall awake, some to everlasting life, and some to disgrace and everlasting abhorrence."[1]

At this stage the conception was widened again; nor does it seem impossible that there were two parallel lines of thought even in Palestinian Judaism, which afterwards were more or less successfully systematized and harmonized with one another. The one line of thought with its results in the Books of Isaiah and Daniel has been indicated above; is there any Old Testament evidence of another?

Prof. Cheyne has argued that there is in certain mystical passages of the Psalter.[2] In the rapture of their communion with God, some Psalmists seem to forget or to ignore death, which they regard only as the doom of the wicked and the apostate. They seem to suggest that this communion and nearness with God will be eternal, unbroken by death, eluding the grasp of Sheol. Their language is by no means clear, and admits of a narrower and purely national interpretation; but when we reflect that these Psalms were written in the late Persian and Greek periods, and that their authors were, therefore, subject to the same influences as the authors of Daniel and Isaiah xxiv.—xxvii., it does not seem unnatural to assign to the passages in question the fuller and more adequate meaning. In that case, the writers of these Psalms hoped that, like Enoch and Elijah, they too

[1] xii. 2.   [2] *Origin of the Psalter*, pp. 381—452.

might find their life with God on earth continued and prolonged in a life yet nearer God in "heaven." "I am continually with thee; thou hast taken hold of my right hand. According to thy purpose thou wilt lead me, and afterward receive me with glory." And again: "I have set Yahveh before me continually: for with him at my right hand I cannot be moved. Therefore my heart is glad and my glory exults, my flesh also dwells in safety. For thou wilt not give up my soul to Sheol, neither wilt thou suffer thy loving one to see the pit; thou makest known to me the path of life; near thy face is fulness of joys; all pleasant things are in thy right hand for ever."[1] While the Sages do not appear to have taken to the idea of this more personal immortality—as apart from the Messianic resurrection—so readily, we yet find that even in Proverbs there is "a mysterious veil thrown over the death of the righteous,"[2] and a noticeable indication of possible escape from Sheol by the discipline of "Wisdom."

Thus even within Old Testament limits, we seem to find evidence of a twofold immortality—a resurrection upon earth out of Sheol at the Messianic age, and an immediate escape from Sheol at death in a continued life of conscious blessedness in heaven. As a matter of historic fact, these were the two elements out of which all the ideas and imaginings in later Judaism upon this high subject did actually arise. They became blended with each other in all sorts of ways, and now the first, now the second, assumed larger proportion and wider

[1] Ps. lxxiii. 23, 24, xvi. 8—11.
[2] Oehler, *Theologie des Alten Testamentes*, 1882, p. 858.

significance. But to pursue their history further cannot be attempted here.[1] The religious effect of anticipations and beliefs such as these can hardly be over-estimated. Earthly suffering and earthly bliss were both transfigured. It was easier to endure calamity and to retain a living faith in God, if one might believe that there would be a personal resurrection to life eternal. Earthly suffering could be complacently regarded as God's chosen method for the education of Israel, so long as, in accordance with the particularist tendencies of the post-Maccabean period, the resurrection and its glories were almost exclusively reserved for the chosen race. The fear of death was lessened: the eagerness to fulfil the law was stimulated by the vivid anticipation, not of mere vulgar reward, but of closer and more permanent communion with God. Again, the estimate set on earthly felicity was changed likewise. For it could not be but that the happiness both of the resurrection and of the heavenly life was conceived more inwardly and spiritually than the ordi-

[1] No one who is at all acquainted with Rabbinic literature will understand on what basis Wellhausen has arbitrarily declared: "Of a general judgment at the last day, or of heaven and hell in the Christian sense, the Jews know nothing." (*History of Israel*, E.T., p. 508; *Abriss*, p. 97.) The Jewish conceptions of heaven and hell, with their odd confusion between immediate immortality after death and the postponed resurrection at the judgment, are in all respects completely parallel to Christian conceptions on these subjects. It is equally amazing that Schwally should lay himself open to the easiest of refutations in saying: "Das Buch Hiob bezeichnet hinsichtlich der Eschatologie die höchste Stufe der Betrachtungsweise, nicht nur im Bereiche des alten Testamentes, sondern auch der gesammten ausserkanonischen Literatur der Judenthums." (*Das Leben nach dem Tode*, p. 112.)

nary external happiness of the life here and now. Earthly pleasures were thus depreciated, just as they also tended to be depreciated in contrast and comparison with the spiritual bliss of studying and fulfilling the precepts of the law. Earth's pleasures and earth's pains, alike transitory, were alike cheapened. The resurrection idea, which had partly been discovered to account for the burden of the one and the unequal distribution of the other, tended to make both of less significance and moment. Hence a permanent phase of Jewish teaching and thought is reflected in the famous saying of R. Jacob: "This world is like a vestibule before the world to come; prepare thyself in the vestibule, that thou mayest enter into the hall." That which is valuable in this world— the spiritual side of it—is to constitute the sum and substance of the happiness of the world to come. Hence, too, the same Rabbi went on to enunciate the notable paradox: "Better is one hour of repentance and good deeds in this world than the whole life of the world to come; better is one hour of blissfulness of spirit in the world to come than the whole life of this world."[1] And thus, too, it was that the purest spiritual bliss which this world can give was conceived as the constant occupation of the world to come. And even as the God of Aristotle, for whom the happiest phase of earthly life is realized in philosophic contemplation, is himself a philosopher, if we may so personify the famous νόησις νοήσεως of the Metaphysics, so the God of the Rabbis, whose highest notion of bliss is the study of the law, is himself a student of his own divine creation. The heavenly life,

[1] Aboth, iv. 23, 24.

or even the divine life itself, is but the reflection of the highest and most spiritual moments in the life of earth.

In any more developed phase of religious thought, the doctrine of a future life is an almost necessary complement of a belief in God. But in Judaism it was not a theoretic atheism against which it was to serve as a bulwark, but the more terrible doubt of the divine goodness. It is, however, noteworthy that the ingrained conviction of God's ultimate justice was continually emerging, even without reference to any life beyond the grave by which to explain or justify its methods. Throughout centuries of calamity, the Jewish community, unwilling to throw the entire burden of equivalence upon the world to come, and unable to deny that even in this world there should be some ethical correspondence between merit and reward, has always tended to emphasize its own sinfulness in order to vindicate the goodness of God. It has always tried to believe that its guilt deserved a fuller meed of punishment than actually it received. And with this belief, backed by the doctrine of the future life and the disciplinary theory of suffering, it has never swerved from teaching and confessing a loving God, the God of the 103rd Psalm, who is "full of compassion and pity, long-suffering and plenteous in lovingkindness," who does not requite according to iniquity, but "as a father has compassion upon his sons, has compassion upon them that fear him."

This, then, was the God of Judaism—no hard and merciless taskmaster, but a loving and compassionate Father, whose law, as we have yet to see, was given for Israel's benefit and happiness. But the double limitation must not be forgotten. God's pitying Fatherhood extends only to those "who fear him." Outside that barrier are the heathen nations and the wicked within Israel. The latter may be roughly defined as those who were at variance with the principles upon which the Judaism of their accusers was sincerely believed to depend. They were those who made no honest and faithful effort to fulfil the law. But this limitation of God's love did not change or spoil its quality within the community towards which it was believed to be directed. And so in general, men think more often and more deeply of the included than of the excluded—of God as loving them that fear him, than of God as punishing their enemies or as hating the wicked.

Thus for the Israelite who seeks, in spite of many lapses, to conform to the dictates of the law, God is loving and God is near. Such is not only the evidence of the Psalter, it is also the evidence of the Wisdom books. And such is not only the evidence of the Old Testament, it is the evidence too of the Apocrypha and the Talmud. Israel was a narrow field for the exercise of God's love, when that God was no longer the patron Deity of a people, but the sole God of earth and heaven. But because the field was narrow, the love was not less real. And in that love of God for Israel—a love, be it remembered, which *within* Israel was an ethical love, demanding righteousness and not detached from goodness—every Israelite who *desired* to do God's will might claim his share; he was gladly conscious that God was cognizant of all, and cared not only for his people in the mass, but for every unit of which it was composed. The individual

Israelite never ceased to give thanks to God because his loving-kindness was everlasting: and, as he fulfilled the law, he never ceased to feel that God was near him. By his own religious experience there was borne in upon him the deep propriety of that title which Rabbinic, no less than Christian, piety has delighted to apply to God: "Our Father who is in heaven."[1]

If, then, God was a father to Israel, and through Israel to every Israelite, was not every Israelite his son? Did not the one term of the relation imply the other? Did not the fatherhood involve a sonship? Or was God Israel's father, but the Israelite God's slave? So say still several Christian theologians. "The Jew is God's servant (*Knecht*), who labours to deserve eternal life by his conformity to the law; the Christian is God's child, who already possesses eternal life, and lives in blissful communion with the Father in time and eternity."[2] To the truth or untruth of this antithesis, and to the general moral and religious relation of the Israelite to God, the final Lecture of this series must be devoted.

[1] "Our Father," but no less the Father of individuals, and so felt to be, than the Father of the community or the race. Cf. the individualist use of the word in Sirach, xxiii. 1, 4; Aboth, v. 30 (ed. Taylor).

[2] *Theologische Literaturzeitung*, December 26, 1891, p. 657.

LECTURE IX.

FROM NEHEMIAH TO THE MACCABEES: THE LAW AND ITS INFLUENCE.

THE key-note of this Lecture must be the Law.[1] With the Law for guide and goal, we have to examine into the average Jew's moral standard and his religious relation to God.[2] It would, perhaps, be both more accurate and more convenient to substitute for the English word Law the Hebrew word Torah. For the connotation of Torah has just that elasticity and width of meaning which are wanting to our English rendering. The Torah is not always the Pentateuch alone, but often includes the entire compass of the Sacred Scriptures. It embraces the oral tradition as well as the written code: above all,

[1] For many of the facts in Lecture IX. and for most of the Rabbinical references, I am indebted to the never-failing knowledge and kindness of my friend Mr. Schechter, without whose teaching and help, indeed, this part of my work could hardly have been written. But Mr. Schechter is in no way responsible for any statement I make, still less for any opinion I offer.

[2] My *terminus ad quem* is limited by the Old Testament, and does not therefore properly extend beyond the Maccabean era. But in order to make the tendencies of that age clear, it will often be necessary to speak of the more developed Rabbinical religion, and to quote or allude to passages from Rabbinical literature.

it is not merely a book or a collection of ordinances, but is identical with religion.[1]

The literature of the Old Testament comes to a close with the Law's final and determinative victory. Although within its compass, except in two or three Psalms, there seems to be but little of that rapturous glorification of the law which is characteristic of the entire Rabbinical period, it is not out of place or inaccurate to consider the religion of the post-exilic period within the Old Testament from the legal point of view. It is true that if Antiochus Epiphanes had never interfered in the internal affairs of his Jewish province, the entire course of religious development might have been wholly different. It is also true that there is some slight evidence of tendencies in the post-Nehemian, but pre-Maccabean period, which ran counter to the prevailing legalism of the age, and which, in combination with a peaceful influx of Hellenism, might, and perhaps would, have directed the religion of Israel into a very different channel. In a detailed history of post-exilic religion these tendencies would have to be carefully noted; but in a rapid sketch like the present, they must, on the contrary, be almost wholly passed over, unless it can be shown that here and there they left their mark upon the final and historic result. For the legal tendency was throughout predominant, and in the end victorious and all-embracing. If the pre-Maccabean period be looked at as the preparation for the later Judaism, then the law may be justifiably considered its most important spiritual factor.

As the canon of Scripture became fixed, the sacred

[1] Cf. a fine passage in Cheyne, *Origin of the Psalter*, p. 349.

IX. THE LAW AND ITS INFLUENCE. 467

writings tended to acquire a more exclusive and overwhelming authority. The Scriptures were for the Jews their all-in-all. From them they sought counsel, edification, enlightenment and happiness; out of them they sharpened their wits and fed their imagination. Intellect and phantasy, head and heart, drew their sustenance from the Torah. Jurisprudence and morality, religious form and religious substance, were all mingled together, for they were all branches of the law, and the study of Scripture was the basis of them all.

This sovereignty of the law in its operations and results is only to be proved and illustrated by the Rabbinical literature. But that literature, as it needs for its intelligent employment one who has been steeped in it from his youth, so does it lie outside the limits of the present inquiry. It cannot be emphasized too strongly that the books of the Old Testament show merely tendencies to a religious development which was not fully matured till considerably later, and that, both for evil and for good, they can give no adequate picture of the Judaism even of Hillel and Akiba. It must be remembered, too, that the apocalyptic writings lie for the most part outside the line of the purest Jewish development, and often present but the fringe or excrescence, and not the real substance of the dominating religious thought. The fact that the originals of those which were written in Hebrew or Aramaic are nearly all lost, partly shows that they had no deep hold on the people, or were off the beaten track of the official religion. It is therefore less proper to characterize the Jewish religion of the time of Christ out of such books as Esdras and

Enoch, than from Pirke Aboth and the Mechilta. And yet these Rabbinical books were compiled at a later date. An historian, even though his period closes with the Old Testament, who has no complete mastery of the Rabbinical literature, must be painfully conscious of his inadequate preparation and equipment for the full delineation of the post-Nehemian era. And if he is not conscious of them, his delineation of that era will in all probability be so much the more inaccurate or misleading.

It will be obvious to the informed reader that these remarks are partly directed against the methods and descriptions of certain Christian theologians. It is excessively difficult to enter upon the discussion of the law, and of its effect upon the whole area of religion or morality, in the proper historic spirit of absolute impartiality. Unceasing and one-sided attack on the one hand has inevitably produced an equally unceasing and one-sided defence upon the other. A good instance of this attitude is the frequent employment of such a phrase as "it must be conceded"—on the one side to preface an acknowledgment of a casual excellence, on the other of a casual defect. But surely historical theology has nothing to concede; its business is to record.

Why is it true that the individual Jew's ethical and religious relation to God and man was dominated by the law? For the following reasons: goodness was the fulfilment of the law; sin was its violation. Man's duties to his neighbour and to God were contained in the law either explicitly or implicitly, and to the Rabbinical Jew this was a distinction without a difference. Again, man's spiritual satisfaction and his communion with God were found in and conditioned by the study and the fulfilment of the law. The law was Israel's prerogative and privilege, his duty and his happiness. It was both means and end—pathway as well as goal. And though Torah in the larger sense included the whole compass of Scripture, in the narrower sense it meant the precepts of the Pentateuch, together with their traditional implications. So far as any generalization can go, it is therefore quite true that in Judaism religion took the aspect of law. Judaism is a legal religion. It began to receive this character on the introduction of Deuteronomy; it was confirmed in it by the reformation of Ezra; while the final triumph of legalism was brought about by the persecutions of Antiochus.

A coincidence of religion with law seems fatal for the excellence of religion. It is very difficult to clear one's mind of all Pauline prepossessions, and simply to observe the results for good or ill, without any attempt to prejudge them by logic or philosophy. It surely is obvious, one might suppose, that legalism in religion must logically produce certain definite and distressing results. But deductive logic is a dangerous guide in the field of historic theology. "In point of fact," says Prof. Toy, the distinguished model of impartiality upon later Judaism, when discussing a certain effect of the law which logically should have been of a particular character, "in point of fact, the result was different."[1] The words are significant; somehow or other it will frequently be found true—" in point of fact, the result was different."

[1] Toy, *Judaism and Christianity*, p. 186.

There is no more illogical religion—is this an unmixed evil?—than Judaism.

A distinction must be made at starting. The Judaism of the Maccabean period, with which the Old Testament practically closes, is a legal religion, and hence there may be discovered in it the qualities of legal religions generally. But it is not only religion as law which has to be considered. Judaism rests on a particular law—a much more significant and influential fact. Supposed effects of legal religion in the abstract must be distinguished from actual effects of *the* legal religion in particular. It will, I think, be found that the evil effects, deducible logically on general principles, of legalism in the abstract, are often "in point of fact" historically non-existent; while the evil effects of the particular law were tangible and real. The particular law was a combination of moral and ritual enactments; the main weaknesses and defects of the Jewish religion resulted from the existence in the law of ritual enactments which, equally with the moral enactments, were regarded as the direct command of God, and thus constantly tended to be put on the same level. It is, however, possible to conceive of a legal religion in which every command would be purely moral, and the general results of legalism as such would be more clearly apparent from it than from Judaism. At any rate, the effects of religion as law, and the effects of the particular law, with its unfortunate combination and co-ordination of moral and ritual enactments, must be carefully and systematically distinguished.

Again, if the evil effects of religion as law—of including the whole religious and moral life in the sphere of jurisprudence—be reckoned up on the one side, it is right to ask whether the same cause might not produce good as well as evil. The effects of an absence of law in religion and morality would have also to be considered. Such an inquiry might be made both historically and in the abstract. Religion in the form of law might be reasonably supposed to stimulate to moral earnestness and to the faithful and adequate discharge of all those elements of morality which admit of being represented by definite injunctions. Moral zeal and a firm grip upon the actual and defined duties of every-day life would be as obvious and logical a result upon the one hand, as externalism and formalism upon the other. And even though the law of the Pentateuch embraces both moral and ceremonial enactments, it would need very delicate investigation to determine whether, during the two thousand years in which it has been the basis of Jewish morality and religion, the evil effects of its legalism have outweighed the good. For if an impartial critic would assign to the Jews certain marked virtues and excellences, as well as certain marked vices and defects, it is only reasonable to suggest that the former are as intimately connected with, and as directly due to, the law as the latter. If religion as law has its good as well as its evil issues, it will probably be fair to suppose that the extremes of either are the exception and not the rule. And in harmony with the conclusions of logic, history will probably decide that, on the whole, the virtues of the Jews in the long Rabbinic period exceeded their vices. Where, finally, there is large agreement as to the content of morality, it is probable that the religious form in which it is cast will make no considerable difference. If at the present day you were to take ten thousand orthodox Jews who believe in the doctrine of justification by works, and were to match them with ten thousand orthodox Protestants who believe in the doctrine of justification by faith, there would be a fringe of peculiar excellence and peculiar viciousness in either, each with its own *nuance* of good and evil; but in the main body of both there would probably be about an equally large number of pious and moral citizens, whose qualities of virtue would be practically indistinguishable.

Meanwhile, the actual law of Judaism was a heterogeneous mass of ethical, political and ceremonial elements. It is necessary to form some conception of the character and extent of the last and largest section, since for our purposes the civil and penal code may be neglected, although it formed an important part of the total Torah, and one of the six divisions of the Mishnah is concerned with it.

Our present object is rather to classify those provisions of the ceremonial law which touched the average Jew's daily experience, and entered practically, and even frequently, into his religious life. In the second and first centuries B.C., these sections would mainly be the laws concerning sabbath and festivals, the agrarian laws, the dietary laws, and the laws of clean and unclean. As to the first, it is probable that in the Maccabean period the minutiæ of sabbatical observance were already for the most part in vogue. It must, however, be understood that these details filtered down gradually from the discussions and determinations of the schools into the actual life of the people. This explains why the rigid observance of the sabbath became part and parcel of the Jewish faith, and yet, though universally fulfilled, was never—a point to which I shall recur—regarded as a burden or a calamity. Of the various laws which are noticed in the Rabbinical literature as having been transgressed by a certain element of the population, to be afterwards defined, the sabbath, the day of delight for rich and poor alike, is never mentioned as one.

About the dietary laws there is a similar silence. These laws included the Pentateuchal distinctions between permitted and forbidden food, whether beast, bird or fish; secondly, the rules as to the proper slaughtering of cattle and birds; and thirdly, the purely Rabbinical prescriptions by which milk and meat might not only never be eaten together, but which even demanded that a certain interval should elapse between the enjoyment of one and the other, and that one set of utensils should be kept for the preparation of all food made with meat, and another for such as might be made with milk or any milky product. No doubt the Hellenistic party disobeyed these laws, but we do not learn that they were objected to or markedly transgressed by the lower or more uneducated portion of the population, whose grievances against the ceremonial law concerned the last two divisions of it, to be now enumerated.

The agrarian laws affected the people in a wholly different way: they touched a man's pocket. By far the most important of them were the dues levied on agricultural produce, for the maintenance of the Levites and the priests.[1] A two-per-cent. tax of the total ingathering had to be deducted for the priest, and of its remainder ten-per-cent. for the Levite. Every third year a further ten-per-cent. was allotted to the poor, according to the law of Deuteronomy.[2] Besides these imposts, there were the first-fruits and the firstlings of cattle, to which may be added the tax at the redemption of first-born sons. But of all these various dues, the yearly tithe seems to have been the one which pressed most hardly upon the poorer cultivator, and which, therefore, was the most frequently neglected. On the other hand, it was precisely this law upon which the strict Pharisees and Rabbis laid the greatest stress. Their insistance led, as we shall see, to a cleavage in the community.

Last, but not least, come the laws of clean and unclean. These, like the agrarian enactments, were clearly connected with the priesthood and the sanctuary, and most of them gradually fell into desuetude after the destruction of the temple. Distinctions of clean and unclean are, as we know, thoroughly characteristic of priesthoods all the ancient world over, and rest in their origin upon a variety of primordial superstitions. Unfortunately, the practices and ideas to which these superstitions gave

[1] I have omitted the dues from cattle and from slaughtered animals.

[2] xiv. 28, 29, xxvi. 12. I have omitted the extra tithe mentioned in Deut. xiv. 22—27, and given four times in every cycle of six years, because, though the tithe had to be eaten in Jerusalem, or its worth in money spent there, it was the owner of the produce who enjoyed it.

IX. THE LAW AND ITS INFLUENCE. 475

birth, survived centuries after the superstitions were past and forgotten. In the Pentateuch, the laws about clean and unclean belong almost wholly to the later code; but they contain, as we have already seen, a record of very ancient priestly practice, and embody rites reaching back ultimately to the pre-prophetic period.

In the post-exilic age, when the separation between priest and scribe began, it might have been supposed that purely priestly enactments, such as the rules about clean and unclean, would have been lightly regarded by the new and secular teachers of the law. This may have been the case in the Persian period; but the opposition to Hellenism probably quickened the growth, and effected the predominance, of a precisely opposite tendency. Some have thought that Zoroastrian influences were also at work. However this may be, the Scribes took up and worked out the laws of clean and unclean with the greatest zeal and zest. They developed them with extraordinary subtlety, and spent upon them the full force of their hair-splitting and casuistical dialectic. It would seem as if the ideal of the rigorists among them in the age of Christ was, as it were, to transform the layman into a priest, or even to transform him, for his whole life, into the condition of a priest when performing the functions of his sacred office.

It is well to point out precisely what a state of ritual cleanness really implies. It means being in a condition to visit the temple, or, at a higher stage, to perform some ceremonial or sacrificial act. The uncleanness of a given object means that contact with it transfers its impurity to the person. According to Pentateuchal ordinances, uncleanness is produced in two main ways : first, by certain sexual impurities and by the plague of leprosy; secondly, by the corpses of human beings, of all animals not permitted for food, and of those permitted animals which have died a natural death or been killed by wild beasts. An ordinary yeoman or artizan was not greatly troubled by these laws. Certain usual uncleannesses he could easily remove by bathing.[1] Towns and villages possessed apparently public baths for these purposes.[2] If somebody died in his house, a special purification was necessary. This was effected by sprinkling within the house some of the ashes of the consecrated red heifer, according to the rite described in Numbers xix. But though the Pentateuch enjoins this purification as strictly incumbent upon all, it is very doubtful whether any need was felt to observe the rite until the temple had to be visited. The statutory limit of time was therefore, we may infer, commonly neglected.[3] The only obligation binding upon all was to be ritually clean before entering the temple. A layman might contract uncleanness without scruple; the traditional law in this point even modified the letter of the Pentateuch, interpreting, for example, the enactment of Leviticus xi. 8 to apply only to the priesthood or to the season of the festivals.[4]

[1] E.g. Lev. xi. 24—28, xv. 16, xxii. 4—7.   [2] Shekalim i. 1.

[3] Numbers xix. 12, 13, 19, "on the seventh day."

[4] Maimonides, *Hilchoth* אוכלין טומאת, xvi. 9; Torath Kahanim (Sifra), 49 a; Rosh ha Shanah, 16 b. Maimonides codifies the Talmudical rulings thus: "It is permitted to every one to touch an unclean thing, and thereby to become unclean. For Scripture only forbids priests and Nazarites from becoming unclean by touching a dead body: hence it is inferred that everybody else may become

IX. THE LAW AND ITS INFLUENCE.   477

For the priests, however, and for those laymen who voluntarily elected to live as if they were priests themselves, the rules of clean and unclean were vastly more rigorous and complicated. Fanatical rigorists, for example, perhaps attempted to remember and observe all those distinctions respecting the various capacities of different utensils to contract uncleanness, over which Prof. Schürer makes merry in the second volume of his History, not realizing, however, that these distinctions and rules did not concern the layman, and are themselves merely the written precipitate of the discussions of the schools, and were probably unknown to nine-tenths of the pious and observant Israelites in the age of Christ.[1] Nevertheless,

unclean. And even the priests and Nazarites are only forbidden to become unclean through a human corpse (i.e. they may, for example, become unclean by touching a dead mouse). Every Israelite is enjoined to be clean at the time of the festivals, in order that he may be able to enter the temple, and eat holy food (i.e. sacrifices). And when it says, 'Their carcase ye shall not touch,' this means at the festivals only."

[1] Schürer says (*Geschichte*, Vol. II. p. 400, E. T. Div. ii. Vol. II. p. 106): "Far deeper was the influence upon daily life of the manifold and far-reaching ordinances concerning *cleanness and uncleanness*, and the removal of the latter, than that of the law of the Sabbath." I hardly think that any one would guess from this language that the laws about clean and unclean did *not* apply to the daily life of the ordinary layman at all. In speaking of the priestly code, Kuenen says (*Religion of Israel*, Vol. II. p. 270; see above, p. 344): "If he (the Israelite) was scrupulously pious, he always continued to regard uncleanness as a real calamity or as a heavy punishment, and considered himself bound to avoid it as much as possible. But this gave rise to another danger. How could he then be free from uneasiness, and petty, anxious precautions? Reflect that all sorts of clothes, household furniture and food, were capable of becoming unclean, and of polluting, in their turn, any one who touched them. What a life he must have had who feared such pollution, and yet could hardly escape it!" But

the existence of a large priesthood who were bound to follow out the rules of clean and unclean to the utmost of their knowledge and capacity, and the existence of an extreme section of Rabbis who even sought to outdo these professional observers, were grave evils. These puerile prescriptions not only interfered with social intercourse, but tended to set up a false ideal of external sanctity. Their baneful influence in helping to drive a certain section of the community outside the recognized pale and limits of the common religion will come before us again.

Such, then, were the chief contents of a law, all parts of which were accredited alike with divine authority. It is clear that the drawback or misfortune of such a code was its equal accentuation of the ceremonial and the moral. More precisely, the evil lay in that mournful relic of outworn paganism—the conception of external holiness and pollution, of clean and unclean. The law was far less a misfortune in virtue of its legalism than because of its heterogeneous contents. Priestly regulations were accepted and developed by the ingenuity of the Scribes. In calmer moments, during the Persian and early Grecian periods, the Scribes, as we have seen, appear to have laid greater stress upon the ethical part of the law than upon its ritual; but when Hellenism became a danger, and still more when apostasy and persecution began, the prescriptions of clean and unclean,

the traditional or Rabbinic explanation of the Pentateuchal law had obviated this danger, and for the great mass of pious Israelites the supposed life of uneasiness never existed or could have existed at all. One needs to be very cautious in writing about the Law.

and all the ceremonialism which pertained to the individual, became of the utmost value and importance in accentuating the difference, as well as strengthening the barrier, between the observing subjects of the law and the polluted outer world of Jewish apostates and Gentile foes. Men died for the law's sake; and when all its enactments were believed to have issued from the same divine source, a single ceremonial injunction could easily be regarded as a type or symbol of the entire code.

What, then, was the effect of the law upon morality and religion? Always careful to avoid the imminent danger of squeezing the undogmatic post-exilic religion into modern categories of thought, we may endeavour to note, first, the effect of the law upon men's conception of goodness, and, secondly, upon the content of morality. Next in order may come the capacity of right-doing, the nature and removal of sin; and lastly, the motives which impelled to the observance of the law. Thus at the end we shall be brought face to face with the problem mooted at the close of the last Lecture: Was the relation of the old Jews to God that of slave to master, or that of son to father? Did they do his will in fear and for hope of reward, or did they do it also and mainly for its own sake, and for the love of the law and of its Giver?

Duty, goodness, piety—all these are to the Jew equivalent terms. They are mere synonyms for the same conception—the fulfilment of the law. A man, therefore, is good who knows the law and obeys it; a man is wicked who is ignorant of it and transgresses it. Apart from the influence of the ceremonial element, the moral dangers of this conception seem obvious and alarming. "Who is the good man?" We tend to give some answer which implies that the stress in goodness must be laid upon spirit rather than form, upon the motive rather than the deed, upon being rather than doing. But the legal tendency would be precisely the opposite. Let us assume there are two hundred moral injunctions in the law, a hundred negative and a hundred positive. The good man would be he who, whenever occasion offers, fulfils the positive commands, and by constant abstinence from evil fulfils the negative commands. Thus even in the Psalms the good man is more than once defined by a catalogue of doings and refrainings. It would, then, seem as if it were the mere letter of the law which needs fulfilment: the spirit is indifferent. While morality needs freedom, the law is a fixed, external standard, which can only be obeyed as a servant obeys his master. A man under the law will do a "good" action in the same way and from the same motive as he pays his taxes. More important still is the supposed effect of legal morality upon the state of a man's soul. It is said to lead either to bland self-righteousness or to irreligious despair. If you are conscious that you have performed the law, you are proud, and yet your heart is bad; if you are fearful that you unwittingly may have transgressed it, you despair, and yet your heart is good. The *real* good man is he who in full consciousness of human frailty does his best and feels at peace with God; but the *legal* good man feels either satisfied when he should not be satisfied, or ill at ease when he might trust in God. Legalism oscillates between self-righteous pride on the one hand, godless despair upon the other.

"In point of fact, the result was different." Where these evil results of legalism became discernible, they were apparently due, not to the legalism as such, but to the ceremonial law. Humility, not pride, was the mark of post-exilic Judaism. Where pride comes in, it is owing, not to a consciousness of having individually fulfilled the law, but to a comparison and contrast between Jew and heathen, or between law-observer and lawbreaker. In the Psalter and the Proverbs, humility is often either directly commended and enjoined, or by implication extolled. The Anavim, the humble and afflicted ones, "became standing designations of the true Israel."[1] "With the lowly is wisdom."[2] The same insistance on humility is characteristic of Rabbinical teaching. Lowliness of soul and humbleness of spirit were regarded as the signs of the disciple of Abraham.[3] Nor is there any evidence that among the observers of the law there was any frequent fear of unconscious transgression. It is true that in the legal 19th Psalm the prayer is uttered, "Clear thou me from secret or unknown faults;" and Prof. Cheyne argues from this that the Psalmist's εὐλάβεια, or scrupulosity, passed the bounds of moderation, and that the law had become a yoke.[4] Of the entire yoke theory, there will be more to say subsequently; but it may here be noted that the same man who seems to show this anxious scrupulosity and a nervous terror of unconscious transgression, is the very man who has just said that Yahveh's law "restores the soul" and rejoices the heart.

[1] Cheyne, *Psalter*, p. 110; cf. p. 98.   [2] Prov. xi. 2.
[3] Aboth v. 28, 29 (ed. Taylor).
[4] *Origin of the Psalter*, p. 365.

It is true, again, that in a thousand-times-repeated story, a certain distinguished Rabbi of the first century A.C. is represented as weeping upon his death-bed, in fear of the judgment of the divine king, before whom his death would bring him; but the very fact of this single story having to serve so continuously is sufficient proof of its exceptional character. Oddly enough, within a few pages of it, there occurs in the Talmud another story with the same framework and the very opposite teaching.[1] If anything, the Jews were somewhat too confident of their assured participation in the blessedness of eternal life; all Israelites, except very exceptional and determined sinners, were believed to have their share in it. Yet within their own community, the Jews, upon the whole, preserved a happy mean between pride and despair: righteous as compared with the heathen, they felt themselves sinners before God. If God, indeed, were to bear transgressions in mind, no man could stand before him, and religion would be impossible. Blithe, though humble, is Israel's hope, because with God there is forgiveness.[2]

This simple confidence accurately represents the attitude of the legalist. He is not puffed up by the consciousness of his own fidelity; if he has learned or practised much Torah, he claims no merit to himself, for "thereunto was he created."[3] His sins and inadvertences do not drive him to despair, for his God is gracious and full of compassion. As we saw in the last

---

[1] Berachoth, 5 *b* (Wünsche, *Der babylonische Talmud in seinen haggadischen Bestandtheilen*, Vol. I. p. 9).

[2] Ps. cxxx. 3, 4.   [3] Aboth ii. 9, with Taylor's note

IX. THE LAW AND ITS INFLUENCE.

Lecture, the doctrine of measure-for-measure retribution was in practice and everyday-life overcome by the doctrine of God's mercy. And thus, though the Rabbis, like the teachers of every other creed which accepts the dogma of a future life, are continually insisting that man will be judged according to his works, they never seem to infer that the Israelite is in any danger of special retribution, still less of eternal woe, because of occasional sins and inadvertent offences, whether of omission or commission. For these, if human means were needed, repentance was ample atonement. Privation and suffering, which gradually became recognized as the habitual and necessary concomitants of Israel, tended to make the Rabbis more and more accustomed to accept and accentuate the doctrine that earthly tribulations were the God-sent trials and chastisements leading to the more certain and universal bestowal of immortal bliss.

If it were true that the later Judaism of the law laid exclusive stress in its moral teaching upon the mere outward act and not upon the spirit—upon doing rather than being, as we might now-a-days express it—we should scarcely find that constant harping upon the heart as the source and seat of good and evil. What more legal book than Chronicles? Yet it is there that we find the earnest supplication for a heart directed towards God.[1] It is there that Hezekiah, on the occasion of a ritual error, prays that "the good Yahveh may pardon every one that directed his heart to seek God, though he was not cleansed according to the purification of the

[1] 1 Chron. xxviii. 9, xxix. 18—19, xxii. 19; 2 Chron. xi. 16, xv. 12 xvi. 9.

sanctuary."[1] And it was a Rabbi who, bidding his disciples "go and see which is the good way that a man should cleave to," approved the answer of him who said, "A good heart," because his words included the words of his companions.[2] Few sayings are, I believe, quoted and applied more frequently in the Rabbinical literature than the adage which closes those tractates of the Mishnah which deal with the sacrificial law: "He that brings few offerings is as he that brings many; let but his heart be directed heavenward."[3] In other words: "All service ranks the same with God."

The casuistic hair-splitting which characterized the legal disputations on the ceremonial law, the penal code, or the agrarian injunctions, does not seem to have entered to any appreciable extent into the field of morality proper. From that casuistry, at any rate, which is popularly supposed to have degraded the morality of the Jesuits, the Rabbis were wholly free. Apart from the influence of the ceremonial law, their notions of goodness were exceedingly simple. They theorized little, but they practised a great deal. Even the Wisdom books of the Old Testament show a considerable range of work-a-day virtues, and these were expanded and refined in the Rabbinical period. Take the thirty-first chapter of Job as an inventory of late Old Testament morality. One main virtue is charity, practical kindness to those in need. Charity became the virtue *par excellence* to the Jewish mind. It is a synonym for goodness. By none than the Rabbis have the grace and power

[1] 2 Chron. xxx. 19.   [2] Aboth ii. 12.
[3] La t words of Mishnah Menachoth (Wünsche, Vol. II. 4, p. 56).

IX. THE LAW AND ITS INFLUENCE.

of charity been more subtly and eagerly extolled; they are, moreover, wont to distinguish, much as does St. Paul, between mere almsgiving, and "the doing of kindnesses," rating the latter far above the former.[1] On three things, said Simon the Just, whose date is disputed, but is at least pre-Maccabean, the world is stayed, on the Torah and on the Worship and on Charity.[2] Another emphasized virtue in Job's catalogue is that of chastity, and this also became a prominent feature in Jewish ethics, to which fact the repulsiveness of Hellenism to the orthodox Jew was at least partly due. Monogamy without concubinage, as we may gather both from Proverbs and Sirach, was gradually becoming the rule in the post-exilic period.

Self-control and moderation were likewise prominent. The spiritual joys of the law crowded out the material joys of earth. What an enormous advance in the 119th Psalm, the hymn of the law—a perfect exemplar of the Rabbinic point of view—over the attitude of Deuteronomy! The lovers of the law had other and better things to rejoice about than that "their wealth was great or that their hand had gotten much." God's commandments were better unto them than thousands of gold and silver. The attitude of Judaism towards "external goods" was, upon the whole, sensible and manly. They were neither over-valued nor despised. Rabbinical religion was far from asceticism, though its followers were ready at a moment's notice to throw all earthly pleasures to the winds for the sake of the

[1] E.g. Succah, 49 *b* (Wünsche, Vol. I. p. 396).
[2] Aboth i. 2.

law.¹ Without splendid assertions on the nothingness of earthly goods, they showed no tendency to accept them above their proper rate, or to compare them with the spiritual satisfactions of the law, and of prayer and communion with God. In his catalogue of sins, whose opposites imply a catalogue of virtues, Job enumerates the rejoicing over the fall of enemies. Its attitude towards enemies is commonly supposed to be a weak spot in the ethics of Judaism. Was it the fault of the law? The truth is that one must, as usual, distinguish between the private enemy and the public enemy—between the foe of the individual and the foe of Israel. Towards the second, the particularist tendency begot all those cries of vengeance and cursing with which we are familiar in the Psalter. But the enemy of Israel was often to be found within Israel. The man who thought himself of the true Israel prayed more eagerly and frequently for the fall than for the conversion of those whom he considered God's enemies as well as his own. The feeling of party, the convinced assurance that there could be neither salvation nor righteousness outside their own way of thinking and doing, were never stronger than among the whole Pharisaic and Rabbinic community. As against the heathen, and as against the Israelite outside the legal fold, they

¹ Put somewhat modernly, their general doctrine seems to have been that man's natural or fleshly desires should be subdued to the service of God; they should not be violently crushed or rooted out. See, e.g., a very curious passage in the Jerusalem Talmud, Berachoth, 14 *b*, the point of which is that it is a higher thing to make one's desires subservient to goodness or God than to destroy them altogether. Cf. also Genesis Rabba, ix. 6, Wünsche's translation, p. 38.

emphatically were in the right. This conviction, with its attendant ethical evils of pride and vindictiveness, was indefinitely strengthened by, even though it was not the direct creation of, the law. But *within* the observing community, Proverbs, Sirach and the Rabbinical literature show good evidence of a very different feeling. Towards a private enemy the famous maxims of the older code were extended and developed. Thus the same Sirach who counts, among the nine causes of happiness to witness the fall of enemies, and who lays down the rule, "Give to the pious, but help not the sinner, for God too hates the sinner," is able in another passage in his book to say : " Forgive thy neighbour. the wrong he has done to thee, so shall thy sins be forgiven when thou prayest. One man retains hatred against another—does *he* ask pardon from God ? To a man who is like himself he shows no pity—does *he* ask pardon for his own sins ?.... Remember the Commandments, and bear no malice against thy neighbour; remember the covenant with the Highest, and overlook the injury."[1] Professor Toy says rightly, that while the Psalms, " profoundly religious " as they are, " do not " (as a rule) " rise above the level of the old prophetic morality," " in Proverbs, Wisdom of Solomon, Ecclesiasticus, and in the sayings of the great lawyers, we find a distincter recognition of individual social relations and of the law of kindness."[2] It is customary to make much of the prudential and eudæmonistic character of the morality taught in the Wisdom literature, and to connect this lack of enthusiasm and

---

[1] xxv. 7, xii. 4, xxviii. 1—7 (A.V.).
[2] *Judaism and Christianity*, p. 293.

"altruism" with the legal standpoint. Of the eudæmonistic motive, something must be said later ; the prudential elements in Proverbs and Sirach, which undoubtedly exist, seem, however, less due to the law than to the general gnomic character of these collections. When righteousness becomes a phase of wisdom and vice a phase of folly, it is natural to prove the excellence of the one and the vileness of the other by pointing to their practical issues. It is noteworthy that the later Rabbis showed much greater warmth in their moral teaching than the sages of the Bible or the Apocrypha. Many illustrations could be drawn from their sayings of that ardent religious enthusiasm—clear evidence of lofty moral purpose and fervid willingness to self-sacrifice—which, in its highest and purest form, is so characteristic a feature in the teaching of Christ.[1]

[1] Cf. the following adage from Sabbath, 88 *b* (Wünsche, Vol. I. p. 150), which sounds quite unlike anything in Proverbs or Sirach : "Of them who suffer humiliation but do not inflict it, who are reviled but revile not, who do all from the love of God and rejoice at their sufferings, the Scripture says, 'They that love him are as the sun, when he goeth forth in his might.'" It is, therefore, very improper to characterize the utilitarian and prudential elements in the teaching of Sirach as specifically Jewish. That is merely using the adjective Jewish as a convenient epithet of depreciation and abuse. I have elsewhere called attention to the wide connotation given to the word in this direction. Cf. the calm remarks of Steinthal in his *Einleitung in die Psychologie und Sprachwissenschaft*, 2nd ed., 1881, p. 217 : "Die Herrschaft der Monomanie (d. h. der Apperception jedes Gegebenen, mag es noch so verschieden sein, durch dieselbige Vorstellungsgruppe) in der Wissenschaft ist nicht geringer als im Leben ; und dann schrumpft freilich die Fülle der Gestaltungen zu den dürftigsten Kategorien zusammen.... [Der eine] hat nur zwei Kategorien für die Auffassung der Geschichte : jüdisch und christlich ; jüdisch heisst unfrei, reactionär, neidisch, zerstörend; christlich heisst frei, revolutionär, schöpferisch."

The small extent of the post-exilic but pre-Christian literature gives us little opportunity of obtaining any extended idea of the moral ideas and practice of the period. And much of the literature which we have, including all the various apocalypses, is useless for the purpose. We are still worse off for that social side of ethics, which was nevertheless not uninfluenced by religion. For the Talmudic period the sources would be far more abundant; and it may be hoped that a good scholar will delineate for us one day a picture of "Social Life in Jewdom from Hillel to Saadia" on the model of Mahaffy's delightful "Social Life in Greece from Homer to Menander." From a general point of view, it may, I think, in justice be maintained that the fulminations of the Prophets concerning justice, kindness and chastity had sunk deep into the national consciousness. Where apostates and enemies are not concerned, the Semitic fierceness of the old pre-exilic days had been greatly modified. Of this change, a clear instance is the transformation— for it amounted to no less—of the old penal law. This transformation must have begun within our period, though its consummation falls without its limits. In violation of the letter of the law, the old *lex talionis*, eye for eye, tooth for tooth, was explained away to signify a monetary payment varying according to the severity of the inflicted wrong. The offences for which the Pentateuch prescribes death as punishment remained the same under the Rabbinic law; but as a matter of fact we know that the death penalty was frequently dispensed with, and that imprisonment—a punishment unknown to the Pentateuch—had been invented in the early Pharisaic or

Rabbinic period.[1] Josephus mentions that the Pharisees "are not wont to be severe in punishments."[2] Again, while all the four methods of execution known to the Pentateuch were still, I suppose, occasionally employed by the authorities of the second and first centuries B.C., the manner of their performance was mercifully modified.[3] Most significant of all was the introduction of a custom according to which the criminal before being led to execution was given a drugged cup of wine, by which he lost consciousness of what was being done to him. The Talmud adds the probably accurate tradition that the rich women of Jerusalem were wont to charge themselves with the preparation and expense of this particular draught.[4]

The respect for human life had deepened. Even in war, while we hear of wholesale slaughters according to the custom of the age, we hear nothing of any refinements of cruelty. Torture, so familiar to the cultivated Greeks, was unknown to Hebrew law. There is no example or instance of infanticide. In respect for old age, decrepitude and helplessness, the Jewish religion from the post-exilic period onwards has yielded to none.[5] Slavery still existed; but the evidence of Rabbinical literature tends to show that upon the whole the slaves

---

[1] Cf. Sanhedrin, ix. 5.   [2] *Ant.* xiii. 10, 6.

[3] Sanhedrin, vi. and vii.

[4] Sanhedrin, 43 a (Wünsche, Vol. II. 3, p. 76).

[5] As Mr. Abrahams has pointed out to me, I ought to have added a few sentences about education in the Rabbinical period. Jewish children were tended and trained with devoted care. There are several monographs on this subject.

IX. THE LAW AND ITS INFLUENCE.

of the Jews had a fairly comfortable time of it, and this improvement in their lot was directly due to the humanizing influences of religion. Both as regards the education of children and the treatment of slaves, Sirach shows a rigour which is not characteristic of the Rabbis. The slave-concubine, a combination obvious to the Pentateuch no less than to other ancient codes, was fast becoming the exception, and not the rule.[1] For concubinage, no less than harlotry, was broken down by that growing sense of the supreme importance of chastity which is one of the noblest ethical elements in the Rabbinical religion. Monogamy was not indeed the law, but it was gradually becoming the practice. This is not the place to say anything—nor have I the requisite knowledge—of the position of women in the Rabbinic religion; but it falls within our period to note how Sirach, if in accordance with his touch of peculiar harshness he speaks with special virulence of the evils of the bad woman, excels Proverbs in his deepened appreciation of the noble wife. The excellence of the virtuous woman of Proverbs lies, after all, mainly in her industry and diligence. She is above all things the good housewife. Sirach strikes a higher note. It is almost surprising, from the old Jewish point of view, to find him not only putting the companionship of a wife above the companionship of a friend, but also above children. "Friends and companions meet from time to time, but above both is the wife with her husband. Children and the building

[1] In Talmudic times the slave-concubine became an impossibility. No Jewish woman could be sold into slavery after the age of puberty; and if she had been sold before, she then attained her freedom.

of a city make a man's name lasting, but a blameless wife is prized above both."[1]

The concrete morality of the post-exilic and Rabbinic religion—the actual bulk and content of its moral and social practices—was indubitably of a high order. Here the law had done well. It was its ceremonial elements which constituted its chief religious and moral danger. External cleanness is obviously much easier than cleanness of heart, and yet the law seemed to make an equivalence of value between the one and the other. Hence the possibility of formalism and pride and hypocrisy and self-righteousness and self-deceit—the evils against which Jesus declaimed, and which do not go without censure in the Talmud. The stricter the rule, the more ready the contempt for those who were less exact, the more violent the loathing of those who had altogether fallen outside the average standard of observance. It was very difficult, moreover, for the higher spirits to correct this evil. To the pre-exilic prophets the way was easy. They knew nothing of a divinely-given ceremonial law; and when Hosea said that God desired loving-kindness and not sacrifice, he was in the position of a modern preacher who might say that God desired goodness and not church-going. The preacher does not want church-going to be abolished, but, on the other hand, he does not believe that it has been ordered by God. But the Rabbi, though quite conscious that "the Most High is not pleased with the offerings of the wicked, or ready to forgive sin by the multitude of sacrifices,"[2] was nevertheless unable to deny that the cere-

[1] xl. 19, 23.   [2] Sirach xxxiv. 19 (A.V.).

IX. THE LAW AND ITS INFLUENCE.   493

monies were divinely ordained. He could not say that that which goeth into a man's mouth defileth not. The strict observer of an elaborate, ceremonial law has a very difficult task before him if he would combat the moral evils arising from the fulfilment of a law which he, no less than the immoral hypocrite whom he condemns, must also rigorously maintain.

If the ceremonial law clearly led to a certain amount of formalism, sanctimoniousness and hypocrisy, because of the very facility with which it could be fulfilled in comparison with the moral law, it is also generally supposed to have been a terrible burden, which only the hope of reward could have induced men to observe. To read the treatises of the Mishnah upon the sabbath and upon clean and unclean produces the impression that such minutiæ of ritual practice must have made of all life an intolerable nuisance. It would seem as if you were always in danger of transgression from forgetfulness, ignorance or mishap.

This supposed evil result of the ceremonial injunctions leads us on to another point, which, though distinct, is so closely connected, that its consideration may fitly be inserted here. As the ceremonial sections of the law obviously constituted its bulkiest portion, so also did they require the most learning. The ordinary elements of every-day morality are tolerably simple, and known to wise and foolish alike; but to know the innumerable cases of ritual uncleanness, or the infinite possibilities of transgressing the sabbath, would seem to demand study and opportunity. If to know them is wisdom, and if wisdom, as the sages taught, is piety, then piety is beyond the compass of the ignorant. Hence the law, it is argued, produced a false and irreligious intellectualism; it led to a perverse glorification of a spurious kind of knowledge, the absence of which separates from God. It is absolutely true that the religious teachers of the post-exilic period laid more and more stress upon the study of the law, in which they included elaborate discussion and careful knowledge of its ceremonial sections. Such a study clearly demanded leisure; and hence Sirach, just like a Greek philosopher, declares that the wisdom of a scribe comes by opportunity of leisure, and only he that has little business can become wise.[1] Although in his depreciation of handicrafts Sirach was conspicuously at variance with the Rabbis, who taught that the study of the law should always be united to some worldly occupation, a few of them tended to look down upon an uncultivated piety, or rather to doubt the possibility of its existence. But, on the whole, the good sense of the Rabbis enabled them to see that great as might be the study of the law, practical goodness was greater still. "He whose works exceed his wisdom, his wisdom shall endure." That is the dominant teaching. And again: "Whosoever wisdom is in excess of his works, to what is he like? To a tree whose branches are abundant, and its roots scanty; and the wind comes, and uproots it and overturns it. And whosoever works are in excess of his wisdom, to what is he like? To a tree whose branches are scanty, and its roots abundant; though all the winds come upon it, they stir it not from its place."[2] Unlike the priests, the Rabbis made no profit from their calling as

[1] xxxviii. 24 (A.V.). [2] Aboth iii. 27 (ed. Taylor).

teachers, and indeed repudiated the sinful idea that the law, as they expressed it, should be made a spade wherewith to dig.[1] They were thus compelled to turn for their subsistence to ordinary occupations and handicrafts. But though doubtless the ideal was " to have little business and be busied in Torah," Rabban Gamaliel, son of Judah the prince, was wont to say : " Excellent is the study of the law combined with some worldly occupation, for the labour demanded by them both makes sin to be forgotten. All study of the Torah without work must in the end be futile and become the cause of sin."[2]

Nevertheless, a strong dash of intellectualism is a prominent feature in the Rabbinic religion. Its highest satisfaction is as much the study as the fulfilment of the law. The learned Rabbi has ever been the subject of the deepest veneration. To this day, among the orthodox communities in the east of Europe, there is no reputation so glorious as that given by knowledge of the law, and every family in all ranks of society is proud to possess some member who is learned in the Torah. To the Jew,

[1] Aboth iv. 7 (Authorized Prayer-book, &c., p. 196).

[2] Aboth ii. 2, iv. 14. The following passage is worth quoting : " R. Eleazar said, Which was the first blessing which Moses said over the Torah ? Blessed art thou, O Lord our God, King of the universe, who hast chosen this Torah and sanctified it, and art well pleased with them that follow it. He did not say with them that trouble themselves about it, or with them that meditate on it, but with them that follow it, that fulfil its words. If a man say, I have learnt neither wisdom nor Torah, what shall become of me ? God says to Israel, All wisdom and all Torah is a simple matter ; for he who fears me and fulfils the words of the Torah, he has already all wisdom and all Torah in his heart." Deuteronomy Rabba, xi. 6 (Wünsche's translation, p. 110, with the necessary correction in the note on p. 137).

the law with its study has ever been the great spiritual stimulus. It has saved him from sacerdotalism and priestcraft. It supplied for him the place of every possible sort of intellectual or artistic or even professional activity, from which his peculiar religion on the one hand, and the intolerance of mediæval society on the other, kept him effectively away. It was the study as well as the fulfilment of the law which prevented the Jews from sinking in the scale of manhood, throughout the middle ages, intellectually and even morally.[1] Like every other ideal, it had its evil side, and was capable of lamentable perversions: ideally, the study of the law is equivalent to the study of perfect truth: practically, it is often the study of puerilities: the evolving of juridic hair-splittings upon the one hand, and fantastic and disordered imaginings upon the other. In this capacity for perversion and degeneration it shared the fate of other ideals, some of which were even nobler than itself.

But how far had the legal spirit and the enthusiasm for the law and its study won a firm hold upon all classes in the Maccabean and post-Maccabean age? It is important to bear in mind that the condition of Jewish society then was in one crucial respect different from what it became after the destruction of the temple. After the final dispersion, the rule of Rabbinism was not only unquestioned, but its own special ideals may be practically said to have become the ideals of all. Everybody

---

[1] Indeed, according to well-known sayings in the Mishnah, the true study of the Law was only possible to men of noble character. See the conditions and results of Torah study in the chapter "On the Acquisition of Torah," Taylor, *Aboth*, pp. 113, 115, 116.

observed the law, and to be learned in its lore was the desire of rich and poor alike. Its study penetrated every class, and its practice was a spiritual bond which knit all classes to each other. But in the early period of the law's domination this was not the case. Then, quite apart from those who may have objected to the law from a universalist or prophetic point of view—a diminishing minority of persons, among whom the authors of the anti-sacrificial Psalms may possibly be reckoned—and apart from those who objected to the oral and traditional additions to the written Pentateuchal code, there apparently existed a class who violated the law through ignorance or indifference, and regarded its teachers with feelings of hatred or contempt. The numerical relation of this "outcast" class to the entire people it is impossible to ascertain, but its existence seems vouched for both by the New Testament and the Talmud. Its origin and nature cannot be passed over here.

It would usually be said that in the Mishnah and the Talmud the outcast fringe which neglected or despised the law was known by the name of *'Am ha-Arets*. Literally this expression means "people of the land;" and in the Books of Ezra and Nehemiah it is used to designate the half-breeds and aliens, whom the exiles on their return from Babylon found settled on or near Judæan territory. But in the Rabbinical literature it clearly designates, not foreigners or even half-castes, but Jews. It is, however, impossible to put together a single and harmonious picture of the *'Am ha-Arets* from the dicta of the Talmud. These often contradict each other. In the Mishnah—the codified Rabbinic law of which the date is

2 K

about 210 A.C., though its contents are often much older—the *'Am ha-Arets* is almost invariably opposed to the *Chaber*, and the questions raised concerning him relate to legal restrictions of social intercourse between the two classes, on the basis of the agrarian laws and the laws of clean and unclean. Who was the *Chaber*? Many scholars suppose that he was practically identical with the Pharisee;[1] but this view is, in all probability, a grave mistake. Neither all Pharisees nor even all Rabbis were *Chaberim*. The *Chaber* was rather a member of a special order, composed of the extreme rigorists before alluded to. They, though laymen, determined to live as priests, and to observe the laws of clean and unclean in their fullest possible development. In their eyes, any person about whom there was a doubt whether he was sufficiently particular in the observance of these laws, as well as in the exact observance of the law of tithe, was an *'Am ha-Arets*, with whom social intercourse was greatly restricted, if not wholly tabooed.[2] It is not implied that the *'Am ha-Arets* generally neglected the law, or that he was an outcast and a sinner. In the body of the Talmud, the date of which is considerably later than the Mishnah, though it preserves a mass of old traditions, a curious uncertainty is evinced as to who the *'Am ha-Arets* actually was. He had apparently become a creature of the past. Discussions are reported on the question what were the par-

[1] So Schürer, *Geschichte*, Vol. II. pp. 319—334 (E. T., Div. ii. Vol. II. pp. 8—25).

[2] For the individualistic use of the word, cf. Schürer, *Geschichte*, Vol. II. p. 331, n. 47 (E. T., Div. ii. Vol. II. p. 22).

IX. THE LAW AND ITS INFLUENCE. 499

ticular ceremonial delinquencies the commission of which stamps a man as an '*Am ha-Arets*.[1] A variety of answers is given, and the entire argumentation wears a very academic air. There is only one considerable passage in the Talmud where virulent hatred is expressed against the '*Am ha-Arets*, and where he is accused of gross immorality and of the bitterest animosity to the Rabbis.[2] It seems clear that in this passage, and in the very few parallels to it elsewhere, a different class of persons is alluded to from those whose intercourse with the rigorists the Mishnah attempts to regulate and restrict. They must, perhaps, rather be identified with the apostates and informers of the later Roman period, and, in that case, they hardly concern us here.[3]

[1] E.g. Berachoth, 47 b; Sotah, 22 a (Wünsche, Vol. II. 1, p. 295); Gittin, 61 a. The passage in Berachoth, 47 b, runs as follows: "There is a tradition (a *Boraitha*): 'Who is the '*Am ha-Arets*? Rabbi Meir says, He who does not eat his ordinary food in a state of ritual cleanness (i.e. in a state in which he could eat holy food), but the Rabbis say, He who does not tithe his produce accurately.'.... The Rabbis have taught: 'Who is an '*Am ha-Arets*? R. Eliezer says, He who does not read the *Shema* evening and morning; R. Joshua says, He who does not put on the phylacteries; Ben Azzai says, He who does not wear fringes on his garments (Numbers xv. 38); R. Nathan says, He who has no *Mezuzah* on his door. R. Nathan ben Joseph says, He who has children and does not educate them in the Torah; others say, Even if a man has read Scripture and Mishnah, but has not associated with the learned, he is an '*Am ha-Arets*.'"

[2] Pesachim, 49 b (Wünsche, Vol. I. p. 216); cf. Baba Bathra, 8 a (Wünsche, Vol. II. 2, p. 120).

[3] The whole question of the Chaber and the '*Am ha-Arets* is very difficult and intricate. Schürer makes it seem too easy. Cf. also Rosenthal, *Vier apokryphische Bücher*, 1885, pp. 25—29; Hamburger, *Real Encylopädie zu Bibel und Talmud*, Vol. II. pp. 54—56, &c.

Thus the evidence of the Rabbinical literature gives no real support to the view that there existed in Judæa a deep social cleavage between a *corps d'élite* of Scribes and Pharisees who strictly obeyed the law, and a mass of good, simple and ignorant people who, on its ceremonial side, neglected and disobeyed it. The Rabbis themselves were mostly men of the people, who still pursued their industrial or agricultural occupations. In its enactments about reading the *Shema*, the Rabbinical law makes provision for the case of handicraftsmen and field-labourers.[1] The institution of the translating *Meturgeman* and of the *Chazan* (reciter) in the synagogues was devised for the sake of the unlearned.[2] At Passover, Pentecost and Tabernacles it is reported that the laws which might have prevented the '*Am ha-Arets* from full participation in the ceremonies and festivities at Jerusalem were wholly suspended.[3] We know from Josephus that the people recognized in the Pharisees or Scribes their own religious leaders. The '*Am ha-Arets* is therefore not to be classed with the "publicans and sinners" of the Gospel; and the famous verse in John, "This people who know not the law are cursed," if "people" be interpreted in its ordinary sense, and not explained to mean a small class of

---

[1] Berachoth: Mishnah, ii. 4; Talmud, 4 *b* and 16 *a*; cf. also Rosh ha Shanah, 35 *a*, *ad fin.*, where it is said that provision was made by Rabbi Gamaliel in regard to the New-year Service for the "people in the fields," i.e. peasants and labourers.

[2] *Zunz Gottesdienstliche*, *Vorträge*, 2nd ed., p. 9. For the *Chazan*, cf. Rosh ha Shanah, 34 *b*.

[3] Chagigah, 26 *a*; Niddah, 34 *a*.

complete outsiders, cannot be regarded as accurate or historical.[1]

From the Mishnah and the older traditions of the Talmud, it is, however, tolerably certain that the agrarian laws and the laws of clean and unclean were, on the one hand, looked upon with exaggerated and fanatical reverence by the rigorists, and on the other hand, comparatively or occasionally neglected by some of the more careless, ignorant or independent elements of the people. The neglect of the law in one particular would lead to the neglect of it in others; and in addition to those who fell far short of the rigorists' standard in those two sections, there were some others who dropped out of the general mass of the law-abiding population. A few there were, such as the tax-farmers, whose occupations

[1] Passages also occur in which a less separative attitude is taken towards the 'Am ha-Arets. "R. Jehuda said, Be careful with the children of the 'Am ha-Arets, for from them Torah is wont to go forth" (Sanhedrin, 96 a, Wünsche, Vol. II. 3, p. 185; cf. Bába Mezia, 85 a, Wünsche, Vol. II. 2, p. 95). "R. Jehuda bar Hai said, A Rabbi's unintentional sins are accounted (by God) as intentional, the intentional sins of an 'Am ha-Arets are accounted as unintentional" (Baba Mezia, 33 b, Wünsche, Vol. II. 2, p. 65; cf. Chulin, 92 a, Wünsche, Vol. II. 4, p. 108; Menachoth, 99 b, Wünsche, Vol. II. 4, p. 51). Interesting is the following extract from the Aboth of Rabbi Nathan (ed. Schechter, p. 64): "A man should not say, I love the Rabbis but hate their disciples, or I love the disciples but hate the 'Am ha-Arets, but he should love them all, and should only hate the heretics and the apostates and the informers, following David, who says, 'Those that hate thee, O Lord, I hate.'" Worth quoting, perhaps, also is the bit in Midrash, Shir ha-Shirim Rabbah, II. 4, Wünsche's translation, p. 59: "An 'Am ha-Arets who in the Shema reads ויאבת, 'thou shalt hate,' instead of ואהבת, thou shalt love,' of him God says Even his error is dear to me.

made them hateful to the bulk of their fellow-citizens. An outcast class of "sinners" exists in every state; and Rabbinic religion was perhaps even less inclined than other religions to show regard or compassion for those who had put themselves quite outside the pale of religious conformity. But the real '*Am ha-Arets* was probably the creation of the burdensome agrarian and purity laws. Most of these enactments gradually became obsolete and impracticable after the destruction of the temple.

Due thus to special causes, the '*Am ha-Arets* slowly disappeared after the second century of the Christian era. Produced by the law, he was nevertheless no necessary and constant product. Through all layers and sections of society the law penetrated down, and all of them found in the faithful fulfilment of it a veritable religious satisfaction. And although the highest ideal even for those who had no chance or opportunity to reach it, was always a special knowledge of the law, it does not seem as if the average Jewish farmer or artizan was plagued by a gnawing sense of religious inferiority.[1] The mere performance of the law, both in its ceremonial and moral elements, was a sufficient privilege, as it was the emblem of a special love.[2] If this be true, it follows that to a growing number, and at last to practically the entire bulk, of the Jewish community, the law, ceremonial as well as moral, was not felt as an irksome burden to which one had to cling from fear of punishment or hope of reward, but as a spiritual satisfaction, a gracious gift

[1] It must be remembered that most of the Rabbis were farmers or artizans themselves.
[2] Aboth iii. 23 (ed. Taylor).

IX. THE LAW AND ITS INFLUENCE. 503

of God through which man might enjoy supreme felicity both in this world and in the world to come. This result seems paradoxical and outrageous. People naturally tend to think of the law in the light of Christ's contrast between his own easy yoke and the heavy burden of the Pharisees, or in the light of Paul's Epistles, with their intense moral recoil against a rejected creed, or in the light of the mere technicalities of the Mishnah and of the legal discussions in the Talmud. But the Pauline attitude by which the ceremonial law was a positive bar to moral progress and spiritual peace seems, even in the age of Christ, to have been very exceptional. To the great bulk of Jews the law was at once a privilege and a pleasure. This fundamental truth of the later post-exilic religion is continually cropping up in every phase of the faith, and needs to be continually reiterated. Prof. Schultz acknowledges the fact, at least for the Old Testament period. He says: "To the true son of Israel the law is no heavy burden or hated compulsion. It is, on the contrary, the most precious and beloved gift of God's grace."[1] Basing his statements on the first, nineteenth and one hundred and nineteenth Psalms, he adds that the Israelite found in the law "a treasure more precious than gold, sweeter than honey, the centre of his thought, whereon he meditates day and night, the delight of his soul, towards which all his longing desires are set."[2] And yet this is the very same law the commandments of which were " in a constantly increasing degree "

[1] *Alttestamentliche Theologie*, 4th ed., p. 475.

[2] "Die Beweggründe zum sittlichen Handeln in dem vorchristlichen Israel," *Theologische Studien und Kritiken*, 1890, p. 42.

obeyed in an "anxious, servile manner."[1] But if the three legal Psalms reflect the point of view of the early Pharisees of the Grecian period, much better and more accurately do they reflect the point of view of the entire Jewish religion throughout the Rabbinic period. The notion that the law was a heavy burden, only endured from special motives outside itself, is radically false. Except for a certain small class, which disappears after the destruction of the temple, it has no historical validity whatever.

But how then, it must be asked, about the burdensome details of the oral law? How about the observance of the Sabbath, with its thirty-nine heads of forbidden occupations, and its subdivisions of these heads *ad infinitum*? How about the laws as to prayer, which with their rulings of season and manner and degree, seem effectively to quench every spark of spirituality? Here is one more of the curious antinomies of the Jewish religion, and one more reason why the truth is so seldom understood. Another difficulty in the way of Christian theologians is that they are necessarily ignorant of the internal life of such Jewish communities as still faithfully believe and practise, with no tincture of modern culture or scepticism, the undefiled religion of the Talmud. Historically the Sabbath has been a day of delight. The injunctions for its observance rapidly became so well known and so universally maintained, that they were no longer felt as an irksome restriction upon liberty, any more than are the social customs and conventionalities of modern times. In the long nightmare of the Middle

[1] *Alttestamentliche Theologie*, 4th ed., p. 459.

IX. THE LAW AND ITS INFLUENCE.

Ages, the sabbath, as the incomparable Heine has truly said, was the day on which the cruel spell of bondage and degradation was for a brief space broken.

> "Er ist geheissen
> Israel. Ihn hat verwandelt
> Hexenspruch in einen Hund.
>
> Hund mit hündischen Gedanken,
> Kötert er die ganze Woche
> Durch des Lebens Kot und Kehricht,
> Gassenbuben zum Gespötte.
>
> Aber jeden Freitag Abend,
> In der Dämmrungstunde, plötzlich
> Weicht der Zauber und der Hund
> Wird aufs neu' ein menschlich Wesen."

Again, as regards prayer, Prof. Schürer says: "When, finally, prayer itself, the very centre of the religious life, is confined in the fetters of a rigid mechanism, then there could no longer be a possibility of living piety. And this fateful step had been already taken by Judaism in the age of Christ."[1] He then goes on to quote several Rabbinic ordinances about prayer, its legal seasons, what sort of prayer is legally adequate, and so on. Some of these determinations are as outward, formal and childish as you could possibly desire. Is the Professor's deduction a true one? One thing is certain: for eighteen centuries the Jews never retraced that fateful step which, as Prof. Schürer says, they had taken by the time of Christ. Was there, then, no living piety among them during all that long period? Were they able to endure the Crusades and the Inquisition without living piety? This would be a paradox even greater than the

[1] *Geschichte*, Vol. II. p. 408 (E. T., Div. ii. Vol. II. p. 115).

IX. THE LAW AND ITS INFLUENCE.

paradox of the existence of living piety in spite of the immense variety of prescriptions. And this second paradox is the truth of which the Jewish liturgy is itself a sufficient proof. Talmudical anthologies contain a number of utterances, proving to the full that the essentials of true prayer, however strange it may seem, were as well known to the Rabbis as to ourselves.[1] The same faults which Jesus, with such inimitable magnificence of scorn, chastises in the hypocritical Rabbis of his day (are there not hypocrites in every church in every age?) are also chastised in the Talmud.[2] "Before a man prays let him purify his heart."[3] This sort of spiritual commonplace was as familiar to the Rabbis as it is familiar to ourselves. And there was surely never a religious community to whom prayer was a more real satisfaction and comfort, and who were, if I may say so, more happy and at home in their houses of prayer, than the Jews.

Upon this most crucial question of the burdensome quality of the law, Mr. Schechter has put the two conflicting views with admirable cogency and force.

"On the one side," he says, "we hear the opinions of so many learned professors, proclaiming *ex cathedra* that the law was a most terrible burden, and the life under it the most unbearable slavery, deadening body and soul.

---

[1] For a later period, cf. Steinthal's essay on *Andacht* in his *Zu Bibel und Religionsphilosophie*, where he shows that the word כונה, exactly answering to the German *Andacht*, was the creation of mediæval Judaism.

[2] Sotah, 22*b* (Wünsche, Vol. II. 1, p. 297); *Talmud of Jerusalem*, Berachoth, 14*b*.

[3] Exodus Rabbah, xxii. 3 (Wünsche's translation, p. 174).

On the other side we have the testimony of a literature extending over about twenty-five centuries, and including all sorts and conditions of men—scholars, poets, mystics, lawyers, casuists, schoolmen, tradesmen, workmen, women, simpletons—who all, from the author of the one hundred and nineteenth Psalm to the last pre-Mendelssohnian writer—with a small exception which does not even deserve the name of a vanishing minority—give unanimous evidence in favour of this law, and of the bliss and happiness of living and dying under it; and this, the testimony of people who were actually living under the law, not merely theorizing upon it, and who experienced it in all its difficulties and inconveniences. The Sabbath will give a fair example. This day is described by almost every modern writer in the most gloomy colours, and long lists are given of the minute observances connected with it, easily to be transgressed, which would necessarily make of the Sabbath, instead of a day of rest, a day of sorrow and anxiety, almost worse than the Scotch Sunday as depicted by continental writers. But, on the other hand, the Sabbath is celebrated by the very people who did observe it, in hundreds of hymns, which would fill volumes, as a day of rest and joy, of pleasure and delight, a day in which man enjoys some presentiment of the pure bliss and happiness which are stored up for the righteous in the world to come. To it such tender names were applied as the 'Queen Sabbath,' the 'Bride Sabbath,' and the 'holy, dear, beloved Sabbath.' Somebody, either the learned Professors or the millions of the Jewish people, must be under an illusion. Which it is I leave to the reader to decide."[1]

As the law tended, ever more successfully, to become less and less a burden, as it became better known and more universally acknowledged, so its diffusion and acceptance tended, though naturally with less prevailing success, to overcome the moral dangers of its ceremonial elements. When the ceremonies were obeyed by all, their distinguishing character within the community was effaced. Though divine laws, they were also communal customs. Where nobody dreamed of eating milk and meat together, to refrain could hardly be regarded as a merit. The differentiation of good and evil inclined once more to become centred on morality. Moreover, the tendency of the law was to deprive the ceremonial injunctions more and more completely of any meaning except that of happening to be God's will. To the priest, with all his old traditional and heathen superstitions, external holiness had a real meaning: to the Rabbi, all these things had to be done, as Sirach says about offerings, just because they chance to be in the code. The original meaning is lost. It was only the moral laws which had worth in themselves as well as value from their inclusion in the law. This distinction not only tended to place the moral laws, such as those of charity and beneficence, above the ceremonial laws, but also to

[1] "The Law and Recent Criticism," *Jewish Quarterly Review*, Vol. III. p. 762. On the question of evasions of the law, which figure so largely in certain books upon Rabbinical religion, I would refer here to the valuable Appendix which Mr. Schechter has kindly written for me upon this subject.

IX. THE LAW AND ITS INFLUENCE.

make men more frequently fulfil the latter from a purely spiritual motive, either from unquestioning obedience to God's decree, or from love of his revealed will.

Strange, too, as it may seem, the Jewish legalists themselves never wholly lost sight of the difference between the ceremonial and the moral, the shadow and the substance. One must not forget that the larger Torah included the prophets as well as the Pentateuch. If they were precluded from saying, "Mercy and not sacrifice," they could at least say that charity outweighed all the other injunctions of the code. And they did say it.[1] Or, again, take the case of fasting. It is notable that a considerable stress is laid upon fasting in the post-exilic literature. There is a solemn fast after Ezra's reading of the law. He himself had proclaimed a fast before he left Babylon, "that we might humble ourselves before God to seek of him a prosperous journey."[2] Nehemiah, on hearing the evil news of Jerusalem's degradation, "sat down and wept and mourned certain days, and fasted and prayed before the God of heaven."[3] Joel, the post-exilic seer, although he bids his readers rend their hearts and not their garments, couples externals and essentials together, when he makes God urge the people to turn unto him "with all their heart, and with fasting and with weeping and with smiting of the breast."[4] Daniel sets his face unto the Lord God to seek for prayer and supplications with fasting and sack-

[1] Baba Bathra, 9 a (Wünsche, Vol. II. 2, p. 124); Succah, 49 b (Wünsche, Vol. I. p. 396).
[2] Ezra viii. 21; Neh. ix. 1.   [3] Neh. i. 4.
[4] Joel ii. 12, 13.

cloth and ashes.[1] In the Apocrypha, we find Tobit urging his son that prayer is good with fasting and almsgiving and righteousness.[2] Judith is held up as a model of piety because all the days of her widowhood she put sackcloth on her loins and fasted, except on sabbaths, new moons and holidays.[3] The predilection of the Rabbis for fasting as an act of outward piety is frequently alluded to in the Gospels and the Talmud. If the autumn rains, for example, were late in falling, public or general fasts were imposed. Some rigorists fasted from sunrise to sunset on every Monday and Thursday throughout the year.[4]

Yet with all this emphasis upon the externals of supplication and repentance, it can hardly be said that the Rabbis ignored the fact that there was no value in them except as concomitants of inward resolve for improvement or of practical manifestation of a better life, both negatively in the relinquishment of sin and positively in the doing of virtue. The ceremonial law had this evil effect—it prevented men from seeing that sackcloth and fasting had no value whatever; but upon the whole it did not prevent them from seeing that the efficacy of these adjuncts was gone if they stood alone and without the support of morality.[5] It is characteristic of the Rabbis that they chose for the prophetic lesson

[1] Daniel ix. 3.   [2] Tobit xii. 8.
[3] Judith viii. 5, 6.

[4] Taanith: Mishnah, i. 4—7; Talmud, 12 a; cf. Schürer, *Geschichte*, Vol. II. p. 411, n. 97.

[5] E.g. Taanith: Mishnah, ii. 1; Talmud, 16 a (Wünsche, Vol. II. 1, pp. 436, 437).

upon the morning of the Atonement-day, the fast *par excellence* of the entire year, the fifty-eighth chapter of Isaiah, in which the true fast is declared to consist exclusively in moral well-doing; and upon the afternoon the Book of Jonah, in which they were well able to point out that God spared Nineveh, not because the people fasted and covered them with sackcloth, but because they turned from their evil way and from the violence that was in their hands. Dr. Edersheim—no friend of the law and the Rabbis—declares in his Commentary that the sentiments of the following passage from Sirach "seem almost to have become proverbial in Jewish theology:"—"He that washes himself because of a corpse and touches it again, what avails him his washing? So is it with a man who fasts for his sins, and goes again and does the same: who will hear his prayer, and what avails him his humbling?"[1]

One other tendency of the ceremonial law must not be lost sight of. The fact that there were so many religious enactments in the perpetually recurrent occupations of ordinary life—such, for example, as in eating and drinking—tended to give a certain dignity and sanctity to life as a whole, and to break down the distinction between holy and profane. Of course this result was only a tendency which became marked in the exceptionally good, just as the evil results became marked in the exceptionally wicked. But as a really existent tendency it deserves notice. The Jew was perpetually reminded of his God. There was no arbitrary separation

[1] xxxiv. 25, 26 (A.V.); xxxi. 25, 26 (ed. Fritzsche). Cf. a very similar passage in Taanith, 16 *a* (Wunsche, Vol. II. 1, p. 438).

between week-day and sabbath in the sense that the work-days lacked the sanctifying spirit of religion. And if this close environment of the law could, on the one hand, become a source of pride and sanctimoniousness or a mere habit without particular effect one way or the other, it could also, on the other hand, be the means of illuminating a life of sorrow by the felt presence of God in the glad fulfilment of his will, or of "gilding" the pale and petty details of every-day existence with the "heavenly alchemy" of religion.

Let us now turn to the question of the effect of the law upon the conception of sin. In no point does the fragmentary and untheoretic nature of the post-exilic religion come out more clearly. There was not only no theory as to the origin of sin, but not even a general and fixed notion of its nature. As I have already indicated, the tolerably certain and universal conviction of individual human frailty was crossed, and to some extent impaired, by the national sense of righteousness as compared with the alien and unbelieving heathen. And secondly, the happy feeling of the individual conscience, not ignorant of error, but yet at peace with God, was crossed and agitated by the national sense of corporate solidarity, and of an accumulated and yet unatoned mass of past and present communal iniquity. For the sense of solidarity and of mutual responsibility with Israel as a whole was never dissolved by the individualism of Ezekiel and the sages. It constituted both the weakness and the strength of the Jewish religion. It made God near, it nerved to self-sacrifice, it prevented religious egoism; but it confused men's notions of sin and recon-

IX. THE LAW AND ITS INFLUENCE.

ciliation, and of the absolutely separate relation of each individual soul to its God.

"In God's sight shall no man living be justified." "Who can say I have made my heart clean, I am pure from my sin?" "What is man that he should be clean? and he that is born of woman that he should be righteous?"[1] These quotations from late post-exilic writings were taken up and enlarged upon by the Rabbis. Thus the old prayer from which I quoted in the last Lecture opens in the same strain: "Sovereign of all worlds! not because of our righteous acts do we lay our supplications before thee, but because of thy abundant mercies. What are we? What is our life? What is our piety? What our righteousness?" And again: "We know that we have no good works of our own; deal charitably with us for thy name's sake." But the old ideas were never fully shaken off; and in spite of a belief in immortality, the sense of sin, reflected in such passages of the liturgy and in the prayer of Daniel, was more often aroused by the pressure of outward and public calamity than by any inward assurance of the natural and innate infirmity of every human soul.[2] By way of compensation, the

[1] Ps. cxliii. 3; Prov. xx. 9; Job xv. 14.

[2] On the other side, however, one must not forget the doctrine of the evil *Yetser*, of which I have spoken later on. The two causes of sinfulness are curiously combined in the supplication which Rabbi Alexander was wont to add to the fixed prayers: "It is known before thee that our will is to thy will; and what hinders us? The leaven in the dough (= the evil *Yetser* or inclination) and our servitude to the kingdoms. May it be thy will to save us out of their hands, that we may again perform the statutes of thy will with a perfect heart." Bera-

idea of original sin and of an historic fall never became a dogma of the synagogue. Judaism was therefore saved from those gloomy and fatalistic consequences so elaborately worked out in Calvinistic theology.

As distinguished from the heathen and from apostates within its own ranks, the true Israel is righteous. Hence the sense of national or communal innocence so prominent in the Psalter. And to that true Israel the writers of these Psalms are fully conscious that they belong. There is thus a sharp separation between good and bad; on the one side is righteous and upright Israel; on the other, the sinner or the persecutor. The one is God's friend in spite of apparent forgetfulness and present calamity; the other is God's foe in spite of present prosperity. In the Proverbs and Wisdom literature the same contrast and cleavage appear: the wise, on the one hand, whose wisdom is identical with virtue; the foolish, on the other, whose folly is coincident with vice. And doubtless the passage was neither distant nor difficult between saying, "My nation and my party is in the right," and feeling, "I individually am righteous." As Prof. Toy has put it, "the sense of individual shortcomings" could easily have been "swallowed up in the conviction of national innocence."[1] This danger was never overcome. It was fostered and kept alive by the growing consciousness of privilege in the possession of the law, just as, on the other hand, the sufferings of

choth, 17 a (Wünsche, Vol. I. 37). The prayers of the Rabbis in this section of Berachoth are very beautiful and well worth reading.

[1] *Judaism and Christianity*, p. 190.

Israel suggested the idea that Israel's sins, more than those of any other nation, are constantly "before the Lord."[1] Perhaps the two ideas together kept the moral balance fairly even.

For even in the Psalter there is evidence that the feeling of communal integrity as towards the outer world was consistent and even coincident with a sense of human frailty as towards God. "Against thee, thee only, have I sinned."[2] Thus in one verse the author of the forty-first Psalm can pray, "Yahveh, have pity on me: heal my soul, for I have sinned against thee;" in another verse he can declare, "Thou upholdest me in my blamelessness, and settest me before thy face for ever." Or, again, in the thirty-first Psalm the author is not separating himself from the true Israel, even if the "I" is a personification, either when he affirms that his strength breaks down because of his "guilt," or when he invokes punishment upon the lying lips who speak arrogantly against the "righteous." It is true that it is frequently difficult to distinguish between the Psalmist's sense of guilt because of his consciousness of sin, and his sense of guilt as the consciousness of calamity. For the same word was used by them to express both iniquity and its penalty. Punishment, in their eyes too often a synonym for suffering, was also the implication of unknown or unrealized sin. When they and Israel were afflicted, they tended to feel sinful; when they and Israel were prosperous, they tended—though in a less degree—to feel righteous and at ease. Yet with the fine instances of the thirty-second and fifty-first Psalms, together with

[1] Sirach xvii. 20 (A.V.). [2] Ps. li. 6.

several touches and hints elsewhere, to support him, Prof. Toy is probably right in saying that "it is hard to resist the impression that we have in some of the Psalms a true spiritual conception of sin as an impurity of soul which makes a barrier between it and God."[1] In the Wisdom books, although there is a lack of enthusiasm peculiar to their species, it is clear that the sins referred to are of a more private and personal nature, and not related to the good or evil fortunes of Israel. Sin became more and more identified with the violation of the law; and while from the national and priestly point of view unconscious or secret transgressions were dreaded as bringing pollution upon land and people, the legalist, though he might pray to be delivered from both, was yet well aware of the moral difference between voluntary and involuntary offences. The true sin was the open and conscious infraction of any commandment in the law.

Did, then, the legal development of post-exilic Judaism in its accentuation of sins lose the sense of sinfulness? Was sin no more than the transgression of an elaborate series of separate and isolated injunctions of equal value and importance? Was the greatness of a man's sin simply measurable by the number of commandments he had overstepped or omitted? Here no doubt was and is the great religious danger of a nomistic religion, still more of a nomistic religion a very large portion of the laws of which is purely ceremonial. Man's sinfulness varies by no means necessarily in direct ratio with the number of his legal transgressions, even if all items in the law are reckoned at the same rate. A man's heart

[1] *Judaism and Christianity*, p. 187.

IX. THE LAW AND ITS INFLUENCE.

may be deep-grained with egoism and selfishness, who yet may have observed the ceremonial law in its entirety, and conformed, outwardly at least, to the moral law. Such a statement, as well as its converse, that an eager and passionate nature may have incurred many lapses and yet be morally superior to the conforming and negative Philistine, is the merest commonplace to us, but to the followers of the law its obviousness was obscured. With regard, however, to the equivalence of moral and ceremonial enactments, it must be observed that if you once believed that God really gave an injunction such as, "Thou shalt not wear a garment of mixed stuff of divers sorts," as directly and emphatically as its immediate predecessor, "Thou shalt love thy neighbour as thyself," its high-handed and intentional violation could hardly be represented to your own conscience otherwise than as deliberate sin. But this very fact shows how the religious element of sin tended in legal Judaism to obscure its vital connection with morality, as well as its deep-seated root within the soul. On the other hand, the simplicity of the Jewish religion enabled it to avoid in considerable measure the logical consequences of its own legalism, and to escape from those hurtful exaggerations of human sinfulness which have so often been visible in Christianity.

We have already seen how the source of goodness was sought in the heart. There also was known to be the source of evil. This conception may be illustrated from the Jewish ideas of man's capacity to fulfil the law and of his tendency to infringe it, as well as of God's necessary part in the overthrow of human sin.

Without ever formulating a theory, the teachers of post-exilic Judaism were inclined to lay the greatest stress upon man's unfettered choice between good and evil, upon his unrestricted capacity to obey the law and to transgress it. Man's will was free. This teaching is nowhere expressed more sharply than in Sirach: "Say not thou, it is through the Lord that I transgressed, for thou oughtest not to do what he hates. . . . He made man at the beginning, and delivered him into the power of his own inclination: if thou wilt, thou canst keep the commandments. . . . Before man is life and death, and whichever he pleases shall be given him."[1] Here human responsibility is strongly emphasized, while the attribution of Israel's sinfulness to God is but of rare and passing occurrence. Happily also, the proneness of man to sin was never formally and officially stiffened into a theory of either devilish temptation or of personified sinfulness, as if there existed a force or principle of evil apart from the sins and sinfulness of individuals. Satan always belonged more to superstition and folk-lore fancy than to the recognized creed of the leading Rabbis. Thus what Holtzmann regards as the religious weakness of the passage in Sirach, that "according to it sin can only be conceived as the act of the individual, and not as a power standing over the individual and enslaving him," seems to me to constitute its merit and value.[2] If it stood alone, the teaching to be deduced from it would be, it is true, one-sided. But it does not represent the whole doctrine of Judaism. For though man's will was conceived as free, and though there was no dogma of man's

[1] xv. 11—17.   [2] Stade, *Geschichte*, Vol. II. p. 304.

innate corruption, it was recognized that the human tendency to evil is very potent, and that to overcome it the help of God is a necessary factor.

Hence we get those frequent prayers to God that he may direct the way and purify the heart, which run like a golden thread through the post-exilic literature. We find them in Chronicles, in David's supplication that God, who tries the heart and has pleasure in uprightness, may give to Solomon a perfect heart to keep the divine commandments, and may direct the heart of the people unto their God.[1] We find them in the Psalter: "Make me to know thy ways, O Yahveh; teach me thy paths;" "Teach me to do thy will, for thou art my God."[2] This supplication for God's needed help is constantly recurrent in the legal Psalm *par excellence*, the one hundred and nineteenth, where the prayer, "Incline my heart unto thy ordinances," is reiterated with almost wearisome monotony. In the Wisdom literature, the same Sirach who accentuates human responsibility can yet pray to the Father and God of his life to keep him from the sins of the flesh and from the evil desires of his lower self.[3] The very conception of wisdom, both in Proverbs and Sirach, is that of a divine force which, if man seek it, will help him to find it. Or, put less abstractly: let a man meditate on God's commands and think continually upon his ordinances, and then God will make his heart strong, and his desire of wisdom will be granted him.[4] In the Rabbinical literature the same thought is also frequent. It appears in the liturgy in the twofold

---

[1] 1 Chron. xxix. 18, 19.　　[2] Psalms xxv. 4, cxliii. 10, &c.
[3] xxiii. 1—6.　　[4] E.g. Sirach vi. 37.

form of a prayer for understanding and a prayer for purity of heart. "Give us understanding, O Lord our God, to learn thy ways: circumcise our hearts to fear thee." "Purify our hearts to serve thee in truth." "Bring us not into the power of sin or of temptation; let not the evil inclination have sway over us; but subdue our inclination, so that it may submit itself unto thee."[1] Repentance needs the same power of divine grace. "Cause us to return, O our Father, unto thy law; draw us near, O our King, unto thy service, and bring us back in perfect repentance unto thy presence. Blessed art thou, O Lord, who delightest in repentance."[2]

It is true that, as we have seen, the doctrine of God's holy spirit remained inchoate, and that the nature of this divine help towards goodness and repentance was not explained to be the presence of the divine spirit within the soul. The prayer of the fifty-first Psalm, "Take not thy holy spirit from me," stands, as Professor Stade has said, isolated in the Psalter. But the essence of the matter was attained without the theory.

As the source of good and evil was sought in the constitution of the will—both on its moral and intellectual side—it is clear that sin was not looked upon as a mere violation of single and separate injunctions. The early Rabbinic prayer just quoted, "Let not the evil inclination have sway over us," implies a religious psy-

---

[1] Cf. the passage in the Grace after Meals in the Portuguese Ritual: "May the most merciful plant his law and his love in our hearts that we sin not." (*Forms of Prayers according to the Custom of the Spanish and Portuguese Jews*, ed. Sola and Artom, Vol. I. p. 169).

[2] Authorized Prayer-book, pp. 7, 46, 55, 74, 139, &c.

chology parallel to, though less dogmatically worked out than, the Pauline doctrine of the inherent and natural corruption of the human heart. It is the conception of two impulses or inclinations within the soul, one evil and the other good, which struggle for the mastery. A complete and scientific delineation of the Talmudic doctrine of the two inclinations—the evil *Yetser* and the good—would not only be of great interest in itself, but would also show how fully the Rabbis understood that the outward violation of the law depended upon an inward tendency.[1]

If, then, sin, proceeding ultimately from the evil element in man's composite nature, is natural and necessary to all, how may it be so far checked and removed that God may pardon the transgressor on the one hand, and that he may lead a better life upon the other? Post-exilic Judaism had two main streams of teaching out of which to form its doctrine of reconciliation and atonement. There was, first of all, the simple prophetic teaching: Repent; do good instead of evil, and God will forgive your sin, and "wipe out" your transgressions. While the earlier prophets never doubted that such repentance and amendment were within the power of all, the exilic teachers, and Ezekiel most prominently, though not omitting the summons to repentance, yet often declared that the new heart must be the gift of God. God's part in human repentance was, as we have seen, recognized both

---

[1] I may note in passing that Mr. Schechter informs me that in a very large proportion of cases in which the evil inclination is spoken of as soliciting to sin, the sin relates to some form of unchastity in thought or deed.

in the later teaching of the Bible and by the Rabbis. But the first element in any doctrine of divine forgiveness which lay ready to hand was that of practical amendment—the deliberate abandonment of sin and the active practice of virtue. Isaiah's explanation of repentance is summed up in the words: "Cease to do evil, learn to do well."

Parallel with this prophetic doctrine went the less ethical teaching of the priestly law. Here the rules of the sin-offering sprang from a totally different order of conceptions, and were liable to lead to unspiritual and unethical results. It is true that the sin-offering was practically limited to unintentional offences, moral carelessness or slipshod flightiness of speech; and it is also true that a main element in the rite was not so much to secure forgiveness for the individual, as the removal of the pollution of his sin from the sanctuary and from the community at large. Nevertheless, although even in the Psalter voices are raised against the efficacy of sacrifice, though the sages repeat the prophetic teaching of the absolute worthlessness of the offerings of the wicked, and Sirach even shows a certain tendency to emphasize the point of view that sacrifices are to be brought because they happen to be ordered in the law and not because of their atoning efficacy,—yet, while the temple existed, the mere continuance of the sacrificial system must have had a certain unspiritual and superstitious effect. Vague ideas about the power of sacrifice were current, which were not even sanctioned by the letter of the code. Of these we may trace a specimen in the prologue and epilogue to Job, where, in the first place, Job is represented as offering a sacrifice after the feastings of his sons, lest "they had sinned and denounced God in their hearts;" and afterwards God orders Job's friends to bring a burnt-offering, while his servant should pray for them to appease his wrath, lest he deal with them after their folly.[1]

When the temple was destroyed, such superstitions tended naturally to die from inanition. But the Day of Atonement remained; and though in the Levitical legislation this annual rite is clearly national and not individual, a deep crust of superstition gradually surrounded it when its celebration was, as it were, transferred from the temple to the synagogue. It was supposed that God went through an annual process of judging and forgiving, and each individual was only too willing to apply to himself the words of the Scripture, "On that day shall he make an atonement for you, to cleanse you, that ye may be clean from all your sins before Yahveh." But, happily for Judaism, the mere sacrificial element in the Day-of-Atonement ritual as well as in the theory of the sin-offering, took no deep hold. It was too purely priestly. The consequence was that it was easy for the Rabbis to teach that charity or repentance was an accepted substitute or equivalent for sacrifice.[2] For according to the prophetic teaching, which was only dimmed but never abrogated by the introduction of the priestly law, repentance had all along been regarded as the true means of reconcilement and forgiveness. While, on the one hand,

[1] Job i. 5, xlii. 8.
[2] E.g. Pesikta, ed. Buber, 158 a (Wünsche's translation, p. 227. The whole 25th section on Repentance is very interesting).

it was an ethical and spiritual loss that the doctrine of conscious self-sacrifice taught in Isaiah liii. was not more widely developed and inculcated by the synagogue, the loss was to some small extent obliterated by a compensatory gain. For Judaism avoided all those ethical troubles and difficulties involved in theories of vicarious atonement and imputed righteousness which have so largely followed from the teaching of Paul and of the Epistle to the Hebrews.

The main doctrine of Judaism on the subject of atonement is therefore comprised in the single word Repentance. And under repentance was included and understood amendment. It was not believed that there is ever any radical impossibility to repent and to reform. It is never too late to mend. The simple adage of the sage sums up the developed teaching of the later Judaism, which, on this side, had nothing to add to it: "He who covers his sins shall not prosper, but whoso confesses and forsakes them shall have mercy."[1] Or, as Sirach has phrased it: "To depart from wickedness is that which pleases God; to give up unrighteousness is atonement."[2]

It was exceedingly fortunate that the sages and Rabbis had such a close grip upon true repentance. It was well that they recognized its import both morally, as indicative of a changed heart, and religiously, as the condition precedent of divine forgiveness. For the legalism of their religion incurred a considerable danger in regard to this very matter, and there is undoubtedly

[1] Proverbs xxviii. 13.

[2] Sirach xxxv. 3 (A.V.), xxxii. 3 (Fritzsche); cf. Pesikta, ed. Buber, 163 a and b (Wünsche's translation, pp. 234, 235).

IX. THE LAW AND ITS INFLUENCE.

some evidence that the danger was not entirely overcome. Goodness, to the legalist, is the performance of the law's injunctions; wickedness or sin is their transgression. Hence, first of all, there was the danger of thinking to acquire credit by the performance of a multiplicity of commands. God might be conceived as keeping an account for and against every individual; every law fulfilled was so much to the good; every law transgressed, so much to the bad.[1] The balance would decide whether a man was good or bad, deserving of punishment or of reward. There are certain indications that from this mechanical externalism Jewish teaching was not wholly free. Yet the peril was often avoided by the continual insistance upon the emptiness of human worth in the eyes of ideal righteousness. Examples of this saving thought have already been quoted from the Jewish liturgy. As an early instance of the false doctrine of merit, the petition of Nehemiah—"Remember this, O God, to my good,"—in other words, "put it to my credit,"—has been repeatedly quoted by modern theologians. But their censure had been anticipated by a Rabbi of the Talmud who when asked, Why was the book of Ezra not called by the name of Nehemiah? replied to the question, "Because he insisted upon his merits."[2] When the idea of merit is applied to the forgiveness of sin, it would assume the form that man might buy off his punishment by a number of virtuous acts. Thus could the taint of sin within the soul be forgotten, and the stress be laid upon the importance of

---

[1] Cf. Aboth iii. 25.
[2] Sanhedrin, 93 b (Wünsche, Vol. II. 3, p. 169).

escaping punishment by an amount of legal performance which would outweigh the amount of preceding iniquity. This is the doctrine of "good works" in its crudest and most unspiritual form. Certain well-known passages from Daniel, Sirach and Tobit are invariably quoted as evidence that in the Maccabean period Judaism had fallen a victim to this unethical and mechanical teaching.

It is twice said in the Book of Proverbs that while riches profit not in the day of wrath, righteousness delivers from death.[1] It is probable that righteousness in these passages is nearly identical with beneficence. In later Hebrew the word *Tsedakah* acquired a more specific meaning, and is commonly translated "almsgiving;" but if this translation be kept, it must be understood that the word was often loosely used to connote not merely the giving of money, but all forms of beneficence to the poor, the dependent and the oppressed.[2] Although by the later Rabbis charity in the higher sense, or the doing of kindnesses, as they called it, was distinguished from almsgiving and appraised above it, still the letter of Scripture was sufficient to make them continually reiterate the doctrine that almsgiving "delivers from death." An immense importance was attached by all Jewish teachers, from the Prophets onward, to the active and friendly succouring of the poor and indigent. Thus Daniel recommends Nebuchadrezzar to "break off, or cancel, his sins by almsgiving, and his iniquities by showing mercy to the poor;" and Tobit advises his son

[1] Prov. x. 2, xi. 4.
[2] Cf. Kethuboth, 50 *a*; Baba Bathra, 8 *a* (Wünsche, Vol. II. 2, p. 121).

to give alms rather than to lay up gold, "because alms deliver from death and will purge away all sin." Sirach teaches that "water will quench a flaming fire, and alms make an atonement for sins." Moreover, the same writer puts another cardinal virtue upon the same level: "Whoso honours his father, makes atonement for his sin; and he that honours his mother is as one that lays up treasure. For compassion to thy father will not be forgotten, and in spite of thy sins thou shalt again be built up. In the day of thy trouble the Lord will remember thee; as warm weather on ice, so shall thy sins melt away."[1]

It is clear that doctrine of this kind was liable to lead to hypocrisy and superstition. It was perhaps the greatest spiritual danger to which Judaism was exposed. It tended to make the hatefulness of sin as a moral disease forgotten and ignored, and to lay the misfortune of it upon the possible evil consequences to the sinner. It tended to make men think that so and so many sins could be cancelled by so and so many meritorious acts, and to attribute a magical effect to the mere external performance of almsgiving. It tended to destroy the unity of human character, as if it were nothing more than a number of actions, law-breaking and law-fulfilling. It tended to make men think that God also, in his capacity of Judge, took the same mechanical view of human nature, and that, keeping a register of every man's acts, both good and evil, he would allow a number of so-called "good deeds" to cancel the punishment, which in another world was supposed to await the evil-

[1] Daniel iv. 24 (Heb.); Tobit xii. 9; Sirach iii. 3, 4, 14, 15, 30.

doer. We can see that superstitions such as these, from which, if the written religious teaching of the Rabbis is not entirely free, we may be certain that the religion of the average worshipper was far less exempted, were precisely similar to those Romanist doctrines against which the fresh Pauline teachers of the Reformation so loudly and so rightly protested.

That the slippery adage, "Almsgiving delivers from death," had less evil effect in the course of Jewish teaching than might have been expected was partly due to the untheoretic nature of Judaism, on which fundamental characteristic it has been advisable to insist so often. No fixed and formulated dogma of "good works" was ever worked out and accepted by the synagogue; and far more frequent than any notion of striking a balance upon the right side in the moral account with God is the doctrine that human merits are as nothing in his sight, and that man depends for his salvation upon God's mercy and loving-kindness.

Nor must it be forgotten that the good works cited in Sirach as efficacious for atonement are, at the worst, moral actions and not ceremonial rites. No doubt the particularizing is dangerous. But the original writers would scarcely have allowed that a perfunctory almsgiving, which was not the visible expression of a "repentance in the heart," as Sirach terms it,[1] would have secured the desired atonement. And the Rabbis taught the same. Their literature is full of adages and stories about the glories and virtues of this sovereign quality. Repentance, as in the doctrine of momentary

[1] Sirach xxi. 6.

conversion, can give immediate entrance to the kingdom of heaven.[1] It can accomplish in an hour what the ordinary individual is not sure of achieving in a lifetime.[2] Where the penitents stand, the faultlessly righteous stand not.[3] "Better," said Rabbi Jacob, in the first half of his famous paradox, "is one hour of repentance and good works in this world than all the life of the world to come."[4]

The effects of the law upon the Jewish conception of righteousness and sin have been, though sketchily and inadequately, yet not, as I hope, partially or unfairly, set down in the foregoing paragraphs. To avoid one-sidedness, to admit an inconsistent variety of teaching, never to forget the undogmatic character of the material before us, or the grave impropriety of forcing it into certain preconceived categories at the risk of misinterpretation and omission, will be as necessary and as difficult when we now come to consider the motives which induced the Jews of the second temple and the long Rabbinical period to observe the law.

If a pious Jew of the Maccabean and post-Maccabean period had been asked why he obeyed the law, he would probably have failed to understand the question. To obey the law was to him absolutely identical with the fulfilment of God's certain will. To ask why he obeyed God's will, would have seemed as meaningless and irreligious a question as to ask an idealist, "Why are you good." The law, in his eyes, was the best and noblest

[1] Cf. Pesikta Rabbathi, ed. Friedman, 185 a; Joma, 86 a.
[2] Cf. Abodah Zarah, 17 a; Genesis Rabba, lxv. 22.
[3] Berachoth, 34 b.   [4] Aboth iv. 24 (ed. Taylor).

and sweetest thing in all the world: it was the *summum bonum*, the supreme good, and for the end in itself there is no accounting. Our pious Jew could, of course, have explained to you what *effects* the observance of the law had upon himself, upon Israel and upon God; but if you could have laid bare the recesses of his heart, you would have found that the law's effects must not be identified, off-hand, with the motives for its observance. Its effect for God was the diffusion of his glory; its effect for Israel was the possible advent of the Messianic age; its effects for the individual were the assurance of present bliss, the possibility of present happiness, and the certainty of future "reward."[1] By "reward," to the developed Rabbinic Jew, must be understood the fuller knowledge and the spiritual beatitudes of the life to come, both immediately after death by the disembodied spirit, and after the resurrection by the risen body once more united with its vivifying soul.

Now several Christian theologians not only identify the motives impelling to the observance of the law with its effects, but they single out of the three effects the egoistic effect alone, that, namely, of the law upon the individual. Moreover, while that effect was explained to consist in the assurance of present bliss, the possibility of present happiness and the certainty of future reward, they entirely omit from consideration the first clause, the assurance of present bliss, and limit the effect—and there-

---

[1] By "bliss," I understand the higher felicity which accompanied the execution of God's commands, be external circumstances what they might; by "happiness," the lower felicity which accompanied such external circumstances if they were prosperous and fortunate.

fore the motive—to the possibility of present happiness and the certainty of future reward.

How far do such an identification and limitation interpret or misinterpret the facts?

The argument, "Obey the law because it will pay you to do so," constitutes unquestionably the fundamental motive of Deuteronomy. Perhaps the authors of that book thought it was the only way in which they could get an idolatrous and recalcitrant population to accept their various and startling innovations; but, however this may be, the motive for observance is clear: "that it may be well with thee"—that "thy days may be prolonged," as it says in the fifth Commandment, and so on. Press this motive home, and you seem to deal a death-blow to goodness and religion. Morals and piety become nothing more than the wiser policy. Above all —a crucial point—the law is no longer an end, but a means, the means to one's own prosperity. Happiness is the end. The more eager you are for prosperity, the more likely will you be to obey the law: the more fearful you are of punishment and of the God who will inflict it, the less likely will you be to infringe the law, on the one hand, but the more servile will be your obedience, upon the other.

Now the Christian theologians appear to suppose, if I rightly understand them, that this motive is the *necessary* religious motive, when religion takes the aspect of law. The more, therefore, the law in later times became the very flesh and blood of the Jewish religion, and the more its ceremonial enactments became regarded as equally divine with its moral enactments, the more did this motive necessarily become the only possible religious motive which induced the Jew to obey the law. Legalism, they assert, brings slavishness and eudæmonism by logical necessity in its train. It is not merely a general conviction, Do God's will and you will prosper; but since a certain meed of punishment is expected for the transgression, and a certain meed of reward is expected for the fulfilment, of each separate legal injunction, in all cases and circumstances the dual motive of fear and hope is always and ever alone before the mind. Thus, after pointing out that the laws of the priestly legislation are almost exclusively ceremonial, Prof. Schultz continues thus: "These laws simply demand obedience. The motives for keeping them can therefore be nothing but the fear of God and the anticipation of reward or punishment. Moreover, as each individual commandment stands by itself and cannot be fitted into the uniform and harmonious body of moral truths, eudæmonistic and heteronomous considerations must come into play in each individual case, and cannot merely form a general presupposition to a man's habitual moral attitude. Hence they become dangerous and enslaving, and tend to degrade the mind."[1] So too, Prof. Schürer, while quoting the famous saying of Antigonus of Socho, "Be not like servants who minister to their masters upon the condition of receiving a reward, but be like servants who minister to their masters without the condition of receiving a reward," goes on to say: "This adage is in nowise a

[1] H. Schultz, "Die Beweggründe zum sittlichen Handeln in dem vorchristlichen Israel," *Theologische Studien und Kritiken*, 1890, p. 41.

IX. THE LAW AND ITS INFLUENCE.

correct expression of the fundamental disposition of Pharisaic Judaism. That Judaism in truth resembled servants who serve for the sake of their reward."[1]

This statement is made with perfect good faith, but in strange violation of the facts. It is curious that these critics are apt to excuse the eudæmonistic and utilitarian motive in Deuteronomy, while they emphasize it one-sidedly in the Rabbis. They are at pains to show that it is not the only motive to be found in Deuteronomy, while they assure us that it constituted the sole motive of Pharisaic Judaism. Whereas the truth is exactly opposite. The eudæmonistic motive is strongest in Deuteronomy; it is weakest with the Rabbis. It was the only motive to which the founders of the legal development could appeal: it was but one among many when the development was completed.

This movement is historically traceable. The doctrine of retribution is not ignored. As we have seen, in one form or another, it is clung to with intense conviction; but to the lover of the law, the *motive* of his obedience detaches itself with ever-increasing clearness from the *effect*. In the priestly code we hear less of the motives of hope and fear than in Deuteronomy. In it, the prevailing motives are rather the honour and glory of God, and in the background the bringing on of the Messianic age,— in the beatitudes of which, however, no resurrection would enable the first observers of the law to join. In the hymn of the law—the one hundred and nineteenth Psalm —the hope of external reward and the fear of punishment occupy a still smaller space; and in the Rabbinical

[1] *Geschichte*, Vol. II. p. 390 (E. T., Div. ii. Vol. II. p. 93).

literature the thought emerges triumphant that the essence of observance lies in itself and not in its external rewards. In other words, the motive became purer as God and his law were loved more deeply, and as they were more implicitly believed to be good.

The law was obeyed because it was the will of God, and God was loved and conceived to be infinitely good and gracious, seeking Israel's welfare and well-being, and loving his people as a father loves his son. It is impossible to deny that these beliefs were really held by the post-exilic community, and through the entire Rabbinical period. But if they were really held, is it not clear that they must have become motives? People say, What has a petty detail of ceremonial observance to do with the reverence and love of God? In our eyes, nothing. But if you came to believe that the good and wise God who loves you, and whom you love, had ordained a certain ceremonial, would you not logically be impelled to execute the rite, even although you knew nothing of its reason—to execute it gladly, for God's sake, because his revealed will must be wise and must be good?

The law, as we have seen, was no burden to the true believer. It was a high prerogative. It was therefore obeyed for its own sake, because the observance of it was an exceeding joy. "Thy law is my delight: thy commandment is exceeding broad. Thy law do I love: great peace have they which love it."[1] Now this loving enthu-

---

[1] Psalm cxix. 96, 163, 165, &c. Mr. Schechter once wrote to me: "I think that Ruskin *felt* his way to a conception of the law truer than the expositions of all our theologians." See *Frondes Agrestes*, ix., § 76.

siasm for the law is commonly allowed to the author of
the one hundred and nineteenth Psalm; why is it denied
to the Rabbis who felt it a thousand times more keenly,
and proved it on a thousand scaffolds by the sacrifice of
their lives? But Prof. Schultz says, the main bulk of
the law is ceremonial, and the ceremonial law can only
be observed out of fear of punishment or hope of reward.[1]
Here we have the logic of theory at variance with the
logic of facts. Prof. Schultz cannot imagine how the
details of the ceremonial law can be anything else than a
sore burden—very tiresome and irksome annoyances, only
submitted to through lust for gain or fear of evil. But
it was precisely the ceremonial law which was most of
all performed for its own sake and for the love of God.
Clothe the naked, feed the hungry, and the end lies
partly in the subsequent effect; but say the sabbath
blessing, lay the *Tefillin*, or cleanse the house from leaven
before the Passover, and the end and the joy lie purely
in the acts themselves. A spiritual bliss was felt in the
execution of each divine command, a true religious rapture in seemingly the most puerile of observances. The
law brought down heaven to earth, and made the presence
of God felt within the soul. The profusion of ceremonial
injunctions is the high privilege of Israel. As the recompence of sin is sin, so the recompence of command is
command.[2] According to R. Eleazar, the true felicity of
the man who delights in God's commandments is due to
this, that he delights in their performance, but does not

[1] "Die Beweggründe," &c., pp. 40, 41.
[2] Aboth iv. 5 (ed. Taylor).

solicit their rewards whether in this world or in the next.[1]

The still prevalent popular usage of the word *Mitsvah* tells its own truthful tale. *Mitsvah* has, on the one hand, acquired the meaning of a meritorious act. This appears to substantiate the critical theory that the motive of the observance was to acquire a store of merit, and therefore of merit's reward. It really only emphasizes the fact that the effect of the observance was never lost sight of, and that the doctrine of retribution was often mechanically interpreted. On the other hand, *Mitsvah* has acquired the meaning of privilege, and hence a ceremonial detail connected with the law is often called a *Mitsvah*, although it is not an ordinance or an act from which any reward is anticipated. A stranger entering an orthodox synagogue, is entrusted, as an honour and a privilege, with some small ceremony in the bringing out of the scroll of the law from the ark, or in its return. Such an honour, though no legal injunction, is yet called a *Mitsvah*.

The question presents itself, whether a full and even exaggerated belief in retribution cannot co-exist with a love of the law for its own sake? Does it necessarily make the lust for reward (*Lohnsucht*) the only motive for the law's observance? Prof. Schultz allows that the law won the love of the Israelites (he does not directly say "of the Pharisaic Jews"), and was adopted by

[1] Abodah Zarah, 19 a (Wünsche, Vol. II. 3, p. 344); cf. Sifri, 79 b, 84 b; Yalkut, i. § 862. Maimonides, on Sanhedrin xi.; Schechter, "Doctrine of Divine Retribution in the Rabbinical Literature," *Jewish Quarterly Review*, Vol. III. p. 49.

them with free resolve as the rule of their lives. But because the law was mainly ceremonial, this love of the law could produce, according to him, no truly ethical motive. It was at bottom "nothing but a purely religious resolve of free and unconditional obedience to the divine will, arising from the admiration of the beauty and wisdom of an ideal life, which God has introduced into the world."[1]

Now a religious resolve of free and unconditional obedience to the will of God would seem to be no bad motive after all. For we know that the Jews believed that God was loving, and that his will was wise and good. Prof. Schultz himself, in the same essay from which I have been quoting, had already said that a religious motive can become truly ethical, if believing in the love of God and in the identity of his will with the good, you freely and inwardly give yourself up to this will. Where, then, is the difference? Prof. Schultz obviously thinks that difference there is, for to the sentence defining what the Jewish motive of loving the law really amounted to, he adds, in brackets, the two bare words: "national pride." Whether the martyrdom and fidelity of centuries are adequately explained by "national pride" may be fairly doubted. It is a matter less of formal debate than of subjective feeling. At any rate, even national pride is something different from the lust of reward. The real connection between the love of the law and the hope of reward was rather that, as piety was the result of the former, it was, and in the last resort needs must be, conditioned by the latter. For Well-

[1] "Die Beweggründe," &c., p. 41.

hausen himself has acknowledged: "Piety cannot maintain itself if God makes no difference between the godly and the wicked, and has nothing more to say to the one than to the other; for piety is not content to stretch out its hands to the empty air—it must meet an arm descending from heaven. It needs a reward, not for the reward's sake, but in order to be sure of its own reality, in order to know that there is a communion of God with man and a road by which to reach it."[1] Surely these words explain the presence of the doctrine of retribution in all theistic religions. As the reward is deferred to a future life, so the eudæmonistic element becomes more spiritual. This was equally the case both with Judaism and Christianity. The teaching of Jesus does not lack the doctrine of punishment and reward. It is prominent even in the Beatitudes. "They that mourn now *will be* comforted; they that do hunger and thirst after righteousness *shall be* filled. They that are meek *shall* inherit the earth. They that are pure in heart *shall see* God." Precisely similar to these utterances is the teaching of the Rabbis. And both they and Jesus, as men of religion and not as philosophers, declared, "Do God's will, his will is good," rather than "Because his will is good, therefore do it."

It is not unnatural that Jews should feel the charge of interested motive somewhat sorely. History assures them of its inaccuracy. Deep-seated particularism is a true count in the indictment of Judaism: the puerility of great sections of the ceremonial law is another. A base motive is not a third. And if it is not accurate,

[1] *Abriss*, p. 92; *History of Israel*, p. 504.

it is insulting. For to say—and this is what the allegation involves—that the faithfulness of centuries has been mere hireling service; that the blood of numberless martyrs was poured out, and that the anguish of myriads of forgotten souls was endured, for greed of gain or for fear of penalties; that the love of God and of his law, which from the Maccabees of old to the Russian Jews of to-day has withstood a hundred persecutions, and triumphed over nameless woes, was no love at all, but a mere yearning for reward—outward, material reward; that all this unselfishness was selfishness, all this devotion, pride, and all this sacrifice a sham,—this is surely one of the most cruel and virulent insults which can be levelled at men created, as well as their maligners, in the image of God.

If the law, then, is a blessed and blissful privilege which God has given Israel because he loved him, did this high privilege make God distant or bring him near? Did it constitute and produce a spiritual communion between God and man, or render such communion unknown and impossible? Was the relation of the Pharisaic Jew to God—the Jew who loved God's law and realized his highest bliss in its fulfilment—that of slave to master, or that of child to father? We recall the pointed antithesis which was quoted at the close of the last Lecture. "The Jew is God's servant, who labours to deserve eternal life by his conformity to the law; the Christian is God's child, who already possesses eternal life and lives in blissful communion with the Father in time and eternity." Have we not been able to see that this crisp antithesis lacks the qualification of a real cor respondence with the facts? "Beloved are Israel, for they are called children of God. Beloved are Israel, for unto them was given the law."¹ The Sonship and the Fatherhood were both realized in the fulfilment of the law. It is very strange that whereas some Protestant theologians have laid it down that present communion with God was made impossible by the law, the Rabbis believed that it was veritably the law which made such communion a full and actual possibility.² Was I not justified in saying that the law, as the mediating link between God and man, fulfilled something of the same office as the person of Christ in the various phases of Christianity? Without ignoring the dangerous particularism of the Jewish mediation, we must not be blind to its spiritual effects within the borders of the community. In the pictorial language of the Midrash, before the law was given, heaven and earth were still separate and apart; but at the season of its bestowal, Moses went up to heaven, and God came down upon the earth.³

"Beloved are Israel, for they are called children of God." Did the Father love the children, but the children tremble before the Father? Is the love of God unknown to Judaism? It is an interesting fact that, frequently as man's love to God is spoken of in Deuteronomy, it is rarely alluded to in the later books of the Old Testament and in the Apocrypha.⁴ The fear of God, on the other hand, is a predominating note in the Wisdom

¹ Aboth iii. 22, 23.
² Cf. Exodus Rabbah, xii. 3; Pesikta, ed. Buber, 1 *b*, 2 *a*.
³ Pesikta, ed. Buber, 105 *a* (ad init.); Wünsche's translation, p. 134.
⁴ In the Rabbinical literature it reappears.

literature, and is also repeatedly mentioned in the Psalms and elsewhere. But this fear was no longer what the fear of Yahveh had been before the exile. It combines reverence and devotion, and it rather includes love than opposes it. The love of God may be known, even if it be not specifically mentioned: who will say that the Jesus of the Synoptic Gospels does not inculcate love to God, and yet, except in his quotation from Deuteronomy, he seems to name it definitely but once?[1] Precisely the same ethical issues are attributed to the fear of God as to the love of God. Thus the Sage declares: "The fear of Yahveh is the hatred of evil;" and the Psalmist exclaims: "Ye that love Yahveh, hate evil." And Sirach uses the two expressions indiscriminately : " They that fear the Lord will not disobey his word; and they that love him will keep his ways. They that fear the Lord will seek that which is pleasing unto him ; and they that love him are filled with the law."[2] Thus the fear of God to the law-loving Pharisaic Jew had practically driven out fear, and through the spiritual joy of fulfilling God's will he lived in blissful communion with the Father in time and eternity.

To give a short and yet true characterization of the post-exilic religion, as a whole, is overwhelmingly difficult. It is so easy to fix attention upon this side of it or on that, and then, according to individual inclination, to praise it or condemn. The danger is greatest for the master of epigram. Hence the comparative failure, even of so great a critic as Wellhausen, to characterize the

[1] Luke xi. 42.
[2] Prov. viii. 13; Ps. xcvii. 10; Sirach ii. 15, 16.

Pharisees. "The sum of the means became the end: through the *Torah* God was forgotten."[1] How telling, and how false! An habitual lack of impartiality upon the Christian side seems mainly due to the influence of St. Paul. The Rabbinic religion is doomed because Paul abjured it. But the verdict of Paul, one of the greatest religious geniuses the world has ever known, cannot be accepted without demur. Wellhausen speaks of him somewhere as the great pathologist of Judaism, who understood and saw through the religion as never another. If this be so, then clearly Judaism is a worthless religion, the followers of which for eighteen hundred years have been puffed up with self-righteousness or crushed with despair. They can never have known what it is to love God in purity and truth. For if you estimate the Judaism of the first century according to Paul's judgment, you estimate at the same value the Judaism of eighteen hundred years! But to accept Paul as a correct critic of Judaism is a fallacy. Do you consider that a convert from Liberalism to Toryism is the most adequate and impartial judge of the political system which he has abandoned? Is a convert from evangelical Protestantism to Roman Catholicism the best judge and critic of evangelical theology? Would you accept his evidence without cavil, and say that just because he abandoned the religion of his fathers for possibly a greater and fuller faith, he was the best possible critic and pathologist of the religion he has forsaken?

The post-exilic religion may be looked at with some

[1] *Die Pharisäer und die Sadducäer*, 1874, p 19.

IX. THE LAW AND ITS INFLUENCE. 543

advantage and comprehensiveness from two general points of view: first, from that of the undogmatic and untheoretic nature of its various beliefs; and secondly, from that of its all-embracing legalism.

A main cause of the chaotic character of its religious beliefs was the heavy burden of a sacred Scripture, whereof every sentence was necessarily true. The Babel of different doctrines in the Canon of the Old Testament was regarded as equally accurate and divine throughout. Notions of sin and of retribution, conceptions of God's nature and character, which at the close of the Canon had been essentially outgrown, hung yet as a confusing and darkening sediment in the wine-cup of religious truth. For as the Bible was practically the total literature of the Jews, and its study their only spiritual and intellectual interest, the leading teachers knew the whole book—which, after all, is not a very large one—by heart, and were weighed down by its authority. Some things, of course, were explained away; but many more were simply accepted as they stood, and the unperceived contrarieties lay all juxtaposed and unharmonized within the believer's mind. But, secondly, the lack of system and precision in religious dogma was a relief to the superabundance of them in religious practice. As the Christian schoolmen argued about subtleties of belief, so the Jewish Rabbis argued about subtleties of practice. Their imagination was given full rein outside the borders of the law.

Both good and evil effects, as we have already perceived, arose from this want of articulation and ordered sequence in the field of religious theory. On the one hand, Judaism was spared the evils which ensue when doctrines, true up to a certain point, but with their own admixture of falsehood, are stiffened into dogmas and pushed to a wild extreme. To this fluidity of teaching, it was partly due that the frequent adage, "Almsgiving delivers from death," was never developed into a hard-and-fast dogma of good works, leading to wide-spread moral corruption. Hence, too, Judaism was spared the moral and religious evils which have resulted from a one-sided exaggeration of such dogmas as those of predestination or justification by faith. It was able to include and find room for various sides of truths, which are perhaps too complex and difficult to be ever harmoniously realized, without defect or excess, by the mind of man.

A typical Jew could pray that God might forgive him his sins or teach him the statutes of life, and yet, in the same breath, he could avouch his unqualified fidelity to the law. He could believe that God leaves no sin unpunished; he could believe that with God is forgiveness. He could fulfil the law and feel at peace with God; he could realize that there is no man who has not yielded to sin. He could pray to a Father who is in heaven, and could assert that God is unconfined by space. He could hope by his own well-doing to merit a place in the world to come; he could aver with pious sincerity that it was only by divine "grace" that he would attain it. He could appreciate Leviticus, and he could appreciate Isaiah. For the prophetic lesson upon the greatest fast-day in the year, he could choose a chapter which asserts the idle inutility of all outward forms. He could welcome the joys of material prosperity; he could despise them in comparison with a single commandment of the law. He could proclaim that man alone is responsible for his deeds; he could urge the necessity of God's help in the triumph over evil. He could loudly asseverate the innocency of Israel; he could earnestly exclaim that Israel is destitute of righteousness. He could believe that calamity betokens sin; he could be convinced that suffering is the gift of love.

For every mood of the human spirit he had a doctrine and a verse to suit. Jewish legalism was systematized by St. Paul, and misinterpreted. An orthodox Jew would have entirely failed to grasp the gist of Paul's diatribes against the law. The doctrine of "the law as the strength of sin" would have had no meaning for him. In its very combination of opposites, Judaism was an admirable religion for the shifting requirements of every-day life.

On the other hand, the dead weight of Scripture and a lack of intellectual interest in the precision of dogma led to many unfortunate results. Some of the old, outworn ideas were never frankly cast off; some of the better ideas never advanced to a clear and unquestioned primacy. Unchecked religious imagination gave birth to many wild absurdities. Numberless superstitions crept in as the centuries rolled on. No great genius arose on native soil, and as a servant of the law. Such minds as Philo, Maimonides, Spinoza, receive their inspiration from the foreigner, and the greatest of them all emancipates himself from Judaism and the law even more thoroughly than St. Paul. No master-mind in post-exilic Judaism set forth with commanding and authoritative utterance a comprehensive doctrine of man's relations to God and to society. Its literature contains an abundant quantity of noble, though conflicting, sayings on morals and religion, but little more. Systematic study was only devoted to religious jurisprudence, and thus it comes to pass that the Rabbinic writings teem with all sorts of heterogeneous ideas upon moral and religious subjects, which are yet only the chance and casual expressions of a myriad different minds. Unity is wanting.

To some extent, indeed, the missing unity of lofty doctrine was supplied by the idealism of the law. Jewish legalism was provocative of a high standard of work-a-day morality, of that morality which is the real salt and substance of human life. We have already seen that the sanctimonious and immoral Pharisee is a ridiculous figure to set up as the proper and necessary product of Jewish legalism. That is the judgment of the Philistine, who can see no good thing outside his own circle. The bad Pharisee of the New Testament is the perversion of legalism; just as the antinomian, on the one hand, or the sanctimonious hypocrite, on the other, who believes his own sect saved and the world damned, is the perversion of St. Paul. It must not be forgotten that the age of Jesus was one of religious ferment and fanaticism. It was an age of violent oppositions, unlike the long Rabbinical period, inaugurated by the downfall of the temple. Sadducee and Pharisee and Zealot, Essene and Outcast, all figure upon the religious stage. The defects of all parties show themselves strongly in fierce antagonism and morbid exaggeration.

IX. THE LAW AND ITS INFLUENCE.

Rabbinic morality was simple and pure. Legalism sanctified the home, and refused to accept a divorce between religion and life. The law transfigured ordinary life; it did not create a sphere of special piety outside it. Yet, earnest as life was, it was nevertheless cheerful. The temple festivities were modified, but not discouraged, by the law.[1] Cheerfulness is, indeed, a marked feature of post-exilic religion. Judaism looks forward, not backward: its golden age is in the future, not in the past: so that man's progress, rather than his mythical fall, has become a dogma of its creed.[2] Its very contrarieties of mood towards outward prosperity produced a happy and satisfactory issue; morality penetrated through Jewish society, and was a potent link or bridge between class and class. It was real, practical and to the point. Men were fitted to the simple duties of everyday life, but also to the sublimest self-sacrifice for the cause of God. The sweet charities which transform existence have perhaps nowhere been more conspicuously or

[1] Cf. Delitzsch, *Iris, Studies in Colour and Talks about Flowers*, in the excellent essay, "Dancing and the Criticism of the Pentateuch." He shows conclusively, as against the too systematizing Wellhausen, that the law by no means crushed out joy and merriment in the various festivals of the temple.

[2] The Jews were not only optimists as to the future of their community, but their religion taught them to believe that life for each individual was, or ought to be, a good thing, a blessing of God. You could not write of the melancholy of the Jews as Prof. Butcher writes of the melancholy of the Greeks. Quite un-Jewish, I imagine, and unparelleled in their literature, except in Ecclesiastes, would be the conduct of the Trausian Thracians who, when a child was born, made lamentation for all the evils of which he must fulfil the measure (Herod. v. 4).

genuinely practised than in the mediæval Jewish communities. To the ethical dangers of legalism I have already called attention. There was the danger of law in itself, and there was the danger of the particular law as mainly ceremonial. But we saw how the first danger was less real than the second, and how the second was partially neutralized, so far as the internal morality of Judaism was concerned, by the acceptance and diffusion of the ceremonial law throughout the entire community.

On the religious side, the chief and permanent defect of legalism was its emphasized nationalism. Orthodox Judaism can never utterly overcome this defect; for though it has ceased to teach that God loves the Jews more than he loves the Gentiles, or deals with them according to a different measure, its law, the embodiment of its religion, the medium of its communion with God, and the source of its highest bliss, remains—and must remain—purely national or sectarian. And yet, for critics of every school, there is no getting over the fact that some of the highest possibilities of religion have been evoked and conditioned by the law. It has been said that the religion of Judaism was a soulless deism. It is a false charge, but false because of the law. It was the law which made God near; it was the law which brought him home; it was the law by which his sanctifying presence was felt within the heart. It was the law which cleansed the religious motive of sordidness and egoism. It was the law under and through which that potent goal of human purpose was devised, the sanctification of God, for the sake of which torture and death were preferable to welfare and dishonour.[1] It was the law which created a spiritual beatitude, independent of circumstance, a beatitude which involved in a single consciousness the doing of God's will and the sense of communion with him. It was the law which destroyed eudæmonism. It called into being an inner life, which, as it hinged on an ideal conception, was unaffected by the ebb and flow of earthly prosperity and adversity. "O Israel, happy are we, for the things which please God are known to us!"[2] "Happy are we, how goodly is our portion, how pleasant is our lot, how beautiful our heritage!"[3] Happy, pleasant, beautiful—wherefore? Because of outward fortune and material success? Not so. Because early and late, morning and evening, we declare: "Hear, O Israel: the Lord our God, the Lord is One." The community prays: "We beseech thee, O Lord our God, to make the words of thy law pleasant in our mouths and in the mouths of thy people, the house of Israel; so that we, our offspring, and the offspring of our offspring, may all know thy name and learn thy law for its own sake."[4]

The law for its own sake. The hope of retribution was not forgotten; but just as to the Christian the love of Christ is its own reward, though he also believes in the

---

[1] קדוש השם.   [2] Baruch iv. 4.
[3] Authorized Prayer-book, p. 8.
[4] *Forms of Prayers according to the Custom of the Spanish and Portuguese Jews*, Vol. I. p. 8. The idea of disinterested love of God, of serving or learning the law *for its own sake* (לשמה) is of very frequent occurrence and very interesting. Rabbi Saphra was wont to pray, "May it be thy will that all who occupy themselves with the law not for its own sake may ultimately come to occupy themselves with it for its own sake." Berachoth, 17 *a*.

recompence of "heaven," so also did the Jew believe that the blessedness of "heaven" was, as it were, antedated or anticipated by the blessedness of the law on earth. The body of religious teaching was, as we know, fragmentary and inconsistent, but the love of the law linked the fragments together, and they shone transfigured in an ideal light. In the law, the various elements—by themselves heterogeneous and contrary—found their union and their harmony.

It is only now that this amazing idealization of the law is slowly breaking down, when the Pentateuch is being estimated at its actual historic worth, and subjected to the scalpel of a criticism which disintegrates its unity and bereaves it of its supernatural glamour, that Judaism will, I think, gradually begin to feel the want of a dominant and consistent doctrine, adequate and comprehensive, soul-satisfying and rational, which can set forth and illumine in its entire compass the relation of the individual to society and to God. I am myself inclined to believe that, from the words attributed in the Gospels to Jesus, important elements towards the formation of such a congruous body of doctrine could well be chosen out, elements which would harmonize, develop and bring together the highest religious teaching in the Old Testament and the early Rabbinical literature, and which a prophetic, though not a legal, Judaism, with full consistency and much advantage, might adopt and cherish as its own. Doctrines and sayings such as, "He who loses his life shall find it;" "Not that which goes into, but that which comes out of, the mouth defiles a man;" "Not my will, but thine;" "Father, forgive them, for they know not what they do,"

IX. THE LAW AND ITS INFLUENCE. 551

—can only, I venture to think, be disregarded with some spiritual detriment to the religion which believes itself compelled to pass them by.[1] Some of the sayings ascribed to Jesus have sunk too deep into the human heart, or, shall I say, into the spiritual consciousness of civilized mankind, to make it probable that any religion which ignores or omits them will exercise a considerable influence outside its own borders. If, then, Judaism be still destined to play a prominent and fruitful part in the religious history of the world, it may, perhaps, be that this new stage in its development will only ensue when it has harmoniously assimilated to itself such of the Gospel teachings as are not antagonistic, but complementary, to its own fundamental dogmas, and has freely and frankly acknowledged the greatness, while maintaining the limitations, of the illustrious Jew from whose mouth they are reported to have come.

But is any permanent reform of Judaism within the limits of possibility? Can Judaism burst the bonds of legalism and particularism and remain Judaism still? That is a question which it is for the future to answer, and for the future alone. It may be that those who dream of a prophetic Judaism, which shall be as spiritual as the religion of Jesus, and even more universal than the religion of Paul, are the victims of delusion. But,

[1] I do not mean to imply that even to these sovereign adages parallels in the Rabbinical literature might not be found. "Not my will, but thine," can, e.g., be imperfectly paralleled in Aboth ii. 4, and more adequately perhaps in Berachoth, 17 a, quoted above. But in the Gospels they are more clearly and closely brought together, their supreme importance more fully established, and they are less clogged with inferior matter.

at any rate, the labour which they may give, and the fidelity which they may show, to this delusion, cannot be thrown away. They will not be the only men who have worked for a delusion, and have yet benefited the world. For their devotion to the cause of an imaginary Judaism remains devotion to the cause of God. They are the champions of Monotheism, herald-soldiers of a world-wide Theism which, while raising no mortal to the level of the divine, can yet proclaim the truth of man's kinship and communion with the Father of all. To that religion let the future give what name it will. But among those who, marching under different banners, shall help to fashion and to diffuse it, may they, too, be found enrolled, the story of whose religious ancestry I have sought to tell, with many and obvious imperfections, but in loyalty, as I hope and would fain believe, to the spirit of all-prevailing truth.

APPENDIX.

I.

THE DATE OF THE DECALOGUE.

I cannot enter here into the question of the extremely complicated critical analysis of Exodus xix., xx., xxiv., xxxiv. For the study of it, I can only refer the reader to the books of Dillmann, Kittel and Driver, upon the one hand, and to those of Kuenen (in the *Onderzoek* or *Hexateuch*), Cornill, Wellhausen, Robertson Smith (*O.T. in the Jewish Church*, 2nd ed., pp. 332—337), upon the other. The second class of scholars, together with Stade, Oort and others (we may now add Mr. Addis in *The Documents of the Hexateuch*, 1892), has abandoned the Mosaic authorship. To show that this view is the more probable is my only object here: the exact date of the Decalogue, its original place and function in the Elohistic narrative, and its relation to the so-called "Book of the Covenant" (Exodus xx. 23—xxiii. 19) and the "Words of the Covenant" (Exodus xxxiv. 12—27), I must leave undetermined.

That the Ten Words in the form in which they now appear in Exodus cannot be Mosaic in their origin, is obvious and almost undisputed. If they were so, the reason for observing the Sabbath in Deuteronomy's version of the Words would not have differed from that now given in Exodus. In fact, the Exodus text of the fourth Word has been enlarged and edited by more than one hand (i.e. both by a "Deuteronomistic" and a "Priestly" editor). As Mr. Addis says: "The 'Words' were originally short precepts like those in the 'Book of the Covenant,' and thus the disproportion in bulk between the precepts of the first and second table disappears" (p. 140). But even if we omit the additions, and suppose that the second Word ran originally, "Thou shalt make thee no graven images;" the third, "Thou shalt not take Yahveh thy God's name in vain;" the fourth, "Remember the Sabbath-day to sanctify it;" the fifth, "Honour thy father and thy mother;" and the tenth, "Thou shalt not covet thy neighbour's house,"—grave difficulties remain in coupling these Words with the name of Moses. Could Moses have forbidden image-worship, when we know that the representation of Yahveh under the form of a bull was a common and scarcely reprehended custom down to the age of Amos? To avoid the difficulty by the assumption that the command was neglected, forgotten or ignored, seems precarious. It is, indeed, true that we do not definitely hear of any animal-symbolizing of Yahveh in the sanctuaries of Shiloh and Jerusalem; but the more I consider the subject, the more I am inclined to think that we must not build too much upon this perhaps accidental omission. It is also doubtful whether the ark was intended to serve as a material substitute for an image of Yahveh. Nor does it seem probable that we may omit the prohibition against image-making altogether, and yet retain the number ten by making the exordium, "I am Yahveh thy God," constitute the first Word. There is another difficulty relative to the fourth Word, "Remember the Sabbath-day to sanctify it." Does not this command, it may well be asked, imply the amplifications which follow it, and thus rest upon conditions of agricultural life unlike those under which Moses could have conceived and promulgated any legislative code? Mr. Addis says, with regard to both the fourth and the tenth Words: The Decalogue "must have arisen long after the Israelites had passed from a nomad to a settled life. It is the house, and not, as in Arabic, the tent, which stands for a man's familia or household, and the Sabbath implies the settled life of agriculture. An agriculturist needs rest, and can rest from tillage. A nomad's life is usually so idle that no day of rest is needed; while, on the other hand, such work as the nomad does, driving cattle, milking them, &c., cannot be remitted on one day recurring every week."

Even if, however, it were assumed that Moses might have

APPENDIX.   555

prohibited the making of images and ordered the observance of the Sabbath (and that a sacred seventh day in each week should have been known to the Israelites ever since their migration from Mesopotamia seems a not improbable hypothesis, partially confirmed by parallel Assyrian observances), we are still far from the positive conclusion that Moses did write the Ten Commandments.

I do not lay very much stress upon the fact that no allusion is made to the Decalogue by the prophets. But unless there were some valid outside testimony, it is hard to see why we should except the Ten Words from the general conclusion that Moses did not write or devise the laws which in the Pentateuch are put forward in his name. The story of the Decalogue with which from childhood we are familiar rests almost entirely upon the Book of Deuteronomy. It is only in Deuteronomy that we are told that the ark was constructed for the reception of the two tables on which the Decalogue was inscribed. In the historical books the sanctity of the ark depends upon quite another cause—upon the presence of the Deity. If the ark contained any stones at all, they were probably sacred in themselves, and not in virtue of any writing graven upon them—perhaps survivals of a pre-Mosaic superstition, according to which certain stones were regarded as the dwelling-places of spirits and gods. (1 Kings viii. 9 is notoriously a Deuteronomistic interpolation.) Moreover, in the Book of Exodus as we now possess it—omitting one very doubtful passage, xxxiv. 28—it is not definitely stated that the Decalogue of xx. 2—17 was written upon the tables, or that the tables were two in number, or that the Words were ten. In our present text of Exodus the Decalogue is not the basis of the Covenant: it is not certain that it ever was so. It is also probable that xx. 18—21 once stood after xix. 19, and that therefore, in the original Elohistic narrative, the people were not supposed to hear the proclamation of the Decalogue, any more than they hear the giving of the "Book of the Covenant."

It is true that in Exodus xxxiv. 28 we read: "And he wrote upon the tables the Words of the Covenant, the ten Words;"

but round this verse, as round the chapter in which it occurs, there rages controversy violent and perhaps unappeasable. Assuming that the verse is to be interpreted along the old lines, that Yahveh is the subject of "he wrote," and therefore that the Words written refer to Exodus xx. 2—17, and not to the Words spoken of in verse 27, viz. commands now incorporated in verses 14 to 26,—yet even in that case it seems hard to deny that the verse was "worked over" or modified when it was removed from its original place by a Deuteronomistic reviser. Why should the earlier narrator only here have spoken of the tables as containing the "Words of the Covenant, the ten Words"?

There is the further question whether the Yahvistic narrative J ever contained the Decalogue of E (viz. Exodus xx. 2—17). On Wellhausen's theory, adopted by Stade, Duhm, Robertson Smith and many others, xxxiv. 28 is not separated from ver. 27, and J's Decalogue, *his* "Words of the Covenant," also "ten Words," and written (by Moses, not Yahveh) upon the tables, are to be picked out of xxxiv. 14—26. (See the enumeration in *Die Composition des Hexateuchs und der historischen Bücher des alten Testaments*, 1889, p. 331.) It is now even customary to contrast the earlier ritual Decalogue of J with the later moral Decalogue of E. I am not persuaded that such a contrast is justifiable. If we believe that the teaching of the priests included "morality" from the first, ever since Moses "connected the religious idea with the moral life," and that moral and juridical laws were codified earlier than ritual enactments, we shall be inclined to suppose that the Decalogue of E dates from an earlier period than the supposed Decalogue of J. It may be older than J, even though J did not know it. But if it were Mosaic, then it would have occupied the same place in J as it does in E; and even waiving this argument, it would have occupied the same place in E as it does in Deuteronomy.

Taking all these considerations together, I think we must abandon the Mosaic authorship of the Decalogue. But I am by no means prepared to admit that its very substance and contents prove that it cannot be earlier than the eighth or seventh century. (So, e.g., Kuenen, *Hexateuch*, p. 244, Stade, Cornill, Addis and many others.) The short lapidary style of the sixth, seventh and eighth Words betokens a comparatively high antiquity. To this may be added the argument of Kittel, *Geschichte*, Vol. I. p. 85, which I have quoted in my article in the *Jewish Quarterly Review*, Vol. III. p. 285. And, finally, if it be true that the religious teaching of Moses did contain an ethical element,—if by the creation of the judicial and pedagogic Torah he practically declared that Yahveh was a God of justice as well as a God of might—and if the priests, his successors, followed, very gradually and with many lapses, but still followed, in his footsteps—then I see no convincing reason why the Decalogue need be assumed to imply and to demand the prophetical movement of the eighth century. It may equally well have been drawn up by some priest of the north, who answered more fully to Hosea's ideal of the priesthood, in the ninth or even in the tenth century.

II.

LEGAL EVASIONS OF THE LAW.

The so-called "Evasion Laws" in Rabbinical Judaism, to which reference is occasionally made in theological works, are very few in number. The Rabbis were too closely attached to the Law to shun what was inconvenient in it. Only in a few cases where the enforcement of the law would, under new conditions, have inevitably compelled people to rebel against its authority, did they try to meet law by law, or even by a legal fiction through which the law in question was indeed partly abrogated, but the authority of the Law as a whole was maintained intact. The evasive laws are usually, though not always with full justice, taken to include certain regulations of the Rabbis concerning oaths and vows, and others relating to the Sabbath and the Sabbatical year.

Most of the definitions by which the Rabbis seek to classify and explain oaths and vows were formulated solely from the juristic side. This must by no means be confounded with their moral aspect, which is equally represented in the Talmud. The general principles of the Rabbis will bear comparison with the highest ideal standard ever attained by any moral teacher. But the Rabbis were also Judges, and when they had to inflict on the transgressor corporal punishment or exact a sacrificial fine, they could—as judges—only be guided by the legal code as they interpreted it. To give an instance. It is an accepted moral principle with the Rabbis that the thought of sin is worse than sin, that an unchaste thought is a "wicked thing" (Abodah Zarah, 20 a), and that an impure word not only brings him who utters it into the very lowest depth of hell, but calls forth the judgment of God upon the whole world (Sabbath, 33 a). This was the teaching of the Rabbis as preachers and moralists; but when they had to decide whether *they* should condemn a man or woman for adultery, they did not allow themselves to be carried away by their lofty moral sentiments, but, like any modern judge, they were guided by the facts of the case and gave their verdict on the basis of the legal code. The same thing may be observed in their procedure with respect to oaths and vows. The general principle is: Let thy yea be yea, and thy nay be nay (Baba Mezia, 49 a); and even a silent determination in the heart is considered as the spoken word which must not be withdrawn or changed (Maccoth, 24 a, and Rashi, ad loc.), for he who changes his word commits as heavy a sin as he who worships idols (Sanhedrin, 92 a), and he who utters an untruth is excluded from the divine presence (Sotah, 42 a). We can thus conceive with what abhorrence the Rabbis must have condemned every false or vain oath. Indeed, such offences belong to the seven capital sins which provoke the severest judgment of God on the world (Aboth, v. 11). A false oath, even if made unconsciously, involves man in sin and is punished as such (Gittin, 35 a).

Such were the views of the Rabbis as to the importance of oaths and of truth-speaking generally. Still, when they acted as judges, they carefully weighed whether the case before them

APPENDIX.   559

fell under any of the four classes of oaths of which the Law speaks (utterance oath, vain oath, witness oath, and trust oath). They would consider under which heading the special case before them might be included, whether the case corresponded in detail—according to their interpretation of the Law—with those for which Scripture prescribes either flagellation or the penalty of a sacrifice. It must be clearly understood that the Rabbis considered the bringing of a sacrifice under a false pretence or doubtful obligation—i.e. in cases where it was not perfectly clear that Scripture required a sacrifice—as sinful and sacrilegious. Hence their compunction against ordering a transgressor to bring a guilt-offering or sin-offering in cases in which there was the slightest doubt, lest the scriptural injunction was inapplicable. The term *patur* (פטור, "free" from bringing an offering) in Rabbinic literature therefore has merely a legal implication: namely, the case in question was not considered analogous to that cited in Scripture. But this term *patur* must not be taken as an equivalent of *muttar* (מותר, "permitted"), i.e. as permitting the man to do the act, or as acquitting him before the tribunal of his conscience. As an illustration showing how little the Rabbis confused the legal element with the moral, the words of Maimonides may be quoted from the *Mishneh Torah* (*Hilchoth Shebuoth*, c. 12, §§ 1, 2), and these words are based upon citations from the Talmud, as may be seen from the commentators to Maimonides' treatise: "Though he who takes a vain oath is punished by flagellation, and he who takes a false oath has to bring a sacrifice, not the whole of the sin is atoned (by these penalties). For it is said that God will not hold him guiltless (Exodus xx. 7). There is thus no escape for him from the judgment of Heaven until he has been punished by God for the profanation of the great name (which is involved in his sin), as it is said, And ye shall not swear by my name falsely, so that ye profane the name of your God (Levit. xix. 13); . . . . . which sin is one of the heaviest, though it is not punished either by *Kareth* (being rooted out) or by execution at the hands of the *Beth Din*." Thus the atonements prescribed by Scripture were not in themselves an acquittal of the offender from the sin of profaning the name of God, which is the moral aspect of the oath. When the moral element was violated the man suffered for it, whether the Beth Din had the right to fine him for the breach of the purely legal element or not. When the Rabbis assigned to every one the duty of immediately, and without further consideration, putting under a ban (see Maimonides, *ibid.* § 9) a man heard to utter a false or vain oath, they probably regarded this as the right way to make the man conscious of the moral offence which he had committed.

As to the admissibility of granting absolution for vows and oaths, the conclusion is clear enough. The Rabbis felt a general repugnance against oaths and vows even when they were kept and fulfilled (Nedarim, 20 *a*, 22 *a*), and there was even a tendency to declare the man who was in the habit of taking vows to be unworthy of bearing the name *chaber* (Demai, ii. 3). But people were not always guided by this advice; and under momentary impulse or in times of danger, men often took vows which they could not possibly fulfil. Some relaxation of the law was therefore necessary unless people were to become downright transgressors. Sometimes their vows and oaths might clash with their domestic duties, or interfere with their proper relations to their neighbours (Nedarim, ix. 4, 5 and 9), and in such cases the Rabbis would consider it their duty to afford people every facility to annul their thoughtless or impossible vows. This was done by the Beth Din or by the Chacham. Now the Rabbis themselves profess their ignorance of the source from which their predecessors derived the authority enabling them to deal with vows in this manner. "The absolving of vows," we read in Chagiga i. 8, "flies in the air, without any support" (from Scripture). Most probably they followed the precedent of Scripture, which allows the father to annul the vows of his daughter and the husband of his wife, and the Beth Din or Chacham, who were considered as in a sense guardians of the people, were invested with similar powers. But if this be the precedent, the absolving of vows cannot rightly be regarded as an evasion of the law, but as providential, and as designed, like the law in the Bible with regard to father and husband, to avert the evil resulting from an unlimited power of taking oaths and vows which might be abused by imbecile and rash minds.

Besides, it was only in certain cases that the Beth Din could exercise its power, and thus the Biblical law, generally considered, was obeyed. An oath or vow, for instance, which a man was charged to make by a court of justice, could not be absolved by any Beth Din or Chacham, or any other authority in the world. And even *private* vows and oaths (those imposed on oneself by oneself voluntarily) could only be annulled under certain conditions and restrictions.[1] The subject is indeed a most complicated one, and a full treatment is here impossible. One instance only of these conditions will be given as an illustration of the opening paragraph of the Mishnah Nedarim, c. ix., which has been the object of much misrepresentation. I refer to the so-called "door case." For the absolving of certain vows, it was necessary to prove that the vows would never have been made if he who made them had realized their evil effect upon him, upon his good name, upon his relatives, &c. I must premise two things: 1, that this had to be proved to the entire satisfaction of the Beth Din, and if they could not rely upon the man's telling the real truth—nay, if there were even a suspicion that a feeling of shame might make him withhold the truth— the court would not absolve his vow; 2, that the habit of taking vows was considered a sign of bad breeding, and affected the honour of the vower's parents, just as swearing would nowadays point to a man's low origin. In the Mishnah to which I have referred, the question is whether the Beth Din may open (the door) to one who has taken a vow of a private nature (*not* directly affecting his relation to his parents) by saying to him: Would you have taken a vow at all had you considered how injurious this very act is to the honour of your parents?—people inferring from this habit that you have been badly brought up. On this, the Wise Men remark that such a question is not permissible, as no man is so bare of all shame that he would

---

[1] The oaths here alluded to partake rather of the nature of vows than oaths. See Z. Frankel's essay, *Die Eidesleistung der Juden in theologischer und historischer Beziehung* (Dresden, 1847).

answer: Yes, he would have taken the vow even at the risk of offence to his parents; and thus the Beth Din could not rely upon getting the whole truth from him. This is the real meaning of the Mishnah, and it is clear enough that it has no relevance whatever to Matt. xv. 5 and Mark vii. 10. Such vows as are referred to in those passages belong to the category of vows which, as I mentioned above, the Beth Din would afford every opportunity of annulling (See Maimonides, *ibid.* c. 6, § 10).

The evasion laws relating to the Sabbath do not affect any Biblical law. The restriction of the Sabbath way to 2000 yards without the town is a Rabbinical restriction (see Jerusalem Talmud Erubin, i. 10, and Maimonides, *Hilchoth Sabbath*, c. 27, § 1), and of a relatively late date (see Herzfeld, *Geschichte des Volkes Israel*, II. 142). Now the legal fiction often alluded to consisted in putting a meal at a certain point (at the end of the 2000 yards' limit). The person so acting was regarded as having removed his habitation from the town, and as having fixed it at the new point. He could thus walk 2000 yards further on, whilst he lost the right to walk 2000 yards in the opposite direction. This was termed *Erub Techumin*. As the *Erub* as well as the Sabbath way were both Rabbinical institutions, the former was hardly an evasion, but a law on equal footing with the law of the Sabbath way itself. But even this concession was only allowed for the furtherance of some religious object; for instance, to pay a visit of condolence, to attend a wedding banquet, to meet a master or friend, or to perform similar acts (Maimonides, *Hilchoth Erubin*, c. vi. § 6).

A really evasive law—one which the Rabbis themselves regarded as such—was the Prosbul ($\pi\rho\sigma\beta o\lambda\eta$), introduced by Hillel. By this, the law in Deuteronomy xv. 1—3 was practically abrogated. The accepted interpretation of the law already was that moneys or fines charged by a public court were not released by the Sabbatical year. By the Prosbul, a kind of registered declaration, the creditor made over all his charges to the Beth Din, so that the court became the creditor and thus secured the debt, despite the incidence of the year of release. (See Mishnah, *Shebiith*, x. § 3.) The cause of this reform was, as the Mishnah points out, that people ceased to lend each other money, and thus transgressed the injunction: "Beware that there be not a base thought in thy heart, saying, the seventh year, the year of release, is at hand" (Deut. xv. 9). It was thus the moral element (not the thought of establishing public credit on a safe basis) that necessitated the reform, and the maintenance of the law was itself a moral principle, while no contradiction, as it would seem, was originally felt in maintaining it by a legal fiction. The later Rabbis (Amoraim), indeed, felt great difficulty about this evasive law, and they tried to explain it in various ways (Gittin, 36 *a* and *b*, and references) into which it is impossible to enter here. But one thing is clear from this sense of difficulty. As they never raised similar objections to the absolution of vows or to the *Erub* (with regard to the Sabbath way), the Rabbinical authorities cannot have regarded them as evasive laws. The effect of evasive laws can only be pernicious in religion when people realize them as such.

S. Schechter.

ADDITIONS AND CORRECTIONS.

P. 47. Wellhausen, in his new edition of the Minor Prophets (*Die kleinen Propheten übersetzt, mit Noten*, 1892), has the following suggestive note upon Hosea ii. 9, A.V. ii. 7 ("I will go and return to my first husband, for then was it better with me than now"): "Der Entschluss zu Jahve zurückzukehren setzt beim Volk ein freilich nur in der äussersten Noth sich regendes Bewusstsein des Unterschiedes zwischen dem alten Jahvedienst und dem seit der Einwanderung übernommenen dionysischen Cultus voraus. Das Bewusstsein ist in der That vorhanden gewesen und hat die innere Spannung erzeugt, aus der die ganze Bewegung der israelitischen Religionsgeschichte sich erklären lässt" (p. 99).

Pp. 59—62. Canaanite religion. Several points here stated seem, on further investigation, to rest on insufficient evidence. The exact relation of Baal to the sun is not ascertained; the meaning of *Chammanim* is doubtful; plain Baal was not the supreme Canaanite god, because no divinity bearing the name Baal, unqualified by a locality (mountain, town, heaven) or a quality (as Baalzebub, Baal berit, &c.), seems known. El should have been included in the list of Canaanite divinities. He, and not Baal, may have been the deity to be identified with the Cronos of Carthage. The whole subject is very obscure and the sources are fragmentary, and thus greater caution was necessary than I, who do not speak of the subject first-hand, have shown. Cf. Ed. Meyer, in his articles on Astarte, El and Baal, in Roscher's *Lexikon der griechischen und römischen Mythologie*. The article on Baal is in the *Nachträge* to Vol. I. (1890).

P. 60. From Hosea ii. 19, it would seem as if the various Baalim had often also their own particular names to boot. So Wellhausen: "Die Baale führen also verschiedene Eigennamen, von denen uns jedoch nur wenige bekannt sind, z. B. Astarte" (*Die kleinen Propheten übersetzt, mit Noten*, 1892, p. 100).

P. 63, n. 1. Add also Wellhausen's note on Hosea ii. 7, in *Kleine Propheten übersetzt*, p. 98.

P. 69. On the oral and legal character of the early Torah of the priests, cf. the admirable chapter of Wellhausen, "The Oral and the Written Torah," in *Religion of Israel*, pp. 392—400.

P. 79. On Nathan, cf. Schwally, *Zur Quellenkritik der historischen Bücher, Z.A.W.*, 1892, pp. 155, 156.

P. 84. The historical truth of 1 Kings xi. 29—39, has been denied. On the divergencies of the LXX., see Robertson Smith, *The Old Testament in the Jewish Church*, 2nd ed., 1892, pp. 117—119. On the other side, cf. Kittel, *Geschichte der Hebräer*, Vol. II. p. 162, n. 1.

Pp. 93, 94. On 1 Kings xxii., cf. Schwally, *Zur Quellenkritik*, &c., pp. 159—161.

P. 99, seq. For an admirable and somewhat more conservative view of the pre-prophetic period in its religion and culture, see Kittel, *Geschichte der Hebräer*, § 38, "Kultur und Religion in der Richterzeit" (pp. 82—90); § 50, "Kultur und Religion der ersten Königszeit" (pp. 169—176); and § 64, "Kultur und Religion der Zeit nach Salomo" (pp. 252—264). The points on which he lays most stress are, that in the sanctuary at Shiloh, where we find the ark of Yahveh and Eli as priest, there is no evidence of any image of Yahveh. Samuel is never brought into connection with the ephod. Moreover, after the ark has been captured and the estrangement between Saul and Samuel begun, ephod and teraphim become more prominent. With the return of the ark they begin to wane. Baal is no longer used in proper names after David (pp. 90, 175, and also pp. 260, 261).

P. 113, n. 1. See also Kittel's article, "Die pentateuchischen Urkunden in den Büchern Richter und Samuel," *Theol. Studien und Kritiken*, 1892, pp. 44—71; and his *Geschichte der Hebräer*, Vol. II. pp. 3—54. The two prophetical narratives in the Pentateuch and Joshua have for the first time been disentangled from the remaining portions, and printed separately, by Mr. Addis in his *Documents of the Hexateuch*, Vol. I., "The Oldest Book of Hebrew History" (1892).

P. 118. On Hosea viii. 12, cf. now Wellhausen (*Die kleinen Propheten übersetzt*, p. 119), who emends rather differently.

P. 128, n. 2. Wellhausen (p. 92) also agrees that if the text be sound, the allusion must be to the golden bulls of Jeroboam. But he

ADDITIONS AND CORRECTIONS. 567

goes on to say: "Dem Amos ist der Ausdruck (die Schuld Samariens) nicht zuzutrauen; denn er gebraucht nie Samarien für Israel, und das goldene Kalb ist ihm keineswegs die Gründsünde des Volks (Hosea x. 10), er polemisirt nie dagegen, überhaupt nicht gegen irgend eine Besonderheit des Cultus. Er wird einen unverfänglichen Namen für den Jahve von Bethel gebraucht haben, der dann später korrigirt worden ist." It may also be noted that Wellhausen (p. 83) suspects the genuineness of Amos v. 26: "Denn Amos macht seinen Zeitgenossen sonst nur übertriebenen Jahvecultus zum Vorwurf, nie den Dienst fremder und gar babylonisch-assyrischer Götter."

P. 130, n. 2. In the Hebrew Dictionary by Brown, Driver and Briggs, it is said that אלילים was possibly originally an independent word = *gods*, but even if so, associated by the prophets with the idea of worthlessness, and used by them in ironical contrast with אלהים אלים

P. 138, n. 1. Wellhausen (*Kleine Propheten*, p. 94) also suspects the authenticity of Amos ix. 8—15.

P. 149, n. 1. Duhm, in his new *Commentary on Isaiah*, also brings forward fresh and, it must be admitted, powerful arguments against the authenticity of Isaiah xix. 16—25. It should be added, however, that he regards these verses as a very late addition (circa 150 B.C.) to a wholly un-Isianic chapter.

P. 163. Hezekiah's reform. It is possible I have followed Stade too closely and been too negative. Cf. Kuenen, *Hexateuch*, § 12, n. 5, p. 218: "Deuteronomy presupposes Hezekiah's partial reformation, for the incomplete and partially defeated practice usually precedes the theory, and not *vice versa*." See also Kittel, *Geschichte*, Vol. II. pp. 301—303.

P. 190, last line. This is exaggerated. I am not sure now whether one should use these catch-word oppositions, "people," "church," even for the priestly code. (It was a *nation* which rose in revolt against Antiochus Epiphanes.) They are certainly out of place for Deuteronomy. Cf. Wellhausen, *Composition*, p. 205: "Israel ist im Deuteronomium wie in JE zwar ein *frommes* Volk, aber doch ein Volk, ein bürgerliches Gemeingewesen—in Q ist es eine Kirche, eine Gemeinde, die rein aufgeht in den geistlichen Angelegenheiten."

P. 206. That Habakkuk was one of the "false prophets" would be convincingly established if Wellhausen's views should prove to be correct. See his notes on Habakkuk in the *Kleine Propheten übersetzt*, p. 161, seq.

P. 215, n. 3. It must be confessed that the two verses, Deut. iv. 39 and xxxii. 39, *seem* almost modelled upon Deutero-Isaiah's language.

P. 234. One of the best arguments *for* the existence of written collections of priestly or ceremonial laws before the exile, seems to be a chapter of Deuteronomy such as xiv. and certain passages in xxii.—xxv. I have not sufficiently alluded to and acknowledged the weight and probability of this argument. Cf. the very temperate remarks of Kuenen, *Hexateuch*, p. 263 fin., § 14, n. 6, pp. 266, 272, and § 15, n. 1, 2, 3, 4, pp. 273—275.

P. 256. Cf. the arguments in Gautier's pleasant book, *Le prophète Ezechiel* (Lausanne, 1891), especially pp. 176—187 and pp. 261—274.

P. 329 and 349. Cf. note on p. 190. For the general effect of the temple legislation, see Delitzsch's admirable essay, in *Iris, Studies in Colour and Talks about Flowers*, on "Dancing and the Criticism of the Pentateuch."

P. 425. Cf. Cheyne, *Origin of the Psalter*, p. 314.

P. 500. The '*Am ha-Arets*. It should perhaps have been said that while originally and technically the '*Am ha-Arets* (as Jew) seems to have denoted the man who was lax in his observance of the laws of clean and unclean and of the agrarian laws, there was also a tendency to use the word (as we may see from the passages quoted on p. 501, n. 1) to denote anybody who was generally both unobservant and ignorant of the law. But nevertheless Rabbinism was never a religion *of* the learned and *for* the learned only.

P. 551. To the saying of Jesus, "Whosoever shall seek to save his life shall lose it," &c., a very interesting parallel may be found in Tamid 32 *a* (Wünsche, Vol. II. 4, p. 165 fin.), in the reply which the "wise men of the south" make to Alexander of Macedon. He asks, "What should a man do that he may live?" and they answer, "Let him kill himself," and *vice versa*. The Hebrew is very pointed and precise: אמר להן מה יעבד איניש ויחיה אמרו ליה ימית עצמו מה יעביד איניש וימות יחיה את עצמו. Cf. also *Aboth de Rabbi Nathan* (ed. Schechter), 36 *a*, where R. Jehuda the Prince gives similar advice. Cf. also Brüll, *Jahrbücher für jüdische Geschichte und Literatur*, II. Jahrgang (1876), p. 129.

INDEX.

A.
Abiathar, 43, 67, 79.
Abijam, 87.
Achimelech, 67.
Agrarian laws, 474; neglect of, 501.
Ahab, 90, 92, 93.
Ahaz, 108, 111.
Ahijah, 84.
Alexander the Great, 362.
Almsgiving, 485,526; delivers from death, 527, 528.
Altars, see High-places.
Amaziah, 97, 98.
'Am ha-Arets, 497; meaning of, 498, 499; laws concerning, 500; sayings about, 501, n. 1; disappearance of, 502.
Ammonites, religion of, 29.
Amon, 167, 171.
Amos, 99, 119, 120, 128, 131, 138, 144, 146, 162.
Anaitis, worship of, ordered by Artaxerxes II., 360.
Angels in post-exilic literature, 429; in Daniel, 430; functions of, 431; bad angels, 453; Satan, 453, 454.
Antigonus, 363.
Antiochus III., 365.
Antiochus Epiphanes, 367, 382.
Apocalypses, place of, in post-exilic religion, 467.
Ark, relation of, to Yahveh, 42; captured by Philistines, 71; taken by David to Jerusalem, 82.
Arpad, battle of, 107.
Artaxerxes I. Longimanus, 307, 359.
Artaxerxes II. Mnemon, 360.
Artaxerxes III. Ochus, 360; deportation of Jews by, 361.
Asa, 87; his religious reform, 88.
Asherah, 87, 89, 164, 181.
Assyria, prophetic view of its relation to Israel, 133,134; judgment on, 144,145.
Astarte, 61.
Asurbanipal, 167, 172.
Athaliah, 92, 96.
Atonement, day of, 333—336, 523.

Augustine, St., 449, n. 1.
Azariah or Uzziah (king of Judah), 98, 108.

B.
Baal, 20, 59, 60; introduction of worship of Tyrian Baal by Ahab into Israel, 92; by Jehoram and Athaliah into Judab, 96; suppressed in Israel by Jehu, 95; in Judah by Jehoiada, 96.
Baasha, 86.
Baethgen, on Semitic religion, 24; on Edomite religion, 28; on Ammonite religion, 29.
Bagoses, 361, 362, 392.
Baudissin, on the god Moloch, 61.
Boissier, on Paul Orosius, 448.
Bulls (images or symbols of Yahveh), 42, 43; Jeroboam's, 84, 85.

C.
Cambyses, 297.
Canaanites, influence of, 20, 31; not destroyed by Israelites, 56, 58; their religion, 59; chief divinities of, 60; their worship, 62; influence of, on Israelite religion, 62, 63.
Carchemish, battle of, 199.
Carpenter, on Isaiah liii., 280, n. 1; on Proverbs, 396, n. 2; on Messianic king, 417, n. 1.
Chaber, 498.
Charity in post-exilic period, 484, 485, 491, 526.
Chavannes, on editors of historical books, 234, n. 1; on lack of mysticism in Judaism, 424.
Chemosh, 29, 35.
Cheyne, on Josiah, 173; on pre-Deuteronomic collection of laws, 178; on hopefulness of Deuteronomy, 191; on Jehoiakim's submission to Nebuchadrezzar, 203; on Lamentations, 210, n. 2; on imperfect moral conceptions of Isaiah, 217; on Deutero-Isaiah, 265; on Isaiah liii., 279; on Jewish revolt under Ochus, 361; on Isaiah lvi., 372

2 P

n. 2; on influence of Hellenism, 378; on Zoroastrian origin of belief in future life, 456; on future life in Psalter, 458; on Psalm xix., 481.
Chronicles, Book of, 348, 403, 447, 454, 483.
Circumcision, 229, 337.
Cleanness, ritual, meaning of, 475, 476; neglect of, 501; see also Law.
Cornill, 410.
Covenant, book of, 117.
Criticism of the Old Testament, general results of, 3.
Cyaxares, 195, 199.
Cyrus, 260, 261; Deutero-Isaiah's conception of, 273; captures Babylon, 283.

D.

Daniel, Book of, 408, 412, 430, 457.
Darius, 277, 301, 302.
Darius II. Ochus, 359.
David, 35, 39, 43, 81.
Davidson, on idolatry in the exile, 226, n. 1; on Ezekiel, 248, n. 1.
Deborah, 75; Song of, 15, 56.
Decalogue, 49, 117, and Appendix I.
Delitzsch, on faith of Old Testament, 455.
Demetrius (son of Antigonus), 363, 364.
Deutero-Isaiah, 264—267; his monotheism, 268; his appeal to previous prophecies, 270, 271; on idolatry, 271, 272; conception of Israel's calling, 274, 275; of the Servant and his work, 277—280; the new Jerusalem, 280, 281.
Deuteronomy, origin of, 177, 178; finding of the Book of the Law, 179; public recital of, 180; account of, 183 seq.; aim of, 184; hatred of idolatry, 185; single sanctuary, 186, 187; sacrifices in, 187; secularization of slaughter, 187; humanity of, 188; priestliness of, 188; introductory chapters of, 189; love of God, 190; not hopeful, 192; first four chapters, 193; school of Deuteronomists, 193; monotheistic verses in iv. and xxxii., 215.
Dillmann, on patriarchs, 12, 13.
Driver, on Priestly Code, 354.
Droysen, 364.
Duhm, on Jeremiah, 213, 221; on Ezekiel, 239; on Deutero-Isaiah, 267; on the Servant, 276, n. 3; on Isaiah lvi., 372, n. 2; on Isaiah lvii. 15, 441, n. 1.

E.

Eben-ha-Ezer, battle of, 71.
Ecclesiastes, Book of, 367, 379, 408, 424, 427.

Ecclesiasticus, see Sirach.
Edomites, religion of, 28.
Elah, 86.
Eli, 67
Eliashib, 351.
Elijah, 91, 92, 94.
Elisha, 94, 95.
Ephod, 43, 67, 69.
Esarhaddon, 167.
Esther, Book of, 412
Ethics, post-exilic, 484; "external goods," 485; attitude towards enemies, 486, 487; enthusiasm, 488; modification of penal law, 489, 490; women and marriage, 491.
Evasions of Law, 557 seq. (Appendix II.).
Exile, Babylonian, 209, 222; causes of special result of, 212; condition of exiles in, 207, 223, 259; religious views among, 224—228; attitude towards victories of Cyrus, 261; restoration of exiles by Cyrus, 284, 285.
Ezekiel, 239; his early life, 240; his prophetic call, 241; his book, 242; his visions, 242, 243; his work among the exiles, 244; his conception of Yahveh, 246, 247; of Yahveh's relation to Israel, 250; his individualism, 251—253; his conception of the new Jerusalem and its sanctuary, 255; position of morality in, 256; his legalism, 257.
Ezra, his journey to Jerusalem, 306; objects of, 307; arrival at Jerusalem, 308; hears of mixed marriages, 309; the special commission, 310; desires to fortify Jerusalem, 311; works with Nehemiah, 313; produces his new lawbook and reads it, 314, 346; his speech, 347.

F.

Fasting in post-exilic religion, 509, 510.
Free-will emphasized by Sirach, 518.
Freudenthal, on moderate Hellenistic party, 377.
Fripp, on composition of Genesis, 316, n. 1.
Future life, 455; rise of belief in, 456; resurrection of body, 457; idea of immortality in Psalter, 458, 459; religious effects of belief in, 460—462.

G.

Gad, 79, 80.
Galilee, Judaizing of, 371.
Gaza, battle of, 363.
Gedaliah, 208.
Gideon, 43. 57.
God, conception of, in post-exilic period, 420; Yahveh now equals God, 421; God still remains Yahveh, 422; God's

nearness, how conditioned, 422; his nature, 423; his transcendence, 423; effects of, 424; God of heaven, 425; his relation to nature, 426; near to Israelite, 432, 434—436; religious effects of his nearness, 439; conception of character of, 442; goodness and compassion of, 443; his rule of Israel in the past, 447; his justice, 462; his love and its limits, 463, 464; a Father to Israel and the Israelite, 464, 539; fear of, 540; love of, 541; see also Yahveh.
Graetz, 363, 365, 366.

H.
Habakkuk, 206.
Haggai, 297, 299.
Hananiah, 206.
Hazael, 97.
Heart, source of good and evil, 483, 484, 519.
Heaven, God's dwelling-place, 425.
Hebrews, original meaning of word, 27.
Hekatæus of Abdera, 382.
Hellenism, influence of, 374; opposition to and attraction of, 375, 376; mediatizing effects of, 377; religious speculation promoted by, 378; gradual Hellenization interrupted by Antiochus Epiphanes, 382, 383.
Hezekiah, 111, 112; his reform, 163—165; effect of, 166; death, 166.
High-places, 87, 103; growing objection to, by prophetical party, 176; idea of their abolition, 177; destroyed by Josiah, 182.
Hilkiah, 173, 179.
Historical books, view of their editors of age between Moses and prophets, 17; editing of, in exile, 231; religious views of editors, 232; their conception of Israel's past history, 233.
Holiness, conception of, in Deuteronomy, 188, 189; law of, 235, 236; conception of, in Priestly Code, 325, 326.
Holtzmann, on Joseph, son of Tobias, 375; on Judæa under Ptolemæan kings, 397; on post-exilic conception of sin, 518.
Hosea, 70, 119, 120, 128, 129, 132, 139, 162.
Hoshea, 108, 109.
Humility a post-exilic virtue, 440, 441, n. 1, 481.
Hunter (Hay), 283.
Hyrkanus, 366.

I.
Idolatry, in pre-prophetic period, 18; character of, 19; idolatrous influence of Canaanites upon Israelites, 20; under Solomon, 83; in 8th century, 115, 128, 130; Assyrian idolatry in Judah, 168; sacrifice of children, 169; under Josiah, 176; Josiah eradicates its symbols, 181; in exile, 226; Deutero-Isaiah's polemic against, 271, 272.
Images (of Yahveh), 42—44; no allusion to, in prophetical narratives of Hexateuch, 116; Hosea's view of, 128, 129; Isaiah's view of, 130; Hezekiah's attack on, 164.
Immortality, see Future Life.
Individualism, growth of, in 7th century, 216, 217; in Jeremiah, 218, 219; in Ezekiel, 251—253.
Isaiah, 119, 120, 130, 132, 136, 139—144, 147, 148, 162, 165, 166, 217. Second Isaiah, see Deutero-Isaiah.
Israel. kingdom of, or northern kingdom. founded by Jeroboam I., 84; religious condition of, 85, 86; under Ahab, 90; fall of, 109; deportations to Assyria; 110, 111; introduction of foreign colonists, 110; relation of returned exiles from Babylon to mixed inhabitants of north, 293.
Israelites, their place among the Semitic races, 27, 28.

J.
Jacob (Rabbi), 461.
Jannai (Rabbi), 451.
Jehoahaz (king of Israel), 97.
Jehoahaz (king of Judah), 196.
Jehoiachin, 204.
Jehoiada, 96, 117.
Jehoiakim, 196, 197, 200, 203, 204.
Jehonadab, 95.
Jehoram (king of Judah), 96.
Jehoshaphat, 88, 92, 93.
Jehu, 95, 97.
Jephthah, 40.
Jeremiah, 173; early prophecies of, 174, 175; relation to Deuteronomy, 194. 201; after Josiah's death, 198; under Jehoiakim, 199, 200; on sacrifices, 201; on inviolability of Jerusalem, 202; lives concealed, 203; under Zedekiah, 207; after fall of Jerusalem, 209; monotheistic implications in, 215; individualism in, 218, 219; new covenant in, 220, 221.
Jeroboam I., 83, 84, 85.
Jeroboam II., 98, 107.
Jerusalem, made capital of kingdom by David, 82; Solomon builds temple at, 82; escapes in Sennacherib's invasion, 112; importance of, to Isaiah, 165; effects of Isaiah's teaching about, 166;

captured by Nebuchadrezzar, 204; again and destroyed, 208 ; walls of, rebuilt by Nehemiah, 313; captured by Ptolemy I., 362, 364 ; by Scopas, 365 ; by Antiochus III., 365.
Jesus, 428, 429, 506, 550, 551.
Jezebel, 90.
Joash or Jehoash (king of Judah), 96, 97.
Joash (king of Israel), 97.
Job, Book of, 367, 408, 453.
Jochanan (son of Joiada the high-priest), 361.
Joel, Book of, 362, 406.
Johanan (son of Kareah), 208.
Jonah, Book of, 371, 408.
Joseph (son of Tobias), 366.
Josephus, on foundation of Samaritan community, 352 ; on Bagoses, 361 ; on Antiochus III., 365 ; on Joseph, son of Tobias, 366, 376 ; on John Hyrkanus, 394 ; on punishments of Pharisees, 490.
Joshua, high-priest, 270, 299.
Joshua (son of Joiada the high-priest), 361.
Josiah, 171—173 ; his reform, 177 seq.; hears the new Law-book, 179, 180 ; his measures to give it effect, 181—183, his death, 196.
Jotham (king of Judah), 108.
Judæa, relation of restored exiles to old population remaining in, 291, 292.
Judah (kingdom of), religious condition after disruption, 85—87; Asa's reform, 88 ; vassal of Assyria, 163 ; Hezekiah's reform, 163, 165 ; religious effects of, 166 ; effects of Josiah's death, 196 ; religious reaction, 197, 198; first deportation under Jehoiachin, 204 ; condition under Zedekiah, 205 ; second deportation, 208 ; religious condition in 7th century, 210 ; religious advance in 7th century, 213—217.
Judaism, its religious development unfinished at age of Maccabees and of Christ, 357.
Judges, nature of so-called, 57.
Judges, Book of, unhistorical conception of history between Joshua and Samuel given by editors of, 57 ; see also Historical Books.
Judgment, conception of, by prophets, 137—143.
Judith, Book of, 408.

K.

Kamphausen, on Mosaic religion, 47.
Kenites, 51.
Kings, Book of, see Historical Books.
Kuenen, on pre-prophetic period, 19 ; on Moses, 46 ; on religious effect of Syrian wars, 97, 99 ; on prophetic monotheism 135 ; on Isaiah xxxii., xxxiii., 218 ; on Sheshbazzar, 289 ; on delay in rebuilding temple, 294 ; on Priestly Code, 341, 343 ; on laws of clean and unclean, 477, n. 1.

L.

Lamentations, Book of, 209—211.
Law, beginnings of written law, 118, collection of laws in exile, 234 ; holiness law, 235, 236 ; teaching of, in postexilic period, 400, 402 ; additions to Priestly Code after Ezra, 402 ; influence of, on outward circumstance, 452; gives new spiritual pleasure, 452 ; place of, in post-exilic religion, 468 ; effect of religion as law, 469—471; ceremonial law, 472 seq.; dietary laws, 473 ; agrarian laws, 474 ; clean and unclean, 474 seq.; effect of law on conceptions of goodness and sin, 479 ; the "legal good man," 480 ; "pride or despair," 481, 482 ; law as spiritual joy, 485 ; effects of ceremonial law, 492, 508 ; was law a burden ? 493 ; "intellectualism" of law, 494—496 ; not disobeyed by mass of people, 500 ; not a burden, 502, 503 ; sanctification of ordinary life by ceremonial law, 511 ; tendency towards doctrine of "good works," 525—528 ; why law was observed, motive for observance, 529 seq.; effects not the same as motives, 530 ; motive not merely mercenary, 531 ; Prof. Schultz on motive, 532 ; mercenary motive in Deuteronomy stronger than with Rabbis, 533 ; law obeyed for God's sake, 534 ; from real religious motives, 537—539 ; God's fatherhood realized by law, 539, 540 ; law moralized life, 547 ; general effects of, 548 ; law for its own sake, 549 ; see also Deuteronomy, Priestly Code, Torah.
Legalism, mark of post-exilic period, 466.
Levites, relation to priests, 66, 70 ; in Deuteronomy, 193 ; in exile and at restoration, 288, 289 ; in Babylon after Zerubbabel's return, 305 ; few accompany Ezra, 308 ; in Priestly Code, 323 ; at reading of law, 346, 347 ; in postexilic period, 393 ; as teachers, 400.
Lot, sacred, 65, 66, 67, 68.
Love of God, in Deuteronomy, 190 ; in later literature, 541.

M.

Mahaffy, 365.
Malachi, Book of, 349.

INDEX. 573

Manasseh (king of Judah), 167, 168, 169, 170.
Manasseh (grandson of Eliashib), 351, 352.
Marriages, mixed, 302, 303, 309, 310, 349.
Marti, on Satan, 454.
Medes, 195.
Megiddo, battle of, 196.
Menahem, 107, 108.
Mesa, 29.
Messiah, Messianic king in Isaiah, 142, 143; conception of, less important in Judaism than in Christianity, 416; Messianic age, priestly conception of, 319; later views of, 416, 438.
Micah (Ephraimite), 43, 66.
Micah (prophet), 119, 120.
Micah, Book of, chapter vi., 171.
Micaiah, 93, 94.
Mitsvah, meaning of, 536.
Moabite stone, 29.
Moabites, religion of, 29; not monolatrous, 30.
Moloch or Milk, 61; worship of, 169, 171.
Monolatry, meaning of, 11; origin of, in Israel, 16, 18; Yahveh Israel's God, 21; origin of, why ascribed to Moses, 31, 32; character of pre-prophetic, 34, 35, 36.
Monotheism, advance towards, by 8th-century prophets, 134—136; in 7th century, 214—216; growth of, in exile, 228; absolute in Deutero-Isaiah, 268; in post-exilic period, 367, 368.
Moses, 14, 15; origin of his monolatry, 33, 50; character of his monolatry, 46; his conception of Yahveh, 47; his religious teaching, 48, 49; his relation to Kenites, 51; opens historic period, 54; his work, 55; founder of priestly Torah, 64, 65, 68.
Myus, battle of, 363.

N.

Nabonnedos, 260.
Nabopolassar, 199.
Nadab, 86.
Nathan, 79, 80.
Nazirites, 80.
Nebuchadrezzar, 199, 200, 203.
Necho II., 155, 196.
Nehemiah, 311; his expedition to Jerusalem, 312; his rebuilding of the walls, 313; at reading of law, 346; leaves Jerusalem, 349; second visit of, 350, 351.
Nehushtan, 164.

Nöldeke, on names compounded with Yahveh or Yah, 21, n.1; on Semitic religion, 24, n. 1.

O.

Old Testament history, closes at Nehemiah, 353, 355.
Old Testament literature extends for 300 years after Nehemiah, 355, 412; classes of, 415.
Omri, 86, 87.
Onias III. (high-priest), 366.
Origin of Israelite religion, why obscure. 4—7.
Orosius (Paul), 448.

P.

Panion, battle of, 365.
Particularism, growth of, in exile, 228; in post-exilic period, 292, 369, 432, 437, 439.
Patriarchs, 11; unhistoric, 12, 13.
Paul, St., 156, 427, 429, 542, 545.
Pekah, 108.
Pekahiah, 108.
Pentateuch, "prophetical" narratives of, 113; final redaction of, 403, 404.
Philistines, 71.
Pietschmann, on early Canaanite religion. 26.
Post-exilic period, religious variety in. 409; explanations of this variety, 410. 411; religious fervour in, 413; points of view from which to regard, 416.
Prayer, character of, in post-exilic religion. 505, 506.
Priest, priesthood, in old Israel, 65; origin of, 66; relation to tribe of Levi, 66; priests as soothsayers, 67; as judges and teachers, 68; their Torah oral, 69; advance between Samuel and Amos, 69; Hosea's conception of priest's office. 70; in 8th century, 116, 117; their written codes, 117, 118; in 7th century, 175, 212; priests of high-places, 182; in Deuteronomy, 188, 193; codify laws in exile, 234; at the return, 287; "sons of Zadok," 288; high-priest, creation of, 290; in Babylon, 304; legal work of, 305; "sons of Aaron," 323; quarrel with Levites, 350; corruption among, 350—352; high-priest, 392; number of, in post-exilic period, 392; position of, 393.
Priestly Code, Ezra's law-book, 315; portions of Pentateuch which belong to, 315, 316, 354; character of, 316; central portion of, 317; account and criticism of, 318—345; deals with community,

318; conception of God, 320; his relation to Israel, 321; Priests and Levites in, 323; morality in, 324; conception of holiness in, 325, 326; of sin and atonement, 327; of uncleanness, 328, 329; place of sacrifice in, 330—332; Day of Atonement in, 333—336; Sabbath in, 338, 339; relation of Israel to outer world in, 339, 340; position of foreigners in, 341; place of ritual in, 342; sin-offerings in, 343; effects of, 344, 345; reading of, 346; covenant signed to observe, 348; additions to, after Ezra, 402.

Prophets of 8th century, 8; their teaching, 9, 10; on Moses and Mosaic age, 16; first appearance of, 72, 76; Canaanite origin of, 77; coalescence with seers, 77, 78; in 8th century, 115, 116; higher movement at that time, 120; character of, 121; teaching of Amos, Hosea, Isaiah, Micah, 121—160; moral ideals of, 126; monotheism of, 134; not statesmen, 150; political teaching of, 151, 152; sympathy with poor, 152, 153; religious teachers, 154; Wellhausen's view of, 154, 155, 158; sudden excellence of, 155; their work and its results, 156—160; in 7th century, 174; alliance with priests, 175; national party among, after Josiah's death, 198, 205, 206; in exile, 237, 238; prophecy aroused by Cyrus' victories, 262; new character of, 262, 263; character of early post-exilic prophecy, 298; editing of prophetical writings in post-exilic period, 405; additions to, 405; their character and purpose, 406, 407; see also Judgment, Yahveh, Messiah, Monotheism, Sacrifices, Universalism, and names of Prophets, Amos, Isaiah, Jeremiah, Ezekiel, &c.

Proselytism, 369, 371, 372.
Prostitution, sacred, 87, 88.
Proverbs, Book of, 362, 367, 380; post-exilic date of, 396; explanations of that date, 397; teaching in, 401, 428, 459, 488, 491, 514.
Psalter, 302, 362, 385, 386, 428, 443, 458, 459, 515.
Psammetichus, 172.
Ptolemy I. Lagi, 362, 364.
Ptolemy II. Philadelphus, 365.

R.

Rabbinical literature, use of, in these Lectures, 465, n. 2, 467.
Rechabites, 51.
Rehoboam, 87.

Religion, between Moses and Samuel, 58; influence of Canaanites, 58, 63; character of pre-prophetic religion generally, 100—105; simplicity of, 104; limitations of, 105; religion in 7th century, 210—212; advance, 213; religious literature of 7th century, monotheistic progress in, 214—216; growth of individualism in, 216, 217; religious views in exile, 224—228; undogmatic character of post-exilic religion, 418, 545; religion only spiritual interest, 419; unsystematized, 543, 544.
Renan, on Semitic religions, 23; on Asa's reform, 88; on prophets, 152.
Repentance, needs God's help, 520; condition of forgiveness, 521, 524; Rabbinic eulogies of, 528, 529.
Resurrection, see Future Life.
Retribution, divine, theory of, in post-exilic period, 444—446, 538.
Reuss, on Priestly Code, 323.
Rezin, 108.
Ruth, Book of, 362, 408.

S.

Sabbath, 56; increased importance attached to, in exile, 229, 230; in Priestly Code, 338; in post-exilic religion, 473; not a burden, 504, 505, 507.
Sacrifices, prophetic attitude towards, 131, 132; in Priestly Code, 330—332.
Samaria, capture of, 109.
Samaritans, foundation of their community, 352.
Samson, 71.
Samuel, 72—76, 80.
Samuel, Books of, see Historical Books.
Sanballat, 350, 351.
Sargon II., 109, 111.
Satan, 453, 454, 518.
Saul, 73—76.
Schechter, on St. Francis of Assisi, 426, n. 1; on Sabbath under law, 506, 507; on Ruskin and the law, 534, n. 1; on evasions of the law, 557 (Appendix II.).
Schrader, on delay in rebuilding temple, 295.
Schultz, on supposed higher conception of Yahveh through Elijah and Syrian wars, 98; on burden of law, 503; on motive for law's observance, 532, 535—537.
Schürer, on influence of Hellenism, 383; on numbers of Levites, 393; on origin of Scribes, 396; on laws of clean and unclean, 477; on prayer in post-exilic religion, 505; on motive for observing law, 532.

INDEX.

575

Schwally, on Job, 460, n. 1.
Scopas, 365.
Scribes, origin of, 394, 395; literary products of earlier Scribes in the Old Testament, 396 seq.
Scriptures, sacred, 212; in post-exilic period, 389.
Scythians, 172.
Seers, 72; their office and methods, 73.
Seleucus I., 363, 364.
Seleucus IV. Philopator, 366.
Semitic religion, 22; names of Semitic deities, 23, 24; no original monolatry, 25; chief divinities, 26.
Sennacherib, 111, 112, 162.
Servant, conception of, in Deutero-Isaiah, 276—280.
Shallum, 107.
Shalmanesar IV., 109.
Shaphan, 179.
Sheol, 102.
Sheshbazzar, 289, 294.
Sin, conception of, in post-exilic religion, 512 seq.; sense of sin, how aroused, 513; national righteousness, 514; guilt and calamity, 515; sin as violation of law, 516; sin and sinfulness, 516, 517; no principle of sin, 518; God's part in its overthrow, 519, 520; evil inclination, 521; theory of "good works," 525, 526; sin and merit, 527, 528.
Sirach, 380—382, 388, 389, 428, 443, 488, 491, 518, 519, 524.
Smend, on Ezekiel, 254.
Smerdis (Pseudo), 297.
Smith (Robertson), on prophets of 8th century, 150; on conception of holiness, 325; on uncleanness, 328, 329; on Day of Atonement, 333, n. 3; 334, n. 1.
Society, condition of, in 8th century, 114; religious decline and advance, 115, 116.
Solomon, 82, 83.
Spirit, divine, 431.
Stade, on pre-prophetic period, 19; on Mosaic religion, 47; on origin of Yahveh, 50; on priesthood in Old Israel, 68, 70, 71; on book of Jeremiah, 214; on monotheistic passages in Deuteronomy and Jeremiah, 214; on Sheshbazzar, 289; on delay in rebuilding temple, 294, 295; on 2 Chronicles xv. 9 and xxx. 5—25, 370.
Steinthal, on Isaiah ii. 2—4, 372, n. 1; on humility, 441, n. 1; on scientific monomania, 488, n. 1.
Suffering, disciplinary view of, 445; problems of, 450; explanations of, 451.
Synagogue, origin of, 390; services in, 390; effect of, 391.

Syrian wars, 97.

T.

Temple, Solomon's built, 82; worship at, in 7th century, 177; made the only legitimate place of worship in Deuteronomy, 186; not rebuilt at once on return, 294, 295; begun in 520 B.C., 299; finished in 516 B.C., 302; in post-exilic period, 383; religious influence of, 385—388; God's presence in, 433.
Teraphim, 44.
Theano, 328, n. 1.
Tiele, on origin of Yahveh, 50.
Tiglath-pilesar II., 107—109.
Tobiah, 350, 351.
Tobit, Book of, 408, 430.
Topheth, 181.
Torah, priestly Torah, 45; founded by Moses, 49; character of his Torah, 55, 64, 65; of that of his successors, the priests, 69, 70; meaning of word in Judaism, 465, 469; see Law.
Toy, on relation of God to nature in postexilic period, 426; on relation of God to Israel, 439; on post-exilic religion, 469; on post-exilic morality, 487; on feeling of national innocence, 514; on conception of sin in Psalms, 516.
Tradition, its view of Old Testament books, 2.

U.

Universalism, origin of idea, 146; universalist passages in Isaiah, 147, 148; growth of idea in exile, 228; tendency towards, in post-exilic period, 353; universalist passages in post-exilic literature, 371, 372, 437; see also Proselytism.
Uriah, 117.
Urijah, 202.
Uzziah or Azariah (king of Judah), 98, 108.

W.

Wellhausen, on Israelite apostasy to Baal, 20; on Moses and his Torah, 49; on origin of Yahveh, 53; on influence of Canaanite religion, 63; on Elijah, 91; on prophets, 126, 154, 155, 158; on the single sanctuary of Deuteronomy, 187; on Jeremiah, 218; on Priestly Code, 345; on Pharisees, 541; on St. Paul as the pathologist of Judaism, 542.
Wisdom, conception of, 380, 399; identified with law and its teaching, 400.
Wisdom literature; see Ecclesiastes, Job, Proverbs, Sirach.

Y.

Yahveh, God of Israel, 21, 35; character of, in pre-prophetic period, 37; connection with fire, 37; wrath of, 38; warlike, 39; human sacrifices to, 40; his form, 41; his relation to the ark, 42; images of, 43; God of justice, 44; his sanctuary, 45; origin of name, 50, 51; meaning of name, 52; name probably pre-Mosaic, 53; Wellhausen's hypothesis, 53; remains God of Israel in spite of Canaanite influence, 56, 64; conception of, raised by Elijah and Syrian wars, 98, 99; at close of pre-prophetic period, 100; gradual moralization of character of, 101, 102; Israelites proud of, 105; conception of his character by prophets of 8th century, 122; relation to Israel, 123—125; object of Israel's election by, 125; true worship of, 127; prophetic attack upon images of, 128—130; conception of, in Deuteronomy, 190, 191; by Jeremiah, 215, 216; increased importance attached in exile to outward worship of, 231; Ezekiel's conception of, 246, 247; Yahveh's honour, 248, 249; as universal Creator in Deutero-Isaiah, 269, 270; conception of, in Priestly Code, 320; Yahveh and God are identical in post-exilic period, 421.

Yetser, good and evil, 513, n. 1; 521.

Z.

Zadok, 67, 69.
Zechariah (king of Israel), 107.
Zechariah (prophet), 297, 300, 301, 453.
Zechariah, Book of, ix.—xi., 149.
Zedekiah, 204, 214.
Zephaniah, 173.
Zerubbabel, 289, 294, 299.
Zimri, 86.
Zoroastrian religion, influence of 373.

www.ingramcontent.com/pod-product-compliance
Lightning Source LLC
Chambersburg PA
CBHW071216290426
44108CB00013B/1198